THE EUROPEAN
INTERNAL
MARKET

THE EUROPEAN INTERNAL MARKET

Trade and Competition

Selected Readings

Edited by
ALEXIS JACQUEMIN
and
ANDRÉ SAPIR

OXFORD UNIVERSITY PRESS
1989

Oxford University Press, Walton Street, Oxford OX2 6DP

Oxford New York Toronto
Delhi Bombay Calcutta Madras Karachi
Petaling Jaya Singapore Hong Kong Tokyo
Nairobi Dar es Salaam Cape Town
Melbourne Auckland

and associated companies in
Berlin Ibadan

Oxford is a trade mark of Oxford University Press

Published in the United States
by Oxford University Press, New York

Introduction and editorial matter © André Sapir and Alexis Jacquemin 1989

British Library Cataloguing in Publication Data
The European internal market: trade and competition.
1. European community countries. Economic
integration
I. Jacquemin, Alexis II. Sapir. André
337.1'42
ISBN 0–19–829532–4
ISBN 0–19–877293–9 (pbk.)

Library of Congress Cataloging in Publication Data
The European internal market: trade and competition/edited by
Alexis Jacquemin and André Sapir.
Includes bibliographical references.
1. European Economic Community. 2. Europe–European integration.
3. Trade regulation—European Economic Community countries.
4. European Economic Community countries—Commerce. I. Sapir,
André. II. Jacquemin, Alex.
HC241.2.E859 1989   337.1'42—dc20   89–9320
ISBN 0–19–829532–4
ISBN 0–19–877293–9 (pbk.)

Typeset by Cambrian Typesetters, Frimley, Surrey
Printed in Great Britain by
Courier International Ltd.
Tiptree, Essex

Contents

Acknowledgements

The editors are grateful to the following for permission to reproduce copyright material in this collection: Société Royale d'Economie Politique de Belgique (Chapter 1 by Jacques Drèze); the University of Chicago Press (Chapter 2 by W. Max Corden); Institut für Weltwirtschaft (Kiel) (Chapter 3 by Richard Pomfret); Basil Blackwell Ltd (Chapter 3 by David G. Mayes and Chapter 6 by Alan L. Winters); North-Holland Publishing (Chapter 7 by Okan H. Aktan, Chapter 9 by Bela Balassa and Luc Bauwens, and Chapter 10 by Alexis Jacquemin and André Sapir); Edition Sigma (Berlin) (Chapter 8 by Jürgen Müller and Nicholas Owen); Harvard University (Chapter 11 by Bob Hamilton and John Whalley); the Commission of the European Communities (Chapter 12 by Pierre Buigues and Philippe Goybet); the Brookings Institution, Washington, DC (Chapter 13 by Robert Z. Lawrence and Charles L. Schultze); Centre for European Policy Research (Chapter 14 by Paul Geroski and Alexis Jacquemin); Centre d'Etudes Prospectives et d'Informations Internationales (Paris) (Chapter 16 by Paul Krugman).

Introduction
1992: A Single but Imperfect Market

Alexis JACQUEMIN and André SAPIR

The keystone of European economic integration is the common market, in which member states have combined to create a unified economic area. Since the Treaty of Rome established the European Economic Community (EEC) in 1957, the development of the internal market has undergone three phases. The first one was the elimination of customs duties and quantitative restrictions within the EEC. This phase was completed in July 1968 with the introduction of a common external tariff. During this period, and until 1972, the EEC witnessed a rapid expansion of intra-Community trade. The second phase, starting around 1973, saw the increasing recourse by member states to protectionist non-tariff barriers due to rising structural problems and unemployment. As a result, there was a slowdown in intra-Community trade, which has been documented by Jacquemin and Sapir (1988). This situation prompted the Commission to prepare a White Paper listing major remaining barriers to intra-EEC trade and a detailed timetable for their removal. The passing of the Single European Act in December 1985, instoring 'qualified majority voting' for the White Paper directives, has provided the institutional framework for completing the final phase in the creation of the internal market.

Creating in the 1990s a single European Community home market of over 320 million people by removing the non-tariff barriers between its twelve national components is expected to lead to substantial gains in economic welfare. It will help bring down costs and prices. With some time-lag, the greater dynamism of the competitive process may also stimulate trade, promote new investments, bring about restructuring and multinationalisation of firms, generate changes in location, and foster technological progress through an increased flow of innovative processes and products. It could also increase growth and employment and contribute to a better balance in the world economy.

But to analyse correctly the theoretical foundations, the empirical consequences and the economic policy implications of the '1992' initiatives, it is necessary to understand the reasons why a group of countries forms a preferential trading arrangement, implying that trade with each other is affected by lower restrictions than trade with the rest of the world.

The analysis of the welfare effects of such preferential arrangements has for long occupied a central position in international trade theory.

However, general results are hard to obtain given the second-best nature of these arrangements. Ever since Viner's contribution, two conflicting effects have been identified. On the one hand, the formation of a customs union is expected to expand trade among the partners as they remove trade barriers with each other (trade creation). On the other, it is expected to increase trade among the partners at the expense of third countries due to discriminatory treatment (trade diversion).

The traditional analysis assumes homogenous products, perfect competition and constant returns-to-scale. In recent years, however, contributors to the theory of preferential arrangements have recognized the need to incorporate product differentiation, imperfect competition and scale economies. Simultaneously, corresponding empirical testing and policy analyses have been developed allowing a more realistic account of the present-day international issues.

The purpose of this volume of readings is to provide a selection of papers that throw light on how one might use the various approaches for grasping 'the economics of 1992'. The volume is divided in three parts. Part One contains seminal contributions to theoretical aspects of preferential trading arrangements and trade in a non-Walrasian context. Part Two deals with various types of empirical research applied to the European economy and incorporating the theoretical features analysed in Part One. Finally, Part Three groups policy papers that refer to the kind of arguments and conclusions emerging from the previous theoretical and empirical research to derive various perspectives for European economic policies.

THEORY: PART ONE

Even after the promised liberalisation in Europe, intra-EC trade will still be affected by extensive product differentiation, nonconvexties in production, incomplete information and various forms of collusive or non-collusive oligopolistic behaviour. The source of these imperfections lies in the exogenous characteristics of the demand and costs functions, as well as in the strategies adopted by private and public agents. In fact the major share of the potential gains from completing the internal market relies on the very existence of such features. On an allocative level, three effects can be identified (Jacquemin 1982): greater production efficiency achieved through the enlargement of the market, reduction in monopoly power in national markets and, enlargement of the range and diversity of available products and services. In addition, distributive effects based on an intra-industry specialisation could be quite different from those stemming from inter-industrial specialisation (Krugman 1981, Helpman 1987).

An implication of this situation is that, in order to understand the mechanisms underlying European trade and identify the relevant issues for the EC common policies, it is necessary to overcome the limits of the traditional models relying on the Walrasian paradigm and take into account the growing variety of economic analysis incorporating the new features of imperfect competition. In fact, the economics of integration has recognized for a long time the importance of imperfect competition. Viner had mentioned scale economies as a possible, albeit minor, source of benefits from customs union. Similarly, several authors had underlined the importance of product differentiation for many internationally trade goods. For example, Johnson (1967) called for general equilibrium models incorporating monopolistic competition.

The opening paper of Part One, appearing here for the first time in English, is important in that it combines economies of scale and product differentiation in exploring an aspect of European economic integration. The main argument developed by Jacques Drèze is that small countries, like Belgium, have to specialise in standardised rather than differentiated products in order to exhaust the benefits of economies of scale. The author has added a post scriptum written for the present volume.

The next two papers, by Max Corden and Richard Pomfret, respectively, are concerned with the introduction of the above features of imperfect competition into the traditional customs union theory. Corden offers the first convincing attempt to show that exploitation of scale economies can be an important motive for such union. In his survey, Pomfret analyses recent efforts to incorporate some missing pieces which would make the theoretical framework more satisfying. These include transport costs, tariffs outside the customs union and bargaining motives for preferential arrangements.

The last paper of the theoretical part, by Wilfred Ethier and Henrik Horn, constitutes a radical departure from the literature on customs union theory. The authors propose several extensions, including considerations of scale economies and product differentiation. These two features are combined in an illustrative model used to examine changes in union commercial policy.

APPLICATIONS: PART TWO

Most observers recognise that empirical implementation and testing of the theories of international trade are rather difficult. The problem is not so much the frequent absence of relevant data, a typical situation at the European level, but the difficulty of agreeing on what would constitute a valid test. This situation characterises the theory of preferential trading arrangements and its application to European integration. The most direct methodology used to test this theory is the construction of a hypothetical view of international trade patterns in the absence of integration, the so-called 'anti-monde', then a comparison with what has really happened and an imputation of differences to the effects of integration.

But as long as economic relationships are not stable through integration and additional variables come into play, the construction of any 'anti-monde' is controversial. This is especially so for ex-ante models intended to predict the likely effects of integration: indeed many variables, potentially important for explaining a future 'normal' evolution in trade flows, without integration, are inevitably lacking.

On the other hand, ex-post models attempt to measure the actual effects of integration and can be more easily expanded to incorporate the more relevant economic variables determining the level of trade between countries. And indeed, the specification of these models has improved over time, including supply as well as demand variables, static and dynamic effects. Plausible estimations of the welfare consequences of integration (trade creation and trade diversion) have been estimated from such models.

In spite of their improvements, these models cannot easily take into account the multiple departures from perfect competition, including scale economies, concentration, product differentiation and barriers to entry. It is therefore not surprising that a large number of econometric models have been developed to test directly various relationships between intra-European trade and factors expressing the existence of imperfectly competitive international trade.

Although these models do not derive rigorously from trade theories, they are piecemeal improvements in their empirical applications. Together they offer a body of evidence that '. . . has fostered a consensus as to what the economic factors are that contribute most to the understanding of international trade' (Deardorff, 1984, p. 469). They include an analysis of the effect of an enlargement of the market, through European integration, on the exploitation of scale economies, identification of variables which tend to be conducive or detrimental to intra-Community trade in comparison with imports from the rest of the world as well as studies of the gains European countries may obtain from international specialisation in general and from economic integration in particular.

The next step was to construct formal models of imperfect competition and to apply them for measuring the effects suppressing of trade barriers between member states. Two types of models can be distinguished: partial and general equilibrium models.

Until now, general equilibrium models of imperfect competition are very rare and none of them has been applied to the European Community. Two recent papers are, however, very relevant for evaluating the effects of completing the Common Market. Goto (1988) develops a general equilibrium trade model under imperfect competition which incorporates labour market imperfection and variable elasticity of substitution. It shows that the opening up of trade brings about the following gains: greater consumer satisfaction due to an increase in the variety of goods; decrease in monopoly power; technical efficiency due to decrease in average costs; decrease in unemployment due to reduced imperfection in the labour market; and contribution to economic growth through the release of capital resources from the distorted sector. These gains, estimated for the U.S. automobile trade, are fully in line with the conclusions derived in the European Commission's report on the benefits of a single market (1988). Similarly, Harris and Kwakwa (1988), have used a dynamic general equilibrium model for a small open economy to analyse the effects of the 1988 Canada–America Free Trade Agreements (CAFTA). This sequenced general equilibrium model incorporating imperfect competition, scale economies, entry and exit dynamics, and some labour rigidities, allows the authors to conclude that there are large gains in production coming from improvements in productivity achieved in the scale-economy-intensive industries through a process of rationalisation, and that the adjustment costs imposed on the Canadian economy in terms of job losses are rather small.

Partial equilibrium models under imperfect competition have also been applied to international trade. Like in the above general equilibrium approach, these models cannot be used to test the theory but give it some realism by using observed data and parameters taken from econometric studies. Several of these models have been calibrated with European data and have been used for simulating the effects of various industrial and commercial policies on welfare. Two recent papers published in a special issue of the *European Economic Review* (d'Aspremont, Jacquemin, and Jaskold-Gabszewicz, ed., 1988) offer fruitful illustrations. Smith and Venables study the welfare effects of changes in the EC internal market, contrasting two scenarios: one in which there are small reductions in barriers to trade and the other where a fully integrated market is created. In the second case, substantial welfare gains are generated. Laussel, Montet and Pequin-Feissolle, following the same methodology as Smith and Venables, show that an increase in the present European tariff with respect to Japanese cars could be welfare-improving, but these gains would be low. When the policies are effective, the best one is a subsidy; quotas and voluntary export restraints are generally inefficient.

In Part Two of the readings, several types of empirical contributions have been selected, all of them with applications to the European situation. Two surveys, one by David Mayes and the other by Alan Winters, present the state of the art in the estimation of the effects of economic integration on trade creation and trade diversion, obtained with ex-ante and ex-post models. These surveys show the progressive improvements of this approach. They are completed by a paper of Okan Aktan on the expected effects of the second enlargement of the EC on the old members and the new entrants. His optimisation model allows to overcome some limits of the 'anti-monde' methodology but does not lead to welfare calculations.

Then a set of econometric papers illustrates a variety of analyses intended to capture the relationships between European integration and imperfect market structure. Nicholas Owen and Jurgen Müller show that, as a result of trade and in particular intra-Community trade, substantial efficiency gains have been obtained by German manufacturing industries due to better exploitation of economies of scale. Bela Balassa and Luc Bauwens, using a two-stage procedure, examine the impact on bilateral trade among European countries, in individual industries, of factors affecting inter-industry and intra-industry specialisation. Their results are interpreted as providing incentives for overall trade liberalisation as well as for the completion of the European integration process. Alexis Jacquemin and André Sapir also conduct an econometric analysis of intra-Community trade but focus on a set of variables that tend to be conducive or detrimental to intra-Community imports in comparison with imports from the rest of the world. A distinction is drawn between two types of factors that favour intra-area trade: those that could foster economic welfare and those that hinder a more efficient world division of labour.

Finally, the paper of Bob Hamilton and John Whalley presents a general equilibrium model of world trade applied to eight trading regions, including the European Community. Although retaining most character-istics of the Heckscher-Ohlin trade model, they assume that products are differentiated on the basis of geographical point of production as well as by physical characteristics. Simulations of two-region free trade areas are reported, including the US-EC and the EC-Japanese cases.

The transition to Part Three of the readings is made by the paper of Pierre Buigues and Philippe Goybet. On the basis of a new analysis of the main trends of intra- and extra-Community trade, broken down on a sectoral and geographical basis, they compare and critically evaluate the patterns of trade specialisation for the EC, the US and Japan. Their conclusions lead to the necessity of European initiatives to overcome the current structural weaknesses still affecting the Community. The move towards a single European market can be part of the answer.

POLICY: PART THREE

The 1992 project can be seen as an adventure in deregulation: most of the 300 directives set out in the EC's 1985 White Paper on 'Completing the Internal Market' are intended to create a common market in which goods, services, people and capital could move without barriers. However, a common market cannot be reduced to a free trade area: it is also characterised by policies, macro and micro, at the national and EC levels.

The role of common economic policies and coordination between EC member states economic policies has always been crucial given the existing high level of interdependance and the corresponding substantial amount of externalities that can be internalized. It is well known that, while the European Community as a whole is only slightly more open than the US and Japan, the intensity of intra-EC trade is quite strong. And one must expect that completing the internal market will accentuate this situation. Furthermore, the challenge of 1992 is not just economic, it is also political and social. Accepting the corresponding social and political costs would require a greater solidarity among the member states.

From that point of view, the recent poor performance of European economies has been analyzed intensely in the mid-1980s. Part Three of the volume opens with two contributions to the debate on the nature of and remedies for Europe's economic problems. The paper by Robert Lawrence and Charles Schultze (hereafter L & S), introducing and summarizing a volume of contributions by a group of American economists on barriers to European growth, is mostly concerned with macroeconomic difficulties, in particular the high unemployment in the EEC (The present readings reproduce only the first and the last sections of the overview chapter by Lawrence and Schultze). On the contrary, the paper by Paul Geroski and Alexis Jacquemin (hereafter G & J) raises the issue of corporate competitiveness in Europe, particularly in high-tech activities.

Despite their different starting points, the papers by L & S and G & J point to the same diagnosis of the European malaise: the existence of market rigidities responsible for the sluggish response of European economies to the shocks of the 1970s and 1980s. Thus, Lawrence and Schultze attribute the rise in unemployment to increasing structural rigidities in European labor markets characterized by a reduction in labor mobility. Similarly for Geroski and Jacquemin, the cause of too slow adaptation of industrial structures in Europe lies in rigidities that prevent the entry/exit of firms and the necessary changes within corporate structures.

From their common diagnosis the two papers deduce a common policy recommendation: a structural reform aimed to enhance market flexibility and reduce barriers to mobility. Both papers insist that these reforms should be coupled with complementary measures. L & S recommend the introduction of expansionary macroeconomic policies designed to raise the growth of output and employment, therefore easing the burden of the required structural adjustment. By contrast, G & J, recognising the imperfectly competitive supply conditions of many markets, strongly argue in favour of a coordinated and cooperative European-wide industrial policy.

The policy challenge of 1992 consists precisely in the implementation of structural changes designed to create the conditions for renewed growth of output and employment in Europe. In the last two papers of the volume, Michel Catinat and Paul Krugman, respectively, analyse in great depth the problems and challenges of the European internal market programme.

The paper by Catinat provides a useful review of four main components of the 1992 initiaitve: the opening up of public procurement, the abolition of internal frontiers, the liberalisation of financial services and, more generally, the improvement in resource allocation. Although all these measures constitute supply-side structural reforms with direct effects on efficiency, Catinat also examines their macroeconomic impact. The message of the paper is that the completion of the internal market—a 'European-style supply-side' exercise—offers two potential beneficial effects: contraction in unit costs and expansion of intra-EEC trade.

Catinat insists, however, that the full realisation of the benefits of the 1992 programme requires the implementation of accompanying measures. The reduction of unit costs would only translate in lower prices if the rules of competition are strictly enforced. Equally, the expansion of intra-EEC trade would only produce an increase in welfare on two conditions: Community commercial policy and macroeconomic coordination. Although most economists recognise the need for competition, external trade and macroeconomic policies at the European level, there is no consensus on the shape of such policies. For instance, it is a matter of lively debate in Europe whether the establishment of a unified internal market should take place at the expense of or in conjunction with greater world integration (Sapir 1989).

The closing paper by Krugman supplies a clear presentation of the microeconomic as well as macroeconomic issues raised by the final stage of economic integration in Europe. The microeconomics of international integration suggests that the completion of the European internal market will give rise to two problems, each corresponding to a different motive for trade. First, contrary to the first phase of integration which produced mostly an expansion of intra-industry trade, the economic disparities among the present twelve member states is more likely to lead to an increase of inter-industry trade based on comparative advantage. The result will be greater problems of internal adjustment than during the earlier phase of integration. Second, in situations where trade results from economies of scale (static and/or dynamic) and imperfect competition, there is a degree of indeterminacy about the future location of sectors often regarded as strategic. There is, therefore, a danger of conflict among member states attempting to secure the desired sectors for themselves.

Increased microeconomic integration makes countries more inter-dependent in product and factor markets, but also in their macroeconomic policies. Krugman insists that economic interdependence creates a need for improved coordination. Along with Catinat, he warns European policy makers that their failure to produce macroeconomic coordination could outweigh the microeconomic gains from 1992.

REFERENCES

Commission of the European Communities (1985), *White Paper on Completing the Internal Market*, Brussels.
Commission of the European Communities (1988), The Economics of 1992 – An Assessment of the Potential Economic Effects of Completing the Internal Market of the EC, *European Economy*, 35.

Deardorff, A., (1984), Testing Trade Theories and Predicting Trade Flows, in R. Jones and P. Kenen (eds.), *Handbook of International Economics*, Volume 1, Amsterdam: North-Holland.

Goto, J. (1988), International Trade and Imperfect Competition: Theory and Application to the Automobile Trade, The World Bank, mimeo.

Harris, R. and Kwakwa, V., (1988), The 1988 Canada-United States Free Trade Agreement: A Dynamic General Equilibrium Evaluation of the Transition Effects, NBER/CEPR, mimeo.

Helpman, E., (1987), Imperfect Competition and International Trade: Evidence from Fourteen Industrial Countries, *Journal of the Japanese and International Economies*, 1, 62–81.

Jacquemin, A., (1982), Imperfect Market Structure and International Trade: Some Recent Research, *Kyklos*, 35, 75–93.

Jacquemin, A. and Sapir, A., (1988), European Integration or World Integration? *Weltwirtschaftliches Archiv*, 124, 127–139.

Johnson, H. G., (1967), International Trade Theory and Monopolistic Competition Theory, in R. Kuenne (ed.), *Monopolistic Competition Theory: Studies in Impact*, New York: John Wiley.

Krugman, P. R., (1981), Intra-Industry Specialization and the Gains from Trade, *Journal of Political Economy*, 89, 959–973.

Sapir, A. (1989), Does 1992 Come Before or After 1990?, in R. Jones and A. Krueger (eds.), *The Political Economy of International Trade*, Oxford: Basil Blackwell.

PART I

Trade Theories and Economic Integration

The Standard Goods Hypothesis

Jacques H. Drèze*

The problems of Belgium at the inception of the Common Market have been the subject of much concern, as this audience is well aware. A particularly brilliant summary and report was, moreover, given in this room last month by Professor Dehem, whom I am happy to greet this evening. Without wishing to take up all of the points raised in his account, I believe there are two central issues to which much reflection has been given: on the one hand, the so-called 'slackening' of growth in the Belgian economy—that is, the relative weakness of its rate of growth in comparison with other Common Market countries (though not with other industrial countries); and on the other hand, the more encouraging factor of Belgium's high standard of living—that is, the high per-capita income that we still enjoy.

I do not aim to give a complete explanation of these two characteristics today. They depend to a large extent, however, on considerations relative to the economic structure of our country, which I shall briefly outline. If we have a high standard of living, it is unlikely to be due—or solely due—to the fact that we are more intelligent, harder-working, or more 'productive' than our neighbours; it is primarily because we are more heavily industrialized. Belgium is practically the most industrialized country in the world, if one considers both the proportion of the population and income devoted to industry, and the comparatively small proportion of income and population associated with agriculture. But not content solely with being heavily industrialized, we are also oriented towards those industrial sectors offering the highest salaries. In international comparisons, the difference between wage levels in different industrial sectors is more striking than the difference between wage levels in different countries.

There are three sectors in particular in which wages are extremely high: coal mining, iron and steel, and metal processing, in which wage levels in Belgium in April 1959 amounted respectively to 60, 55 and 50 Fr., in comparison with 43 Fr. in all other manufacturing industries.[1] These three industries alone represent 63 per cent of our industrial production, by comparison with 43 per cent for the entire EEC.[2] Thus we have a

* Translation, by P. and E. Kreager, of the lecture given by J. H. Drèze to the Société Royale d'Economie Politique de Belgique in November 1960 under the title 'Quelques réflexions sereines sur l'adaptation de l'industrie belge au Marché Commun', *Comptes Rendus de la Société d'Economie Politique de Belgique*, 275: 3–37.

[1] Figures for April 1959, cited in 'Les coûts de la main d'oeuvre dans l'industrie manufacturière des pays Européens et des Etats-Unis', *Etudes et conjonctures*, March 1960.

[2] According to OECD data. See *Statistiques Industrielles*.

specialization in high-salary sectors which, naturally, translates into relatively high incomes—even if the general level of our salaries is today comparable with that of our principal neighbours.

I believe that these two structural elements (industrialization and specialization in high-salary sectors) are sufficient to account for another Belgian characteristics: the relatively small proportion of our population in active employment. Our rates of employment are approximately 5 per cent lower than those of the Common Market as a whole, due chiefly to the low employment figures among our female population.

I.2. Structural considerations also provide a partial explanation for the apparent decline in our industrial production. As it happens, we are oriented towards, and specialize in, those sectors which, in the Common Market, show the lowest rates of growth. According to OECD statistics, if we separate industrial sectors into those with a lower and those with a higher than average rate of grwoth, the former represent 5 per cent of the industrial activity of Belgium by comparison with only 37 per cent for other Common Market countries.[3]

If all industrial sectors within the Common Market developed at the same rate as in Belgium, the economic growth of the Common Market would not necessarily slow down; similarly, the rate of Belgian economic growth would scarcely alter if our industrial sectors were to develop on a par with the general rates of the Common Market. A different distribution of our industrial production amongst the several sectors would be required to improve our growth appreciably. Quantitative measurement of this structural pattern poses delicate statistical problems which are far from being resolved,[4] but the partial explanation I have advanced is at all events too significant to be ignored.

Along with the characteristic pattern of our production is a second pattern, the structure of our consumption, which equally deserves emphasis. Many observers have drawn attention to the fact that the growth rate of our exports is strikingly higher than that of our production. This means, on the one hand, that countries buying from us (almost 50 per cent of which are our Common Market partners) possess a higher growth rate than our own, but also that the *increase* in Belgian consumption depends to a larger extent on importation than on national production. In other words, our marginal propensity towards importing is extremely marked. I emphasize this fact as I shall have occasion to return to the structure of our consumption; this marked propensity towards imports is, to my mind, easily explained.

Still on the subject of the declining economic growth of Belgium, the

[3] According to OECD data, loc. cit.

[4] A. Camu, in his 'Essai sur la situation économique de la Belgique', *La Revue Nouvelle*, November 1960, rejects this explanation, based on OECD data for 1938–58. The same data, analysed for the period 1938–57, lead to a contrary conclusion. In any case, these data are aggregated at too high a level (10 industrial sectors only) to be conclusive.

structural factors I have outlined above are probably more important and more fundamental than others often advanced. Thus, it is said that the rate of investment in Belgium is too low, that we do not invest enough (either in quantity or scale). This is in no way an established fact. Gross investment in fixed capital, expressed as a percentage of the gross national product, is inferior to the same percentage for all the other Common Market countries, computed on the basis of their own national accounts. But if one computes this investment and national product not in terms of the domestic prices of each country, but in terms of American or average European prices,[5] *the rate of Belgian investment in fixed capital comes out at the top of the EEC.* This reversal amply illustrates the ambiguous nature of the issue. I must thank Mr Jean Van der Rest, who is here today, for drawing my attention to this point—too-often-ignored—and which certainly deserves closer examination.

I.3. Thus embarked on a line of structural explanation in which Belgium's high standard of living and low rate of growth are attributed to its industrial orientation, and certain industrial sectors in particular, I must of course explain precisely what the industrial structure of Belgium is, and why it has these characteristics.

You will all know—for by now the observation is banal—that the industrial structure of Belgium is characterized by specialization in semi-manufactured products—that is, unprocessed or semi-processed, as opposed to finished products. There is also a tendency to specialize in products for industry, as opposed to those destined for consumption.

This specialization in semi-manufactured production would appear to derive essentially from our orientation towards industries such as coal, metal and glass, all naturally given to half-finished products. In fact, this is not the case: the studies to which I referred earlier* have shown that, in Belgian industries as diverse as organic chemistry, rubber, leather, wood, paper, non-metallic minerals or non-ferrous metals, one finds the same specialization at the level of semi-manufactured products, rather than in finished ones. It is this which characterizes our industrial structure, and which in its turn exerts a profound influence on our situation today.

I.4. You are all doubtless familiar with the classic and often-rehearsed explanations of this phenomenon. There is the early date of Belgium's development, which meant that it was oriented naturally towards the first sectors to industrialize; our dependence on coal, the one major natural

---

[5] Cf. Milton Gilbert and Associates, *Comparative National Products and Price Levels,* OECD, 1958.

* *Note to translation:* In his opening remarks, not reproduced here, the author referred to joint work at Université Catholique de Louvain, on which this speech is based. See 'Les exportations intra-CEE en 1958 et la position belge', *Recherches Economiques de Louvain,* 27: 717–738, 1961; 'Analyse de la balance commerciale de l'UEBL en 1958', *Recherches Economiques de Louvain,* 27: 739–766, 1961 (with Jean Van Der Rest and John Van Overbeke).

resource of which we have made use; and, finally, geographical disposition, our proximity to the sea and abundance of rivers, which oriented development naturally towards heavy products.

These three elements explain in part our attachment to coal, steel, and some other basic products. However, they certainly do not explain why we stop short at semi-manufactured products in areas such as leather, wood, or paper.

One could introduce, then, a second set of explanations: it is likely that the rise of the Belgian manufacturing industry was impeded by the successive events of the First World War, the Great Depression, and the Second World War. The consequences of these three events may be observed, on the one hand, in the relative advance of those countries not unduly affected by the wars or economic depression, and, on the other hand, by the setting-up of protectionist policies. But one must add that this explanation is insufficient because it cannot be applied equally to all our industries, or to other countries. It is therefore inevitably in the incompetence of our economic advisors and industrial leaders, indeed, in the malfunctioning of our social and political institutions, that one searches for the final explanation. In most explanations put forward there is, I believe, a set of complementary factors which I shall call deterministic: these include basic constraints borrowed from history and geography, and the dim view taken of the natural capacities of our politicians and industrialists.

To this lack of national pride (perhaps regrettable—I do not wish to pass any judgement), of which certain of our economists give evidence, I cannot resist comparing the position of an Italian economist, met three years ago in the States, who proposed the following theory: 'I contend', he said, 'that economic development is characterized by increasing returns and not by diminishing returns, as most textbooks teach us. Why? Because, if this were not the case, I could find no explanation for the relative sluggishness and structural unemployment in the Italian economy, other than the imbecility of Italians. This second explanation I refuse to allow, for sentimental reasons. Thus, there are increasing returns.' You can imagine this theory raised certain smiles; an American colleague remarked quite fairly, 'When you come down to it, this theory, evolved by an Italian, confirms precisely the hypothesis that the Italians are imbeciles.'

In the hope of presenting you today with a new approach to the problem, which exonerates to a certain degree those responsible for our industrial and economic policies, I hasten to assure you that my view is not founded on sentimental reasoning, but firmly upon economic thinking.

II.1. I should like you to take, as the point of departure for our considerations, the subject indicated by the title of this [original] paper, 'Our Prospects in the Common Market'. After all, what is the Common Market? What changes will it introduce? What effects will it have?

This question is a simple one. The very idea of the Common Market is to replace an *international* market composed of the juxtaposition of four or five national markets—four or five depending on whether we consider Benelux as one or two markets—by a single market which would be in essence a *national* market composed of some 160 million inhabitants. As a matter of principle, then, the existence of differences between an international and a national market is posited. Such differences do exist, and several could be listed. I shall regroup them under two titles, for reasons which will soon become apparent.

The first difference between an international market and a national market is that the former is 'fragmented' by the existence of customs regulations and, sometimes, quotas, which act as artificial barriers restricting the circulation of goods, and limiting the uniformity of the market. To these objective obstacles may be added a number of further impediments of a psychological, administrative, institutional or similar nature. If there are customs duties there are also formalities of customs clearance, the obligation to fill out certain forms. The difficulties of payment are much greater, since it is necessary to pass through banking channels for exchange purposes. Greater psychological difficulties are involved in dealing with a foreigner than with a compatriot. There are also added difficulties of transport: despite much recent progress the international coordination of transport remains less perfect than national coordination (in the organization of tariffs, for example). There are inevitably problems of language, etc. In brief, the objective obstacles of customs duties and quota systems are reinforced by subjective and institutional factors, rendering an international market necessarily less perfect than a national one.

To this series of imperfections the Common Market hopes to bring—and to bring rapidly—a remedy.

II.2. There exist, however, an additional series of imperfections distinguishing the international from the national market; if these imperfections are not present in all cases, they occur with sufficient frequency to merit the analysis I shall now put forward. These additional imperfections relate to the *qualitative differentiation of products* recorded when one passes from one national market to another. This differentiation occurs whenever it is not economically possible to take the products consumed in one country and use them without alteration to suit consumer demand in another country. Of course we are all aware that no market is perfect: there is often a qualitative differentiation between products which, ultimately, answer the same needs or serve the same purposes. Such differentiations are sometimes purely artificial, the result, for example, of advertising. Sometimes they are real. But I introduce here a slightly different notion—that of differentiations which emerge *when one passes from one country to another*. That products exchanged on the national market are more or less perfectly substitutable is one thing; that this transfer from one national market to another entails new qualitative differences, linked as it were to the threshold of the frontier, is quite a separate consideration, to my mind too little emphasized in the past. For there do exist, for numerous products, significant qualitative differentiations bound up with our international frontiers. One of the clearest indications of this is the lack of uniformity in prices at the international level.

When one calculates the exchange equivalents required to even out prices of the same article in two given countries, even neighbouring ones, considerable discrepancies frequently emerge between results obtained for pairs of goods which are essentially substitutable in their production as well as their consumption. These differences, sometimes exceeding 100 per cent, are far too significant to be attributed exclusively to customs duties and allied complexities.[6]

Casual observations of daily life also confirm this fact. A striking example is provided by the cigarette. The American, English, French, and Egyptian cigarette are four very different things: all you need to do to convince yourself of this is to offer a Gauloise to an American. . . . Another example, equally clear, is the car. Here the reasons are not solely attributable to consumer tastes, which in certain countries give preference to the driving properties of a vehicle and in others to its interior finish, but reflect tax advantages, the price of petrol, the varying standard of roads, differences in average distance covered, etc. Automobile consumption in the United States corresponds in no way to that of Italy, for example, and that of France in no way to that of Germany. One could not satisfy Americans, therefore, with Italian cars, or Germans with French cars.

On the other hand—and I insist equally on the existence of non-differentiated products as on differentiated ones—each car contains components which are interchangeable from one country to another. The clearest example is the battery. Almost everywhere in the world one now finds six-volt batteries of identical format. Americans could use Italian batteries. The fuel is practically the same in all countries, except in certain particulars concerning the quantity of octane. Moreover, if one considers not private vehicles, but industrial ones, lorries hoists, and handling equipment, considerable diversity exists within each country, but little difference is added by transfer from one country to another.

I could cite other examples from the domestic sphere, notably, electrical fittings. Try plugging your razor into an American socket: you won't have much luck. Furthermore, the voltage, amperes, and wattage available to the consumer differ. All these elements, while undifferentiated within a country (save perhaps in Belgium?), become so when they pass from one country to another. And if I had more time today, I would ask my wife to

---

[6] See in particular on this subject the results of the studies carried out by CECA, especially in *Informations Statistiques*, July–August 1957.

take my place here on the rostrum to report on likely adventures when trying to make a washing machine imported from America work in Belgium.

Having outlined some of the differences that affect electrical appliances, I could add that electric cables and wires are fairly readily substitutable from one country to another, or that industrial machines such as transformers, converters, and so forth are far less subject to typically national differences. These examples sufficiently illustrate, I believe, the existence of important qualitative differences from country to country, and of a range of products exempt from them.

Two large groups of products can be immediately distinguished, for which these differentiations are often present but also less extreme. To the first belong semi-manufactured products, such as iron and steel products, plate glass, etc., which have not yet undergone final processing and are essentially standardized, as much within countries as between them. To the second belong products for industrial as opposed to domestic use. I think that, on the whole, there is greater homogeneity and more standardization between countries for industrial articles than for consumer goods. This is quite simply explained by the fact that the industrial sector, more than the consumer, turns to the international market for its purchases.

These two categories of products are, however, only specific instances, not exhaustive, of a larger group for which few qualitative differentiations exist between countries, and which I shall call internationally standardized products.

The notion of the international standardization of products thus plays an important role in evaluating the efficiency of an international market; it throws into relief a second source of problems, which distinguish international from national markets, and which one could try to rectify by a programme of integration.

This idea is, moreover, a classic one amongst economists. I shall simply cite Alfred Marshall who, in his *Principles of Economics*, remarks, 'There are many special causes which may widen or narrow the market of any particular commodity: but nearly all those things for which there is a very wide market [and I have in mind here a more or less perfect international market (author's note)] are in universal demand, and capable of being easily and exactly described . . . so that they can be bought and sold by persons at a distance from one another . . . [and] so that the purchaser may be secure that what he buys will come up to a given standard' (pp. 325–6 of the 8th printing). So, already in Marshall, the idea of the perfection of the market is bound up with the notion of the standardization of products.

II.3. My perhaps too lengthy insistence on this point, you will realize, is evidence of the importance I attach to it, for our national economy at the inception of the Common Market. I expect that you have also already guessed the form in which this importance will manifest itself. But in order to proceed logically, I must now draw upon another set of considerations—also very classical—that is, the presence in industry of economies of scale. By economies of scale, I understand not so much the fact that production costs are lower in large enterprises than in small ones, but that costs are typically lower for mass production than for small-scale production.

This particular interpretation of economies of scale is not universal, but it is frequently encountered. Each time, for example, that assembly line production is mounted, entailing the often high cost of setting up or adjusting a production line prior to manufacture, and each time it is necessary to finance the design and production of a prototype, it is clear that the unit cost decreases in ratio to the quantity of production. For the most part, these economies of scale do not continue indefinitely as the scale of production increases, but there is a point at which unit costs cease to decrease. Thus, in the case of lot size production, once the production line is used continuously, its assembly costs cease to exist: any new increase in production would require simply the installation of a second production line alongside the first, without achieving further economies of scale.

II.4. The existence of these economies of scale naturally interacts with the phenomenon of the national differentiation of products mentioned earlier. The first consequence of this is that clearly differentiated national markets will normally be the attribute of large countries, because the desire in small countries for a national consumption different from that of other countries often restricts them to a level of production too low to take advantage of economies of scale. On the other hand, in a large country one can pay for the luxury of having an autonomous structure of consumption, without losing any of the benefits of these economies of scale—insofar, of course, as one is dealing with limited economies of scale, such as I have suggested and which are normally the case, and not with infinitely self-perpetuating ones.

One would thus expect to see all the branches of industry which involve economies of scale becoming the monopoly of large countries which have at their disposal, from the start, a sufficiently large domestic market to reach the optimum level of production. Any surplus, produced under the most favourable conditions, would then be sold to foreigners. In fact this is not the case. There are a number of small industrial countries specializing in the manufacture of products in which, quite clearly, economies of scale exist, and they do not seem to suffer for it. I think this is simply explained as follows: when a small country specializes in industries in which there are substantial economies of scale, it is because they are dealing with products not differentiated from one country to another—that is, internationally standardized products for which there is an international market rather than solely a domestic one. The theory of comparative advantage, which has such a long economic history, and the theory of monopolistic competition, effectively support this explanation. I shall begin by referring to Chamberlain who, in his *Theory of Monopolistic Competition*, having stressed that pure competition presupposes the complete standardization of large groups of products, goes on to say 'when products are differentiated, buyers are given a basis for preference and will therefore be paired with sellers, not in random fashion (as under pure competition) but according to these preferences . . . the whole is not a single large market of many sellers, but a network of related markets, one for each seller' (p. 69 of the 6th printing).

One expects, then, to see a differentiated international market parcelling itself out: if certain producers specialize in the consumer needs of certain countries, they will doubtless be that same country's own producers; they enjoy the comparative advantage of being on the spot and of not having to contend with the inherent imperfections of an international market. In relation to the producers of large countries, those of small countries suffer an absolute disadvantage in those sectors characterized by economies of scale, since they have to overcome the inherent imperfections of the international market in order to attain a profit-earning level of production. But the less imperfect the international market is, the less significant are these disadvantages; this is particularly the case when there exist fewer qualitative differentiations between the demand of different countries. Hence lesser absolute disadvantages may be regarded as comparative advantages. Thus *small industrial countries enjoy comparative advantages in those sectors where international demand is standardized, whenever economies of scale are present.*

This conclusion, ladies and gentlemen, which I wish to call the *standard goods hypothesis*, appears to me to be so obvious and logical, that I wonder whether I am not wasting my breath on tautologies. My hypothesis should nonetheless be carefully interpreted. Like most economic theories, and like all good ones, it exists *ceteris paribus*, that is, with the qualification of 'all things being equal'. Indeed, if I emphasize a comparative advantage of small industrial countries, it exists as an element alongside others— elements which derive from the availability of raw materials or other production factors, the proximity of the market, or the natural capacities of economic agents, etc. So I am focusing on one element among others. If the other elements are not very marked, this particular element can become dominant and exert a preponderant influence on the industrial specialization of a country. The non-tautological part of my paper will consist precisely in the assertion that *in the case of Belgium this element has been dominant.* Henceforth, in any study of the comparative advantages of Belgium within the framework of the Common Market, this element must first be recognized, and no proper investigation of the other elements is possible without first taking it into account.

In addition to the restriction of *ceteris paribus*, it must also be remembered that I am speaking here of comparative advantages (not absolute ones) enjoyed by small industrial countries, not large countries, and specific small countries at that; what is at issue is the comparative advantages for goods for which international demand is standardized in the sense alluded to earlier; that is, not necessarily goods standardized 'full stop', but goods for which the qualitative differences from country to country are insignificant by comparison to those already present within these countries.

Again, it is necessary to remember that this advantage is connected with the existence of economies of scale, brought about by mass production but not necessarily by large-scale enterprises. Indeed, when economies of scale are associated with the size not of production but of the enterprise, a small country may well reach a level of importance equal to that of a large country—excepting, of course, very small countries like Lichtenstein or the Principality of Monaco, where productive resources would be insufficient. Countries like Luxembourg, Belgium, and Switzerland have large-scale firms; but if their market is not sufficiently wide they will not attain a level of mass production conducive to maximum economies of scale, their size thus arising more from the diversification of activities.

II.5. Having formulated the standard goods hypothesis, and stressed that it is particularly important in the case of Belgium, I am now presented with a very simple problem. We established at the outset that Belgium specializes in semi-manufactured, and industrial, products: these represent particular instances of internationally standardized products. It remains, therefore, to establish whether, in the sphere of consumer goods, Belgium still tends to specialize in products in which the qualitative differentiations between countries are the weakest. If this is the case, the hypothesis would be confirmed and would merit our adherence.

The data assembled within the scope of the study to which I referred earlier* allow a first response to this question. We have identified, in Belgium's foreign trade, the products for which we are net exporters (that is, those products in which we specialize) and the products for which we are net importers (that is, those in which we do not specialize). I shall select a certain number of the former and compare them with the latter. I think that, as we proceed, I will have cited significant number of consumer goods in which our specialization corresponds to the element of international standardization. Likewise, you will see that my hypothesis is quite distinct from the more established view that we specialize in unfinished manufactures.

I begin with a glaring example. We specialize in photographic products, but not in pharmaceuticals. These represent two examples of consumer goods deriving from the *chemical* sector. The first is a perfect example of the *internationally standardized product*. Of course differences exist between the 8 mm and the 16 mm, or the 6 × 6 and the 24 × 36, and so on. But these are differences encountered *in every country*; at least in the

* See note to translation on p. 12.

Western world, there are not any national peculiarities. Thus, Gevaert films (naming no names) may be used equally by the French, the Germans, and the Americans. Pharmaceutical products, on the other hand, present distinct national peculiarities. If you want to see for yourself, ask your doctor for a special prescription and present it to a French pharmacist; nine times out of ten he will not recognize the brand. This is a particularly clear example.

Where *leather* is concerned, we tend to specialize in products for technical as opposed to domestic use. While it is hardly possible here to single out different consumer products, it is nevertheless useful to point out that the more standardized industrial products are Belgian specialities, while consumer products are not, and this relationship holds at every level of sophistication of these products.

Regarding *wood* products, we specialize in laminates, of course, and also in furniture beading and frames. On the other hand, we have no specialization whatsoever in the making of furniture, doors, or windows. The case of furniture is very interesting. We are no less capable than others of producing good furniture, but we make scarcely any for which there is foreign demand. The particularization of our habits of national consumption works aginst us.

In the *paper* industry, we make fancy paper and boxes of very fine quality; but we do not specialize in packaging or household articles. Now the size and quality of commercial paper or writing paper are practically the same in all countries, while packaging products are subject to very different national uses and specifications. You can't have 'all-purpose' packaging in the same way as you can stationery. But there are exceptions. Internationally, cement sacks appear to be perfectly standardized; by chance, we happen to have specialized in the manufacture of cement sacks, of which we are net exporters. The other exception relates to household goods; we are net exporters of cigarette-rolling papers, a finished consumer product. Even if tastes in tobacco differ from country to country, the length and diameter of cigarettes are luckily the same—which opens a market for us.

A still more typical case perhaps is that of *chinaware*: we export plain crockery *of one colour*, but we import the same crockery when it is *multi-coloured or decorated*; that is, when an element of personal taste is introduced which is susceptible to differences from one country to another.

I will not linger over *metal* products, citing simply one or two curiosities. We make bottle-tops, those small internationally standardized caps which seal bottles of mineral water or Coca-Cola, yet we import articles belonging to the same category, such as tin cans, foil, or churns. Where non-ferrous metal is concerned, we export copper cables, yet we import copper tap fittings. Altogether, Belgium's annual import of the latter amounts to almost half a milliard. This is certainly an area in which standardization could be encouraged further, thereby enabling the substitution of a national product for an imported one.

I cite, just for the record, the *car* industry, in which as I have said, scarcely any international standardization exists—save in certain details. What parts of the car do we manufacture? Very few, in fact, despite our growing assembly industry. We manage to supply our own tyres, batteries, car windows, upholstery, and electric cables. These are about the only really standardized parts of a car. We also produce radiators.

To finish, I shall cite a particular instance from the large sector devoted to *textiles*: billiard cloth, a speciality of a firm in Verviers (also renowned for its cassock cloth). I cite it because we should rejoice in the existence, in the sporting world, of international norms adopted world-wide. Sport (like religion?) is an important factor in consumer homogenization. If the Belgians love sport, it's not simply for sport itself, but as 'Standard' supporters.*

II.6. Here, ladies and gentlemen, you have a list of instances which appear to 'prove' my hypothesis, to the extent that proofs may be inductive. However, I must be honest, which is to say, modest. I do not consider these cases sufficient to confirm my theory, since their identification was not sufficiently independent, at least in time, of the mental process by which I arrived at it. If I had not been unconsciously struck by the several particularities of our foreign trade, I would perhaps never have formulated the standard goods hypothesis. That is why I am eager for further substantiation. It is perfectly feasible to subject it to statistical tests, for example, by investigating the international homogeneity of prices as an index of the perfection of the market. The hypothesis could also be tested by seeing if it applied to Switzerland. Until we are better informed I have no reason to believe that my hypothesis is not applicable to Switzerland, bearing in mind the several reservations with which I have qualified it. But I have not had the opportunity to proceed to this test before speaking to you tonight, and indeed I have not wished to wait on its results, being more anxious to hear your opinions than to surround myself with statistical evidence.

I am going to prevail upon you, however, to accept provisionally my hypothesis so I can examine its consequences in the third part of my paper.

III.1. The first consequence, for me, is the discovery of a new explanatory factor for Belgium's industrial specialization. Instead of saying: we make semi-manufactured products and industrial products because of historical and geographical factors and because we have been insufficiently dynamic and far-sighted to change the trend, I now say: in the production of internationally standardized goods (of which the above are particular instances) we are rationally exploiting our comparative advantages. Enjoying comparative advantages in the manufacture of these products, we would have been wrong not to have specialized in them. This throws a totally different light on Belgium's industrial specialization to that cast by

* Note to translation: 'Standard' is the name of a popular soccer team in Liège, Belgium.

traditional explanations. In a way I have reached the same point as my Italian colleague, but via a totally different route.

This is why, Mr President, ladies and gentlemen, I have dared to put forward a quietly optimistic viewpoint this evening. I believe I have introduced an explanation—certainly not the only one but an important one—which places us on a distinctly calmer footing for examining the problems of our industry, than the explanations more frequently advanced.

I am encouraged, first, as an economist. When one works within a discipline founded on rational hypotheses, it is pleasing to find facts confirming rationality. To propound such hypotheses to students, only to add that Belgian industrialists are not rational, would create a certain malaise.

I am also encouraged because this represents an *economic* explanation of an *economic* phenomenon. As an economist I am generally dissatisfied to hear attributed to causes of an institutional or political nature situations characteristically belonging to the economic domain.

But I am further encouraged for Belgium's sake. If valid, the standard goods hypothesis would exonerate our past and present industrialists from a too-frequently levelled criticism: that of being incapable of successfully manufacturing finished or sophisticated products. They would not be held less responsible for having incorrectly anticipated the development of demand, or for having adapted themselves too slowly to this development, when today they find themselves engaged in those areas of production characterized by a relatively slow rate of growth. It is certainly helpful to be more aware of one's weaknesses. But it is another thing again—and it is here especially that I *am* encouraged where Belgium is concerned—to put forward a hypothesis which allows the definition of a new perspective on the future.

III.2. After all, how did we arrive at our specialization in this family of products which affords us comparative advantages? Often enough, through the classic mechanism of competition, that is, by a succession of trial-and-error. The moment economic development ceases to be the simple elimination of weaker rivals, and is guided by the foresight on men aware of their advantages, better perspectives are opened. Does this mean that if we wish to continue to benefit from the situation created by our comparative advantages, and to exploit this situation, we should continue to specialize in semi-manufactured or industrial products, producing consumer goods solely to the (inevitably limited) extent that they become objects of an internationally standardized demand? Certain reservations should, obviously, be formulated.

If, a few moments ago, I praised the rationality behind the individual decisions of Belgian investors, I should add, on the other hand, that *the juxtaposition of individual rational decisions expresses itself, for the economy as a whole, in terms of a structural weakness.* This weakness has in part caused our slower rate of growth, but has other well-known consequences: the over-sensitivity of the Belgian economy to business fluctuations (semi-manufactured products are more vulnerable to these than consumer goods); the threat of competition from young and developing countries (which are naturally going to specialize at the outset in industrial and semi-manufactured products, before proceeding to consumer goods); and finally the narrower profit margin which generally accompanies the manufacture of products that are fairly standardized. Let us emphasize, however, that this last remark applies to semi-manufactured products, but not necessarily to all internationally standardized products. There exist highly finished products which certainly offer the potential of advantageous profit margins and royalties, but for which no qualitative differentiation exists between national demands. Photographic film and hunting guns are two examples.

There exist, besides, a number of advantages linked with the evolution towards more finished, and consumer, products. The first of these is the possibility of substituting a national product for an imported one. It has often been remarked, notably by Kuznets, and more recently by Chenery and his collaborators in the Stanford Project for Quantitative Research in Economic Development,[7] that the replacement of imports by national products is an easier course of industrialization than conquering the export market. This holds for Belgium, which should on the whole reduce its marginal propensity towards importation; it is true also for the Common Market, which still imports highly finished consumer goods from the USA. Articles of European manufacture are progressively replacing those of American manufacture, and it is to be hoped that Belgium will participate in this trend.

A final, and to my mind, most important, reason for desiring a reorientation of Belgium's industrial structure lies in *the concern for optimum utilization of the workforce*. If we have a low level of female employment it is probably due to the fact that we have a lot of heavy industry, in which the employment of women is not general, and insufficient light industry. I also think that we have probably—and unwittingly—sent down the mine-shafts or consigned to the factory floor men whose talent would have been better employed in precision mechanics or in the laboratory. With an ageing and nearly stationary population, if we wish to increase our economic growth rate we must aim at more efficient exploitation of our workforce, which would certainly be facilitated by a greater diversification of our products.

Thus, *we cannot confine ourselves to profiting from comparative advantages. We now enjoy, but must strive to create new ones.* Our policy at the inception of the Common Market should be to strengthen our comparative advantages, to profit judiciously from them, and to create

[7] Cf. H. B. Chenery, 'Patterns of industrial growth', *American Economic Review*, September 1960.

new advantages in those sectors most beneficial and most indispensable to our industrial reorientation.

III.3. Finally, we arrive at the question which doubtless occurred to you at the beginning of this talk. Will the Common Market change all this? My feelings are as follows. The Common Market will enable the rapid disappearance of the first category of market imperfections to which I alluded, namely, customs duties, the complexities of payment, etc. But it will take a much longer time to do away with the second set of imperfections, the qualitative differentiation of products. We will perhaps have to wait a whole generation before demand within the Common Market is as unified as, for example, in a large market like the United States. I hope that our consumption never becomes quite as homogenized as in America; but I hope also, for Belgium's sake, that qualitative national differences in consumption diminish under the Common Market. We are, however, bound to add that this process will not occur directly and automatically when the Common Market comes into force. The disappearance of customs-related and other barriers will certainly help to resolve qualitative differences, but this will be a secondary effect which proceeds rather slowly. Let us see how we might accelerate the process, and what measures we should adopt in the meantime.

III.4. First, Belgium's approach to Common Market policy should not be focused on this or that customs duty, but above all on *the creation of a homogeneous market*, which is not simply a market free of customs barriers. We can certainly influence this by encouraging the international standardization of all public procurement goods. For example, the system of road signs could be standardized throughout the Common Market, which could only serve to profit Belgian industry. I believe that a commission has recently been established in the Common Market to study the regularization of pharmaceutical products used in different countries. The realization of this objective represents, to my mind, the *sine qua non* for significant development of our pharmaceutical industry.

Along with public initiatives there are also private ones. Allow me to recall one such voluntary effort resulting in a greater standardization of products: the use of the oxygen furnace in the manufacture of Thomas steel. The discovery of this process has been a technical innovation of double advantage for Belgium. Firstly, it has enabled the Belgian steel industry to valorize its own product; being the first to use this technique we enjoy a comparative advantage over our competitors. Secondly, and perhaps above all, it has enabled Thomas steel to become perfectly interchangeable with Siemens Martin steel. In the iron and steel industry, national differences in production and consumption are well known, certain countries having specialized in Thomas steel, others in Siemens steel. Certain users accustomed to the latter have refused to use the former. In rendering these two types of steel perfectly substitutable, the

Thomas process automatically created a new internationality standardized
product.

People frequently say there is not enough scientific research in Belgium,
without always specifying where we should concentrate. An emphasis on
innovations of this kind would, I believe, accelerate processes of
homogenisation in the Common Market.

III.5. Second, we should find out *the products or areas of production in
which, at the present moment, none of the Common Market countries has
yet attained a domestic market size sufficient to take complete advantage of
economies of scale.* If we identify such products we will have possibly a
comparative advantage in establishing their manufacture in Belgium,
straight away at the Common Market level.

A typical instance of such products is represented by those goods which
we continue to import from the United States. We should aim systematically
to create in Belgium domestic industries manufacturing those products
which the Common Market imports from America. Our strength there lies,
not as some might wish in specialized small sums, but rather in mass
production itself: to derive optimum advantage from economies of scale it
is necessary to exceed the absorptive capacity of any of our partners'
markets. In this category would come equipment used for civil engineering,
construction, and so forth, which the Common Market buys for a milliard
francs per year from the United States. On this subject it has been said,
and rightly, that we do not possess a sufficient national market to justify
such production. But we can and must work at the level of the Common
Market, because neither do our partners possess a sufficiently wide
national market. (In the sphere of durable consumer goods, one might
suggest lawnmowers and speed-boat engines.)

III.6. Third, in adapting to the Common Market, let us try to *predict the
manner in which product standardization will occur.* If we have set
ourselves somewhat apart from many branches of industry, certain of our
neighbours are perhaps worse off insofar as they specialize in products
which have no future in the Common Market.

I would like to cite an amusing case which springs to mind: that of
spectacle frames. Belgium imports all its spectacles, half of which come
from Germany, and the other half from France. This suggests that the
design of spectacles made in Germany (and sold in Belgium) is different
from that of glasses made and worn in France. Which of these two will be
the 'European' norm a few years hence?

If we can correctly predict consumer trends in the process of market
standardization, we may once again take advantage of our foresight. Just
as I pointed out that certain new directions should be assigned to scientific
research, I stress here the need for a similar redirection of market research.
The important thing, for us, is not simply to predict which products will be
most heavily in demand, but to single out those in which our chances of

specialization are good—which is to say, those products for which there exists or will exist a sufficiently homogeneous international demand.

III.7. Of course, these measures and suggestions have a weakness: their aim is to accelerate the homogenization of the Common Market and to improve our state of preparedness for it, but they will not bring about concrete results immediately. In the meantime we shall have to pass through a *period of transition*. A-propos this transition, I would like here to challenge an idea too often advanced (which I noted just a moment ago) according to which Belgium should specialize in small-scale production. I am of course referring to our exports, and not to production designed to satisfy domestic demand. Should we specialize in exporting small product lines? I consider this alternative to be fundamentally wrong and dangerous. In effect 'small-scale production' means manufacture on commission, according to the client's specifications; in other words, production which depends on a close liaison between seller and buyer. Here is a typical area in which national producers will always have an advantage over the foreign producer, precisely because the liaisons—as much psychological as technical—between the producer and his client are far easier to organize when both are of the same nationality than when the transaction involves international exchange.

I think, on the contrary, but recognizing the need for some caution, that we should direct our interests towards *production under foreign licence*. Why? Because we must not aim, in the context of the Common Market, to export our own tastes. We are too small a country to be able to do that. What we must export is our own products. Even if our tastes in certain cases are 'superior' to those of our neighbours, the simple fact that they differ will be a constant handicap for us, and one not easily surmounted. Let us manufacture, rather, under licence—and I suggest even under licence of firms established in the Common Market, i.e. firms already enjoying significant national demand within this market. But, of course, let us also try to choose firms with a 'good' demand, one which extends to the entire market.

III.8. I fear, Mr President, I have already over-taxed the patience of my listeners. So I will not develop this idea further, although there is still one last issue to discuss. During the transition period we must also direct our energies towards the composition of our domestic consumption. If you observe the latter, you will find in Belgium a diversification probably unparalleled by any other country in the world. I shall illustrate this with examples already cited. In Belgium we smoke English, American, and French cigarettes—and I don't know how many other brands—Belgian, Dutch, German, Egyptian, and so on. If there exists a cigarette of which only a thousand packets a year are made, you may be sure that one of those thousand packets may be found right now within ten kilometres from here. As for cars: we have models from all over the world. I admit many of them are assembled in Belgium. But if we are scarcely able to manufacture the components needed for assembly, it is doubtless because we assemble far too many different cars, models, and makes, from different countries. It is regrettable that our customs policy, while stressing the importance of setting up assembly plants in Belgium, has meanwhile inadvertently left the door open by allowing the annual importation, at low duties, of 250 vehicles of the same model. This encourages diverse consumption. It means that in Belgium we encourage the importation of 250 units of all the different cars in the world, for which spare parts, dealers, and so on are needs, and whose presence will reduce still further the effective size of an already too narrow market.

One could cite examples ad infinitum. You will forgive me if I make a small confession: I am regularly irriated by the fact that, when my wife buys me a new shirt, the tab collars of the previous ones do not fit it. I have never had two shirts that used the same tabs, unless both were bought at the same time!

We are all aware of retailing problems in Belgium. This deficiency is partly a cause and partly an effect of diversification, and rationalization is called for. Let us benefit from this effort to reduce the diversity of our consumption: enlarging the domestic market will enable our producers better to enjoy economies of scale in their national marketing which, in turn, will benefit export strategies.

In many areas, as you have seen, the hypothesis advanced this evening opens up a precise and new selection of economic policies. If in the process I have managed to sketch out a line of conduct for the policies Planning Office and the Belgian Foreign Trade Office, I have not had the time to develop other issues. Thus, it seems to me far more important for the Port of Antwerp to have a large number of regular shipping lines with foreign countries than to have large tonnage. Tonnage in itself has little importance; it only exists to support dockers. But the existence of regular links with a large number of foreign countries allows us to export simultaneously and rapidly into a large number of countries, and represents a desirable factor for a large number of our industries.

Without wishing to extend this list of implications and consequences of standardization, I shall limit myself, Mr President, ladies and gentlemen, to thanking you for your attention, and to asking you, in closing, whether I should wish to be right or wrong in my reflections. Indeed, if they have appeared unperturbed on a number of points concerning the past, and to some extent the future, they are also rather pessimistic about the period of transition between the realization of the Common Market which everyone is talking about, and the realization of the Common Market of which I have spoken, especially the homogeneous market for products. Perhaps, I should also hope, for Belgium's sake, to be wrong? I shall admit, however, that I sometimes feel I am more an economist than a Belgian, and as an economist—even as a Belgian economist—I truly hope that I am right. I wish it primarily in order to confirm that it is at the level of the *integration of theory and observation* that significant and interesting economic progress is made. It is neither on the grounds of pure theory nor observation alone that the foundations of sound economic policies are based. It is only by analyzing the data furnished by observation in the light of all available theories, and by integrating it into a theoretical framework, whilst adjusting this framework as the need arises to meet particular situations, that a strong national economic policy can be developed.

There lies, for all young Belgian economists, a vast territory for research. So I hope, Mr President, that I am right, if only to demonstrate that it is still possible to say something new about the Belgian economy.

Thank you very much.

POST SCRIPTUM (July 1988)

I am grateful to my friends Alexis Jacquemin and André Sapir, for taking the initiative of having this paper translated (competently so) and reprinted. In this way they correct my inexcusable mistake of publishing in a distinctly national journal a paper stressing the fact that goods with idiosyncratic national characteristics do not circulate internationally.

It was fun to read the paper again, after so many years, and to be reminded of the exciting discussions with Luc de Voghel, Michel Falise, Jean Paelinck, Emile Quevrin, Jean van der Rest, and John van Overbeke in the course of which the 'standard goods hypothesis' emerged as the organizing principle through which an array of scattered findings became meaningful. The paper was initially published at the same time as Linder's book[8], and the two sources are sometimes quoted jointly as forerunners of what has become the mature industry of 'intra-industry trade'. Still, there are distinct differences; the specificity of the 'standard goods hypothesis' lies in the joint emphasis on product differentiation *as between countries* and *increasing returns* to scale. My interest in the economics of increasing returns has not faded since[9].

Others could assess, better than I could myself, the extent to which the hypothesis has been validated in further work on the comparative advantages of small industrial countries and on intra-industry trade. Perhaps I may add a few comments on the extent to which the impact of the Common Market on Belgian industry has confirmed the views put forward 30 years ago. The structure of Belgium's foreign trade today is quite different from what is was then. A major force in shaping the difference has been the intense activity in Belgium of multinational firms, which located new plants there or acquired Belgian firms. These

[8] S. B. Linder, *An Essay on Trade and Transformation*, Uppsala, 1961.
[9] Cf. P. Dehez and J. H. Drèze, 'Distributive production sets and equilibria with increasing returns' and 'Competitive equilibria with quantity-taking producers and increasing returns to scale', forthcoming in *Journal of Mathematical Economics*.

multinational firms took advantage of the 'customs union' side of the Common Market to relocate their activities, and to produce in Belgium (and elsewhere) goods sold throughout the Common Market—including goods meant largely for national markets, like automobiles. As a consequence, Belgium has become a net exporter in sectors, like chemicals and indeed automobiles, characterized by net imports 30 years ago. It is fun to find among these firms specific examples announced in the paper—like American scrapers or outboard motors. It is also interesting to note that the port of Antwerp has developed precisely in the announced direction.

It has been sobering to discover that some multinational firms adopted nationalistic policies when the recession came, closing down their Belgian plant to protect employment at home, often at an avowed loss in overall productivity. That aspect, closely linked to disequilibrium, was not part of my 1958 frame of reasoning.

Beyond its customs union role, with profound influences on the location of production, the Common Market has also been instrumental in bringing about more homogeneous consumption patterns. But the pace is surprisingly slow, especially in some countries (like France). Even in the field of public procurements, progress has been limited. There is scope for a refined empirical analysis of these developments, and I regret not having kept up with the relevant literature.

A fresh look at these issues is timely, as we ponder today the extent to which the process of market integration will accelerate after 1992. Judging from past experience the acceleration will be gradual, except in specific areas where geographical mobility entails little cost, like capital markets or air transportation. But the regional competition for location of production activities will continue to increase. It will progressively encompass more and more service activities. It now extends over a larger and less homogeneous geographical area, where low-wage Mediterranean countries carry relatively more weight. And it operates in the disequilibrium context of substantial unemployment everywhere. So it has become increasingly important for each region to reassess its ability to attract geographically mobile investment, and for the Community as a whole to implement macroeconomic policies supportive of the overall growth without which the benefits of market integration might fail to outweigh its cost.

The paper ended on the methodological creed that rewarding discoveries await those capable of integrating imaginatively theory and observation. Thirty years of further experience do not lead me to revise that statement.

Economies of Scale and Customs Union Theory

W. M. Corden

Nuffield College, Oxford

Internal economies of scale are incorporated systematically into customs union theory. The familiar concepts of trade creation and trade diversion remain relevant, but two new concepts are added, the *cost-reduction effect* and the *trade-suppression effect*. Each has a production and a consumption component. Two union countries facing given world prices from outside are assumed. The main analysis is partial equilibrium and verbal. Three cases are considered: initial production of the importable in both union countries, in one only, and in neither. Some account is taken of oligopoly, product differentiation, and general equilibrium in a multigood model.

Orthodox customs union theory assumes constant or increasing costs for each industry and is frequently criticized for failing to allow for economies of scale. The aim of this article is to incorporate economies of scale systematically in customs union theory. In particular, we want to see whether the familiar concepts of *trade creation* and *trade diversion* are still relevant.[1]

The approach will initially be partial equilibrium and static, this being also the way in which the principal propositions of established customs union theory were originally expounded. The economies of scale will be assumed to be *internal* to firms, so that the traditional assumption of perfect competition cannot be maintained. A crucial simplification will be the assumption that the countries forming the union face given prices from the outside world, economy-of-scale effects in the outside world as a result of the formation of the union being insignificant. We shall assume

---

[1] Viner (1950, pp. 45–46) has a substantial discussion of economies of scale, but this has not been followed up in the literature. Some of his conclusions differ from those in the present paper, possibly because his (unspecified) assumptions differ. See also Johnson (1962, pp. 60–61).

actual or potential production. If this average cost is less than the domestic price, there will be domestic production and no imports; and if the average cost of the potential domestic producer exceeds the domestic price at that quantity, there will be imports and no domestic production.[3] The qualification is that the price of imports from C, including tariff, sets only an upper limit to the price a domestic producer can charge. It might pay a profit-maximizing producer to charge less. But we assume at this stage that he maximizes profits by charging right up to the "import-preventing" price. The same analysis applies once the customs union is formed, provided we assume no transport costs within the union. Either the union demand will be supplied wholly by imports from C, or there will be a single domestic producer within the union. In the latter case he might price below the price set by imports from C, but we shall assume at this stage that he prices up to the limit price. This has the important implication that the prices facing consumers are not affected by the establishment of the union: hence (a) the total market for the product in each country remains unchanged and (b) there are no welfare effects on consumers. This assumption will be removed in the next section.

Now we come to the main analysis, which can be very brief. Initially there may be production of the product in both countries, in one only, or in neither. We consider each of these three cases briefly.

1. Initial Production in Both Countries

When the union is formed, one of the two producers, say country A's, will capture the whole union market, the other going out of business. Hence the average costs of country A's producer fall. Total costs of producing the product in the union thus decline because of specialization. This effect can be decomposed into two parts. (a) Country B's expensive domestic production is replaced by imports from A which are cheaper to produce; hence there has, in a sense, been a movement to a cheaper source of supply through the opening up of trade between A and B, and hence an orthodox *trade-creation effect*. But it must be remembered that the domestic price in B is assumed to be given at this stage. So none of the gain will go to B; it will all go to excess profits in A, and indeed B may lose, since its expelled producer may have earned excess profits. (b) Country A obtains its domestic supplies at lower cost of production. This can be called the *cost-reduction effect*. While it is a consequence of the creation of trade with B, it is not an orthodox trade-creation effect, since it is the result not of a movement to a cheaper source of supply

---

[3] See Corden (1967). The present article is essentially an extension of the analysis of this earlier paper to customs union theory.

three countries, countries *A* and *B,* which form the union, and country *C,* representing the rest of the world.

I. Simple Model: Two New Effects Introduced

We begin with a single homogeneous product which is produced in country *C* and is at least capable of being produced in the two union countries. There is a single actual or potential producer in each of the union countries. He has a declining average cost curve which indicates private and social average costs. He is assumed to pay constant prices for his factors of production whatever the scale of output, so that there are no factor rents. The average cost curve is assumed to include normal profits. Each union country faces a given c.i.f. import and f.o.b. export price set by country *C;* because of transport costs and *C*'s tariff, the export price is below the import price. It is convenient, though not essential, to assume that the two countries face the same import and export prices for the product. The average cost curve in each country is assumed to reach its minimum at a level above the export price, so that exporting the product to country *C* is ruled out. We also assume that, because of their tariffs and their relatively high costs, neither country initially exports to the other.[2]

We must now introduce tariffs. We have a choice of two simple assumptions. (1) We could assume that the two countries have the same tariff rate on the product before the union is formed. This is not a very realistic assumption, but it is implicit in much of orthodox customs union theory and means that one can focus on the effects of the freeing of trade within the union and need not be concerned with the establishment of a common external tariff, since such a tariff already exists. Since we want to define precisely what has to be added to orthodox theory when economies of scale are introduced, we should explore this case. (2) Alternatively, we could assume that tariff rates are "made to measure" at levels designed to make the tariff-inclusive import price just equal to average costs, including normal profits, hence avoiding any excess profits. If there is no domestic production, there will be no tariff. This may be a more realistic assumption, and we consider it in the next section. But we begin with assumption 1.

Subject to a qualification to be considered below, in each country the domestic price is determined by the cost of imports from *C* plus the given tariff on imports from *C*. At this price there is a given quantity of domestic demand, and at this quantity there will be an average cost of

---

[2] The requirements for this condition emerge precisely from the diagram in the Appendix.

but rather of the cheapening of an existing source of supply. Country
A's consumers will gain nothing (because they face the same price as
before), and the whole gain will go in profits to the producer.

2. *Initial Production in Country* A *Only*

There are two possibilities now. The most likely is that country A's producer captures the whole union market.[4] The effects can again be decomposed: (*a*) Country B replaces imports from C with imports from A.
The latter are dearer than imports from C, since otherwise A would not
have needed the formation of the union to break into B's market. Hence
B loses from *trade diversion,* a dearer source of imports replacing a
cheaper source of imports. The trade diversion loss to B will be equal to
the loss of tariff revenue on imports from C. For the union as a whole
the trade diversion loss may be less, since A's producer may earn some
excess profits on imports to B. (*b*) As in our earlier example, A obtains
its own product at lower cost now, so that there is a *cost-reduction effect*
equal to the extra profits earned on sales at home.

The other possibility—*production reversal*—seems less likely. When
the union is formed, production in B may start, and B's producer may
drive A's producer out of business and capture the whole union market.
His costs will be less than A's were before the union was formed, so that
this time there is a trade-creation gain through A obtaining its needs
from a cheaper source (though this gain will go wholly to B), while B
loses through the replacement of cheap imports from C with somewhat
dearer domestic production. The costs of its newly established producer
when he is supplying the whole union market must be greater than the
cost of imports from C, for otherwise he could have become established
even before the union was formed. When imports from C are replaced by
domestic production, there is a *trade-suppression effect.*[5] It is akin to the
trade-diversion effect, since a dearer source replaces a cheaper source,
but this time the dearer source is a newly established domestic producer,
not the partner country.

3. *Initial Production in Neither Country*

When the union is established, production in, say, country A may begin
for the first time, since its average costs may now fall below the given
domestic price. They will still be above the costs of imports from C, excluding duty, for otherwise A could have broken into B's market even

---

[4] See the Appendix for a geometric exposition of this case. This case is also expounded geometrically in Johnson (1962, p. 59) and is described in Viner (1950, pp.
45–46).

[5] The term comes from Viner (1950, p. 45).

without the union and so obtained the benefits of the combined market. In this case there is a *trade-suppression effect* for *A* (more expensive domestic production replaces cheaper imports from *C*) and a *trade-diversion effect* for *B* (more expensive imports from the partner replace cheaper imports from *C*). In both countries the whole loss is reflected in the loss of tariff revenue; this revenue loss will exceed the combined real income loss if the new producer earns excess profits.

Our conclusion is that the trade-creation and trade-diversion concepts are still relevant but that they must be supplemented by two other concepts, the "cost-reduction effect" and the "trade-suppression effect." This is the main conclusion of this paper and remains even when some of the awkward or limiting assumptions are removed. Our examples suggest that the *cost-reduction effect* is likely to be the more important of the two.

II. Made-to-Measure Tariff Making: Consumption Effects Introduced

The assumption that the tariffs in country *A* and country *B* are the same initially, so that a common external tariff already exists, and that domestic producers always price up to the tariff-inclusive price, has conveniently eliminated any consumption effects but has led to the peculiar result in our first example that the trade creation gain through *B* getting its product from a cheaper source goes wholly to country *A*. It seems more sensible to assume that the purpose of tariffs is protection, not revenue, and that either a tariff will be high enough to bring domestic production into being (with imports wholly excluded) or it will not be imposed at all. Furthermore, we can now assume, as an interesting limiting case, that if a tariff is provided, it is just high enough to allow the domestic producer to cover his costs plus normal profits. These are the two components of what can be called *made-to-measure tariff making.*[6] Thus there are now no tariff revenues and no excess profits. All gains and losses will be borne by consumers. With this revised approach let us look at two of our cases.

1. Initial Production in Both Countries

The average costs of country *A*'s producer when he supplies the whole union will be less than his costs when he supplied only his home market, and less than the costs of the former producer in *B* when he was supplying *his* own market. Thus the union domestic price can be less than the

---

[6] The term comes from Australia; the complicated structure of the Australian tariff system can be explained partly by an attempt to apply (not entirely consciously) the made-to-measure principle.

domestic price ruling initially in either country. Given made-to-measure tariff making, the common external tariff will thus be less than the two initial tariffs and consumers in both countries will gain from the establishment of the union. (*a*) In country *B* there is a familiar trade-creation gain having two components: the production effect results from the replacement of dearer domestic production by cheaper imports from *A*, and the consumption effect results from the increased consumption induced by the lower domestic price. (*b*) In country *A* there is a cost-reduction gain going to its consumers; this has also a production and a consumption component. The production effect is that the original amount of production sold domestically is now obtained at a lower price, while the consumption effect is that at the lower price an extra amount is purchased on which consumer's surplus is obtained.

The fact that the made-to-measure policy requires the common external tariff to be less than both initial tariffs suggests that made-to-measure tariff making may not be a wholly realistic assumption. In practice the result may be intermediate to that of this model and the previous one: the tariff may fall in at least one country, the gain going mainly or wholly to consumers there, while in the other country the gain goes in excess profits to the union producer (who may not belong to that country).

2. *Initial Production in Country* A *Only*

The made-to-measure model is applied quite easily to this case. Only one point need be noted here. If country *B* initially did not have domestic production, then its tariff will have been zero. If country *A* is to capture *B*'s market—which *A* is assumed not to have captured before—this will result not from the freeing of trade within the union but from country *B* imposing a tariff—that is, from the establishment of the common external tariff at a positive level. The price to domestic consumers in *B* will then rise, and their losses can be divided into production- and consumption-effect components: the new, lower, amount consumed is now obtained at a higher cost than before, this being a shift to a dearer source of supply—the familiar trade-diversion effect—and in addition there is a loss in consumer's surplus on the reduced amount of consumption induced by the higher price. This latter consumption effect of trade diversion does not emerge in orthodox partial-equilibrium customs union theory.

We can conclude that our four effects—trade creation, trade diversion, cost reduction, and trade suppression—each have a production and a consumption component. In a limiting case (the model of Section I) the consumption components disappear. In another limiting case (the present section) all the gains and losses (whether from production or consumption effects) are borne by consumers. One can conceive of intermediate cases where there are some consumption effects and where some of the gains go in excess profits and some of the losses are borne by the government through loss of customs revenue. The extent of consumption effects and of excess profits depends on the extent to which the tariff system permits monopolists to exploit their position and whether they choose to do so. The distribution of gains and losses among government, producers, and consumers is crucial, since it affects the distribution of the gains and losses between the partner countries.

III. Oligopoly and Product Differentiation

We now depart from the assumption of a single producer in each country and in the union and allow for oligopoly and product differentiation.

1. Initial Production in Both Countries

Suppose that there are initially *two* producers in each country. It can no longer be assumed that the increased size of the market must lead to scale economies; if the two firms in each country did not amalgamate originally, or one of them did not attempt to out-compete the other, there is no strong reason to assume that amalgamation or competition would operate in the larger area. Of course, in the world of oligopoly anything is possible, but it is conceivable that the four producers all stay in business, dividing up the market of the union among them. They may do this by differentiating their products, and since there can now be four versions of each product available to each consumer instead of two, there will be a welfare gain; this is essentially a trade-creation effect. There need be no cost-reduction effect, since the increased trade in differentiated products need not necessarily be associated with increased output by any firm.

There may initially have been more than one firm in each country because the potentially dominant producer was reluctant to swallow up the weaker firms for fear of public hostility to monopoly, leading possibly to public intervention. When the customs union is established, it becomes possible to preserve the semblance of competition while eliminating all but one producer in each country; indeed, a government may urge the national firms to amalgamate so as to strengthen the competitive power of domestic production. The two remaining firms—one in each country—may not combine either because of fear of antimonopoly action or because of the difficulty of arranging amalgamations of firms across countries, combined with hostility to, or legislation against, takeovers by foreign firms. The reduction in the number of producers will then lead to a cost-reduction gain. In addition, trade across the borders may increase, or start for the first time, as a result of product differentiation. This may or may not represent a trade-creation gain. On the one hand, the number of firms the consumer can choose to purchase from is the same as before, so he may have no more choice in variety of product; but, on the other hand, he can now choose between products made in different countries.

2. Initial Production in Country A Only·

There may be several producers in country A; when the union is formed, they all enter B's market, and there is the usual cost-reduction gain for A and trade-diversion loss for B. Two complications can be noted. (a) If the expansion of output by the various producers has brought them all closer to scales of output where average costs are at the minimum, the joint loss that they incur by failing to amalgamate is reduced; hence it becomes likelier that the oligopolistic situation will persist. (b) Some of the cost-reduction gains may be lost because producers in B may enter the field for the first time, since they now have a larger potential market available.

IV. General Equilibrium

A really satisfactory general-equilibrium customs union model with economies of scale is difficult to produce. Some of the propositions of orthodox customs union theory have been expounded in terms of the two-good model, and this has led to results similar to those that emerge from the partial-equilibrium exposition. Models with more goods become rather complicated and tend to be expounded in a piecemeal way. There seems little point in developing the economies-of-scale argument in terms of a two-good model; it generally leads to the result that a country produces only one product, though no doubt many of the results produced so far in partial-equilibrium terms could be obtained. Here an alternative approach will be sketched out. It should be borne in mind that the aim is to isolate economy-of-scale effects.

There are many import-competing products; each product is produced, or potentially produced, in each country by only one firm. For each product the average cost curve is downward sloping up to a point, the curve turning upward eventually, so as to rule out exports of the product to country C. In addition, there is an export product with constant costs. There is a single mobile factor of production—labor—and its money wage is given. The cost curves for each product are thus independent of each other, since they depend only on the given money wage and the relevant production functions. In the initial situation each country has a made-to-measure tariff structure, leading to domestic production of some products and imports of others. Our partial-equilibrium analysis can now be applied directly. When the union is formed, production of some products will expand as the partner's market is taken over (cost reduction), production of others will cease as the domestic market is vacated for the partner (trade creation), and imports from C may cease because they are replaced either by imports from the partner (trade diversion) or by domestic production (trade suppression). All our four effects will happen at the same time.

Are there any general equilibrium complications? First, the demand curves for different products may shift because real income as a whole and income distribution may change, and because there are cross-elasticities. A fall in the price of one product would shift the demand curve for another product to the left. For any particular product the level of demand is crucial in determining either the tariff rate required to sustain a domestic industry or, alternatively, whether a domestic industry can be sustained with a given tariff rate. Furthermore, it determines the actual volume of output. Because of these demand relationships one cannot look at each product separately as if the general-equilibrium story were just made up of a set of separable partial-equilibrium stories. But it remains true that there are our four effects.

A second general-equilibrium complication is the need to maintain balance-of-payments equilibrium, which (with constant money wages) would be brought about through exchange-rate adjustment. In the first instance, with a given exchange rate, many of country A's industries might expand into B's market, while many of B's industries close down. Such a situation will then provoke appreciation of A's and depreciation of B's currency, and hence declines in the prices facing A's producers and increases in the prices facing B's producers (each in terms of their own currencies). This will then cause some of A's industries to go out of business and some of B's industries to revive again. In considering our effects in a general-equilibrium model, we should compare the initial preunion situation with the situation after the union is formed, each situation having its own equilibrium exchange rate.

V. Dynamic Considerations

There is nothing essentially "dynamic" about economies of scale. The whole of the analysis so far has been comparative static. But it is true that in a comparative-static model when there are economies of scale it is not possible to describe precisely the equilibrium that will be reached in a customs union. If initially our product is produced in both partner countries, we can say that when the union is formed one country might take over the whole market. But we cannot say which country it will be: that depends on dynamic considerations—on the nature of oligopolistic competition, the relative rates of gross investment in the two countries, and so on.[7] In the comparative-static model it is clear that, if only one firm survives, there will be trade-creation and cost-reduction effects, both of which represent gains to someone, but one cannot say which country will obtain the trade-creation and which the cost-reduction effect.

More generally, customs union theory may not tell us much about the reallocation of existing resources, owing to their immobility, but it can tell us something about the allocation and productivity of new investment. In the short run capital is immobile and industries do not just "take over" the whole market in another country or "close down" as neatly as a comparative-static model might suggest. Assuming a "putty-clay" model, the more gross investment there is in proportion to existing output, the more outputs will respond over a given period to price changes. Hence the effects described in this paper will take time, how much depending on the rate of gross investment.

Appendix

In figure 1, DD' is country A's demand curve for the product, and LL' is the horizontal sum of country A's and country B's demand curve. The c.i.f. import price (when importing from C) is OP_m, and the f.o.b. export price (to C) is P_x. These prices are identical for countries A and B. We illustrate the argument of Section I of the paper here. The given tariff is P_mT. Before the union is formed B has to pay this tariff on imports from A as well as from C, so that the combined demand curve facing A's producer is $TQRVZP_x'$. Once the union is formed, the demand curve facing him is $TWZP_x'$.

Curve AA' is country A's average-cost curve. If it cuts DD' below Q (as drawn) then there is domestic production in A before the union is formed; if it cuts DD' above Q, the whole amount of domestic consumption TQ will be imported (unless there are exports to B). If AA' cuts LL' above V (as drawn), there will be no exports to B in the absence of the union (unless there are exports to C) because B will find imports from C cheaper, while with the union production will depend on a positive common external tariff. If AA' cuts LL' below V there will be exports to B even in the absence of the union, and with the union production will not depend on a positive common tariff; furthermore, there will be production in A even if AA' happens to cut DD' above Q. If

---

[7] One might envisage a process of cutthroat competition to decide which of the two firms will survive. The firm that would have the relatively lower average costs if it supplied the union market on its own will have an advantage; this may depend on relative factor intensities, and so on. If "learning by doing" counts for anything, and provided it is related to output, one might expect (other things being equal) the firm that initially enjoyed the larger home market to have the lower costs after the union is formed, and so to survive. Relative financial resources to bear temporary losses are also relevant. During the process of "sorting out," the union price may fall substantially, so that there may be a temporary income redistribution from producers to consumers.

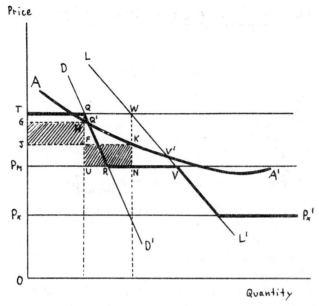

FIG. 1

AA' cuts *LL'* above *W* (which it can do only if there is no production initially, *AA'* also cutting *DD'* above *Q*). then there will be no production even with the union. Provided the minimum-cost point on *AA'* is above $P_x P_x'$ (as drawn), there will be no exports to *C*.

The diagram assumes (*a*) that even though *B* may have produced initially, it vacates production once the union is formed, and (*b*) that there are no transport costs within the union.

If (1) the producer prices right up to the import-preventing price *OT* and (2) *B* imported from *C* before the union, then the cost-reduction effect is *GHFJ* and the trade-diversion effect for the union as a whole is *FKNU* (both shaded). The loss of customs revenue to *B*, and hence the total loss to *B*, is *UQWN*, of which the trade-diversion effect *FKNU* is a net loss to the union countries combined and *FQWK* is a redistribution toward *A*'s producer, who gains *FQWK* plus the cost-reduction effect. From the point of view of *B* alone, one would describe the customs revenue loss *UQWN* as the "trade-diversion effect."

If the made-to-measure system operated, the price to *A*'s consumers before the union is formed would be given by the point *Q'*, and the price to *A*'s and *B*'s consumers after the union is formed, by *V'*. Bearing this in mind, the diagram could be used to illustrate the various arguments of Section II.

References

Corden, W. M. "Monopoly, Tariffs and Subsidies." *Economica* 34 (February 1967): 50–58.

Johnson, H. G. *Money, Trade and Economic Growth*. London: Allen & Unwin, 1962.

Viner, J. *The Customs Union Issue*. London: Carnegie Endowment Internat. Peace, 1950.

The Theory of Preferential Trading Arrangements

By

Richard Pomfret

Contents: I. Introduction. – II. Some Pre-Vinerian Contributions. – III. Mainstream Customs Union Theory. – IV. The Vanek-Kemp Branch. – V. The Search for the Missing Prince. – VI. Why Do Preferential Arrangements Exist? – VII. Conclusions.

I. Introduction

In view of the proliferation of preferential trading arrangements since the war, one might expect the analysis of discriminatory trade policies to occupy a central position in international trade theory[1]. In fact it was a backwater during the late 1960s and the 1970s. The accepted theory had limited applicability, there was little consensus on the reliability of existing measures of the welfare effects even of the most important preferential arrangements (such as the European Community), and the conventional explanation of the establishment of such arrangements rested on "non-economic" arguments. Recent theoretical developments have improved the situation by incorporating new elements into the theoretical framework, which provide the basis for more convincing explanations of why discriminatory trade policies exist. In conjunction with growing disrespect by policymakers for the nondiscrimination principle which is the cornerstone of the GATT, these developments indicate the need for an up-to-date survey of the theory of preferential trading arrangements.

There are some good reasons for the deficiencies of this branch of international trade theory. The theory of trade preferences belongs to the

---

Remark: I am grateful to Dermot McAleese, Jim Riedel, Ed Tower and Alan Winters for helpful and encouraging comments on earlier drafts, even if not all of their advice was acted upon.

[1] The terms preferences, discrimination and preferential trading arrangements are here used interchangeably to refer to different treatment for different trading partners; nondiscrimination and MFN treatment are used for the opposite situation. The list of postwar preferential arrangements is too lengthy to reproduce, but by the 1980s the majority of international trade was being conducted on a preferential basis [Pomfret, 1985]. For the European Community, half of members' imports were intra-EC trade and over half of the remainder was covered by the EFTA agreement, the Lomé Convention, Mediterranean agreements, the Generalized System of Preferences (GSP), the Multi-fibre Arrangement (MFA), and trade with Comecon – "most-favored-nation" treatment applied to a residual seven countries. For the United States, the main proponent of nondiscrimination, ten percent of imports are covered by the MFA, the Autopact with Canada, GSP and Comecon trade, while many non-tariff barriers are discriminatory and there is current pressure in Congress for reciprocity in commercial policy (i.e. discriminatory measures against countries not granting "fair" treatment to U.S. exports). On other major preferential schemes see El-Agraa [1982].

world of second-best, and generalizations are hard to make[2]. The 2 x 2 x 2 model is not applicable, since at least three countries must be involved[3]. Even granted these obstacles of outcome and method, however, the literature has made disappointing progress, primarily because inappropriate assumptions have been overused in order to surmount the methodological problem; these have enabled some strong conclusions to be reached, but they are divorced from many practical cases. In particular, international price changes have often been ruled out by assumption, which in turn ensures that analytical attention is focused on the preference donor rather than the recipient and biases the analysis against finding welfare gains from preferences. To the extent that the literature looks beyond the donor, it is to analyze the global welfare effects of preferences, obviously a useful goal, but in avoiding the distribution of welfare gains and losses, it sheds little light on the political economy of preferences.

The aim of this paper is, by surveying the literature on preferential trading, to identify the reason for this lackluster performance. Section II resurrects three earlier contributions which remain relevant. The third and fourth sections survey the literature of the 1950s and 1960s in order to trace the genesis of the situation described above. During the 1970s and early 1980s there were signs of dissatisfaction and attempts to incorporate some missing piece which would make the theoretical framework more satisfying; four types of pieces are examined in Section V. After relaxing the assumption of constant costs and giving price changes a larger role, discrimination in international trade may be rational from a national perspective; Section VI sketches the economic motives for preferences and applies them to the major postwar preferential trading arrangements. The main conclusions are summarized in the final section.

II. Some Pre-Vinerian Contributions

The theory of preferences (or customs union theory) is frequently interpreted as beginning de novo with Viner's 1950 book. This is clearly a simplification; most tariff regimes before 1950 had been discriminatory, proposals for customs unions had been frequent and some important ones had been implemented, and there had been informed discussion of all this. Yet there had been no resolution of the fundamental dilemma posed to advocates both of free trade and of protection: are preferential tariff reductions better than no tariff reductions or, alternatively expressed, is protection against some foreign suppliers better than no protection? Neither from a national nor a

---

[2] Thus a movement towards one condition for Pareto optimality by reducing tariffs on imports from some sources may not be welfare-improving when other conditions are not fulfilled (which they necessarily are not when tariffs remain on non-preferred imports) [Lipsey, Lancaster, 1956/57].

[3] There is some debate over the minimum number of commodities (see Section V.1 below).

global welfare perspective could this be categorically answered. Viner's great contribution was to prove indeterminacy, and, by introducing the concepts of trade creation and trade diversion, to provide tools for identifying conditions under which preferential arrangements are welfare improving[4]. Nevertheless, there had been important insights before 1950, three of which will now be described.

The controversy which Viner resolved had focused on a preferential tariff's impact on the donor. Some consideration had been given to global considerations, but most contributors took a nationalist viewpoint. Little attention was paid to the impact on the preference recipient, perhaps because it appeared obvious and had been spelled out long ago: "When a nation binds itself by treaty ... to exempt the goods of one country from duties to which it subjects those of all others, the country, or at least the merchants and manufacturers of the country, whose commerce is so favoured, must necessarily derive great advantage from the treaty" [Smith, 1776, Book IV, Ch. 6]. By emphasizing the gain to the preference recipient Smith makes an important point about the distribution of gains (both among and within affected countries); the point aroused little controversy, but by the 1960s it appeared to be largely forgotten, or assumed away.

The most controversial word in the above quotation is "great". The direction of change seems incontrovertible, but its magnitude is not. In an article foreshadowing Viner, Taussig [1892] showed that the incidence of the costs and benefits from preferences depends upon the market share of the recipient. He illustrated this with two examples. Preferences given by the USA to Hawaiian sugar in 1876 scarcely affected American prices (because the Hawaiian market share remained small) but yielded a windfall gain to the Hawaiian producer, i. e. the welfare effect was a transfer from U.S. government revenue to Hawaiian producer surplus. Taussig [1892, p. 28] concluded that "... any remission of duty which does not apply to the total importations, but leaves a considerable amount still coming in under the duty, puts so much money into the pockets of the foreign producer". His second example concerned the other extreme where the preferred partner provides almost all imports, illustrated by the U.S. granting preferential treatment to imports of wool from Australia. In this case, if the price elasticity of import supply is high, the primary beneficiaries are domestic consumers. Taussig's examples

---

[4] O'Brien [1976] has argued that the concept of trade diversion was discussed by classical economists from Hume and Smith on, and especially by McCulloch in the nineteenth century. In the first half of the twentieth century it is less prominent, and many writers only emphasized the trade creation aspects of preferences. To me, O'Brien's limited concession to Viner's originality in focusing attention on trade creation and trade diversion, in contrast to previous references which were "short discussions in the context of rather wider issues" [*ibid.*, p. 560], underrates the key insight that it is the possibility of either outcome which is the source of ambiguity of welfare effects; previous writers tended instead to argue for or against preferential arrangements, stating only one side of the argument.

indicate that the distribution of the preferences' welfare effects depends upon what happens to prices, i.e. upon whether the exporter is "large" or "small". Taussig's paper is a precursor of Viner's work insofar as it identifies the ambiguous impact of preferences on the donor (in his examples the USA), although in less general terms than Viner's[5].

Along a different track, Torrens [1844] developed an argument for preferences based on the nationally optimum tariff in the presence or absence of other countries' reactions. He opposed unilateral tariff abolition on the grounds of negative terms of trade effects and increased vulnerability to other countries' manipulation of the terms of trade, and advocated bilateral negotiation of commercial treaties on a reciprocity basis. Torrens rejected charges that he was opposed to free trade in general; free trade was the ultimate objective but it could only be imposed upon political dependencies, while independent (large) countries could gain by levying their nationally optimum tariff unless this was made costly by retaliatory tariffs[6]. Torrens' analytical contribution is valuable because he recognized the argument that a country could maximize national welfare by operating as a discriminating monopolist even though the global optimum was free trade, and because he related preferences to changes in the terms of trade, which occupied center-stage in his policy discussion; a position which they vacated, with unhappy consequences, in later work.

III. Mainstream Customs Union Theory

Viner's distinction between trade creation and trade diversion as effects of a preferential tariff reduction was seminal. The distinction is important because the resource misallocation associated with trade diversion is the fundamental cost of discriminatory trading arrangements which has to be weighed against the benefits of a lower tariff on some imports. Unfortunately, however, the branch of economics opened up by Viner proved disappointing, partly because of its focus on trade diversion and trade creation. The most powerful apparatus for illustrating these concepts involved assumptions which ruled out many interesting aspects of discrimination and which focused exclusively on the situation of the preference donor. After classifying and clarifying the trade diversion / trade creation aspects of discrimination, the literature centered around the proposition that customs unions were irrational in the standard economic sense.

---

[5] For other precursors see O'Brien [1976].

[6] "It is by the enforcement of retaliatory duties throughout the ports of the British empire that free trade is to be conquered" [Torrens, 1844, p. 67]. On page 102 he calls for "a British commercial league – a colonial Zollverein" to counter foreign rivals' hostile tariffs. His analysis of commercial policy is contained particularly in letters II, III and the postscript to letter IX; the clearest statement of policy recommendations is on pages 47–48. For a modern commentary on Torrens' work see Robbins [1958, Ch. 7].

Jacob Viner's seminal contribution is contained in the fourth chapter of *The Customs Union Issue*[7]. Despite the book's title, Viner emphasizes that the customs union is but one of possible preferential trading arrangements whose economic differences are slight [Viner, 1950, p. 4]. The key passage concerns his explanation of the trade creating and trade diverting effects of a customs union on p. 43: "There will be commodities, however, which one of the members of the customs union will now newly import from the other but which it formerly did not import at all because the price of the protected domestic product was lower than the price at any foreign source plus the duty. This shift in the locus of production as between the two countries is a shift from a high-cost to a lower-cost point... There will be other commodities which one of the members of the customs union will now newly import from the other whereas before the customs union it imported them from a third country, because that was the cheapest possible source of supply even after payment of duty. The shift in the locus of production is now not as between the two member countries but as between a low-cost third country and the other, high-cost, member country" and his initial evaluation on p. 44: "From the free-trade point of view, whether a particular customs union is a move in the right or in the wrong direction depends, therefore, so far as the argument has yet been carried, on which of the two types of consequences ensue from that customs union. Where the trade-creating force is predominant, one of the members at least must benefit, both may benefit, the two combined must have a net benefit, and the world at large benefits; but the outside world loses, in the short-run at least .... Where the trade-diverting effect is predominant, one at least of the member countries is bound to be injured, both may be injured, the two combined will suffer a net injury, and there will be injury to the outside world and to the world at large".

Viner goes on to discuss two other sources of benefits from customs union, scale economies [pp. 45–47] and terms of trade changes [pp. 55–56], but he downplays the former as unlikely to be substantial and the latter as a welfare transfer involving "corresponding injury to the outside world". His prime interest in chapter 4 is in assessing the net impact of a customs union compared to the pre-union situation and he concludes that confident judgment "cannot be made for customs unions in general and in the abstract, but must be confined to particular projects" [p. 52]. He does not explicitly compare customs unions with unilateral commercial policies, although he does advocate the preferability of multilateral nondiscriminatory tariff reductions [p. 135].

---

[7] The possibility of trade diversion had been briefly raised in an earlier article [Viner, 1931, p. 11], but Viner acknowledges in his book [1950, p. 53] that his mind was still unclear on the issue in the early 1930s.

During the decade following Viner's book emphasis was largely on clarifying the concepts of trade creation and trade diversion and identifying situations under which each would be more likely. The major theoretical development was to identify a possible welfare-increasing aspect of trade diversion; the lower price in the preference-donor would encourage additional consumption of the imported good, involving increased consumer surplus whether or not the additional imports were from the least-cost supplier[8]. Meade referred to this as "trade expansion", and later commentators found the amendment largely semantic (because trade creation could be extended to include all post-preference imports which were not previously imported) without altering Viner's basic evaluation[9]. Meade's 1955 lectures contained the fullest tracing out of preferences' effects through the primary impact of trade flows in the preferred goods, the secondary impact on substitutes and complements, and the tertiary impact via any need for balance-of-payments adjustment, although his verbal reasoning did not make a lasting impression. Other writers, notably Scitovsky [1956; 1958], focused on the realization of scale economies and increased efficiency due to greater competition in domestic markets as the major sources of welfare gain from customs unions. The domination of trade creation and trade diversion is, however, reflected in Lipsey's influential 1960 survey of the field, which mentions the scale economy, technical efficiency, terms of trade and growth aspects, but whose analytical core is related to the resource allocation aspects of customs unions.

The year 1960 represented a watershed in customs union theory (as the theory of preferences had come to be known) in that it saw the popularization of the diagram which dominated future textbook presentations of the theory. One problem with Vinerian theory was the lack of rigor of the original exposition, almost all the relevant parts of which have been quoted above. As Meade [1955, p. 36] pointed out, Viner's analysis is most suitable where demand elasticities are zero and supply elasticities are infinite. Whether Viner made these assumptions is doubtful and Meade certainly saw any analysis based on them as incomplete, but it became the practice to base customs union theory on infinite supply elasticities of all foreign suppliers[10].

---

[8] The point was made at more or less the same time by Meade [1955], Gehrels [1956/57] and Lipsey [1957].

[9] This definition was proposed by Johnson [1960a] and endorsed by Corden [1965]. The issue returned in a fruitless debate over welfare improvements from trade diversion [e.g. Bhagwati, 1971; 1973; Kirman, 1973], which had to be settled by Johnson [1974]. In terms of Figure 1 Johnson defines both CB and GH (and not just the former) as trade creation; this is the definition adopted in the remainder of the present paper.

[10] Arguments over "What Viner really said" still continued a quarter of a century later. Viner [1965] denied making either assumption, although Michaely [1976] shows that Viner neglected demand changes and was inconsistent and ambiguous about whether costs were constant or increasing. See also the Bhagwati [1971; 1973] and Kirman [1973] debate.

Given this assumption, Figure 1 illustrates trade creation, trade diversion and the primary consumption effect in the simplest manner, with the standard conclusion that the net welfare effect (ABC + FGH − BEJG) may be positive or negative[11]. Although the diagram is a splendid heuristic device, it is ironic that its method runs counter to that of Viner and Meade, its putative fathers. In a long footnote Viner [1950, p. 53] criticized previous analyses of customs unions for, among other things, "applying the standard techniques of partial equilibrium analysis ... to the tariff problem where its findings are either totally without significance or of totally indeterminable significance". Meade [1955], by his emphasis on the secondary and tertiary impacts, also saw preferences as requiring a general equilibrium framework of analysis. Even within the partial equilibrium framework Humphrey and Ferguson, for example, recognized the restrictiveness of assuming horizontal supply curves from the preference recipient and the rest of the world, but their Model II incorporating increasing costs did not provide any real insights and was largely forgotten[12].

Figure 1 − *Partial Equilibrium Analysis of Discrimination with Perfectly Elastic Supply of Imports*

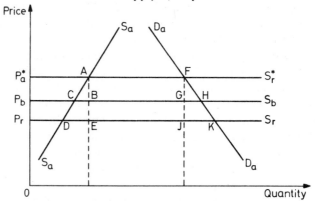

Note: S_a and D_a are domestic supply and demand curves in A. S_b is the supply of imports from the preferred source, B, which is perfectly elastic at a price P_b. S_r is the supply of imports from the rest of the world, and P_r is the world price; S_r^* is the tariff-inclusive supply curve, and P_a^* is the pre-preference domestic price in A.

[11] The use of producer and consumer surplus (and the welfare triangles) had already been described by Meade [1955, pp. 35–43], but he had not drawn the diagram. Figure 1 appears in Johnson [1960a] and Humphrey, Ferguson [1960]. Whether either article was the source of its popularity is impossible to say, as Lipsey's survey (which used a constant cost example to explain Viner's argument) and Johnson's influential costs of protection article (which applied the same technique to nondiscriminatory trade barriers) appeared in the same year, and it is a short step from them to Figure 1.

[12] A similar approach had been used by Johnson [1957; 1958] in articles which also remained neglected. See Section V.3. (below) for further developments.

Both the mainstream theoretical and empirical literature of the next dozen years could be placed within the framework of Figure 1. The net welfare effect of the preferential tariff reduction in Figure 1 can be no better (and will normally be worse) than that of unilaterally eliminating the tariff on a nonpreferential basis, i.e. ADE + FJK. The implication is that preferential trading arrangements are economically irrational and can only be explained by noneconomic motives [Johnson, 1965; Cooper, Massell, 1965]. The disappointingly small estimates of the welfare triangles (ABC + FGH) for such a major customs union as the European Community led more empirically oriented authors to conclude that scale, technical efficiency, or other considerations were the key ones, but little progress was made in quantifying these so-called dynamic effects[13].

IV. The Vanek-Kemp Branch

Figure 1 and its progeny (specifically the Cooper-Massell-Johnson proposition about the noneconomic motivation for preferential trading) dominated preferential trading theory through the 1960s and 1970s, and became the textbook presentation of the subject. There was, however, a substream which developed along its own lines more or less independently of the mainstream literature; its primary source was Vanek's 1965 book.

Vanek uses the neoclassical 2 x 2 general equilibrium model with production possibility frontiers and community indifference curves, extended to include a third country. The advantage of this approach is to bring prices back to center-stage, a point emphasized by Vanek [1965, p. 26]: "... perhaps the most important... [economic variables] ... are the terms of trade prevailing within the union, and in world markets after integration". The drawback of Vanek's approach is that in a two-commodity world pre-union trade patterns can only take two possible forms (see below); either A and B trade with one

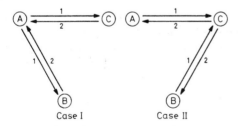

Case I   Case II

Legend:
1 and 2 are
the two *goods;*
A, B and C the
three *countries*

---

[13] The distinction between static and dynamic effects was popularized by Balassa [1961]. Kreinin [1964] tried to pin down the dynamic effects (although why, say, scale economies are dynamic remains a mystery) and pointed out the possibility of negative dynamic effects on the rest of the world; Kreinin's empirical work is brought together in his 1974 book. Balassa [1975] is a useful collection of empirical studies. Pelkmans, Gremmen [1983] provide a critique of work on the static effects.

another or they do not: The second case is almost trivial (unless trade reversal occurs and B starts to export good 2 to A)[14], while the first case will likely have strongly asymmetrical effects.

These effects are explored by Vanek, Negishi [1969] and Kemp [1969]. The propositions which emerge are typically second-best: "The only general conclusion as to the welfare effects of customs unions is that they can be either beneficial or detrimental to the world as a whole. Any more specific statement must contain further qualifications" [Vanek, 1965, p. 6]. Kemp [1969, p. 31] derives a stronger conclusion about the impact on A and B individually: "Strong inferiority aside, the creation of the preferential trading club operates to the advantage of whichever member trades only with the other member, and operates to the disadvantage of the latter". But this only holds if trade with C does not fall sufficiently for A's terms of trade to improve enough for A to gain and B to lose. He also shows that A and B together will normally gain vis-à-vis the pre-union situation, in the sense that the loser can be compensated and the gainer retain a net benefit, but even this is not necessarily true if capital flows exist and B is a net creditor [*ibid.*, p. 49].

The strongest conclusion arises when not only the disadvantaged partner is compensated, but also the rest of the world is compensated by setting the union's common external tariff so that external terms of trade are unchanged. Under these conditions the post-union utility-possibility function is consistently superior to the pre-union utility-possibility function; i.e. if the welfare of B and C is held constant then A will be better off after forming a customs union than before it [Vanek, 1965, Ch. 7]. This elementary proposition was restated in a more general form by Kemp, Wan [1976], who went on to ask why we do not observe continuous customs union formation culminating in free trade. They mention difficulties of partner selection, noneconomic objectives, and international restrictions on preferential arrangements, but the central point seems to be what they refer to as ignorance and inertia, especially with respect to "the long list of lump-sum compensatory payments required". Thus the Vanek-Kemp-Wan proposition, which is potentially interesting as an economic justification for preferential trading arrangements, has an esoteric air as an explanation of preferences in the real world[15]. A further practical problem is that the compensating common external tariff is not necessarily the welfare-maximizing tariff from the union members'

---

[14] One feature of case II is that A and B in unison can impose an optimum tariff on good 2. This is analyzed in Section V.3. below.

[15] Grinols [1981] has proposed a feasible compensation scheme and applied it to British accession to the European Community [Grinols, 1984], which to some extent could overcome Kemp and Wan's complexity and ignorance point but which does not resolve the problems caused by lack of respect for other countries' interests.

perspective; so, if there is the global consensus for other countries' interests to be respected, why not agree to move directly to universal free trade?

It is easy to see why the Figure 1 literature with its simple exposition and strong (but limited) conclusions remained popular while, at the same time, articles kept emerging in the Vanek-Kemp tradition since this was the only general equilibrium branch of the literature. The two branches of the literature were brought together by Berglas [1979], who used a variant of Vanek's case I to show that anything A and B could gain by preferential trading could be gained by unilateral tariff reduction. Berglas' conclusion is based on the assumption that world prices do not change; in his model A or C is a large country and the others small, so that the only domestic prices to change are those of B, whose export good's price goes up by the amount of A's tariff and whose import good's price falls by the amount of her own tariff. After A and B form a customs union A will lose tariff revenue, while there is a presumption that B gains both A's foregone tariff revenue and from her own tariff reduction (depending on unknown income effects). Berglas demonstrates that, if B compensates A for the latter's loss, then all remaining gains to B could be achieved by unilateral nonpreferential tariff reduction. Constant terms of trade thus yield the Johnson-Cooper-Massell unilateral tariff reduction (UTR) proposition either in a Figure 1 framework or in a Vanek framework.

V. The Search for the Missing Prince

In contrast to the landmark contributions between 1950 and 1965 by Viner, Meade, Lipsey, Johnson, Mundell, Vanek and Cooper and Massell, the next fifteen years saw a marked lack of advances in preferential trading theory. Kemp and Berglas developed Vanek's model, the Wonnacotts and Corden cast further light on the relevance of scale economies, and Krauss' 1972 survey attracted some attention (but less than Lipsey's 1960 survey had)[16]. In the late 1960s Caves and Johnson [1968, p. viii] could still refer to the "large and fast-growing literature" on customs union theory, but during the 1970s disillusionment with this branch of economic theory grew. The cause was not a lack of preferential trading arrangements[17], but rather the twin conclusions of customs union theory that (a) a preferential tariff reduction could be either better or worse than no tariff cut from the home

---

[16] Krauss also attracted criticism for non sequitur [Michaely, 1976] and for missing the point of one paper and other "interpretative lapses" [Bhagwati, 1973, p. 897].

[17] Existing arrangements were extended, e.g. the enlargement of the European Community, the Lomé Convention and the Multifibre Arrangement, and the Generalized System of Preferences for developing countries (GSP) was implemented. The major studies on GSP were concerned with how restricted the actual schemes were [Murray, 1977], how inferior they were to MFN tariff reductions [Baldwin, Murray, 1977], and how the developing countries would do better to participate in

country's and the world's perspective, and (b) a nondiscriminatory tariff reduction will never be inferior to the preferential reduction from these perspectives. Thus, the only generalization that seemed to emerge was that in the absence of domestic distortions a preferential trading arrangement was inexplicable for a welfare-maximizing importing country.

This unhappy state of the art engendered a belief that something must have been omitted from the analysis; customs union theory was "Hamlet without the prince", in the words of Wonnacott, Wonnacott [1981, p. 705]. Their own candidate for the prince's role is tariffs in the rest of the world, but there were other candidates too. Lipsey [1960] had already suggested possible terms-of-trade effects, scale economies, improved technical efficiency and higher growth rates, and although the latter two have not attracted much interest among economists (in contrast to among policymakers) the first two have received some attention[18]. Another direction in the search for a missing component was to increase the dimensionality of models.

1. Higher Dimensionality

The theory of preferential trading must diverge from the two country / two commodity (2×2) trade theory model by introducing a third country, but there is little agreement as to whether more commodities (or countries) are desirable. An analytical framework with more commodities permits complements as well as substitutes, whose significance Meade [1955] described in his secondary effects, which in turn suggests a need for at least two outside countries to capture the different impact on producers of complements and substitutes [Arndt, 1969]. Nevertheless, the *essential* elements of preferential trading could possibly be dealt with in a 3×2 model, as Vanek [1965, p. 13] and Kemp [1969, p. 21] believed. A series of authors during the 1970s challenged this belief by gaining new insights through 3×3 models, but the

---

multilateral GATT bargaining than to seek preferential treatment [Balassa, 1980]. There was little attempt to analyze (or measure) the welfare effects of GSP or to explain why GSP was introduced; Blackhurst [1972] took the welfare analysis some steps further (see below), and McCulloch, Pinera [1976] tackled the motivation issue, but despite an economic apparatus their main conclusions relied on noneconomic factors.

[18] Technical inefficiency is not readily explained within standard microeconomic models unless markets are not competitive. Several writers have referred to the gains from reducing domestic monopoly power as a possible side-benefit from freer access to preferred imports, as they are with any tariff reduction, but this argument has not been formally developed. Growth effects independent of the resource allocation effects are also difficult to formalize within standard models. The main practical case is when preferences stimulate a relocation of investment from outside to within the preferred area (as seems to have happened in the EC and with other preferential trade agreements [e.g. Pomfret, 1982]); this will increase GDP and growth within the preferred area but with an offsetting cost to the rest of the world if it is capital diversion – indeed the global effect may be negative if the productivity of the investment was higher in a nonpreferred location [Kreinin, 1964, p. 195].

overall record was clouded by the startling differences in conclusions reached by different authors.

There are four new elements which three-ness permits. Firstly, it can avoid the asymmetry of most two-good models (as in Vanek–Kemp dissimilar economies), although not all 3 x 3 models are symmetrical. The possibility of symmetry was recognized by Vanek [1965, p. 13], emphasized by Collier [1979], and used by Riezman [1979], but ruled out by assumption by Berglas [1979]. Secondly, if a country can have more than one import, then changes in import structures are a possible source of welfare change [Corden, 1976; Collier, 1979]. Thirdly, complementarity relationships can be analyzed, as emphasized by Meade and taken up by Berglas [1979]; McMillan, McCann [1981]; and Ethier, Horn [1984, pp. 213–217], in whose models the degree of substitutability between countries' products becomes a determinant of the welfare changes. Fourthly, the introduction of more than one relative price introduces further second-best possibilities due to divergences between the ratio of marginal rates of substitution in consumption and marginal rates of transformation [Lipsey, 1970]. Lloyd [1982, p. 62] concludes that "3 x 3 are the minimum dimensions for models of customs unions". Yet the outcome so far has been disappointing because the operation of the last three elements just described depends upon the assumed trade patterns, so that each model (because based on different assumptions) can generate different conclusions; "every 3 x 3 model is a very special case" [Lloyd, 1982, p. 62]. Thus, despite the advantages of higher dimensionality, such models have had limited influence[19].

2. Tariffs in the Rest of the World

Wonnacott, Wonnacott [1981] provide a trenchant criticism of the proposition that, if a preferential trade agreement does not affect the terms of trade, then it does not allow for any mutually beneficial policy opportunities which are not open to each of the member countries separately by unilateral tariff reduction[20]. Their main argument is based on the existence of a tariff in (or net transport costs to) C which opens up a wedge between the price which A receives from her export to C and the price which B pays to import the same good from C. By forming a customs union to divert trade to one another A and B can trade within the wedge, gaining out of C's foregone tariff revenue.

---

[19] This summary treatment is not to deny the potential of these models nor the value of existing explorations; rather it reflects that this branch of the literature has already been the subject of an excellent survey [Lloyd, 1982], to which there is nothing to add in the present paper's context. Lloyd also points out that further benefits could come from introducing intermediate inputs (or service payments on imported capital), which would allow shifts in the transformation surface.

[20] This is Berglas' [1979, p. 329] formulation, which subsumes the earlier Johnson-Cooper-Massell proposition. Domestic distortions (including scale economies) are assumed absent.

In a two-good world the wedge is formed by B and A facing different tariff-inclusive offer curves from C, and the mutual gain from preferential trading is easily demonstrated. The main caveat to this argument is that in practice the rest of the world (C) is not a single country and part of the burden of tariffs will be borne by domestic consumers in the rest of the world. In such a case Wonnacott, Wonnacott argue that differences in net transport costs will still create a wedge, which explains why geographical neighbors tend to form customs unions. This is not completely satisfactory insofar as the narrower the wedge becomes, the smaller the welfare gains from trading within it, and because geographically dispersed countries have formed preferential trading arrangements (e.g. the British Commonwealth, the Lomé Convention, Comecon), suggesting that there is something else involved.

The Wonnacotts' analysis is hampered by the self-imposed limitation in their terms of reference. To refute the proposition on its own grounds, they exclude any changes in the terms of trade. Yet this, in combination with the existence of tariffs in the rest of the world, provides a more potent argument for preferential treatment; the point being to reduce the welfare gains to the rest of the world from levying a tariff which improves its terms of trade (as Torrens had argued much earlier). If there are other barriers to equal multilateral trade (e.g. some currencies are not convertible), then there is also a benefit from discrimination[21]. Indeed, it would be surprising if the move toward Pareto optimality by nonpreferential tariff reductions were necessarily welfare improving in a tariff-ridden world, since the foreign tariffs exclude the first-best outcome. In sum, the Wonnacotts' wedge is sufficient to refute the UTR proposition, but alone it is an unconvincing reason for widespread discrimination.

3. The Terms of Trade

Building higher-dimensioned models and introducing foreign tariffs into the analysis indicate dissatisfaction with existing theory, but do not get to the heart of the matter. One reason for the lacunae in preferential trading theory is the analytical apparatus of Figure 1, which highlights the trade diversion / trade creation concept by making assumptions which rule out other effects of preferences. The horizontal import supply curves exclude price effects or any welfare implications of change in exports. This is not just a result of the partial equilibrium framework, but rather concerns assumptions about costs and about how prices are set. In the general equilibrium framework of Figure 2 a

---

[21] This was generally recognized by postwar policymakers as a source of conflict with the IMF's position in favor of nondiscrimination. If country A had insufficient hard currency to pay for imports from the United States, but could pay for the same imports from a soft currency country (B) by exports to B, then A, B and the world would be made better off by A discriminating in favor of imports from B [Patterson, 1966, Ch. 2].

customs union between two small countries (A and B), with prohibitive external tariff, would bring A and B to point S, where B is better off than with nonpreferential tariff elimination (point L) but A is worse off (than at point M); B cannot compensate A sufficiently, so the welfare optimum is L and M, i.e. the situation after nonpreferential removal of tariffs by A and B.

Figure 2 – *General Equilibrium (Offer Curve) Analysis of a Customs Union Involving Two Small Countries*

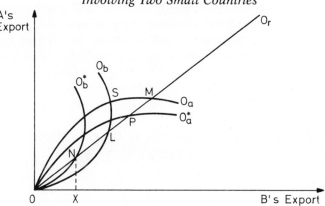

Note: O_a^* and O_b^* are the initial tariff-inclusive offer curves of A and B. O_a and O_b are their tariff-exclusive offer curves. O_r is the rest of the world's offer curve. Initially A trades at point P and B at point N. Their welfare-maximizing positions, given the world price ratio, are M and L.

In the recent debate over the UTR proposition between the Wonnacotts [1981] and Berglas [1983] both sides agree to assume no changes in the terms of trade, and this represents the central tradition of the postwar literature. This is, however, an implausible assumption for general analysis of preferential trading arrangements[22]. One symptom of the implausibility of Figures 1 and 2 is the stories they tell about the sources of imports (which is after all what discrimination is all about); in Figure 1 all of A's imports come from the rest of the world when there is no discrimination and they all come from B with preferential treatment, while in Figure 2 the source of A's imports and destination of B's exports up to quantity OX is indeterminate before the customs union. The all or nothing import share stories are tied to the simple treatment of prices[23].

---

[22] The assumption may, of course, be justified and useful in specific cases. Berglas [1979] appears to have in mind an arrangement such as the EC-Israel free trade area, where terms-of-trade effects may well be minimal [Pomfret, 1978], but this is not a general case.

[23] Vanek [1965, p. 30] allowed the terms of trade to change, although the direction of change can go either way. As mentioned above, however, this branch of the literature failed to reach firm conclusions, until Berglas [1979] introduced assumptions which ruled out international price changes.

The introduction of increasing costs is sufficient to create the possibility of both B and the rest of the world exporting to A. This can be analyzed within a partial equilibrium framework (Figure 3)[24]. With a uniform tariff A imports CE from B and P_1C from the rest of the world. If B is granted duty-free access, her exports to A increase to FK, while the rest of the world continues to export P_2F. The welfare gain to B arises from a better price on her previous exports (GJYW) plus the producer surplus on her additional exports (HKX). The welfare effect for A consists of the triangles (CGF + EJK) minus the higher expenditure on goods previously imported and now bought from B (FJYV) plus the lower expenditure on remaining imports from the rest of the world (P_4VZP_5), whose net sign is indeterminate. The rest of the world unambiguously loses from the preferential tariff cut (by $P_4VZP_5 + VWZ$), and the global welfare effect may be positive or negative. Thus Viner's central insight remains, although in slightly different terms, since it is no longer possible to identify high and low cost foreign suppliers. The terms of trade

Figure 3 – *Partial Equilibrium Analysis of Discrimination with Upward Sloping Supply Curves*

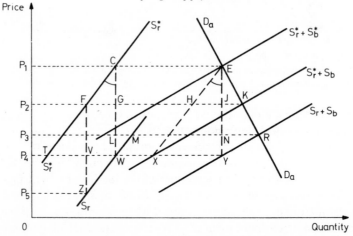

Note: D_a is A's import demand. S_b is the supply of imports from preferred sources and S_r is the supply of imports from the rest of the world; S_b^* and S_r^* are the same including A's tariff. Assuming no nontariff barriers or transport costs and no exchange rate changes, E, K and R represent demand/supply equilibria with A's tariff, with free access for B's goods and without A's tariff, and P_1, P_2 and P_3 are the corresponding domestic prices. P_4 is the price received by exporters to A when A's tariff is in place, and P_5 is the price received by nonpreferred exporters to A when B receives preferential access.

---

[24] Variations of Figure 3 have appeared in the literature several times, apparently independently, without displacing Figure 1 as the norm; e.g. Johnson [1957; 1958]; Humphrey and Ferguson's Model II [1960, pp. 205–210]; and Blackhurst [1972]. One indication of how little impact the analysis has made is that a recent article in a major refereed journal could call B's producer surplus on increased exports an effect "neglected by previous contributors" [Collier, 1979, p. 92].

effects, however, which from a global perspective must net out, introduce distributional effects on B and in third countries, while B also benefits from the producer-surplus on new exports[25].

Blackhurst [1972] uses the Figure 3 to compare the welfare effects of preferential and nonpreferential tariff cuts by A. From a global perspective the latter effect is positive and must be at least as big as the welfare effect of a preferential tariff reduction. But from A's perspective this is not necessarily the case because one positive aspect of a discriminatory tariff cut is lost if the cut is nonpreferential, viz. the improvement in A's terms of trade with third countries. The partner, B, is, of course, better off with the preferential reduction. Thus, the introduction of increasing costs, and hence changes in the terms of trade, qualifies the UTR proposition, since A (and B) may gain more from a preferential than from a nonpreferential reduction in A's tariff.

The preceding analysis is partial equilibrium, but it can readily be turned into general equilibrium on the assumptions of low initial tariffs, a small tariff change and all exports are gross substitutes in world consumption. Now B's terms of trade improve, and the rest of the world's deteriorate. The sum of these changes is equal to the initial change in A's terms of trade, although the final outcome also depends on a budget effect, i.e. how A reacts to her reduced tariff revenues. The terms of trade between A and the rest of the world may end up going either way, but this does not affect "the most important proposition about discriminatory tariff reductions: a tariff reduction in a member country unambiguously improves the terms of trade of the partner country" [Mundell, 1964, p. 5].

Mutual preferential tariff reductions between A and B can change the partners' terms of trade with the rest of the world in either direction. This is in contrast to a popular view that formation of a customs union will improve the members' terms of trade with the rest of the world, although they can be reconciled under certain conditions[26]. With Mundell's assumptions some sets of reductions necessarily improve both members' terms of trade with the rest of the world [Mundell, 1964, p. 7]. These sets congregate around the case where the terms of trade between A and B are unchanged, which may be a plausible outcome from a preferential trade arrangement based on roughly reciprocal "concessions". Even if A and B do not both improve their terms of

---

[25] The unambiguous gain to B, the clearest message from Figure 3, recalls the passage from Adam Smith quoted in Section II. If the rest of the world consists of several countries then some of these clearly may gain, viz. those importing the same good as A [Arndt, 1969].

[26] The popular view is usually a variant of the argument by Viner [1950, p. 55] that formation of a customs union would, *ceteris paribus,* increase the improvement in members' terms of trade resulting from their tariff, because a larger economic unit faces a less elastic offer curve. Riezman [1979] sets up a 3 x 3 model where the terms of trade of A and B improve vis-à-vis C but not necessarily vis-à-vis one another; in this case mutually profitable customs unions are most likely among countries which trade mainly with nonmembers (e.g. LAFTA).

trade, mutual preferential tariff reductions will always improve the terms of trade of one of the two countries.

So far I have considered the terms of trade changes likely to result from preferences, but it may be that the terms of trade are themselves the objective. Two variations of the optimum tariff argument are relevant to preferential trading. Melvin [1969] has argued that the terms-of-trade effect will usually reduce A's welfare gain from a preferential tariff reduction because her MFN tariff may be optimal (from a national welfare perspective) and any change will be welfare-reducing. This is not necessarily so. Even if A's tariff is optimal, like any wielder of monopoly power A could improve her welfare by market segmentation if different partners have different offer curves: the less elastic the partner's offer curve, the higher A's optimum tariff on imports from that source[27]. A second optimum tariff argument is that A and B in combination can wield greater market power than either can alone. Thus, if A imposes a tariff on goods which her suppliers can also sell to B, then the impact will be to change trade patterns, restricting the improvement in A's terms of trade; but if the two similar economies A and B form a union then they can set a union-welfare-maximizing common external tariff; in this situation "what country A really desires from country B is an appropriate protective policy against the outside world" [Arndt, 1968, p. 976][28].

4. Economies of Scale

A final missing player in preferential trading theory is scale economies. The earlier literature on European integration gave it a large role [e.g. Scitovsky, 1956; 1958; Balassa, 1961], but most writers have left it out or kept it in the background[29]. To some extent this reflects a wider problem: Scale economies can be a source of gains from trade, but lead to indeterminacy – a problem usually evaded in international trade theory by assuming that the closed economy conditions for Pareto optimality are met (including perfectly competitive markets). The same assumption could be made in analyzing preferences, but, given policymakers' emphasis on scale economies as a

---

[27] Caves [1974] analyzes within a Vanek-Kemp framework the gains from market segmentation. See also Michaely [1977, pp. 214–215]. McCulloch, Pinera [1977] suggest this as a possible motive for GSP schemes (assuming a high elasticity of supply of exports from developing countries).

[28] Similar arguments are made by Viner [1950], and by Spraos [1964]. Although these are part of the customs union literature [see also Michaely, 1977, pp. 215–216; Riezman, 1985], cartel behavior by countries with common interests does not require preferential treatment; OPEC members, for example, try to agree on a common price and to minimize the free-rider problem without forming any economic union or necessarily discriminating among oil purchasers.

[29] One example is Massell [1968] who after discussing noneconomic and terms-of-trade arguments devotes one sentence to scale economies as a third reason for customs unions, saying that these may be the most important! In Lipsey's 1960 survey they are listed as one of the five sources of welfare gain or loss but only appear in the (inconclusive) next-to-last paragraph.

reason for, say, joining a customs union, reference is often made to the importance of scale economies (without analysis). The two major analytical contributions are those of Corden and the Wonnacotts, although future developments within the framework of Chamberlinian monopolistic competition trade models seem likely [e.g. Ethier, Horn, 1984, pp. 217–225].

Corden [1972] introduced scale economies into basic theory of preferences and found that trade creation and trade diversion remained relevant concepts but should be supplemented by two other effects. If preferred imports from B replace A's domestic production, then the cost-reduction effect of realizing scale economies yields additional gains. If B's exports are replacing goods previously imported by A from a third country (C), there may be trade-suppression if B's lower costs and C's higher costs lead to further reductions in C's exports to A and B (even though C may remain the lowest-cost producer). Corden's cost-reduction and trade suppression effects leave intact Viner's fundamental insight about the sign of the welfare effect, although they accentuate the gains from trade creation and losses from trade diversion[30].

Figure 4 – *An Industry with Decreasing Costs Facing Trade Barriers*

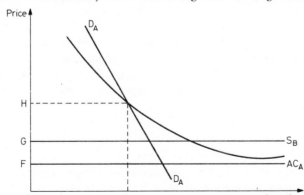

Note: D_A is domestic demand in country A and AC_A is the decreasing average cost curve of the producer in A. Producers in B operate under constant cost conditions with a supply curve S_B at a price of OG. FG is B's tariff. Assuming average cost pricing, barriers to imports and no opportunity to segment markets, A's firm will produce OK and sell at a price OH. Removal of B's tariff permits A's producer to increase output, selling at a price between OF and OG in B's market.

Wonnacott, Wonnacott [1967] provide empirical support for the common presumption that countries gain from joining a free trade area or customs union via access to a wider market. From their studies the Wonnacotts find

---

[30] Viner [1950, pp. 45–47] had recognized the former point and Meade [1955, pp. 93–94] described the magnification of trade creation and trade diversion with two examples, although neither treated the matter as thoroughly as Corden.

most Canadian industries to have cost curves such as that in Figure 4. Removal of the United States' tariff would permit expansion of Canadian output on the basis of exports, leading with a fixed exchange rate to higher wages in Canada (or with a flexible exchange rate to improved terms of trade). The Wonnacotts estimate the gain to Canada from a North American free trade area at 10.5 percent of GNP of which around 4 percent comes from Canadian tariff cuts and the remainder from the effect just described, i.e. the realization of scale economies is the main source of Canadian gain. This analysis is, however, distinct from all the literature so far discussed insofar as the effects of scale economies do not arise from the home country's preferential trade reduction. What the analysis does do, is to emphasize the gains from freer access to other countries' markets (in Figure 4 this does not have to be preferential access). The only sense in which the Wonnacotts' study provides a case for preferential treatment is if reduction in one's own tariff is a critical bargaining counter in convincing other countries to reduce their trade barriers.

VI. Why Do Preferential Trading Arrangements Exist?

Three sets of motives explain the existence of most preferential trading arrangements. Firstly, arguments for nondiscriminatory trade barriers can be adapted to preferences. Secondly, preferential treatment can be used as a bargaining tool. Thirdly, the terms of trade changes and gains to exporters described in the previous section yield benefits from preferential arrangements which are not to be gained from unilateral policies. Each of these will be considered in turn, and then the role of noneconomic motives will be assessed.

The optimum tariff argument's extension to discriminatory monopsonistic behavior has already been mentioned. There may also be a case for forming a customs union to realize administrative economies and increase net revenue. In practice, however, the main motivation for postwar trade barriers has been the protection of import-competing sectors, especially when they have well-organized and effective lobbies. For institutional reasons new trade barriers have frequently taken the form of orderly marketing arrangements or voluntary export quotas, negotiated on a bilateral basis and hence discriminatory. Whether such measures are effective in providing protection depends upon the size of the cross-price elasticities among trading partners. If these elasticities are large, then the barrier must be extended to all significant suppliers (in the limit becoming nondiscriminatory) or it will provide little protection[31]. If substitution possibilities are small, then a discriminatory

[31] A perfect example of proliferation is the history of textiles and clothing protection from the first Japanese voluntary export quotas to the USA in the 1950s through the cotton textile arrangements of the 1960s to the MFA in the 1970s [Keesing, Wolf, 1980]. Similar tendencies were

barrier will provide protection, but its impact differs little from a nonprefer-ential measure[32]. In sum, the protection argument is not a strong one for discrimination *per se*, although apparently discriminatory measures may be adopted or actually discriminatory measures taken as the first steps towards general barriers.

The bargaining motive for preferential treatment of trading partners has a long history[33] and follows naturally from policymakers' view of trade barrier reductions as concessions. Economic rationale for this motive is provided by Torrens' emphasis on the incentives for countries to levy nationally optimal tariffs if these are not contingent on tariff levels abroad and by the Wonna-cotts' emphasis on the importance of gaining market access for exports. Presumably, however, the argument is about means rather than ends – Torrens, for example, continually proclaimed his belief in free trade as the *optimum optimorum*. Whether the goal can be better achieved by bilateral confrontation or via multilateral GATT negotiations is not self-evident, nor is it readily analyzed by economists' tools[34]. My impression is that economists tend to favor the GATT approach, but the "reciprocity" proposals in Congress suggest that American policymakers are tilting towards the bilateral threat approach[35].

The clearest economic arguments for discrimination arise from the gain to the preference recipient as exporter. If the preferences are reciprocal then all partners will be the favored exporter of some products, and in nonconstant

---

observed during the 1977–1981 footwear OMAs imposed by the USA on Taiwan and South Korea [Pearson, 1983], and seem to be happening in the wake U.S. restrictions on steel imports from Europe.

[32] Quotas on Japanese autos to the United States seem to have had this effect during the 1980s (although it may be that short-run and long-run cross-price elasticities differ in the auto industry and given time Korean or Brazilian autos would replace barred Japanese autos).

[33] It lay behind French and Spanish opposition to unconditional MFN treatment during the interwar years (they argued that high tariff countries, such as the USA, should lower their tariffs, before they could expect equal access to low tariff countries' markets) and behind American use of conditional MFN clauses before 1919.

[34] Cline [1982] draws up a taxonomy of outcomes, but the key issue is the probability of each outcome. In a two-country model there must be a negotiated agreement which dominates the Nash equilibrium outcome of a tariff war [Mayer, 1981], which is consistent with Whalley's [1985, Ch. 14] high estimates of post-tariff-war U.S. and EC tariffs and the associated welfare loss relative to free trade. Generalization of these results to threatened discriminatory tariff increases is difficult because in a multi-country world the scope for imposing costs on other countries by own-welfare-increasing tariff hikes is negatively related to the number of substitute markets.

[35] The stated arguments emphasize that GATT negotiations have been biased against U.S. interests (by omitting, for example, trade in services and foreign investment) and that other countries have circumvented GATT concessions by nontariff barriers [Hay, Sulzenco, 1982]. This may be a result of distorted vision [Cline, 1982] or a route to disguised protectionism, but even if the arguments are valid it is unclear whether reciprocity measures would produce the desired effect on other countries.

cost industries will enjoy gains from increased exports. From a macroeconomic perspective, as long as internal terms of trade are unchanged all partners in the preferential trading area enjoy improved terms of trade with the rest of the world. This may be a sufficient explanation of economic benefits from the European Common Market which could not be realized by unilateral policies[36]. The potential importance of these effects is also illustrated by the application of computable general equilibrium models. Hamilton and Whalley [1983] found that bilateral free trade areas among the major trading nations may or may not raise global welfare, but in all cases one of the FTA members (and usually both) gains, while outsiders usually suffer welfare losses[37].

The major new preferential agreements of the 1970s (GSP and Lomé) involved nonreciprocal preferential treatment of developing countries' exports. Here the gain to exporters explains the recipients' lobbying for the GSP and acceptance of the Lomé Convention. There is, however, little economic gain to the preference donor; indeed in the case of a large country giving preferential treatment to a small supplying country, all the gains go to the latter, while the large country loses tariff revenue on preferred imports. Thus this type of arrangement has a noneconomic motivation on one side. The history of the GSP negotiations is one of political accommodation by the industrialized countries to one aspect of the demands for New International Economic Order; in view of the small size of the foregone tariff revenue due to actual GSP schemes, the economic cost of political accommodation has not been large. The Lomé Convention (and also the bilateral agreements with Mediterranean countries) reflects political motivation on the European Community's part, as it uses one of its limited arsenal of policy tools to create spheres of influence[38]; again the cost from the donor's perspective is not

---

[36] Petith [1977] applies Mundell's model to the EC case and finds terms of trade gains to be substantially larger than the welfare triangles from trade creation.

[37] This paper and Whalley's 1985 book point to the importance of the participating countries' initial levels of protection and relative size, while they downplay the Vinerian trade creation/trade diversion effects of preferential trade agreements. Such conclusions may reflect the simplicity of their model and are sensitive to key parameter values (in this context particularly the elasticity of substitution between imports from alternative sources), but the Whalley model exhibits some robustness and yields plausible results in other contexts. There is also a problem in identifying the Vinerian effects in a computable general equilibrium model, as Meade's identification of tertiary effects due to macroeconomic adjustment implies.

[38] The Mediterranean agreements are discussed in Pomfret [1986]. The argument in this paragraph was also made by Viner [1950, pp. 91–92]: "Of the more serious movements which involved a great power and a small country or a number of small countries, it appears to have been the case without exception for the great power that political objectives were the important ones", while for the small countries in such arrangements "only the economic consequences as a rule were regarded as attractive, while the political aspects were thought of as involving risks which might have to be accepted for the sake of the economic benefits with which they were unfortunately associated".

large, while the gain from increased export earnings is economically riskless and may be substantial compared to economic magnitudes in the preference recipient.

What role is there here for the Johnson-Cooper-Massell argument? Starting from the UTR proposition this argument relates the motivation for preferences to internal divergences of prices from social opportunity costs, e.g. because of a desire for industrialization. Such a desire could be fulfilled by subsidizing production, but if the home market is limited then GATT restrictions on export subsidies deter this strategy. Customs union provides a solution to the dilemma because preferential market access is equivalent to an export subsidy in this context, and customs unions are permitted under GATT. The argument can be generalized insofar as in the presence of a domestic distortion a discriminatory tariff charge may or may not be superior to a nondiscriminatory tariff change. It's dominance of the field is, however, surprising given its second-best nature even from a national perspective; especially as it seems difficult to explain in these terms customs unions and free trade areas among developed countries or one-way preferences such as the GSP and Lomé Convention. Given the three sets of motivation described above it also appears unnecessary to invoke purely noneconomic motives for preferential trading arrangements.

VII. Conlusions

The theory of preferential trading has been one of the more disappointing branches of postwar economics. That is despite Viner's great insight about the ambiguity of welfare effects, which led to the theory of second best. Indeed, ironically, it was the codification of Viner's concepts in the form of Figure 1 which may explain the subsequent stultification. By assuming constant costs the terms of trade effects were limited and the possibility of gains from increased exports eliminated. Yet these should be two key features of the theory of preferences. Terms of trade changes, while not altering the global evaluation, have distributional effects such that costs are imposed on third countries while the participants in a preferential arrangement may enjoy gains not available from nondiscriminatory policies. Either increasing or decreasing costs open up the prospect of welfare gains to a preference recipient from increased exports, and the export expansion will be at least as great as from nonpreferential tariff reduction by the donor. Once these two features are permitted it becomes easier to explain why preferential trading arrangements exist (and are increasing) in terms of the economic gains to the principal parties. These modifications do not, however, improve the global assessment of discriminatory practices – rather by pointing out conflicts between national and global interest they reinforce the case for a framework such as the GATT to set and arbiter the rules.

66 *Richard Pomfret*

References

Arndt, Sven W., "On Discriminatory versus Non-Preferential Tariff Policies". *The Economic Journal,* Vol. 78, 1968, pp. 971–979.

–, "Customs Union and the Theory of Tariffs". *The American Economic Review,* Vol. 59, 1969, pp. 108–118.

Balassa, Bela A., *The Theory of Economic Integration.* Homewood, Ill., 1961.

– **(Ed.),** *European Economic Integration.* Amsterdam 1975.

–, "The Tokyo Round and the Developing Countries". *Journal of World Trade Law,* Vol. 14, 1980, pp. 93–118.

Baldwin, Robert E., Tracy Murray, "MFN Tariff Reductions and Developing Country Trade Benefits under the GSP". *The Economic Journal,* Vol. 87, 1977, pp. 30–46.

Berglas, Eitan, "Preferential Trading Theory; The n Commodity Case". *Journal of Political Economy,* Vol. 87, 1979, pp. 315–331.

–, "The Case for Unilateral Tariff Reductions: Foreign Tariffs Rediscovered". *The American Economic Review,* Vol. 73, 1983, pp. 1141–1142.

Bhagwati, Jagdish N., "Trade-Diverting Customs Unions and Welfare Improvement: A Clarification". *The Economic Journal,* Vol. 81, 1971, pp. 580–587.

–, "A Reply to Professor Kirman". *The Economic Journal,* Vol. 83, 1973, pp. 895–897.

Blackhurst, Richard, "General versus Preferential Tariff Reduction for LDC Exports: An Analysis of the Welfare Effects". *Southern Economic Journal,* Vol. 38, 1972, pp. 350–362.

Caves, Richard E., "The Economics of Reciprocity: Theory and Evidence on Bilateral Trading Arrangements". In: Willy Sellekaerts (Ed.), *International Trade and Finance.. Essays in Honour of Jan Tinbergen.* London 1974, pp. 17–54.

–, **Harry G. Johnson (Eds.),** *Readings in International Economics.* Homewood, Ill., 1968.

Cline, William R., *"Reciprocity": A New Approach to World Trade Policy?* Washington 1982.

Collier, Paul, "The Welfare Effects of Customs Unions: An Anatomy'. *The Economic Journal,* Vol. 89, 1979, pp. 84–95.

Cooper, Charles A., Benton F. Massell, "A New Look at Customs Unions Theory". *The Economic Journal,* Vol. 75, 1965, pp. 742–747.

Corden, W. Max, *Recent Developments in the Theory of International Trade.* Special Papers in International Economics, 7. Princeton 1965.

–, "Economies of Scale and Customs Union Theory". *Journal of Political Economy,* Vol. 80, 1972, pp. 456–475.

–, "Customs Union Theory and the Nonuniformity of Tariffs". *Journal of International Economics,* Vol. 6, 1976, pp. 99–106.

El-Agraa, Ali M. (Ed.), *International Economic Integration.* New York 1982.

Ethier, Wilfred J., Henrik Horn, "A New Look at Economic Integration". In: Henryk Kierzkowski (Ed.), *Monopolistic Competition and International Trade.* Oxford 1984, pp. 207–229.

Gehrels, Franz, "Customs Unions from a Single Country's Viewpoint". *Review of Economic Studies,* Vol. 24, 1956/57, No. 63, pp. 61–64.

Grinols, Earl L., "An Extension of the Kemp-Wan Theorem on the Formation of Customs Unions". *Journal of International Economics*, Vol. 11, 1981, pp. 259–266.

–, "A Thorn in the Lion's Paw. Has Britain Paid too much for Common Market Membership?" *Journal of International Economics*, Vol. 14, 1984, pp. 271–293.

Hamilton, Bob, John Whalley, *Geographically Discriminatory Trade Arrangements*. University of Western Ontario Centre for the Study of International Economic Relations Working Paper, No. 8321C. London, November 1983.

Hay, Keith A. J., Andrei B. Sulzenco, "US Trade Policy and 'Reciprocity' ". *Journal of World Trade Law*, Vol. 16, 1982, pp. 471–479.

Humphrey, Don D., Charles E. Ferguson, "The Domestic and World Benefits of a Customs Union". *Economia Internazionale*, Vol. 13, 1960, pp. 197–216.

Johnson, Harry G., "Discriminatory Tariff Reduction: A Marshallian Analysis". *Indian Journal of Economics*, Vol. 38, 1957, No. 148, pp. 39–47.

–, "Marshallian Analysis of Discriminatory Tariff Reductions: An Extension". *Indian Journal of Economics*, Vol. 39, 1958, No. 59, pp. 177–181 (reprinted in Johnson, 1962).

– [1960 a], "The Cost of Protection and the Scientific Tariff". *Journal of Political Economy*, Vol. 68, 1960, pp. 327–345.

– [1960 b], "The Economic Theory of Customs Union". *Pakistan Economic Journal*, Vol. 10, 1960, pp. 14–32 (reprinted in Johnson, 1962).

–, *Money, Trade and Economic Growth*. London 1962.

–, "An Economic Theory of Protectionism, Tariff Bargaining and the Formation of Customs Unions". *Journal of Political Economy*, Vol. 73, 1965, pp. 256–283.

–, "Trade Diverting Customs Unions: A Comment". *The Economic Journal*, Vol. 84, 1974, pp. 618–621.

Keesing, Donald B., Martin Wolf, *Textile Quotas against Developing Countries*. Thames Essays, No. 23. London 1980.

Kemp, Murray C., *A Contribution to the General Equilibrium Theory of Preferential Trading*. Amsterdam 1969.

–, **Henry Y. Wan, Jr.,** "An Elementary Proposition Concerning the Formation of Customs Unions". *Journal of International Economics*, Vol. 6, 1976, pp. 95–97.

Kirman, Alan P., "Trade Diverting Customs Unions and Welfare Improvement: A Comment". *The Economic Journal*, Vol. 83, 1973, pp. 890–894.

Krauss, Melvyn B., "Recent Developments in Customs Union Theory: An Interpretative Survey". *Journal of Economic Literature*, Vol. 10, 1972, pp. 413–436.

Kreinin, Mordechai E., "On the Dynamic Effects of a Customs Union". *Journal of Political Economy*, Vol. 72, 1964, pp. 193–195.

–, *Trade Relations of the EEC: An Empirical Investigation*. New York 1974.

Lipsey, Richard G., "Mr. Gehrels on Customs Unions". *Review of Economic Studies*, Vol. 24, 1956/57, No. 65, pp. 211–214.

–, "The Theory of Customs Unions: Trade Diversion and Welfare". *Economica*, Vol. 24, 1957, pp. 40–46.

–, "The Theory of Customs Unions: A General Survey". *The Economic Journal*, Vol. 70, 1960, pp. 496–513.

–, *The Theory of Customs Unions: A General Equilibrium Analysis*. London 1970.

Lipsey, Richard G., Kelvin Lancaster, "The General Theory of 'Second Best'". *Review of Economic Studies*, Vol. 24, 1956/57, No. 63, pp. 11–32.

Lloyd, Peter J., "3 × 3 Theory of Customs Unions". *Journal of International Economics*, Vol. 12, 1982, pp. 41–63.

McCulloch, Rachel, José Pinera, "Trade as Aid: The Political Economy of Tariff Preferences for Developing Countries". *The American Economic Review*, Vol. 67, 1977, pp. 959–967.

McMillan, John, Ewen McCann, "Welfare Effects in Customs Unions". *The Economic Journal*, Vol. 91, 1981, pp. 697–703.

Mayer, Wolfgang, "Theoretical Considerations on Negotiated Tariff Adjustments". *Oxford Economic Papers*, Vol. 33, 1981, pp. 135–153.

Meade, James E., *The Theory of Customs Unions*. Amsterdam 1955.

Melvin, James R., "Comments on the Theory of Customs Unions". *Manchester School of Economic and Social Studies*, Vol. 37, 1969, No. 2, pp. 161–168.

Michaely, Michael, "The Assumptions of Jacob Viner's Theory of Customs Unions". *Journal of International Economics*, Vol. 6, 1976, pp. 75–93.

–, *Theory of Commercial Policy, Trade and Protection*. Chicago 1977.

Mundell, Robert A., "Tariff Preferences and the Terms of Trade". *Manchester School of Economic and Social Studies*, Vol. 32, 1964, pp. 1–13.

Murray, Tracy W., *Trade Preferences for Developing Countries*. London 1977.

Negishi, Takashi, "The Customs Union and the Theory of Second Best". *International Economic Review*, Vol. 10, 1969, pp. 391–398.

O'Brien, Denis, "Customs Unions: Trade Creation and Trade Diversion in Historical Perspective". *History of Political Economy*, Vol. 8, 1976, pp. 540–563.

Patterson, Gardner, *Discrimination in International Trade: The Policy Issues 1945-1965*. Princeton 1966.

Pearson, Charles S., *Emergency Protection in the Footwear Industry*. Thames Essay, No. 36. London 1983.

Pelkmanns, Jacques, Hans Gremmen, "The Empirical Measurement of Static Customs Unions Effects". *Rivista Internazionale di Scienze Economiche e Commerciali*, Vol. 30, 1983, pp. 612–622.

Petith, Howard C., "European Integration and the Terms of Trade". *The Economic Journal*, Vol. 87, 1977, pp. 246–272.

Pomfret, Richard W., "The Economic Consequences for Israel of Free Trade in Manufactured Goods with the EEC". *Weltwirtschaftliches Archiv*, Vol. 114, 1978, pp. 526–539.

–, "Trade Preferences and Foreign Investment in Malta". *Journal of World Trade Law*, Vol. 16, 1982, pp. 236–250.

–, "Discrimination in International Trade: Extent, Motivation, and Implications". *Economia Internazionale*, Vol. 38, 1985, pp. 49–65.

–, *Mediterranean Policy of the European Community: A Study of Discrimination in Trade*. London 1986.

Riezman, Raymond G., "A 3 x 3 Modell of Customs Unions". *Journal of International Economics*, Vol. 9, 1979, pp. 341–354.

–, "Customs Unions and the Core". *Journal of International Economics*, Vol. 19, 1985, pp. 355–365.

Robbins, Lionel C., *Robert Torrens and the Evolution of Classical Economics.* London 1958.

de Scitovsky, Tibor, "Economies of Scale, Competition, and European Integration". *The American Economic Review,* Vol. 46, 1956, pp. 71–91.

–, *Economic Theory and Western European Integration.* Stanford 1958.

Smith, Adam, *An Inquiry into the Nature and Causes of the Wealth of Nations.* London 1776.

Spraos, John, "The Condition for a Trade-Creation Customs Union". *The Economic Journal,* Vol. 74, 1964, pp. 101–108.

Taussig, Frank W., "Reciprocity". *Quarterly Journal of Economics,* Vol. 7, 1892, pp. 26–39.

Torrens, Robert, *The Budget: On Commercial and Colonial Policy.* London 1844.

Vanek, Jaroslav, *General Equilibrium of International Discrimination: The Case of Customs Unions.* Cambridge 1965.

Viner, Jacob, "The Most-Favoured-Nation Clause". *Index VI,* 1931, No. 61, pp. 2–17.

–, *The Customs Union Issue.* New York 1950.

–, "Letter to W.M. Corden of 13 March 1965". *Journal of International Economics,* Vol. 6, 1976, pp. 107–108.

Whalley, John, *Trade Liberalization among Major World Trading Areas.* Cambridge, Mass., 1985.

Wonnacott, G. Paul, Ronald J. Wonnacott, "Is Unilateral Tariff Reduction Preferable to a Customs Union? The Curious Case of the Missing Foreign Tariffs". *The American Economic Review,* Vol. 71, 1981, pp. 704–714.

Wonnacott, Ronald, J., G. Paul Wonnacott, *Free Trade between the United States and Canada: The Potential Economic Effects.* Cambridge, Mass., 1967.

※　※　※

Zusammenfassung: Die Theorie der Präferenzabkommen. – Hier wird ein Überblick über die Theorie der geographisch diskriminierenden Handelspolitik gegeben. Der rote Faden ist, daß es im Laufe der sechziger Jahre auf diesem Gebiet der Außenhandelstheorie zu einem Stillstand kam, weil die grundlegende These, Präferenzzollsenkungen müssen einseitigen nicht-diskrimierenden Zollsenkungen unterlegen sein, mit dem rapiden Anstieg der Präferenzhandelsabkommen unvereinbar zu sein schien. Es werden Versuche zu einer Auflösung dieses Stillstands erörtert, wobei das Schwergewicht auf die Notwendigkeit gelegt wird, in die Analyse wieder internationale Verteilungswirkungen einzubeziehen.

※

Résumé: La théorie des accords commerciaux préférentiels. – L'auteur présente un aperçu sur la théorie des politiques commerciales géographiquement discriminatoires. Le sujet unifiant est que pendant les années soixante cette approche théorique s'arrêtait parce que la proposition centrale (c.-à-d. réductions tarifaires préférentielles doivent être inférieures aux réductions unilatérales non-discriminatoires) semblait être inconsistante avec la prolifération des accords commerciaux préférentiels. L'auteur discute des approches pour résoudre cette difficulté en soulignant la nécessité de réintroduire des effets de distribution internationale dans l'analyse.

Richard Pomfret

Resumen: La teoría del comercio preferencial. – Se presenta la teoría del comercio discriminatorio según regiones geográficas. La necesidad de tratar este tema deriva del hecho de que durante la década del sesenta perdió fuerza la proposición central de esta teoría (reducciones arancelarias preferenciales son inferiores a reducciones arancelarias unilaterales y no discriminatorias) al ser inconsistente con la proliferación de acuerdos sobre comercio preferencial observada. Se presentan varios intentos de resolver esta dificultad, poniendo énfasis en la necesidad de reintroducir efectos distributivos internacionales en el análisis.

13

A New Look at Economic Integration*

Wilfred Ethier and Henrik Horn

The literature on customs unions theory is gargantuan. Nevertheless it strikes us as inadequate, both in the theoretical cases it addresses and in the actual circumstances of the world economy to which it is commonly thought relevant. This paper aims to spell out the details of this inadequacy and to indicate some lines along which the theory ought to be developed.

Section 1 very briefly describes basic ideas in contemporary customs union theory, and Section 2 then discusses at some length necessary extensions. Two general propositions are advanced in the next section, and proved in Section 4. Section 5 develops a specific model incorporating the new features, and Section 6 then exhibits aspects of this model via some special comparative-statics exercises.

1. BASICS OF CUSTOMS UNION THEORY

There is a huge literature in this area for three distinct reasons: (i) the *institutional* fact that there are many types of discriminatory trade besides customs unions proper (preferential trading arrangements, free trade areas, common markets, economic unions, and so on), (ii) the subject demands disaggregation beyond two-country, two-commodity models, and therefore gives rise to *many conceivable combinations* of characteristics of countries, commodities, and trade flows, and (iii) the subject requires comparisons of *distorted* equilibria which, in particular in conjunction with the second point, increases the mathematical complexity of the analysis. In practice the latter two factors have proved decisive, with analysis concentrated disproportionately upon the case of a customs union proper (free internal trade combined with a common external tariff).

Two basic ideas stand out from the wealth of specific analysis. The first, which might be called the *Vinerian Description*, is the notion that the net effect of a customers union is dependent on the balance of trade creation and trade diversion. This idea is in truth the very core of customs union theory.

(A) *Vinerian Description.* Formation of a customs union produces trade creation between the partners, in response to the mutual elimination of tariffs on one another's goods, and trade diversion from third countries to the partners, in response to the tariff discrimination produced by the union.

Trade creation is by presumption beneficial and trade diversion harmful. Union formation is thus seen as a second-best exercise, with one distortion replaced by another. This, together with the need for at least some disaggregation, accounts for the multitude of separate possibilities. Other aspects of union formation have of course also received attention. Notable examples, to which we shall return, include changes in the terms of trade — both within the union and *vis-à-vis* the outside world — and also economies of scale and the degree of competition.

Mention of the terms of trade relative to the rest of the world brings us to the second basic idea, due to Kemp, Vanek, Ohyama, and Wan. Setting the external tariffs at appropriate levels can cause the member countries, in the aggregate, to trade with the rest of the world exactly the same collection and quantities of goods that, in the aggregate, they traded prior to the union. Then the union will have no effect at all on the rest of the world, and the members must in the aggregate benefit, because the only effect they experience is the freeing of mutual trade. In essence, manipulation of the external tariff schedule allows any customs union to eliminate all trade diversion and so consist only of trade creation. By allowing a small deterioriation in its external terms of trade, the union can ensure that also non-members benefit.

(B) *Kemp–Vanek–Ohyama–Wan.* By an appropriate choice of common external tariffs and of lump-sum transfers among members, any customs union can assure that no countries in the world lose, and that some gain, as a result of the formation of the union.

This proposition applies irrespective of initial conditions, and so establishes a sense in which the countries of the world always have incentives to form additional unions until global free trade is achieved.

2. DESIRABLE DEPARTURES

Although the two ideas discussed above hardly begin to do justice to the vastness of customs union theory,[1] they do indicate the distinguishing features of the subject and are its most important conclusions. Thus we take the pair as a benchmark from which to enquire in what direction contemporary problems mandate that the subject be further developed. We indicate four directions. The four have by no means been completely ignored by the literature; and in some cases have received formal treatment, but they do depart substantially from the core of received customs unions theory.

(i) Trade Modification

The basic element of the conventional theory is tariff discrimination: the *same* good that can be imported free of duty from a partner faces a tariff when it comes from a non-partner country. But partners also trade among themselves some goods which they do not import at all (either before or after the union) from outside countries. For want of a better term, we describe as *trade modification* the change in trade with outside countries due to the elimination of tariffs on goods traded only within the union.[2] Thus trade modification differs from its familiar sister concept of trade diversion in that it can be produced by tariff changes consistent with the Most Favoured Nation clause and with the GATT, that is, by economic integration resulting from the non-discriminatory elimination by the partners of tariffs on goods they import only from each other.

Suppose, as an example, that France and Germany form a customs union, with France eliminating its tariff on German automotive supplies, also initially imported from America. This discriminatory tariff change would presumably induce trade diversion, with imports of German automotive supplies replacing some or all of the imports from America. Now suppose in contrast that France initially imports small cars from Germany and large cars from America, and that the integration takes the form of a French abolition of the tariff on small cars. Such a non-discriminatory tariff change is not usually considered as within the domain of customs union theory, even though it is likely to deflect French demand from American to German automotive products in about the same way as the previous case. Next, suppose instead that there is a unified world automobile industry, with France importing engines from Germany and bodies from America, and that France abolishes its tariff on engines. This again causes trade modification, but now French imports of American bodies will likely rise along with French imports of German engines.

Trade modification differs from trade diversion in that it is not the result of geographical tariff *discrimination* but rather of the replacement of one set of tariffs by another, with the property that the tariffs which are changed apply directly to trade flows between a strict subset of countries. As the example makes clear, degrees of substitutability and complementarity between goods become crucial.

Extending the scope of the theory to encompass trade modification might well therefore open the gates to another flood of special cases — hardly welcome in this field especially. And the bulk of empirical work in the area cannot be interpreted as distinguishing trade diversion from trade modification. But there are good reasons why the theory should include both. First, of course, is that both are in principle part of the problem. More significant is the large volume of empirical work, by Kravis and Lipsey (1971) and many others, that in the last decade has revealed extensive international price discrimination at even quite disaggregated levels. As a result economists now tend, much more than before, to think of international trade as the exchange of differentiated products, rather than of homogeneous goods. This shift in perception calls for a shift in emphasis from trade diversion towards trade modification.

But the most important consideration is the range of phenomena to which the theory of economic integration ought to apply. Although many attempts at customs unions and free trade areas have been made since the Second World War, the only actual, substantially successful, instance to which the theory reflected in the Vinerian Description literally applies is western European integration. An important instance, to be sure, but past history. Customs union theory thus appears seldom to be used as a framework for thought about contemporary problems. But issues to which a theory of economic integration *ought* to apply are legion. As a glaring example, consider the dominant post-war exercise in global commercial policy: the cumulative tariff reductions produced by successive GATT rounds. As often emphasized by economists and men of affairs alike, these reductions have concentrated on trade in manufactures among the developed countries and have been much less relevant to the trade of LDCs. Thus we have experienced on an historical scale (and continue to do so as the Tokyo Round cuts are implemented) the very sort of nationally biased tariff reductions that are the very essence of the theory of economic integration. But our theory has not been thought relevant because those cuts, implemented under the Most Favoured Nation clause, directly conflict with the Vinerian Description. The incorporation of trade modification in addition to (or instead of) trade diversion is essential to the practical relevance of customs union theory.

(ii) Intra-Industry Trade and Product Differentiation

Related to the distinction between trade diversion and trade modification is the observation that customs union theory assumes trade in homogeneous products whereas product differentiation and intra-industry trade are pervasive in actual commerce. Theoretical models of these latter phenomena have been developed in recent years, and extension of these models to the theory of economic integration is obviously called for. Recall that our present widespread appreciation of the large and growing significance of intra-industry trade in the industrial world actually dates from studies of the effects of economic integration in Europe.

(iii) Imperfect Competition and Scale Economies

These phenomena have been considered in the light of customs union theory in the past. What is clearly called for now is the application of recently developed general equilibrium approaches.

(iv) 'Small' Tariff Changes

Customs union theory has generally considered only 'large' tariff changes between partners: the complete elimination of internal trade barriers. Exceptions[3] have usually been accompanied by apologetic explanations of the convenience of marginal analysis. Large changes have been considered an essential aspect of the problem because theorists have often had in the backs of their minds the example of European integration, with free internal trade an objective from the start, and because the GATT rules permitting customs unions and free trade areas require the abolition of internal tariffs: mere reciprocal tariff preferences are ruled out. But the latter consideration is eliminated by our interest in trade modification. Furthermore, a concern with contemporary problems should redirect attention towards small changes, rendering marginal analysis of interest in its own right. The successive GATT rounds have, at each stage, constituted an incremental change toward free trade among the developed countries. If translated into tariff equivalents, the numerous voluntary export restraints of the 'new protectionism' of recent years likewise constitute incremental changes, though in the direction of economic disintegration. Another potentially important example is furnised by the codes of conduct regarding non-tariff barriers formulated during the Tokyo Round. These codes are not automatically binding on the GATT nations, or limited to them, but are to be individually acceded to by individual states. Thus each code seems likely to develop a circle of participating countries applying *vis-à-vis* one another the provisions of the code as regards the respective non-tariff barrier, but applying more restrictive prior standards toward non-participating countries. Thus the codes might well produce non-tariff equivalents of preferential trading areas.

It is easier to undertake by stages the departures recommended here. Therefore, in the following two sections we ignore imperfect competition and scale economies, but allow trade modification and enquire into the consequences of a small preferential change in tariffs, in a conventional context. Two general propositions, analogous to results well known in the theory of trade and domestic distortions, follow easily once attention is directed towards small tariff changes; these proportions are stated in Section 3, and are formally proved in Section 4. In the rest of the paper we consider also the remaining two suggested departures from the standard treatment of economic integration: product differentiation, and imperfect competition and scale economies. To highlight the impact of these additions, we construct in Section 5 a special formal model that incorporates all four departures, but that abstracts from some features already studied. In Section 6 we analyse properties of this model by means of comparative-statics experiments. Finally, some brief concluding remarks are given in Section 7.

3. TWO ADDITIONAL GENERAL PROPERTIES

Consider first an initial state of non-discriminatory (but tariff-ridden) world trade. Suppose that some subset of countries then initiates a marginal mutual reduction of tariffs on trade with one another. (Since the role of the external terms of trade is understood, suppose for simplicity that no change takes place in the terms at which these countries deal with the rest of the world.) Since trade is initially non-discriminatory, an additional unit of imports or exports by any country has the same effect on the welfare of residents of that country regardless of with whom the additional trade takes place. Thus the trade diversion and/or trade modification generated by the marginal preferential tariff reduction must have a zero first-order effect on welfare. But since trade is tariff-ridden, an additional unit of imports will cost any country less than that unit's contribution to welfare: any trade creation must have a positive first-order effect.

(C) *Preferential Trade is Better than Free Trade.* If tariffs are positive but non-discriminatory, any sub-group of countries can raise its joint welfare by means of marginal preferential tariff reductions that increase the gross value of their total trade (in the specific sense that the new trade flows yield the partners more tariff revenue than the old flows, at the initial tariffs and prices), if the prices of goods exchanged between those countries and the rest of the world do not change.

This proposition differs from the result of Kemp and Wan (1978), Ohyama (1972), and Vanek (1965) in that it is limited to small tariff changes, whose relevance we have just advocated. What this limitation buys us is a dispensation from the need to adjust external tariffs so as to eliminate trade diversion and trade modification: their welfare effects will be swamped by those of trade creation.

Now consider the opposite initial situation: a group of countries, in a tariff-ridden world, have formed a customs union with free internal trade. Suppose these countries stage a 'marginal retreat' from the union by imposing a small tariff on imports from one another. Free initial internal trade implies that a marginal import by any member from a partner yields a welfare increase equal to the welfare loss due to the exports required in payment. Thus the 'trade destruction' caused by the marginal internal tariff will entail a zero first-order effect on welfare. But any increased trade with the rest of the world produces a positive first-order effect since the initial external tariffs imply that an additional import increases welfare by more than the sacrifice required to pay for it.

(D) *Preferential Trade is Better than a Customs Union.* If any group of countries has free mutual trade in a tariff-ridden world, their joint welfare will be increased by a marginal tariff on one another's goods that raises total trade with the rest of the world (in the specific sense that the new volume of trade yields the partners jointly more revenue than the old, at the original tariffs and prices), if the prices at which the partners trade with external countries do not change.

In essence, the net benefits from 'undoing' some trade diversion and trade modification necessarily swamp the losses entailed by 'trade destruction', for a small retreat from a customs union. This partially undercuts the consistent motives for union formation that seem to be supplied by idea (B). Also (C) and (D) together imply a motivation for tariff preferences that fall short of complete union. This is quite consistent with the prominent contemporary issues that the previous section argued ought to be addressable by the theory of economic integration.

4. A FORMAL TREATMENT

4.1. The model

This section supplies explicit proofs of propositions (C) and (D) and discusses them further. Assume three countries: two partners (A and B) and the rest of the world (distinguished by an asterisk). There is a total of n traded goods, divided into the twelve groups described in Table 13.1. Groups 1 to 5 contain goods imported by country A, exportables are collected in groups 6–10, whereas country A does not trade in groups 11 and 12.

For each group i, Q_i denotes the n-vector with a zero in each component corresponding to a good not in group i, and with the country A domestic price of the respective good in each component that does so correspond. Thus $Q = \Sigma_{i=1}^{12} Q_i$ is the vector of country A domestic prices. Vectors P_i apply analogously to the partner country, so $P = \Sigma_{i=1}^{12} P_i$ denotes the vector of country-B domestic prices.

In like fashion, P_i^* denotes the vector of prices actually paid to the rest of the world, or received from the rest of the world, for goods in group i (with zeros in components corresponding to other goods). Let $R^A = P_1 + P_2^* + P_3^* + P_4^* + P_5^* + Q_6 + Q_7 + P_8^* + P_9^* + P_{10}^*$. Then R_A is the vector of prices at which country A actually transacts with foreigners, *except* possibly for those goods in group 5 that are imported from country B. In like manner, $R^B = P_1 + P_2^* + P_4^* + P_5 + Q_6 + P_7^* + P_9^* + P_{10}^* + P_{11}^* + P_{12}^*$ denotes B's actual international transaction prices, *except* possibly for goods in group 7 imported from A.

T_i^A, for $i = 1, \ldots, 4$, is the $n \times n$ diagonal matrix with *ad valorem* tariff rates of country A on goods in group i as the appropriate diagonal elements, and zeros elsewhere. T_{5B}^A and T_{5*}^A likewise denote tariff matrices of country A on goods in group 5 imported from B and from the rest of the world respectively. Country B tariff matrices T_4^B, T_6^B, T_{10}^B, T_{12}^B, T_{7A}^B, and T_{7*}^B are defined analogously. Let $T^A = T_1^A + T_2^A + T_3^A + T_4^A + T_{5*}^A$ and $T^B = T_4^B + T_6^B + T_{7*}^B + T_{10}^B + T_{12}^B$. Then

TABLE 13.1. *Description of the Commodity Groups*

Group	Commodity description
1	B exports only to A
2	B exports to A and to the rest of the world
3	the rest of the world exports only to A
4	the rest of the world exports to A and B
5	the rest of the world and B both export to A
6	A exports only to B
7	the rest of the world and A both export to B
8	A exports only to the rest of the world
9	A and B both export to the rest of the world
10	A exports to both B and the rest of the world
11	B exports only to the rest of the world
12	the rest of the world exports only to B

$$Q = (I + T^A) R^A,$$

$$P = (I + T^B) R^B.$$

Note also that $(I + T^A_{5B}) P_5 = (I + T^A_{5*}) P^*_5$ and $(I + T^B_{7A}) Q_7 = (I + T^B_{7*}) P^*_7$.

M^A_i is the n-vector of country A net imports of goods in group i (with zeros elsewhere), and $M^A = \Sigma^{10}_{i=1} M^A_i$. Also $M^A_5 = M^A_{5B} + M^A_{5*}$ and $M^A_{10} = M^A_{10B} + M^A_{10*}$ where the two vectors on the right in each case record trade with country B and the rest of the world respectively. Analogously for M^B_i, for $M^B = M^B_1 + M^B_2 + M^B_4 + M^B_5 + M^B_6 + M^B_7 + M^B_9 + M^B_{10} + M^B_{11} + M^B_{12}$, and for both $M^B_2 = M^B_{2A} + M^B_{2*}$ and $M^B_7 = M^B_{7A} + M^B_{7*}$. (Note that $M^A_1 = -M^B_1, M^A_2 = -M^B_{2A}, M^A_{5B} = -M^B_5$, $-M^A_6 = M^B_6, -M^A_7 = M^B_{7A}$ and $-M^A_{10B} = M^B_{10}$).

In country A, total expenditure – denoted by the national expenditure function $e^A(Q, u_A)$, where u_A denotes the vector of utilities of A residents – must equal income, composed of tariff revenue plus the value of national production, the latter given by the national product function $y^A(Q)$. Thus

$$e^A(Q, u_A) = y^A(Q) + T^A R^A [M^A - M^A_{5B}] + T^A_{5B} P^A_5 M^A_{5B}. \qquad (13.1)$$

Analogously for the partner country:

$$e^B(P, u_B) = y^B(P) + T^B R^B [M^B - M^B_{7A}] + T^B_{7A} Q_7 M^B_{7A}. \qquad (13.2)$$

4.2. A basic expression

Differentiating (13.1), noting that $\partial e^A/\partial Q - \partial y^A/\partial Q = M^A$ and that $dQ = dR^A + d(T^A R^A)$ gives

$$\frac{\partial e^A}{\partial u_A} du_A = -M^A\, dR^A - M^A_{5B} [d(T^A R^A) - d(T^A_{5B} P_5)] + T^A R^A\, d\bar{M}^A$$
$$+ T^A_{5B} P_5\, dM^A_{5B}, \qquad (13.3)$$

where $\bar{M}^A \equiv M^A - M^A_{5B}$. In a like manner, we obtain for the partner country

$$\frac{\partial e^B}{\partial u_B} du_B = -M^B\, dR^B - M^B_{7A} [d(T^B R^B) - d(T^B_{7A} Q_7)] + T^B R^B\, d\bar{M}^B$$
$$+ T^B_{7A} Q_7\, dM^B_{7A}. \qquad (13.4)$$

Equations (13.3) and (13.4) supply measures of the welfare effects on the partners of changes in commercial policy. The sources of these effects, spelled out on the right-hand sides of the equations, are analogous to the sources of welfare effects commonly discussed in conventional tariff theory.[4]

We measure the change in the joint welfare of the partner countries by $dW = (\partial e^A/\partial u_A)\, du_A + (\partial e^B/\partial u_B)\, du_B$. Remember that we suppose constancy in the prices at which A and B transact with the rest of the world, implying

$$M^A\, dR^A + M^B\, dR^B = -M^A_{5B}\, dP_5 - M^B_{7A}\, dQ_7.$$

With goods in group 5 (or group 7) being bought from the rest of the world at prices assumed to be unchanged, $d(T^A R^A)(d(T^B R^B))$ will have zero elements corresponding to positive entries in M_{5B}^A (or M_{7A}^B), and therefore

$$dW = M_{5B}^A [dP_5 + d(T_{5B}^A P_5)] + T_{5B}^A P_5 (dM^A - d\bar{M}^A) + T^A R^A \, d\bar{M}^A$$
$$+ M_{7A}^B [dQ_7 + d(T_{7A}^B Q_7)] + T_{7A}^B Q_7 (dM^B - d\bar{M}^B) + T^B R^B \, d\bar{M}^B,$$

$$(13.5)$$

where $T_{5B}^A P_5 (T_{7A}^B Q_7)$ has zeros corresponding to non-zero elements of $d\bar{M}^A$ $(d\bar{M}^B)$. Furthermore,

$$dP_5 + d(T_{5B}^A P_5) = d[(I + T_{5B}^A)P_5] = d[(I + T_{5*}^A)P_5^*] = P_5^* \, dT_{5*}^A,$$

$$dQ_7 + d(T_{7A}^B Q_7) = d[(I + T_{7A}^B)Q_7] = d[(I + T_{7*}^B)P_7^*] = P_7^* \, dT_{7*}^B.$$

Since also M_{5B}^A (M_{7A}^B) has zero elements corresponding to non-zero elements in $P_5^* \, dT_{5*}^A$ $(P_7^* \, dT_{7*}^B)$, our expression for the effect of tariff changes on the partners' joint welfare simplifies to

$$dW = (T_{5B}^A P_5) \, dM^A + (T_{7A}^B Q_7) \, dM^B + (T^A R^A) \, d\bar{M}^A + (T^B R^B) \, d\bar{M}^B.$$

$$(13.6)$$

This is our basic result. We now apply it to two special cases in order to derive propositions (C) and (D).

4.3. The propositions

Suppose first that all tariffs are initially non-discriminatory, so that $T_{5B}^A = T_{5*}^A$, $P_5 = P_5^*$, $T_{7A}^B = T_{7*}^B$, and $Q_7 = P_7^*$. Equation (13.6) then reduces to

$$dW = (T^A R^A) \, dM^A + (T^B R^B) \, dM^B.$$

$$(13.7)$$

Thus a small discriminatory tariff change (or any other small change) raises joint welfare if and only if the changes in trade volume would increase joint tariff revenues at the initial rates and prices, as was stated in proposition (C) above. Note in particular two aspects of this result.

First, the degree of trade diversion — reflected in the *composition* of dM_5^A between dM_{5B}^A and dM_{5*}^A and in the composition of dM_7^B between dM_{7A}^B and dM_{7*}^B — has no influence at all on dW. This is to be expected in the light of the previous section's informal discussion.

Second, trade modification — reflected in the magnitudes of dM_3^A, dM_4^A, dM_4^B, and dM_{12}^B — will add to or subtract from dW according as the goods involved are in this sense complementary to or substitutes for intra-union trade. This, again, is not surprising in view of the earlier discussion. Indeed, if the goods which countries A and B trade exclusively with the rest of the world are sufficiently strong substitutes for the goods they exchange with each other, they could have an incentive to form an 'anti-union', that is, to *add* a marginal discriminatory tariff on each others' goods. The two would have reason to seek separate preferential arrangements with the rest of the world, rather than with each other.

Suppose next that A and B initially have a full free trade area and impose marginal internal tariffs. Then $T_1^A = T_2^A = T_{5B}^A = T_6^B = T_{7A}^B = T_{10}^B = 0$ and (13.6) reduces to

$$dW = (T^A R^A) \, d\bar{M}^A + (T^B R^B) \, d\bar{M}^B. \tag{13.8}$$

Thus a marginal retreat from internal free trade will raise the partners' joint welfare if and only if it raises total tariff revenue collected on trade with the rest of the world, as stated above in proposition (D). It is instructive to decompose the right-hand side of (13.8) as follows:

$$dW = (T_5^A P_5^* \, dM_{5*}^A + T_7^B P_7^* \, dM_{7*}^B) + (T_3^A P_3^* \, dM_3^A + T_4^A P_4^* \, dM_4^A$$
$$+ T_4^B P_4^* \, dM_4^B + T_{12}^B P_{12}^* \, dM_{12}^B). \tag{13.9}$$

Note that an 'undoing' of trade diversion – indicated by positive terms within the first set of parentheses on the right-hand side of (13.9) – must increase W regardless of how great the accompanying reduction in intra-union trade in the same goods happens to be. This is a consequence of the initial free internal trade, as discussed in the previous section.

The influence of trade modification is summarized by the second parenthesized term on the right-hand side of (13.9). Joint partner welfare is thereby raised or lowered according as this term is positive or negative, that is, according as the goods traded exclusively with the rest of the world are in this sense on balance substitutes for or complementary to intra-partner trade.

Trade diversion and trade modification are central in both exercises. The presumptive role of trade diversion is clear: it should cause both a marginal reduction of a discriminatory tariff and a marginal retreat from a free trade area to raise joint partner welfare. But the role of trade modification depends crucially upon whether the goods traded exclusively with the rest of the world are on balance substitutes for or complements to intra-union trade, in the sense that discrimination in favour of the latter reduces or increases the volume of the former, with the change in this volume measured by the net changes in partner tariff revenue it would generate at initial prices and tariffs.

Neither non-discrimination nor a free trade area would constitute an optimal policy – for A and B jointly, given tariffs on goods from the rest of the world – without a very special balancing of the various influences discussed above. If exclusively external trade is on balance neither strongly substitutable for, nor complementary to, internal trade, optimal policy for the partners will presumably entail tariff preferences that fall short of a full free trade area, so that both non-discrimination and customs unions should be unstable.

Significant net *substitutability* both reduces the gain from initial preferences and increases the gain to a retreat from a full union. Thus one expects it to cause optimal policy to feature a lower degree of preference. Sufficient substitutability should make optimal an 'anti-union' with the members actually discriminating against one another. Significant net *complementarity*, finally, increasing the gain from initial preferences and reducing that from a retreat, presumably causes the optimal policy to approximate more closely free internal trade. Large enough complementarity could cause the optimal policy to be a 'super union' with internal trade actually stimulated by subsidies finance by tariffs on external trade. Note that the European Community's Common Agricultural Policy − which does not naturally come to mind in a discussion of optimality − does in fact possess some of the characteristics of such a case.

5. SCALE ECONOMIES AND PRODUCT DIFFERENTIATION: A SPECIAL MODEL

The previous sections focused on trade modification as well as trade diversion and considered small tariff changes rather than large ones. But we said nothing about induced change in the *number* of distinct commodities (that is, in the degree of product differentiation), and, more prominently yet, imperfect competition and scale economies are foreign to the optimality conditions central to the logic of the propositions. Thus we have set off on some but not all of those departures from standard theory that we have argued for.

We have no wish to construct the awesome structure that would simply add our further suggested innovations to what we have already done in the previous section. Instead we now consider a special model that incorporates our four desired departures in as sharp a fashion as possible: by abstracting from other features. For better or worse, this is also the strategy used in the recent literature on international trade and scale economies, imperfect competition, and product differentiation.

We continue to suppose three countries: the partners (A and B) and the rest of the world, denoted by an asterisk. A and B can be thought of as DCs, the rest of the world as an LDC. A and B produce goods in two common sectors: manufactures and food. There are n and m different variants of manufactures produced in A and B, respectively. They are all (equally) imperfect substitutes to each other from the consumer's point of view, although they are produced with the same homothetic technology, characterized by internal, increasing returns to scale. Food, on the other hand, is produced in all three countries, under constant returns to scale.

We consider the following special trade pattern. A and B export their respective manufactures to each other and to the rest of the world, and both countries import food from the latter. We assume furthermore that A and B have formed a customs union with their internal tariff τ set at zero, and with a common external tariff t. The rest of the world imposes no trade restrictions.

It is clear that, with such a trade pattern, this customs union does not cause any trade *diversion*, since the non-member country exports a different good from that exported by the union countries. But the union will give rise to trade *creation* and trade *modification*.

Following, e.g., Dixit and Stiglitz (1977), we assume the preferences of each country's representative consumer to be given by

$$U^k = \left(\sum_{i=1}^{n} (X_i^k)^\beta + \sum_{j=1}^{m} (Y_j^k)^\beta \right)^{\alpha/\beta} (Z^k)^{1-\alpha}; \quad k = A, \dot{B}, * \quad (13.10)$$

with $0 < \alpha < 1$, and $0 < \beta < 1$, and where X_i^k is the amount of the country A-produced manufacture i that is consumed in country k, Y_j^k is the amount of the country-B produced manufacture j that is consumed in k, and Z^k the consumed quantity of food in k.

Let us now turn to the production side. The production process for manufactures can be thought of as consisting of two stages: first primary factors are used to produce a (non-traded) intermediate input under constant returns to scale, in the amounts M^A and M^B in the two DCs. This input is transformed to final differentiated goods under increasing returns. Since the equilibrium under study is characterized by strong symmetry, in the sense that $X_i^k = X^k, \forall i$, and $Y_j^k = Y^k, \forall j$, each firm in the manufacturing sector in A employs M^A/n of the intermediate good, and correspondingly M^B/m in B. We assume that entry is free, so the condition for industry equilibrium is that profits are zero

$$PX = r^A \frac{M^A}{n}, \quad \text{and} \quad QY = r^B \frac{M^B}{m},$$

where P and Q are the prices received by producers of manufactured products in A and B, respectively, r is the price of the intermediate input, and where $X \equiv X^A + X^B + X^*$, and $Y \equiv Y^A + Y^B + Y^*$. The internal increasing returns to scale stem from a fixed cost a, coupled with a constant marginal cost b. We could therefore alternatively simply define

$$M^A \equiv n(a + bX), \quad \text{and} \quad M^B \equiv m(a + bY),$$

and consider r^A, and r^B, as the 'factor-price index' in the separable cost function.

The conditions for profit-maximization in the two manufacturing industries can be stated as

$$P\beta = r^A b, \quad \text{and} \quad Q\beta = r^B b. \quad (13.12)$$

To express the conditions in this form we use the fact that each firm will adjust its quantities in the three markets in such a way that it receives the same price everywhere.

Now, from (13.11) and (13.12) we immediately get that the total output volume of a firm in the manufacturing sectors is fixed.

$$X = Y = \frac{a}{b} \frac{\beta}{1 - \beta}.$$

This is in particular due to the homothetic technology. It then follows that

$$n = \frac{1-\beta}{\alpha} M^A, \quad \text{and} \quad m = \frac{1-\beta}{\alpha} M^B.$$

The union countries' respective output of food is given by the transformation functions $T(M^A)$ for A, and $S(M^B)$ for B. The domestic produce is sold at the same price as imported food: $P_F(1 + t)$, where P_F denotes the price of food excluding the union's external tariff t. The price of the intermediate good must be the value of the alternative use of the resources devoted to the production of one unit of the good, or

$$r^A = -P_F(1 + t) \, T'(M^A),$$
$$r^B = -P_F(1 + t) \, S'(M^B). \tag{13.13}$$

The rest of the world is assumed to use one factor only, with the reward r^*, and with the fixed supply L^*. It takes one unit of this factor to produce one unit of food, and the condition for profit maximization (and industry equilibrium) is therefore simply

$$P_F = r^*.$$

Two variables that will be of interest in the comparative-statics exercises are the internal and external terms-of-trade, $q \equiv Q/P$, and $p \equiv P_F/P$, respectively. With the aid of (13.11) and (13.13), and recalling the definitions of M^A and M^B, the two variables may be expressed as

$$q = \frac{S'(M^B)}{T'(M^A)} \tag{13.14}$$

$$p = \frac{-\beta}{b P_F (1 + t) \, T'(M^A)}. \tag{13.15}$$

Let us finally, before proceeding to the comparative-statics exercises, give the clearing conditions for the goods markets (the respective demand functions are given in the Appendix)

$$X = \frac{\alpha}{P} \left[\frac{I^A}{n + m y_A^\beta} + \frac{I^B/(1 + \tau)}{n + m y_B^\beta} + \frac{I^*}{n + m y_*^\beta} \right] \tag{13.16}$$

$$Y = \frac{\alpha}{Q} \left[\frac{I^A/(1 + \tau)}{n y_A^{-\beta} + m} + \frac{I^B}{n y_B^{-\beta} + m} + \frac{I^*}{n y_*^{-\beta} + m} \right] \tag{13.17}$$

$$L^* + T(M^A) + S(M^B) = \frac{(1 - \alpha)}{P_F} [I^A/(1 + t) + I^B/(1 + t) + I^*], \tag{13.18}$$

where τ denotes the union's internal tariff.

Comparative-statics exercises will be conducted to expose the basic nature of our model. To have a recognizable point of departure and standard of comparison, we shall conduct an exercise similar to that of proposition (D) discussed in Sections 3 and 4. Thus we start with internal free trade ($\tau = 0$), and with a common positive external tariff ($t > 0$). We first increase the common external tariff and then increase the common internal tariff. To facilitate matters we make the following assumption: the partners have a transfer scheme such that the relative changes in their incomes I^A and I^B are identical and equal to $\hat{I}$. This reflects our concern with the partners' *joint* experience, but is not without practical relevance: the Common Market is an example of a union with an internal transfer scheme.

The rest of this section presents the comparative-statics results. Discussions of these results are postponed to Section 6.

Since we use P_F as the numeraire, we have from (13.18):

$$\frac{\hat{I}}{(1-\alpha)} = -\frac{PnX}{I^A + I^B}\hat{M}^A - \frac{QmY}{I^A + I^B}\hat{M}^B + \hat{t}, \tag{13.19}$$

where $\hat{t} \equiv dt/(1 + t)$.

The numbers of firms in the manufacturing sectors are proportional to the outputs of the two intermediate goods

$$\hat{n} = \hat{M}^A,$$

$$\hat{m} = \hat{M}^B.$$

The terms-of-trade changes are directly obtained from (13.14) and (13.15)

$$\hat{q} = \sigma^B\hat{m} - \sigma^A\hat{n}, \tag{13.20}$$

$$\hat{p} = -\hat{t} - \sigma^A\hat{n}, \tag{13.21}$$

where

$$\sigma^A \equiv \frac{M^A T''(M^A)}{T'(M^A)}, \quad \text{and} \quad \sigma^B \equiv \frac{M^B T''(M^B)}{T'(M^B)}.$$

The changes in trade and consumption patterns are given by

$$\hat{y}_A = (\sigma^B\hat{m} - \sigma^A\hat{n} + \hat{t})/(\beta - 1), \tag{13.22}$$

$$\hat{y}_B = (\sigma^B\hat{m} - \sigma^A\hat{n} - \hat{t})/(\beta - 1), \tag{13.23}$$

$$\hat{y}_* = (\sigma^B\hat{m} - \sigma^A\hat{n})/(\beta - 1), \tag{13.24}$$

$$\hat{z}_A = \hat{n} + \frac{m}{n+m}\left(\frac{\beta}{1-\beta}\sigma^A - 1\right)(\hat{n} - \hat{m}) - \frac{m}{(n+m)}\frac{\beta}{(1-\beta)}\hat{t}, \tag{13.25}$$

$$\hat{z}_B = \hat{n} + \frac{m}{n+m}\left(\frac{\beta}{1-\beta}\sigma^A - 1\right)(\hat{n} - \hat{m}) + \left(1 + \frac{m}{n+m}\frac{\beta}{1-\beta}\right)\hat{t}, \tag{13.26}$$

$$\hat{z}_* = \hat{n} + \frac{m}{n+m}\left(\frac{\beta}{1-\beta}\sigma^A - 1\right)(\hat{n} - \hat{m}),\tag{13.27}$$

where $\hat{\tau} \equiv d\tau/(1+\tau)$, and $z_k \equiv Z^k/X^k$ for $k =$ A, B, *.

The following two expressions are reduced forms of the market equilibrium conditions for X- and Y-goods, respectively, and they will be the starting point of the proceeding analysis:

$$-\theta^*\hat{\imath} - \left[\theta^B + (\theta^B - \theta^A)\frac{\beta}{(1-\beta)}\frac{m}{(n+m)}\right]\hat{\tau} = \left[\sigma^A + \frac{1}{1-\alpha}\right]\hat{n}$$

$$+ \frac{m}{n+m}\left[\frac{\beta}{1-\beta}\sigma^A - \frac{1}{1-\alpha}\right](\hat{n} - \hat{m})$$

$$+ \frac{m}{(n+m)(1-\beta)}\frac{\beta}{}(\sigma^A - \sigma^B)\hat{m},\tag{13.28}$$

$$-\theta^*\hat{\imath} - \left[\theta^A - (\theta^B - \theta^A)\frac{\beta}{(1-\beta)}\frac{n}{(n+m)}\right]\hat{\tau} = \left[\sigma^B + \frac{1}{1-\alpha}\right]\hat{m}$$

$$- \frac{n}{n+m}\left[\frac{\beta}{1-\beta}\sigma^B - \frac{1}{1-\alpha}\right](\hat{n} - \hat{m})$$

$$- \frac{n}{(n+m)(1-\beta)}\frac{\beta}{}(\sigma^A - \sigma^B)\hat{n},\tag{13.29}$$

where θ^k is the share of world income for country k.

We subsequently make the special assumption that $\sigma^A = \sigma^B \equiv \sigma$, i.e. that the elasticities of the slopes of the transformation curves are the same at the equilibrium point, in the two union countries. This has the merit, aside from increased analytical tractability, of highlighting aspects of particular interest: the importance of the degree of product differentiation and the importance of asymmetries between the member countries in the relative sizes of their manufacturing sectors and also in their relative incomes.

(13.28) and (13.20) give the following solution for relative changes in the number of variants in the member countries:

$$\hat{n} = -\frac{\theta^*}{\Delta}\hat{\imath} - \left[\theta^B + (\theta^B - \theta^A)\frac{1}{(1-\alpha)\sigma}\frac{m}{(n+m)}\right]\frac{1}{\Delta}\hat{\tau}\tag{13.30}$$

$$\hat{m} = -\frac{\theta^*}{\Delta}\hat{\imath} - \left[\theta^A - (\theta^B - \theta^A)\frac{1}{(1-\alpha)\sigma}\frac{n}{(n+m)}\right]\frac{1}{\Delta}\hat{\tau}\tag{13.31}$$

$$\hat{n} - \hat{m} = \frac{(\theta^A - \theta^B)}{\sigma}\hat{\tau}\tag{13.32}$$

and

$$\hat{N} = -\frac{\theta^*}{\Delta}t - \frac{\Gamma}{\Delta}\hat{\tau}, \qquad (13.33)$$

where

$$N \equiv n + m,$$

$$\Delta \equiv \sigma + \frac{1}{1-\alpha} > 0$$

and

$$\Gamma \equiv \theta^A \frac{n}{n+m} + \theta^B \frac{m}{n+m} > 0.$$

The Appendix gives some intermediate steps in the derivation of the following two expressions for the relative changes in the indirect utilities V^A and V^*:

$$\hat{V}^A = \alpha \frac{\theta^*}{\Delta}\Lambda\,\hat{t} + \alpha\left(\frac{\Gamma}{\Delta}\Lambda - \frac{m}{n+m}\right)\hat{\tau} \qquad (13.34)$$

$$\hat{V}^* = \alpha\left(\left(\sigma - \frac{1-\beta}{\beta}\right)\frac{\theta^*}{\Delta} - 1\right)\hat{t} + \alpha\left(\sigma - \frac{1-\beta}{\beta}\right)\frac{\Gamma}{\Delta}\hat{\tau}, \qquad (13.35)$$

where

$$\Lambda \equiv \sigma - \frac{1-\beta}{\beta} + \frac{1}{\theta^A + \theta^B} \cdot \frac{1}{1-\alpha} \gtrless 0.$$

6. TARIFF CHANGES

Our comparative statics experiments incorporate the two types of changes in union commercial policy that are of interest: changes $\hat{t}$ in the common external tariff on imports of food, and the marginal imposition $\hat{\tau}$ of a mutual internal tariff on the exchange of differentiated manufactured goods. Consider each in turn.

6.1. An Increase in the Common External Tariff

Let us first examine the implication of an increase in the already positive common external tariff t. From (13.30) and (13.31):

$$\hat{n} = \hat{m} < 0.$$

The numbers of varieties of both types of differentiated goods fall as, in each partner country, resources are pulled from manufacturing into the now more highly protected agricultural sector. The contraction of manufacturing is entirely a reduction in the number of product varieties; each produced variety experiences no change in its level of production. With a common external tariff on food, (13.20) implies that $\hat{q} = \sigma(\hat{m} - \hat{n}) = 0$, so that no substitution between product varieties is induced.[5]

Our assumption about the third country ensures that it continues to export αL^* units of food. The shift of demand in A and B away from food turns the terms of trade in favour of the union. We have $\hat{p} = -\hat{t} - \sigma\hat{n}$, and substitution of (13.30) into this expression reveals that the relative price p of food in terms of manufactures does indeed fall, though by less than the tariff increase. The member countries hence have a terms-of-trade gain to set against the welfare loss from less product variety. But there is, of course, an additional source of gain: the increase in income. This source is partly reflected by the third term of Λ in (13.34). The direction of change in a member country's welfare is therefore ambiguous. We see that the total effect is more likely to be positive (i) the more sensitive the terms of trade are to given changes in product variety (higher σ), (ii) the less the evaluation of this variety (higher β), and (iii) the larger the share of the rest of the world in world income (smaller $\theta^A + \theta^B$).

The rest of the world has to face both a detrimental terms of trade effect and a reduction of product variety, and is therefore clearly worse off. Algebraically this is immediate from (13.35), noting that $(\sigma\theta^*/\Delta) - 1 < 0$.

6.2. A Marginal Internal Barrier

Now turn at last to the exercise treated by proposition (D) and suppose that $i = 0$ but $\hat{\tau} > 0$. As a starting point, assume that the partners have equal national incomes: $\theta^A = \theta^B$. Then again the numbers of varieties produced in the two member countries decline by a common amount, so that $\hat{q} = \sigma(\hat{m} - \hat{n}) = 0$.

Each partner attempts to protect manufacturing, but with resources shifting over to the agricultural sector the result is just the opposite! The reason is as follows. The tariff causes each union member to divert spending from the manufactures of its partner to its own manufactures, and the fact that $\hat{q} = 0$ means that the outside country has no reason to substitute between X goods and Y goods. Thus from (13.22)–(13.24) we see that $\hat{y}_A = -\hat{\tau}/(1 - \beta) < 0$, $\hat{y}_B = \hat{\tau}/(1 - \beta) > 0$, and $\hat{y}_* = 0$. As the partners are of equal size, these effects just cancel.

The higher price of the partner's manufactures reduces demand, so that with constant output volumes of individual firms there is downward pressure on the number of firms. This is reinforced by the fact that the proportion $(1 - \alpha)$ of the tariff revenue raised in the manufacturing sector is channelled into the agricultural sector. Thus the net effect is to protect food, not manufacturing. From (13.22)–(13.26) we have that $\hat{y}_A - \hat{z}_A < 0$ and $\hat{y}_B - \hat{z}_B > 0$, that is, a 'reversal' of trade modification.

It is instructive to compare the discussion in Sections 3 and 4 of proposition (D) with behaviour in the altered context of the present model. First, recall that in the earlier context gains actually resulted when the reversal of trade modification caused the union to import more from the rest of the world. The structure of the present model allows us to concentrate on what is new by ensuring that such gains shrink to zero: our assumptions about the third country imply that it exports an unchanged quantity of food to the union. Exclusively external trade is neither a substitute for nor complement to internal trade, to use our earlier terminology, and there is also now no trade diversion to 'undo'. Second, the terms of external trade were assumed fixed in proposition (D), but now the shift of demand toward food turns the terms of trade in the outside world's favour. From (13.15), $\hat{p} = -\sigma\hat{n} > 0$. This could of course be neutralized by an appropriate increase $\hat{t}$ in the common external tariff. But the most significant difference follows from the role of imperfect competition, scale economies, and the endogenous number of product varieties. As in the conventional analysis, zero first-order welfare effects are caused by shifts in union expenditure between existing X goods and Y goods. But in our model the output levels of all product varieties which continue to be produced are unchanged, and instead the number of varieties of manufactures falls. This is deleterious. The total effect on the welfare of country A or B is ambiguous, as can be seen from (13.34). There is now one additional term, compared to the case with the external tariff, which influences the direction of change in welfare: the relative sizes of the manufacturing sectors. The larger the partner's share of total manufacturing output, the larger the share that will be hit by the tariff, and the more likely it is that the internal tariff will actually reduce welfare, and that a 'super-union' will be optimal.

The external country is affected in an ambiguous way. Its terms of trade improve, so that it consumes more manufactures than before along with the same quantity of food. But, on the other hand, those manufactures possess less product diversity than before. In summary, it is possible that all countries lose from the internal tariff, or that all gain, with $\theta^A = \theta^B$. It is also possible that the member countries gain and the rest of the world loses. But, if the member countries lose, then so must the external country, rendering a 'super-union' beneficial to all!

Thus far we have supposed that $\theta^A = \theta^B$. The role of size disparities between partners is now easily exposed. (13.30)–(13.33) show that the internal tariff will still cause a decline in total output of manufactures, but that the smaller country will have to adjust its manufacturing sector more than proportionally: $\hat{n} > \hat{m} < 0$. There is hence a *reallocation* of manufacturing from the smaller (in terms of national income) partner to the larger. Intuitively, small-country-located firms will have a larger share of production hit by the tariff, inducing more exit to keep profits at zero. Indeed, it might possibly be the case that the larger partner's manufacturing output actually rises, if the difference in national income is sufficiently large. This reallocation of production might be one reason why customs unions tend to be formed by similar economies.

6.3. Intermediate goods

There is an alternative interpretation of our model. Assume only two consumption goods, food and a final manufacture, but many differentiated intermediate goods, or components, used to assemble the final manufacture. This interpretation is entirely consistent with our formulation if we let the CES part of the utility function (13.10) be the assembly function for the final manufacture, X_i^k and Y_j^k represent the inputs of components i and j, and the parameter β reflect the degree of substitutability between different components. The technology is then such that each single producer of an intermediate good faces internal increasing returns to scale available when the production process is geographically concentrated: an example of 'national' economies of scale.[6] Assembly of the final manufacture is costless, and exhibits increasing returns to scale in the number of different components that are used. To see this, note that the CES assembly function gives an output of $n^{1/\beta}X$ in the symmetric version, and hence the output increases faster than the input nX. These economies of scale are 'international', since the size of the world market for the manufacture determines n, and they also reflect the benefits of an increased division of labour in the world economy; they are assumed to be external to individual assembly firms.

There is, in this interpretation, trade both in intermediate goods, and in the final good food. There is initially a tariff only on the latter good, which is exported by the external country. It is immaterial whether finished manufactures are assembled where consumed, or whether they are all assembled in one partner country and then exported. But in the latter case the interesting possibility of tariffs on final manufactures is not covered by our analysis, the components must be taxed the same whether imported directly or embodied in final manufactures, and exports of the latter must be allowed drawbacks of tariffs paid for imported components. The total impact on each country's welfare of tariff changes is, of course, the same irrespective of model interpretation. What differ are the sources of welfare changes. We saw above that an increase in either the internal or external tariff reduced both n and m unless the partners were too different in terms of their national incomes. Here this means that fewer components will be used in the production of manufactures, leading to a situation with less exploitation of international returns to scale. The main welfare-reducing effect of the tariffs is thus that they are detrimental to the division of labour by diminishing the world market for the final manufacture. But, there is no loss here stemming from reduced exploitation of the traditional, national returns to scale. The two developed countries are trying to protect their home industries, and manage in the sense that a higher proportion of inputs are locally made. But with both countries acting in a similar fashion no overall gain is ensured.

7. CONCLUDING REMARKS

We live in a multilateral world. Therefore any non-universal change in commercial policy — and they are all in fact non-universal — ought to fall within the domain of the theory of economic integration. But it has not been so, since that theory usually has been too narrowly conceived. We have argued for four extensions: trade modification, consideration of small changes in policy, scale economies, and product differentiation under imperfect competition.

Adding the first two of these suggested extensions to the conventional framework we derived two basic propositions, suggested by familiar second-best theory, that are central to the characterization of the optimal policy for a subset of countries considering some degree of integration in a tariff-ridden world. We then developed a special, but illustrative, model incorporating all four of our suggested extensions and put it through its paces. Such an exercise is no more than an uncertain first step. But it is in the direction that must be followed, we maintain, if the theory of economic integration is to achieve the relevance to contemporary issues that it long since ought to have possessed.

APPENDIX

1. THE DEMAND FUNCTIONS

$$PX^A = \frac{\alpha I^A}{n + my_A^\beta}, \quad \text{where } y_A \equiv \frac{Y^A}{X^A}$$

$$Q(1 + \tau)Y^A = \frac{\alpha I^A}{ny_A^{-\beta} + m}$$

$$P_F(1 + t)Z^A = (1 - \alpha)I^A$$

$$P(1 + \tau)X^B = \frac{\alpha I^B}{n + my_B^\beta}, \quad \text{where } y_B \equiv \frac{Y^B}{X^B}$$

$$QY^B = \frac{\alpha I^B}{ny_B^{-\beta} + m}$$

$$P_F(1 + t)Z^B = (1 - \alpha)I^B$$

$$PX^* = \frac{\alpha I^*}{n + my_*^\beta}, \quad \text{where } y_* \equiv \frac{Y^*}{X^*}$$

$$QY^* = \frac{\alpha I^*}{ny_*^{-\beta} + m}$$

$$P_F Z^* = (1 - \alpha)I^*.$$

2. THE RELATIVE CHANGE IN THE INDIRECT UTILITIES

The indirect utility function for country A is

$$V^A = \gamma (R^A)^{-\alpha}(1 + t)^{-(1-\alpha)}I^A,$$

where

$$R^A \equiv (nP^\rho + m(1 + \tau)^\rho Q^\rho)^{1/\rho} = p^{-1}(n + m(1 + \tau)^\rho q^\rho)^{1/\rho}$$

and

$$\rho \equiv \frac{\beta}{\beta - 1}$$

and for the third country

$$V^* = \gamma (R^*)^{-\alpha}I^*,$$

where

$$R^* = p^{-1}(n + mq^\rho)^{1/\rho}.$$

γ is a constant, and R^k is a price index defined over the differentiated goods. These expressions become, when differentiated logarithmically,

$$\hat{V}^A = -\alpha \hat{R}^A - (1 - \alpha)\hat{t} + \hat{I}$$

and

$$\hat{V}^* = -\alpha \hat{R}^*,$$

where we use that $\hat{I}^A = \hat{I}^B \equiv \hat{I}$, and that $\hat{I}^* = 0$.

Concentrate for a moment on the change in the price index R^A. The relative change can be split up into two components:

$$\hat{R}^A = \left[\frac{m}{n + m}(\hat{q} + \hat{\tau}) - \hat{p} \right] - \frac{1 - \beta}{\beta}\hat{N}. \tag{13.A1}$$

The second term is the effect on the index of a change in the number of varieties available to the consumer, at given relative prices. This term is of course not present in the traditional analysis of customs unions, but will prove to be of considerable importance here.

Returning to the change in utility we get by substitution

$$\hat{V}^A = -\left[\hat{t} + \alpha \frac{m}{n + m}\hat{\tau} + \alpha\sigma\hat{N} \right] + \hat{I} + \alpha \frac{1 - \beta}{\beta}\hat{N}. \tag{13.A2}$$

By substituting (13.10) and (13.A1) into (13.A2) we arrive at expressions (13.34) and (13.35) in the text.

NOTES

*   The authors received useful comments from Elhanan Helpman and from participants at a seminar at the Institute for International Economic Studies, University of Stockholm. Henrik Horn gratefully acknowledges financial support from Humanistisk-Samhällsvetenskapliga Forskningsrådet, Sweden.
1.   For recent examples see Wonnacott and Wonnacott (1981) and Lloyd (1982).

2.   See Meade (1955, 1956) and Ethier (1983, ch. 12).

3.   The most notable exception is no doublt James Meade (1955, 1956), who was criticized in this regard. For example Lipsey (1968, p. 271) refers to this 'very serious, possibly crippling, limitation'. The subsequent literature has largely avoided marginal analysis. See, however, Berglas (1979), Reizman (1979), McMillan and McCann (1981), and Lloyd (1982).

4.   For such a discussion, see section A.6 of Appendix I in Ethier (1983).

5.   In the more general case $\sigma^A \neq \sigma^B$ we would have $\sigma^A \hat{n} = \sigma^B \hat{m}$ so that manufacturing contracts relatively more in the country with the greater ease of substitution of food for the non-traded manufacturing intermediate good; the structure of such economies remains irrelevant. Also we would still have $0 = \hat{q} = \sigma^B \hat{m} - \sigma^A \hat{n}$.

6.   See Ethier (1979, 1982).

REFERENCES

Berglas, E. (1979), 'Preferential Trading Theory: The n Commodity Case', *Journal of Political Economy*, 87, 315–31.

Dixit, A. K. and Stiglitz, J. (1977), 'Monopolistic Competition and Optimum Product Diversity', *American Economic Review*, 67, 297–308.

Ethier, W. (1979), 'Internationally Decreasing Costs and World Trade', *Journal of International Economics*, 9, 1–24.

Ethier, W. J. (1982), National and International Returns to Scale in the Modern Theory of International Trade, *American Economic Review*, 72, 389–405.

Ethier, W. J. (1983), *Modern International Economics* (New York: W. W. Norton).

Kemp, M. C. (1964), *The Pure Theory of International Trade* (Englewood Cliffs: Prentice-Hall).

Kemp, M. C. and Wan, H. Y. (1976), 'An Elementary Proposition Concerning the Formation of Customs Unions', *Journal of International Economics*, 6, 95–8.

Kravis, I. B. and Lipsey, R. E. (1971), *Price Competitiveness in World Trade* (New York: National Bureau of Economic Research).

Kravis, I. B. and Lipsey, R. E. (1978), 'Price Behavior in the Light of Balance of Payments Theories', *Journal of International Economics*, 8, 193–246.

Lipsey, R. E. (1968), 'The Theory of Customs Unions: A General Survey', in R. E. Caves and H. G. Johnson (eds.), *Readings in International Economics* (Homewood: Richard D. Irwin).

Lloyd, P. (1982), '3 x 3 Theory of Customs Unions', *Journal of International Economics*, 12, 41–63.

McMillan, J. and McCann, E. (1981), 'Welfare Effects in Customs Unions', *Economic Journal*, 91, 697–703.

Meade, J. E. (1955), *Trade and Welfare* (London: Oxford University Press).

Meade, J. E. (1956), *The Theory of Customs Unions* (Amsterdam, North-Holland).

Ohyama, M. (1972), 'Trade and Welfare in General Equilibrium', *Keio Economic Studies*, 9, 37–73.

Reizman, R. (1979), 'A 3 × 3 Model of Customs Unions', *Journal of International Economics*, 9, 341–54.

Vanek, J. (1965), *General Equilibrium of International Discrimination* (Cambridge, Mass.: Harvard University Press).

Viner, J. (1950), *The Customs Union Issue* (New York: Carnegie Endowment for International Peace).

Wonnacot, P. and Wonnacot, R. (1981), 'Is Unilateral Tariff Reduction Preferable to a Customs Union? The Curious Case of the Missing Foreign Tariffs', *American Economic Review*, 71, 704–14.

PART II

Empirical Implementation of Integration Theories

THE EFFECTS OF ECONOMIC INTEGRATION ON TRADE

By David G. Mayes*

Department of Economics, University of Exeter

ABSTRACT

This article provides a critical analysis of the models and methods which have been used to estimate the effects of economic integration on trade and suggests the most fruitful lines of further development. Both the problem of the examination of the effects of past events and problems in the prediction of future changes are tackled. In particular the drawbacks of the method of estimation of the effects of previous integration as a residual from models which explain what would have happened had the integration not taken place are shown. It is concluded that the most fruitful avenue of approach lies in the estimation of models which provide an economic explanation of trade flows and their changes, and can hence be used for both the explanation of the effects of previous integration and the prediction of future events.

Over the past twenty years a vast literature has sprung up attempting to explain what happens to trade when countries reduce or abandon some or all of the barriers to free trade between them. Although the subject is by no means so new the upsurge in interest stems from the formation of trading areas in many parts of the world. The irony of the situation is however that despite such an accumulation of effort there is widespread disagreement between investigators as to the most appropriate method of analysis. To some extent this disagreement stems from the pursuance of different aims; however, most of it revolves round the lack of any yardstick against which to measure the accuracy of any results. Furthermore, since most estimates belong to different time periods and are recorded in different units of measurement it is extremely difficult to make meaningful empirical comparisons between the results. It is therefore the purpose of this article to appraise the methods of analysis which can be used and to see which differences have any bearing on the quantitative results so that conclusions can be drawn on the most profitable line of further advance.

* I am grateful for the helpful comments of John Black, John Kay, Frank Oliver, Paul Richards and the SSRC International Economics Study Group on earlier versions of this paper.

David G. Mayes

1. THE TWO METHODS OF APPROACH

In most areas of economic analysis it is possible to use models which have been developed to estimate the effects of events in the past to predict the results of similar behaviour in the future. This is not true of the majority of estimated models of the effects of economic integration on trade because they estimate (ex-post) the effects of integration to be the residual between what actually occurred and the trade predicted on the basis of the continuation of previous economic relations. The remaining models (let us call them 'analytic') which can also be used for predictive purposes provide a direct economic explanation of the value of trade flows after economic integration.[1]

In general, despite their great variety, the determination of the level of trade between countries in the models considered here stems from some or all of four categories of variables:

(1) economic variables explaining behaviour in the importing country (economic activity, population, prices, pressure of demand, etc.)

(2) economic variables explaining behaviour in the exporting country (economic activity, population, prices, pressure on supply, etc.)

(3) variables explaining specific characteristics of trade between the two countries (geographical separation, trading preferences, etc.)

(4) variables explaining relevant behaviour in third countries (imports, exports, prices, economic activity, etc.).

We shall argue that unless the full range of these variables is included in the model, the estimation of the effects on trade cannot hope to be unbiased, but we shall also consider how valid simplifications of this structure are in producing results where the biases are unimportant. Of necessity ex-ante models consider fewer of the variables as prediction requires not only a model to predict the future values of endogenous variables but also the derivation of a set of future values of the exogenous variables in the model. The degree of heroism required in this latter derivation is such that most authors wisely keep it to a minimum. This also helps to explain why so much more effort has been expended on the ex-post models.

[1] Running right across these two categories are differences in aggregation by country and industries, in static or dynamic form and in whether more than just the effects of changes in tariffs is considered. The flavour of the model is also greatly affected by whether it seeks to explain trade flows for a single country or the world at large.

2. THE EFFECTS OF ECONOMIC INTEGRATION

The theory underlying our expectations of the effects of economic integration is well known,[2] all we need to note here is that if barriers to trade, tariffs, quotas, national buying policies, etc., are removed then we would expect trade to expand (trade creation), and if barriers are removed from trade with one country but not from trade with another we would also expect imports from the first country to increase at the expense of imports from the second (trade diversion).[3] Further effects will also stem from 'positive' actions in integration—such as the adoption of common standards—in addition to the 'negative' actions of merely abandoning discrimination.

In view of the concentration in empirical work on short-run effects on trade flows it is easy to lose sight of the fact that these are only one type of effect. Furthermore the use of simple measures such as trade creation and trade diversion tends to obscure the existence of several causes of the one event. The formation of a trading area, Lipsey suggested (1957), results in changes in the international economy from five main sources:

(1) the specialisation of production according to comparative advantage which is the basis of the classical case for the gains from trade (2) economies of scale (3) changes in the terms of trade (4) forced changes in efficiency due to increased foreign competition (5) a change in the rate of growth.

The bulk of the empirical work which has been undertaken so far is concerned with sources (1) and (3), some of the other sources are included in passing but not often dealt with specifically. It is only right, however, that in a general appraisal such as this that all these factors should be borne in mind. In particular influences on the rate of growth will have important repercussions on trade.

It is a matter of major importance to distinguish between short-run static effects, whereby a change in the barriers to trade result in a single change in trade and its pattern, and longer-run dynamic effects, where the rate of change of economic variables over time is permanently altered by economic integration. We shall therefore examine both of them with respect to trade.[4]

By drawing the line at the consideration of the effects on trade we must also be aware that we are omitting consideration of other

[2] See for example, Balassa (1961), Krauss (1972; 1973) and Robson (1972).

[3] These two terms have many different detailed definitions, see Truman (1972) for example, we have merely opted for the most straightforward.

[4] Some of the controversy over estimation methods (see Sellekaerts (1973) for example) stems from whether the intention is to measure the static effects alone or the static and dynamic effects combined (a common result in residual methods).

factors which may be of greater importance. Much of the theoretical interest in customs unions stems not from the fact that the balance of trade of participants may be affected either positively or negatively, but that the overall effect on world welfare is contingent upon the particular relationship. Also, there is what Kaldor (1971) terms a 'resource cost' for some of the participants in economic integration. In so far as the static trade effects are negative a country will have to indulge in offsetting economic policies if it wishes to rectify the situation. The cost of this rectification is the resource cost of integration, the value of the resources which have to be used in sustaining integration.

3. RESIDUAL MODELS

Let us turn our attention first to residual models as they form the bulk of estimated models and then extend it to consider models which can also be used for prediction. Residual models have the common characteristic that they seek to quantify the hypothetical situation (often referred to as the anti-monde) of what would have happened had the trading agreement not been implemented. As with any such hypothetical circumstance we have no means of testing its validity other than the plausibility of the results and the behaviour of the model in different observable situations. The problem of establishing such an anti-monde is expressed excellently by Duquesne de la Vinelle (1965) in a survey of some early attempts:

La philosophie profonde de cette aporie se trouvait déjà chez le philosophe Heraclite lorsqu'il écrivait 'on ne se baigne deux fois dans le même fleuve'.

Clearly we would expect that the more of the explanatory variables we set out on p. 21 are taken into account the better determined the anti-monde, so we have structured the rest of this section by considering the problem in increasing order of complexity of model.

3.1 *Import Models*

There is a strong tendency to concentrate on explanatory variables drawn from the importing country alone as this considerably reduces the complexity of data collection. Our concern here is to establish whether the gains from convenience are outweighed by the losses in accuracy.

(a) *The demand for imports*

The form of argument which is used is that imports would have increased over time without the trading agreement at exactly the same rate as they did before the agreement came into effect. Clearly such trend extrapolation will have severe drawbacks for a cyclical activity like international trade, so authors such as Clavaux (1969), Walter (1967) and Wemelsfelder (1960) have assumed that imports will retain the same linear relation to total expenditure, GDP and GNP respectively in the anti-monde as they did in the pre-integration period. These studies, as pointed out by Williamson and Bottrill (1971), make the thoroughly unlikely assumption that the marginal propensity to import remains constant, whereas the evidence points to its rising with income. Further, any estimation of the actual marginal propensity to import over previous periods will always be clouded by the other changes in trading arrangements which took place then, and will not represent an anti-monde where no change takes place.

While it is possible to make a critical examination of these hypotheses purely on the basis of economic theory and experience without any consideration of the numerical values of their results, the relative importance of changes in the assumptions can only be shown by looking at their quantitative effects. We have therefore drawn up in Figure 1 a graph comparing the published results of the various models for the effects of the formation of the EEC. The choice of the EEC is dictated purely by the relatively larger number of results relating to that grouping than to any other. Obviously the best form of comparison would be to use each of these models with the same set of data, and where the amount of recomputation involved is small, this has been done and is included in specific tables in the text. However in many cases the data required are so different that we have chosen to use the original results, and these are included in Figure 1, with a time axis to denote the year for which they are estimates.

It is possible to improve the results by use of more observations; Sellekaerts (1973) for example uses ordinary least squares to estimate a linear relation between imports from extra-area suppliers and GNP in the EEC allowing for a shift in both parameters in the period after the formation of the EEC, but interestingly enough he estimates that in aggregate trade diversion is in favour of non-members to the tune of $24,037 mn– $26,404 mn by 1967, not at their expense.

FIGURE I

PREDICTIONS OF TRADE CREATION AND TRADE DIVERSION IN THE EEC

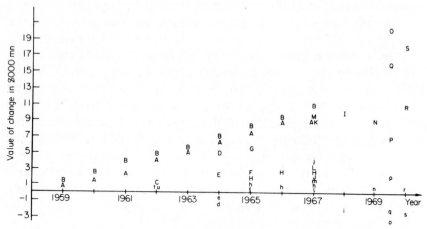

KEY TO FIGURE I

Capital letters denote Trade Creation and small letters Trade Diversion

A Aitken (1973) (projection)
B Aitken (1973) (dummy variable)
C Waelbroeck (1964) (method 1)
D Truman (1969) disaggregated 1958 base
E as D 1960 base
F Balassa (1967c)
G Clavaux (1969)
H EFTA (1972)
I Major-Hays (1970) 1958 base
J Resnick-Truman (1974)
K Truman (1972)

L K (adjusted)
M Verdoorn-Schwartz (1972)
N Williamson-Bottrill (1971)
O Kreinin (1972) not normalised
P O US normalised & adjusted
Q O UK normalised
R Balassa (1964)
S Prewo (1974)
t Lamfalussy (1963)
u C method 2

Values denoted:

(i) Trade Creation						(ii) Trade Diversion		
Year	Estimate	Value in $000 mn	Year	Estimate	Value in $000 mn	Year	Estimate	Value in $000 mn
1959	A	0·9	1965	H	1·7	1962	t	0·5
	B	1·1	1966	A	8·6		u	0·5
1960	A	1·6		B	9·8	1965	d	−1·6
	B	2·5		H	2·2		e	−0·3
1961	A	2·3	1967	A	9·2	1965	f	0·1
	B	3·3		B	11·1		h	0·6
1962	A	3·2		H	2·3	1966	h	0·7
	B	4·1		J	1·8	1967	h	0·9
	C	1·0		K	9·2		j	3·0
1963	A	4·7		L	2·5		k	−1·0
	B	5·2		M	10·1		l	0·5
1964	A	5·7	1968	I	10·8		n	1·1
	B	6·4	1969	N	9·6	1968	i	−2·9
	D	4·5	1969/70	O	20·8	1969	n	0·0
	E	2·6		P	7·2	1969/70	o	−4·0
1965	A	6·9		Q	16·0		p	2·4
	B	8·2	1970	R	11·4		q	−2·8
	F	1·9		S	18·0	1970	r	0·1
	G	5·0					s	−3·1

(b) *Shares in Apparent Consumption*

The problem can also be approached by considering the relative shares of the various suppliers in total consumption, rather than the absolute value of imports. Truman (1969) takes the simplest solution and assumes that the shares of each supplier will remain constant over time, but it is clearly preferable to allow for some change in the ratio over time on the basis of historical change. The EFTA Secretariat Studies (1969, 1972) incorporate this by assuming that the linear trend in shares between 1954 and 1959 would have been maintained by the member countries in the anti-monde. The particular trend they estimate is open to objection on the grounds, first, that the two years chosen may not lie on the actual trend, and second that the form of the trend is too simple. Further estimation by say regression is not really profitable given the simplicity of the original assumption.

The effect of assuming a linear trend in the shares in the anti-monde as opposed to no change from the pre-integration period on the aggregate trade flows is shown in Table 1 for EFTA. Both Truman (1969) and EFTA (1969) disaggregate their analysis by manufactured commodities, but while this prevents some of the bias from aggregation, it makes the rigidity of the hypotheses about import shares rather more unlikely. We must therefore emphasise that the basis of the comparison in Table 1 is in aggregate. All the same the dissimilarity of the results and the almost random distribution of positive and negative signs is striking.

These projections of trade flows relating solely to the performance of import demand in previous periods make too strong assumptions for their validity to be very great. They assume that past trends will continue into the future without considering either the exact nature of the relationship[5] or whether it is really likely that events such as multilateral tariff reductions can be expected to continue at the same rate in the anti-monde. Furthermore, they tend to assume that many of the determining variables, GNP, apparent consumption, etc., would be unchanged in the anti-monde from their actual observed values. Since we would expect these variables themselves to be affected by economic integration this assumption will not be valid. The use of shares rather than absolute values does not avoid the problem

---

[5] Sellekaerts (1973) is an exception to this as he does allow for cyclical factors.

104 *David G. Mayes*

TABLE I
Alternative estimates of aggregate effects of EFTA, 1965 $mn

Country	Trade creation		Trade diversion	
	Hypothesis		Hypothesis	
	(1)	(2)	(1)	(2)
Austria	−121·5	163	178·3	79
Denmark	−180·6	−122	322·1	−166
Finland	−204·9	−59	149·0	−136
Norway	−32.7	63	261·6	−73
Portugal	63·8	62	−15·1	43
Sweden	364·4	276	96·5	−110
Switzerland	−357·8	218	288·3	117
United Kingdom	831·0	−343	−619·1	−594
Total	361·7	258	661·6	−840

SOURCE: EFTA (1969).
(1) Using the EFTA (1969) method.
(2) Assuming that shares in 1965 would have been the same as those in 1959 in the anti-
monde.

unless we can assume that income (and to some extent substitution) effects are zero. Yet EFTA (1969, 1972) explicitly
include an income effect.

(c) *Changes in the Income Elasticity of Demand for Imports*
It is also possible to look at the problem of changes in shares from
the opposite direction, and see what the actual changes imply for
the elasticity of demand for various sorts of imports with respect
to income. Balassa (1969b, 1974) estimates separately income
elasticities of demand for imports from fellow members and for
imports from non-members. He argues that a rise in the elasticity
of demand for imports from all sources indicates trade creation,
and that a fall in the elasticity of demand for imports from non-
members, while the elasticity for imports from other members
shows a rise, indicates trade diversion. It is presumably these
results which are reported, Balassa p. 115, and are reproduced here
in Figure 1. The anti-monde is thus that income elasticities of
demand would not have changed. Since the estimated elasticities
are not unitary and not equal for imports from member and non-
member countries, this means that changes in the shares of total
imports in apparent consumption and imports from non-member

countries (and hence member countries) in total imports can and do take place in the anti-monde. Allowances are made for changes in prices and the effects he calculates are similar to the general trend in Figure 1 although both positive and negative effects occur.

Whether the problem of the anti-monde is approached by Balassa's (1967b) method or the EFTA (1969) method it is still clear that the period before the formation of EFTA and the EEC was one of considerable trade liberalisation, and hence the estimation of trade relationships during that period will be affected by it. The implicit assumption of the anti-monde may in fact be that nothing new occurred, but that liberalisation continued at previous rates. Clavaux (1969) estimates that if we take into account the existence of liberalisation in the estimation period and exclude it from the anti-monde then Balassa's estimates of trade creation by 1966 should be more than doubled. It is not clear that the bias that Clavaux claims is actually so important. In the light of the other drawbacks we have mentioned it is clear, however, that precise elasticities suggest a degree of sophistication which is not really present in these models. As Orcutt (1950) points out, if there are no supply equations there is an identification problem which biases estimates of price elasticities towards zero. The neglect of supply conditions implicitly rests on the strong assumption of infinite supply elasticities. Balassa's (1974, p. 93) estimation of ex-post income elasticities will take supply constraints into account implicitly, but so will it of course for the pre-integration period.

Balassa's approach is also questioned closely by Sellekaerts (1973) who suggests (p. 526) that the estimates will be biased unless 'the following ceteris paribus assumptions are realistic: no autonomous changes in relative prices, no changes in exchange rates, no changes in extra-area trade flows caused by the dynamic effects of a customs union'. Clearly any trends in relative prices either before or after the formation of the area will bias estimates based on income elasticities of demand alone. The third point about dynamic effects merely makes the point that since Balassa is using a 'residual imputation model' all effects, not just the static ones will be included in the residual. Far more important is Sellekaerts' clear demonstration, (pp. 529 and 544), that income elasticities vary widely over both the pre- and post-integration periods. Thus the choice of periods for comparison is crucial. Elasticities will vary with the pressure of demand and it is thus important either to compare time periods where activity was in the same sort of phase of the economic cycle, or to allow for changes in the economic cycle explicitly in the estimation.

3.2 *The Inclusion of Supply Variables*

All these models we have mentioned so far only consider the first area of economic variables affecting trade, namely the variables in the importing country. They are thus largely demand determined, although *ad hoc* supply constraints were introduced in some cases. Obviously the specification of the model will be improved if explicit allowance is made for supply conditions. Thus trade between any pair of countries is a function of variables within both of them.

The simplest approach has been to suggest that under 'normal' circumstances trade between any pair of countries is purely a function of the total trade of each of the two countries. In particular, in the anti-monde the trade between any pair of countries will vary proportionately with total exports of the exporting country and total imports of the importing country. The original model, dubbed RAS, was developed by Stone and Brown (Cambridge, 1963) in the context of input–output analysis, and was turned to the present context by Kouevi (1965) and Waelbroeck (1964).[6] Its major drawback is that total predicted imports and exports are constrained to their actual values so it is not possible to measure trade creation. Further, the whole point of the original RAS was to minimise the errors in the predictions rather than our current purpose. This can be overcome to some considerable extent as is shown in Baron (1968) and Mayes (1971; 1974) in a model which I christened RASAT by adding a commodity dimension and relaxing some of the constraints, but the estimated results for trade diversion are small. In a 32 commodity breakdown for EFTA, however, substantial trade diversion was observed for most of the major categories (Mayes, 1974, Table 5).

A much more satisfactory means of incorporating determining variables from both the importing and the exporting countries is the so-called 'gravitational' model pioneered by Tinbergen and developed by Pulliainen (1963), Poyhonen (1963) and Linnemann (1966) with a large number of applications to the present context.

---

[6] A somewhat similar model to RAS was proposed by Savage and Deutsch (1960) and used to measure changes in the trade of EFTA and the EEC after their formation by Carney (1970).

A major advantage is that the model is no longer 'mechanical' and incorporates explicit economic variables in both countries which makes its interpretation much easier. The gravitational model suggests that the trade flow between any pair of countries is a multiplicative function of their respective national incomes, populations and the distance between them (thus also incorporating part of our third category of explanatory variables (see p. 21) relating to specific factors affecting trade between a pair of countries). The model is estimated using cross-section data and the effects of any trading arrangements are calculated by the unexplained residual in the regression, or, as suggested in Aitken (1973) and Aitken and Lowry (1973), by the inclusion of a dummy variable for trade between partner countries. These two methods can give strikingly different results as the parameters of the model seem to vary substantially over time. Aitken (1973) estimates that trade creation by EFTA in 1967 using the 1958 parameters is $1264 mn (this method is labelled 'projection' in Figure 1) while using the 1967 values themselves and the dummy variable the result is 92% greater (labelled 'dummy'). Since Aitken's results are the only ones which are estimated for a sequence of years they have a heavy influence on the overall pattern of Figure 1. While in general they are coherent with other estimates although they form the upper bound, in some cases, e.g. 1965, they are 3 to 4 times as large as the lower bound. Against this substantial relative difference must be held the fact that the absolute magnitude of all the results is small. The main reason for these differences, as is confirmed by Bluet and Systermanns' (1968) disaggregated study, is the variability in the estimated parameters from year to year, hence projection with fixed parameters should be treated with care. Much of the variability in the estimators occurs because a

TABLE II

Gross trade creation in the CACM and the LAFTA, $ mn

Year	CACM	LAFTA
1963	55·1	239·4
1964	97·0	297·4
1965	121·3	404·9
1966	160·5	503·2
1967	200·0	357·5

Source: Aitken and Lowry (1973, p. 334)

David G. Mayes

cross-section cannot represent a relationship which responds to cycles in economic activity and the very process of trade liberalisation in general. Pooling data helps to some extent but the model's main disadvantage is the omission of relative prices.

This deficiency is overcome by Verdoorn and Schwartz (1972) in the second of their models. They combine the advantages of the gravitational model with the effects of price, both on the overall demand for imports and the substitution between imports from various sources. This model really provides the link between the residual models and the analytic models in the next section. While results are still largely calculated on a residual basis, two dummy variables are used to explain some of the 'residual', although they are only explanatory in a statistical rather than an economic sense. The results are shown in Table 3 and, as can be seen from Figure 1, they correspond with the general run of results, which is comforting in the sense that the different methods agree, but it also implies that this more highly developed model does not tell us much which is new. The unexplained variation is still large (22%) so there is still room for considerable improvement particularly in the rather harsh constraint that the parameters of the model shall be the same for all countries.

TABLE III

Resnick and Truman's (1974) estimates of trade creation and trade diversion in EEC and EFTA compared with those of Verdoorn and Schwartz (1972) $ mn

Country	Trade creation		Trade diversion	
	R & T *1968*	*V & S* *1969*	*R & T* *1968*	*V & S* *1969*
EEC				
BLEU	152	913	281	183
Netherlands	93	868	190	216
W. Germany	−659	3,874	1,732	267
Italy	1,022	1,336	62	154
France	582	3,073	737	248
Total	1,190	10,064	3,002	1,068
EFTA				
UK	81	204	394	249
Other EFTA	131	161	231	547
Total	212	365	625	796
EEC+EFTA	1,402	10,429	3,627	1,864

3.3 *The Incorporation of Information from Third Countries*

We argued on p. 21 that relevant behaviour in countries excluded from the trading area both before and after the agreement comes into force should be incorporated into the analysis. While the share approach to estimation does not include supply factors directly it can include third country behaviour as is shown with great clarity by Lamfalussy (1963). He showed that if we take the change in shares of trade of non-members and member countries of the EEC in other markets, where neither suffers nor benefits from discrimination, as the basis of our expectation about how shares in the member countries' markets would have changed without integration, we get a very different set of answers from those from trend extrapolation in the members' markets alone. This can be seen in Table 4. The differences have a fairly clear pattern: the share of EEC exports in both EEC and EFTA imports is substantially greater under the first hypothesis and the share of ROW in both markets falls under the first hypothesis but rises under the second. EFTA shares in both markets are greater under the second hypothesis but only very marginally so in the case of intra-EFTA trade. It is also clear, as Williamson and Bottrill (1971) demonstrate, that Lamfalussy's pessimistic con-

TABLE IV

A comparison of the effects of different anti-mondes on the imports of the EEC and EFTA in 1969 ($ mn)

Anti-monde	Exporter	Importer EEC	Importer EFTA
(1)		5,091	−1,042
(2)	EEC	1,018	−3,610
(1)/(2)		5·00	0·29
(1)		−2,258	2,542
(2)	EFTA	−1,594	2,644
(1)/(2)		1·42	0·96
(1)	Rest of world	−2,833	−1,500
(2)		576	966

(1) Share of exporter i in the market of importer j would change between 1959 and 1969 at the same linear rate as the share of i's exports in the imports of Rest of World (ROW) changed during the same period (shares constrained to sum to unity).

(2) Share of exporter i in the market of importer j would change between 1959 and 1969 at the same linear rate that it did between 1954 and 1959.

Source: Data drawn from Williamson and Bottrill (1971).

clusions are largely due to the fact that he was only able to consider the first three years of the Common Market's existence; over a longer period an obvious EEC effect would have been observed. They, therefore, develop his method further by using a long run of data and more sophisticated extrapolation methods of the anti-monde shares. However, this method does not enable us to determine the derivation of trade creation and diversion until further assumptions are made about their relative sizes. This is not, however, too dramatic a drawback for as is shown in Mayes (1976), the estimates are not unreasonably sensitive to the choice of the relative magnitudes.

The idea of the use of non-member countries as a control group or form of 'normalisation' in order to estimate what the anti-monde would have been, can be incorporated explicitly into the model, and is done so most thoroughly by Kreinin (1972) where he adapts the technique of projecting the anti-monde on the basis of predicted import/consumption ratios described at the beginning of Section 3.1. This enables us to see far more clearly how the normalisation procedure works, so that we can evaluate the plausibility of the assumptions on which it rests. It is too easy to assume that we can actually find a control group for arrangements such as the EEC, because the control variables themselves are affected by the very experiment we are seeking to isolate. In the case of say the CACM and LAFTA the particular arrangement does not have important feedback effects on the control variables, but there again the control variables are affected by other examples of economic integration which occurred simultaneously during the period of estimation. Kreinin in seeking to estimate the effects of the EEC on imports of manufactures uses the US, the UK and Japan as normalisers. The percentage increases in the total import/consumption ratio and the ratio of imports from non-members to consumption are reduced by the increase in the normalising country's import/consumption ratio. From these two normalised ratios he estimates trade creation and trade diversion respectively. Additionally, in the case of normalisation by the US alone he further adjusts the EEC import/consumption ratio firstly for the fact that the real GNP of the US had grown more slowly than that of the EEC during the period and that its income elasticity of import demand is 1·69, and secondly for the different rates of inflation and hence competitiveness. This second change is estimated by assuming that US imports should be reduced by the same percentage as the decline in the US share in third markets. These adjustments are rather ad hoc and it is helpful to see the full range of estimates set out in Table 5.[7] 'Normalisation' is highly dependent upon the choice of normaliser, as is suggested in Mayes (1974); it is unfortunately true that no one country appears to be 'normal'. Hypothetical normality is bound to be difficult to assess, and unless a model is used which explains differences from the norm such attempts at normalisation will be unsatisfactory.

TABLE V

Estimates of trade creation and diversion in the EEC in manufacturing industry in 1969/70 ($ mn)

	Trade creation	Trade diversion
Not normalised	20,777	−4,024
Not normalised but +		
income adjustment	10,481	1,431
US normalised	8,543	1,721
US normalised		
+adjustments	7,256	2,426
UK normalised	16,044	−2,848
Japan normalised	20,500	−4,161

Source: Kreinin (1972): Tables VI, VII, VIII

3.4 *The Estimation of the Anti-Monde*

In Sections 3.1–3.3 we have shown that the number and range of estimates of the effects of economic integration by imputation of the unexplained residual are large, and it is evident that the more of our four categories of variables included in the estimation of the anti-monde the more satisfactory is the result. Further refinements such as disaggregation and the incorporation of a clear distinction between final and intermediate products should further improve the estimates, although the work by Prewo (1974) shows a strikingly different pattern of results from the other models (see Figure 1), probably due to the simplicity of some of his other assumptions. Yet the problem of estimating a hypothetical anti-monde is in itself not an attractive proposition. While it is possible to point out the existence of biases it is not possible to know whether an unbiased estimate has been achieved, one can merely judge on the grounds of plausibility. Plausibility depends upon the factors taken into account not just in the importing and exporting countries, but as they affect the trade cycle and movements in world prices. There is therefore a considerable incentive to find an analytic model which can explain actual trade flows and their

[7] These results are deliberately chosen to show how wide the range of estimates can be, they do not represent Kreinin's considered views in his article—the subtraction of processed foods has a considerable equalising effect on the results.

changes, rather than to have to resort to the derivation of an anti-monde and the imputation of residual differences to the effects of integration.

4. ANALYTIC MODELS

We have already suggested that some of the models which employ the residual form of analysis are partly analytic, for example there is the demand analysis side of Verdoorn and Schwartz (1972) second model (p. 31). However, let us repeat the meaning of 'analytic' in this context, namely 'providing an economic explanation of the actual post-integration situation'. This is a necessary requirement for all ex-ante models as of course the actual values of trade flows in the future are unknown. Because of the difficulties inherent in prediction ex-ante models are usually simple, concentrating on economic behaviour in the importing country. In particular[8] it is suggested imports are a function of some measure of income or economic activity and the relative prices of imported and domestic products. Hence trade creation can be predicted from the change in tariff levels if the relation between tariff changes and price changes is assumed and trade diversion can be estimated if the elasticity of substitution with respect to price changes between partner and excluded countries is known.

This approach is clearly simplistic and although it can be improved by the use of more sophisticated import demand functions it will not give really satisfactory estimates until the relation between tariff changes and price changes can also be explained. The expectation which is normally used—that prices fall by the full amount of tariff changes—is shown in EFTA (1968) to be an overestimate; only part of the tariff change appears to be passed on. There is considerable evidence at a micro-economic level that the pricing of imports of many products depends largely on the prices of existing competing domestic products. Walter (1967) suggests that the problem is even worse as importers tend to anticipate tariff changes and hence trade growth will lead the 'determining' tariff changes. Thus not only is price used as a proxy for all the other non-price factors in economic integration, such as decisions to set up marketing networks, which affect trade flows but it is not the true measure of the actual change in 'price' either.

---

[8] See Houthakker and Magee (1969), Ball and Marwah (1962), Kreinin (1969), Mayes (1971) and Barker and Lecomber (1967).

Attempts (Krause, 1962; Kreinin, 1961) to estimate tariff elasticities directly have not been very successful and as Mayes (1971, 1974) shows, the results from this approach do not correspond closely with those from residual models.

The greater the degree of disaggregation the more plausible the results as there is no reason to expect different commodities or countries to behave in an identical manner. The results from Mayes (1971) for a projected 'Atlantic' Free Trade Area composed of US, Canada, EFTA and Japan are shown in Table 6 for a 97 commodity breakdown of manufactured products. Not only do the results have the expected pattern of signs for overall trade creation and diversion but they are fairly robust to quite substantial changes in the parameters. While I tried to allow for a complete system of demand equations with the volume and price of imports from each country being distinguished to give a whole matrix of direct and substitution elasticities[9] other authors have tried to use more global values based either on assumption or crude extrapolation from estimates for the United States. The effects on the estimates of using three different sets of assumptions proposed by Balassa (1967), Kreinin (1967) and Krause (1968) are shown as columns (2), (3), and (4) respectively in Table 6.[10] To quite an extent the similarity between the various results is due to offsetting changes, greater trade creation is balanced by greater trade diversion. The main feature of the results is their smallness compared with residual models (Kreinin (1969), for example, gives estimates for the effects of the formation of the EEC during the period 1962–65 which are all less than $100 mn).

More substantial models which allow for the determination of import levels by a series of allocative decisions have been developed, Armington (1970) and Resnick and Truman (1973, 1974) and simple assumptions can be made for supply constraints as in Balassa and Kreinin (1967), but as can be seen from Table 3 and Figure 1 these results do not accord well with those from the residual models. Compared with Verdoorn and Schwartz (1972), for example, Resnick and Truman's estimates for trade creation in the EEC are only one-eighth the size (although the ratio is three-fifths for EFTA). Second because Germany had to revise its tariffs upward to the CET, trade creation is negative in the analytic case

[9] Along the lines of Barten (1970). It was also shown that the hypothesis that elasticities of substitution are the same for all countries should be rejected.

[10] It should be stressed that the results shown are the results of my calculations based on my interpretation of their assumptions and not the published results of the authors themselves.

David G. Mayes

TABLE VI

A comparison of ex-ante predictions of the effects of economic integration on trade

An Atlantic free trade area[1] (Effect on total exports) ($ mn) 1972 (estimated)

Country	(1)	(2)	(3)	(4)
US	2,454	2,318	2,509	2,645
Canada	2,141	2,610	2,547	2,650
Belgium-Luxemburg	−88	−124	−93	−117
France	−127	−146	−159	−199
Germany	−444	−538	−538	−673
Italy	−131	−144	−163	−204
Netherlands	−48	−56	−64	−80
TOTAL EEC	−838	−1,008	−1,017	−1,273
Denmark	22	30	24	24
Norway	15	23	18	18
Sweden	128	156	144	148
UK	607	821	726	756
Rest of EFTA	241	263	225	269
TOTAL EFTA	1,013	1,293	1,167	1,215
Japan	1,879	2,380	2,301	2,448
Rest of the world	−646	−806	−719	−898
TOTAL	6,002	6,786	6,786	6,786

[1] Defined here as an area comprising US, Canada, EFTA and Japan—this corresponds closely to the definitions used by Balassa (1967a) and Maxwell-Stamp (1967).
[2] Commodity categories are different so these results do not represent an exact up-dating of the original results.

(1) Mayes (1971).
(2) Using elasticities used by Balassa (1967b).[2]
(3) Using same import elasticity as Balassa but assuming elasticity of substitution is −2·5 as does Kreinin (1967b).[2]
(4) As (3) but assuming elasticity of substitution is −2 as does Krause (1968).

but the largest positive effect for any country in the residual model. This tells us that other factors besides tariff changes had a strong positive effect on Germany's trade after the formation of the EEC. There is clearly much more to be explained which *is not* covered by the analytic models and *cannot* be covered by the residual ones.

The major advantage of the analytic models is that they can be tested after the event and can be used for forecasting as well as ex post estimation. Clearly they need substantial improvement and some hope lies in the detailed work on particular industries,[11] especially since Williamson (1971), for example, has found that the formation of the EEC has resulted in intra-industry specialisation rather than the *inter*-industry specialisation we might have expected. Further they must make allowance for supply factors, the behaviour of third countries and cycles in trade (Adams et al (1969) points the way forward) and most important they must try to reduce the disparity between their results and those of residual models caused by factors other than the impact effect of tariff changes.

5. DYNAMIC EFFECTS

It is clear that in concentrating on the impact effect of price changes alone, the largest part of the total effect may be omitted altogether. The feedback on to incomes and the rate of economic growth or the need for expenditure switching policies to accommodate movements in the balance of payments may be substantial and either positive or negative—Kaldor (1971), for example, in his gloomy assessment of the likely effects of UK entry into the EEC, thinks that adverse impact effects will be aggravated by adverse dynamic effects. Despite this there are very few attempts to estimate such dynamic effects. The most important exception is by Krause (1968) who seeks to explain changes in the rate of real economic growth in EFTA and the EEC by increasing business investment and increasing efficiency. The impact of these factors is straightforward, an increased ratio of investment to GDP leads to an increase in the capital stock, and if the marginal capital output ratios are constant, then output and hence the rate of growth must increase. This fixed relation between capital and output of course automatically excludes economies of scale, one of the factors we specifically wanted to include. The increase in efficiency comes from a decrease in input costs from imports, hence the increase in the ratio of imports to output is calculated and this, multiplied by the average tariff rate, gives the income effect of the reduction in costs which can be expressed as an annual rate.

This analysis is clearly crude in that it makes the assumptions we have considered before about the equality of tariff changes and

[11] Bond and Wonnacott (1968), Haviland et al. (1968) and Singer (1969) in the 'Canada in the Atlantic Economy' series, for example, and the detailed studies of comparative competitive position in Han and Liesner (1971) and Wonnacott and Wonnacott (1967).

consequent price changes. As is shown in Mayes (1971) these two effects can also be applied to Japan where over the same period Japan shows a larger rate of growth effect from the establishment of the EEC and EFTA than do all of the actual members.[12] It is clear that the procedure of attributing all changes which occur during the period after formation of the two areas to their formation is not satisfactory; other economic factors are at work and a satisfactory model must explain them. In Mayes (1971) I attempted a simple calculation of such effects over a limited time horizon of 10–12 years using a truncated dynamic model, and showed what the resulting changes in trade flows would be if each participant country were to alter their exchange rate in such a way as to return to their original balance of trade before the formation of the trading area, but this does not provide a full explanation of the factors at work. This area of growth is probably the most important for future research as its effects can prove far more substantial than any once and for all static effects on trade flows which at maximum result in a gain of around 1% of GNP.

6. CONCLUDING

It is clear after such a wealth of research that bounds of magnitude have been established for the effects of economic integration on trade. If we take the many estimates shown in Figure 1 we can draw arbitrary bounds of the form suggested in Figure 2.[13] Several of the more extreme results lie outside these bounds, yet the range for 1970 is approximately $8–15,000 mn, so it is clear that we are a long way from achieving an agreed point estimate. However, the only really satisfactory bounds that we would wish to use would take the form of an interval estimate where a statement can be made in probability. To obtain this, whether by means of direct estimation with an 'analytic' model or imputation from a 'residual' model, requires a more carefully specified and estimated set of equations than have been presented here. These equations must, as we have established, explain both demand and supply factors and take account of cycles in world trade. The width of the interval estimate could then be brought down to a more reasonable figure.

[12] The respective figures for Japan are approximately 0·19% for the investment effect and 0·08% for the efficiency effect, 0·27% in total, the highest total effect for a member country is 0·25% for Denmark (Krause, 1968, p. 44).

[13] A number of the lower estimates for 1967 lie outside the bounds. To some extent their exclusion is deliberate but it is also somewhat arbitrary, the bounds have been drawn linear, but there is no reason to expect that they should have any such rigid functional form over time.

FIGURE 2

APPROXIMATE BOUNDS TO PREDICTIONS OF TRADE CREATION
AND TRADE DIVERSION IN THE EEC

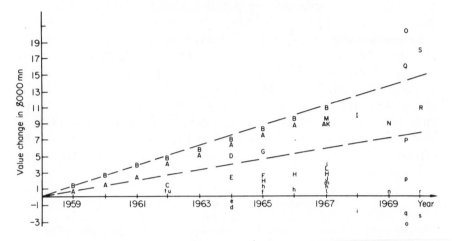

Furthermore it is also clear that the effects on trade flows are by
no means simple. Models seeking to isolate 'static' effects rarely do
so. Changes in trade flows will occur not only as a result of the
exploitation of comparative advantage when international discrimination is reduced or altered and from changes in the terms of
trade, but also from derived effects on variables such as business
efficiency, the exploitation of economies of scale, the abolition of
non-tariff barriers, international standardisation and changes in
the rate of economic growth. These derived or feedback effects
may far outweigh the simply static effects and for our estimates to
have any real meaning they must be included. Since integration
occurs over a period of time any ex post estimation is bound to
include an amalgam of the two types of effects, so any attempted
division between them is likely to be extremely difficult. It is clear
therefore that there is ample scope for further research.

We have expressed throughout a preference for an analytic
approach to the problem, not so much because of the substantial
problems in estimating a hypothetical anti-monde but because of
the unattractive nature of the estimation of an effect such as that
which cannot be explained by the model. There will always be an
unexplained residual in any stochastic model of economic
behaviour and it is therefore inevitable that the residual imputed
to the effect of integration will also include residuals due to other
unknown influences. It is intellectually far more satisfactory to be

able to explain the effect of integration rather than to explain everything else instead. We have shown that it appears to be possible to estimate satisfactory price effects, but that the estimation is complicated by problems such as the inequality of price and tariff changes, the tendency of price to act as a proxy for other effects and the poor determination of equations as the model distinguishes between a larger number of different countries of origin of imports. However, analysis has not progressed far beyond price, because we become involved with the dynamic effects beyond this point, but also because income is not taken fully into account. What is clear from Figure 1 and elsewhere is that the 'residual' models show that there is much more of the effects of economic integration for the 'analytic' models yet to explain.

TABLE VII

The effects of the enlargement of the EEC on the imports of manufactured goods (SITC 5–8)

Importing country	Trade creation			Trade diversion		
	(1)	(2)	(3)	(1)[1]	(2)	(3)[2]
Belgium-Luxemburg	52	68	—	—	58	—
France	39	126	—	152	104	—
Germany	273	314	—	236	249	—
Italy	124	97	—	34	77	—
Netherlands	58	134	—	15	111	—
TOTAL EEC	546	739	2,187	438	599	2,727
Austria	78	—		—	—	
Denmark	0	27	1,661[3]	48	51	698[3]
Norway	74	56		—	38	
Sweden	24	87		—	113	
United Kingdom	346	406	1,058	45	109	1,501
TOTAL EFTA	523	576	2,719	94	311	2,199
TOTAL	1,069	1,316[4]	4,906	531	910	4,926

[1] From rest of world only.
[2] These figures are derived and may underestimate trade diversion as calculated by Kreinin through aggregation.
[3] Continental EFTA + Eire.
[4] Does not sum through rounding error.

(1) Resnick and Truman (1974, p. 86), $ mn 1968.
(2) Mayes (1971, Ch. 6, p. 29), $ mn 1972 (estimated).
(3) Kreinin (1973, p. 95), $ mn 1970.

In order to end on a speculative note and to keep as many issues as possible open we can look ahead to the assessment of the effects of the enlargement of the EEC to include Denmark, Eire and the United Kingdom together with the free trade arrangements between the EEC and the rest of EFTA. The integration began in 1973 and Table 7 gives three ex-ante predictions on the likely effects on the imports of the participating countries. All three models are analytic and measure the static effects alone, although a medium term estimate for the years 1981/2 is given by Mayes (1971, Ch. 7, p. 34) incorporating some dynamic effects. All these results should be testable in the light of experience over the next few years by ex-post methods. Resnick and Truman (1974) and Kreinin (1973) do not quote the years by which these effects can be expected to be observed, but provided the existing schedules of integration are followed I suggested (1971, Ch. 6, p. 29) that the results are for the years 1977/8. It will be interesting to see how wrong they are proved to be.

REFERENCES

Adams, F. G., Eguchi, H. and Meyer-Zu-Schlochtern, F. (1969) 'An Econometric Analysis of Trade: An interrelated explanation of imports and exports of OECD countries', Paris: *OECD* (Jan.).

Aitken, N. D. (1973) 'The Effect of the EEC and EFTA on European Trade: A Temporal Cross-Section Analysis', *American Economic Review*, (Dec.), Vol. LXIII No. 5.

Aitken, N. D. and Lowry, W. R. (1973) 'A Cross-Sectional Study of the Effects of LAFTA and CACM on Latin American Trade', *Journal of Common Market Studies*, (June) 11(4), pp. 326–36.

Armington, P. S. (1970) 'Adjustment of Trade Balances: Some Experiments with a Model of Trade among many Countries', *IMF Staff Papers* 17, pp. 488–523.

Balassa, B. (1961) *The Theory of Economic Integration*, London: Allen and Unwin.

Balassa, B. ed., (1967a) *Studies in Trade Liberalisation*, Baltimore: Johns Hopkins.

Balassa, B, (1967b) 'Trade Creation and Trade Diversion in the European Common Market', *Economic Journal* (March).

Balassa, B. (1967c) *Trade Liberalisation among Industrial Countries—Objectives and Alternatives*, New York: McGraw-Hill.

Balassa, B. (1974) 'Trade Creation and Trade Diversion in the European Common Market: An Appraisal of the Evidence', *Manchester Sch. Econ. Soc. Stud.*, (June), 42(2) pp. 99–135.

Balassa, B. and Kreinin, M. E. (1967) 'Trade Liberalisation under the Kennedy Round: the Static Effects', *Review of Economics and Statistics*, (May), Vol. XLIX No. 2.

Ball, R. J. and Marwah, K., (1962) 'The US Demand for Imports, 1948–58', *Review of Economics and Statistics* (Nov.).

Barker, T. S. and Lecomber, R., (1967) 'British Imports, 1972', University of Cambridge Department of Applied Economics, Report to National Ports Council, (Aug.).

Baron, C. G., (1968) 'A Multiproportional Growth Model for International Trade Flows', M.Sc. thesis, University of Bristol.

Barten, A. P., (1970) 'Maximum Likelihood Estimation of a Complete System of Demand Equations', *European Economic Review*, 1 (1).

Bluet, J. C. and Systermanns, Y. (*1968*) 'Modèle gravitationnel d'échanges internationaux de produits manufacturés', *Bulletin du CEPREMAP*, (Jan.) Vol. 1 (new series).

Bond, D. E. and Wonnacott, R. J. (1968) *Trade Liberalisation and the Canadian Furniture Industry*, Toronto: University of Toronto Press for the Private Planning Association of Canada, No. 6 'Canada in the Atlantic Economy'.

Cambridge, Department of Applied Economics (Stone, J. R. N. and Brown, J. A. C.) (1963) 'Input–Output Relationships', London: Chapman and Hall, No. 3 in *A Programme for Growth*.

Carney, M. K. (*1970*), 'Developments in Trading Patterns in the Common Market and EFTA', *Journal of the American Statistical Association*, (Dec.) 65 pp. 1455–59.

Clavaux, F. J. (1969) 'The Import Elasticity as a Yardstick for Measuring Trade Creation', *Economia Internazionale*, (Nov.).

Duquesne de la Vinelle, J. (1965) 'La Création du Commerce Attribuable au Marché Commun et Son Incidence sur la Volume du Produit National de la Communauté', *Informations Statistiques*, EEC, Brussels, No. 4.

EFTA Secretariat (1968) *The Effects on Prices of Tariff Dismantling in EFTA*, Geneva.

EFTA Secretariat (1969) *The Effects of EFTA on the Economies of Member States*, Geneva. Jan.

EFTA Secretariat (1972) *The Trade Effects of EFTA and the EEC, 1959–1967*, Geneva. June.

Han, S. S. and Liesner, H. H. (1971) 'Britain and the Common Market', Cambridge: Cambridge University Press—Cambridge University Department of Applied Economics Occasional Papers, 27.

Haviland, W. E., Takacsy, N. S. and Cape, E. M. (1968) *Trade Liberalisation and the Canadian Pulp and Paper Industry*, Toronto: University of Toronto Press for the Private Planning Association of Canada, No. 5 in 'Canada in the Atlantic Economy'.

Houthakker, H. S. and Magee, S. P. (1969) 'Income and Price Elasticities in World Trade', *Review of Economics and Statistics*, Vol. LI, No. 2 (May).

Kaldor, N. (1971) 'The Dynamic Effects of the Common Market' in Evans, D. ed. *Destiny or Delusion: Britain and the Common Market*, London: Victor Gollanz.

Kouevi, A. F. (1965) 'Essai d'application prospective de la methode RAS au commerce international', *Bulletin du CEPREL*, No. 5 (Oct).

Krause, L. B. (1962) 'US Imports, 1947–58', *Econometrica*, (April).

Krause, L. B. (1968) *European Economic Integration and the United States*, Washington: Brookings Institution.

Krauss, M. B. (1972) 'Recent Developments in Customs Union Theory: An Interpretive Survey', *Journal of Economic Literature*, (June), Vol. X, No. 2.

Krauss, M. B., ed. (1973) *The Economics of Integration*, London: George Allen and Unwin.

Kreinin, M. E. (1961) 'The Effects of Tariff Changes on the Prices and Volumes of Imports', *American Economic Review*.

Kreinin, M. E. (1967) 'Trade Arrangements Among Industrial Countries: Effects on the US', in Balassa (1967).

Kreinin, M. E. (1969) 'Trade Creation and Diversion by the EEC and EFTA', *Economia Internazionale*, (May), Vol. XXII No. 2.

Kreinin, M. E. (1972) 'Effects of the EEC on Imports of Manufactures', *Economic Journal* (Sept).

Kreinin, M. E. (1973) 'The Static Effects of EEC Enlargement on Trade Flows', *Southern Economic Journal* (April), 39(4) pp. 559–68.

Lamfalussy, A. (1963) 'Intra-European Trade and the Competitive Position of the EEC', *Manchester Statistical Society*, 13th March, 1963.

Linnemann, H. (1966) *An Econometric Study of International Trade Flows*, Amsterdam: North Holland.

Lipsey, R. G. (1957) 'The Theory of Customs Unions: Trade Diversion and Welfare', *Economica*, Vol. 24.

Major, R. L. and Hays, S. (1970) 'Another Look at the Common Market', *National Institute Economic Review* (Nov.).

Maxwell Stamp Associates (1967) *The Free Trade Area Option*, London: The Atlantic Trade Study.

Mayes, D. G. (1971) 'The Effects of Alternative Trade Groupings on the United Kingdom', PhD thesis, University of Bristol.

Mayes, D. G. (1974) 'RASAT, A Model for the Estimation of Commodity Trade Flows in EFTA', *European Economic Review*, Vol. 5, pp. 207–221.

Mayes, D. G. (1976) 'The Estimation of the Effects of Trading Areas on Trade', mimeo, University of Exeter.

Orcutt, G. H. (1950) 'Measurement of Price Elasticities in International Trade', *Review of Economics and Statistics*, (May).

Poyhonen, P. (1963) 'Towards a General Theory of International Trade', *Ek. Samf. Tidskrift*, No. 2.

Prewo, W. E. (1974) 'Integration Effects in the EEC: An Attempt at Quantification in a General Equilibrium Framework', *European Economic Review*, (3).

Pulliainen, K. (1963) 'A World Trade Study: An Econometric Model of the Pattern of the Commodity Flows in International Trade, 1948–60', *Ek. Samf. Tidskrift*, No. 2.

Resnick, S. A. and Truman, E. M. (1973) 'An Empirical Examination of Bilateral Trade in Western Europe', *Journal of International Economics*, Vol. 3, pp. 305–35.

Resnick, S. A. and Truman, E. M. (1974) 'The Distribution of West European Trade under Alternative Tariff Policies', *Review of Economics and Statistics*, No. 1. 56 pp. 83–91.

Robson, P., ed. (1972) *International Economic Integration*, Harmondsworth: Penguin.

Savage, I. R. and Deutsch, K. W. (1960) 'A Statistical Model of the Gross Analysis of Transaction Flows', *Econometrica* (July) 28, pp. 551–72.

Sellekaerts, W. (1973) 'How Meaningful are Empirical Studies on Trade Creation and Diversion?', *Weltwirtschaftliches Archiv*, (Dec.) 109 (4) pp. 519–53.

Singer, J. (1969) 'Trade Liberalisation and the Canadian Steel Industry', Toronto: University of Toronto Press for the Private Planning Association of Canada.

Tinbergen, J. (1962) *Shaping the World Economy*, New York: Twentieth Century Fund.

Truman, E. M. (1969) 'The European Economic Community: Trade Creation and Trade Diversion', *Yale Economic Essays*, Spring.

Truman, E. M. (1972) 'The Production and Trade of Manufactured Products in the EEC and EFTA: A Comparison', *European Economic Review*, Vol. 3, pp. 271–90.

Verdoorn, P. J. and Schwartz, A. N. R. (1972) 'Two Alternative Estimates of the Effects of EEC and EFTA on the Pattern of Trade', *European Economic Review*, 3, pp. 291–335.

Waelbroeck, J. (1964) 'Une nouvelle methode d'analyse des matrices d'échanges internationaux', *Cahiers Economiques de Bruxelles*, 21, I.

Walter, I. (1967) *The European Common Market: Growth and Patterns of Trade and Production*, New York: Praeger.

Wemelsfelder, J. (1960) 'The short term effect of lowering import duties in Germany', *Economic Journal* (March).

Williamson, J. (1971) 'On Estimating the Income Effects of British Entry to the EEC', Warwick: *Survey Papers in Economics*, No. 5 (June).

Williamson, J. and Bottrill, A. (1971) 'The Impact of Customs Unions on Trade in Manufactures', *Oxford Economic Papers* (Nov.), 23(3).

Wonnacott, R. J. and Wonnacott, P. (1967) *Free Trade between the U.S. and Canada: The Potential Economic Effects*, Cambridge (Mass.): Harvard University Press.

Britain in Europe: a Survey of Quantitative Trade Studies*

L. ALAN WINTERS

University College of North Wales, Bangor

The fourteen years since Britain acceded to the European Community have seen fundamental shifts in the pattern of her international trade, with both exports and imports becoming more heavily concentrated on her new partners. It is natural that economists and policy-makers should wonder to what extent these changes are due to the institutional arrangements implied by accession, and what the benefits of such changes are. This article offers a methodological and interpretive survey of empirical work on the effects of the Common Market on British trade in manufactures. The economic theory of customs unions is very large and still growing, and prior to British accession there was a commendable number of predictive, *ex ante*, studies of the likely effects on UK trade. This article ignores both these literatures, concentrating instead on the approaches and the results of the few studies that have sought to measure the actual effects of accession *ex post*. This is not to denigrate theoretical and *ex ante* research — nor the large literature on the effects of the Common Agricultural Policy, which is also ignored — but merely to recognize that, as well as presenting interesting methodological challenges, measuring changes in manufactured trade is necessary to both our understanding of integration and our testing of economic hypotheses.

The article starts with a very brief methodological introduction. It then describes the main quantitative estimates of the effects of UK accession to the EC on manufactured trade, surveying their results and analysing their techniques. Most of the studies conclude that Britain's trade balance in manufactures declined as a result of joining the EC. The final section considers the normative conclusions that can be drawn from the previous

*Thanks are due to Douglas Jay, David Mayes, Ann Morgan, John Rhodes, Peter Robson and John Williamson for comments on an earlier draft of this paper.

positive analyses. It concludes that accession has probably been beneficial in respect of its consequences for the production and consumption of manufactures. It also notes, however, that the welfare analysis of accession is very complex, and that, to date, economists have not made the best job possible of it.

The Analytical Background

Despite four decades of subsequent research, the basic tools for analysing the effects of customs unions remain Viner's (1950) trade creation and trade diversion. Each entails an increase in trade between the newly associated, or partner, countries, but in the former case the new imports displace sales previously internal to the partners' economies, whereas in the latter they displace imports previously bought from third, non-partner, countries. Trade creation can also occur if the decline in tariffs on partner imports stimulates consumption, or if the custom union's common tariff against third countries is lower than one of the partner's pre-union external tariff. The latter circumstance is referred to as external trade creation. Further changes in trade patterns can result from integration if the increase in market size induces large economies of scale, significant dynamic effects (such as shifts in investors' sentiments), or important changes in macro-economic policy. These effects may include trade suppression by which domestic producers are stimulated to recapture home markets from third country suppliers.

Ex post studies of economic integration, which form the subject of this article, are not always able to distinguish the full range of possibilities enumerated above. However, some attempt to do so is desirable, first to facilitate the construction of a hypothetical view of international trade patterns in the absence of integration — the so-called *anti-monde* — and secondly, to permit conclusions to be drawn about the consequences of integration for economic welfare.

Table 1 presents a simple accounting framework for analysing the effects of Britain's accession to the EC on patterns of manufactured trade. It comprises a matrix of transactions disaggregated by three areas: Britain, the EC and the rest of the world (ROW). Down the columns it records the sources of goods consumed in each area, and along the rows the purchasers of each area's output. The final row and column represent total consumption and production respectively. In the notation, S_{ij} represents sales by i to j; hence S_{BE} is Britain's exports to the EC. The additional symbols represent certain transactions from the British point of view in more obvious notation.

Ignoring the problems of how the transactions in the table are measured (e.g. net vs gross, constant vs current prices, etc.), figure 1 can help us make simple predictions about the effects of economic integration. Accession should raise both X_E and M_E. If this is at the expense of other imports, S_{RE} and M_R respectively, trade diversion has occurred, whereas if it is at the

Alan L. Winters

Table 1

A simple accounting framework

buyer seller	Britain	EC	ROW	TOTAL
Britain	H S_{BB}	X_E S_{BE}	X_R S_{BR}	Y $S_{B\cdot}$
EC	M_E S_{EB}	S_{EE}	S_{ER}	$S_{E\cdot}$
ROW	M_R S_{RB}	S_{RE}	S_{RR}	$S_{R\cdot}$
TOTAL	C $S_{\cdot B}$	$S_{\cdot E}$	$S_{\cdot R}$	$S_{\cdot\cdot}$

S_{ij} sales from i to j
$S_{\cdot B}$ total purchases in Britain
$S_{B\cdot}$ total sales by British producers
In the text, S^*_{EE} and S^*_{RR} represent the international trade components of S_{EE} and S_{RR}, which arise because in reality Europe and ROW comprise many countries.

expense of home sales, H and S_{EE}, or is purely additional, trade creation has occurred. Rises in imports from ROW — M_R and S_{RE} — would indicate external trade creation, while rises in home sales — H and S_{EE} — at the expense of ROW exports would indicate trade suppression. All of these changes must be measured not just through time, but rather relative to what trade would have been in the absence of integration. Thus to calculate integration effects one needs measures of trade both under integration and also under identical circumstances but with no integration. In *ex post* exercises the 'with-integration' data are firm, but the 'no-integration' figures require estimation. The estimation of such *anti-mondes* is the most crucial and difficult part of detecting integration effects: it relies not only on data, but also on having a satisfactory model of the processes determining international trade. However, it is also indispensable: behind any statement about the quantitative effects of Britain joining the EC lies an *anti-monde*, even if it is merely a crude one of no change.

The principal contrast between different studies of integration lies in their treatments of the *anti-mondes*, but one further distinction is also useful. Having designed the basic model of trade, one can calculate integration effects in two ways. First, one could estimate the *anti-monde* by setting all variables affected by integration to 'non-integration' values, solving the trade model, and subtracting the resulting predicted value of trade from the actual (integration-inclusive) trade data. Known as residual imputation (see Mayes, 1978), this method attributes all of the difference between a non-stochastic *anti-monde* and a stochastic actual observation to economic integration. Conceptually, although not necessarily numerically, it thus includes 'too much' in its estimate of integration effects, for both random shocks and any effects excluded from the model of trade get added in.

The second approach is to model integration analytically, for example by comparing two runs of the trade model, one using *anti-monde* (i.e. non-integration) tariff rates and the other using actual (integration) tariff rates. This is theoretically superior to imputation, but much more difficult to implement because it requires the explicit identification and modelling of every change entailed in integration. Consequently, researchers have tended towards an intermediate or hybrid approach, in which dummy variables are included in the trade model to represent the difference between 'integration' and 'non-integration' observations. These variables make explicit allowance for integration but in a rather agnostic fashion.

British Accession to the EC

There have been a large number of informal analyses of UK accession to the EC in 1973. They are well represented by the majority of submissions to two Parliamentary enquiries — House of Lords (1983) and House of Commons (1984). Almost all rely implicitly on residual imputation and 'no change' *anti-mondes* — "look how things have changed since 1973", they say, usually continuing with "dreadful, isn't it". I shall not survey these studies here, but will concentrate on the few that are both more sophisticated and more explicit in their methodology. I have been able to identify only four research programmes that have published quantitative estimates, although no doubt many more exist in private and official filing cabinets. Each of the four treats exports and imports quite independently, and despite its obvious theoretical limitations, I follow that practice here.

Table 2

British Imports of Manufactures 1962–84[a]

	SHARES OF IMPORTS			RATION OF IMPORTS TO GDP[b]
	EC(6)	EFTA and IRELAND	REST OF THE WORLD	
1962	30.0	15.3	54.7	18.2
1965	28.3	15.7	56.0	19.1
1968	27.3	18.0	54.7	30.0
1970–72	31.4	22.1	46.5	31.9
1973–75	37.9	20.6	41.5	46.2
1976–78	43.2	18.9	37.9	51.2
1979–81	45.1	17.1	37.8	55.0
1982–84	45.9	17.4	36.7	67.1

[a] Source: Department of Trade and Industry in House of Lords(1983), author's calculations from CSO Blue Books and Pink Books, and Overseas Trade Statistics
[b] GDP deriving from manufacturing industry

Before discussing estimates of the effects of accession, I consider very briefly the prima facie evidence that such an effect exists. Table 2 reports various suppliers' shares in UK manufactured imports and the imports/ GDP ratio for manufacturing. In our previous notation, the former are $M_E/(M_E + M_R)$ and $M_R/(M_E + M_R)$ while the latter proxies $(M_E + M_R)/C$ or $1 - (H/C)$. Prior to 1970 the EC(6) provided a fairly steady 27 per cent to 30 per cent of UK manufactured imports, but since then its share has risen rapidly. EFTA and Ireland, on the other hand, experienced rising shares during the 1960s with subsequent falls after 1972. This pattern presumably reflects the establishment of EFTA and AIFTA (the Anglo-Irish Free Trade Agreement) during the 1960s and their dilution in 1973 as the Six received comparable treatment in British markets.

The final column of Table 2 shows the imports/GDP ratio in manufactures. It reflects the frequently noted tendency for manufacturing industry to become more open since the 1950s, but again the rate of change appeared to rise very significantly just after 1973. In fact the import/GDP ratio is not an ideal reflection of the displacement of home sales by imports, for the GDP derived from manufacturing includes exports as well as home sales, and is based on value-added rather than the gross output concept used to measure imports. However, the ratio of imports to total domestic sales of manufactures, shown in Winters (1983, 1984a) for years up to 1979, tells the same story.

Table 3 presents similar data for manufactured exports, $X_E/(X_E + X_R)$, $X_R/(X_E + X_R)$. It reveals very similar patterns: a noticeable drift towards Europe, especially EFTA, during the 1960s, followed by an obvious switch towards the Six and away from EFTA, Ireland and the rest of the world since

Table 3

British Exports of Manufactures 1962–84[a]

	SHARES OF EXPORTS			RATIO OF EXPORTS TO GDP[b]
	EC(6)	EFTA AND IRELAND	REST OF THE WORLD	
1962	18.5	14.5	67.0	38.3
1965	18.6	15.1	66.3	37.8
1968	19.7	16.1	64.2	45.2
1970–72	21.2	17.8	61.0	48.3
1973–75	24.0	16.8	59.2	56.5
1976–78	27.3	16.4	56.3	65.4
1979–81	30.8	16.5	52.7	64.7
1982–84	31.6	15.1	53.3	

[a] and [b] see notes to Table 2.

accession. The increasing openness of manufacturing is also evident, especially after 1973, but not as marked as for imports, for which the initial trade/GDP ratio was much lower.

Table 4

UK Share of Countries' Imports of Manufactures

	Germany	France	Italy	Netherlands	Belgium Luxembourg	Denmark	Ireland	USA	Canada	Japan
1965	7.0	8.5	9.9	8.3	10.3	15.9	63.4	9.5	8.3	7.6
1968	6.1	6.4	7.4	7.1	9.9	14.8	62.5	7.6	6.2	6.0
1970–72	5.2	6.2	6.2	7.3	7.7	14.1	59.4	6.4	5.7	6.3
1973–75	5.0	6.2	5.8	7.1	8.0	11.2	54.9	6.1	4.3	5.4
1976–78	5.8	6.7	6.6	8.2	10.1	11.0	52.4	5.0	3.4	4.8
1979–81	6.8	6.8	7.2	8.8	9.1	9.3	49.5	4.9	3.2	4.6
1982–83	6.7	6.2	7.0	8.3	8.7	8.5	40.7	4.3	2.5	3.6

Source: Monthly Review of External Trade Statistics, Annual Supplement, 1985

If, as is often maintained, export performance is determined as much by demand stimuli as by supply pressures, Table 3 should be supplemented by Table 4, which shows the UK share of various countries' imports of manufactures — $X_E/(X_E + S^*_{EE} + S_{RE})$ and $X_R/(X_R + S_{ER} + S^*_{RR})$. It too supports the thesis that accession had significant trade effects. Prior to 1973 British market shares declined apparently inexorably almost everywhere, but subsequently, while the decline continued elsewhere, it was, at least temporarily, reversed for every one of the original Six members of the EC. In fact, consistent with Britain's loss of preference in these markets, the decline in her share of Danish and Irish imports accelerated after 1973.

Merely 'eye-balling' the evolution of market shares over a period of economic integration is not a sufficient means for isolating integration effects, but Tables 2 to 4 do suggest that, at a minimum, there is something to be explained. Table 5 summarizes the four groups of publications which estimate the extent to which British accession to the EC can explain these patterns of trade. Several of the studies quote ranges of outcomes — often very large ranges — but the Table reports what I infer to be the authors' 'central', 'preferred' or 'most likely' outcomes.

The first quantitative estimate of accession effects was that of Fetherston, Moore and Rhodes (1979) (FMR). They defined 'EC trade' to include both the original EC (6) and the other two 1973 entrants, Denmark and Ireland. Thus their measures combine both the positive and negative elements described above. Their time-series *anti-monde* related British imports to total final expenditure, time, and relative unit labour costs between the United Kingdom, the EC(8) and the rest of the world (Canada, Japan, Sweden and USA). For exports, they considered UK exports relative to total EC exports

Table 5

Ex Post Studies of UK Accession to the EC: Trade in Manufactures

	Variable	Nature	Anti-monde	Method	Year	Change in Trade Flows	
						imports	exports
Fetherston, Moore and Rhodes (1979)	M_E, M_R $X_E/(X_E + S^*_{EE})$	time-series	f (demand, costs time)	residual imputation	1977 (1970 prices)	$M_E + 2549^a$ $M_R - 494$	$X_E + 507$ $X_R - 396$
Morgan (1980)	$(M_E + M_R)$ $(X_E + X_R)$	time-series time-series	f (demand, relative prices) f (demand, time)	analytic residual imputation	1977 (1977 prices) 1977 (1977 prices)	$(M_E + M_R) + 800$	$(X_E + X_R) + 1,100$
Daly (1978)	$\dfrac{M_E}{M_E + M_R}$	time-series	f (time)	residual imputation	1981 (1981 prices)	$M_E + 5,000^b$	
Mayes (1983b)	$\left(\dfrac{X_E}{X_E + X_R}\right)$						$X_E + 4,750$
	$\left(\dfrac{X_E}{X_E + S_{RE}}\right)$						$X_E + 7,000$
Winters (1983)	$(X_E), \left(\dfrac{X_R}{X_E + S_{RE} X_R + S_{ER} + S^*_{RR}}\right)$	time-series	f (demand, costs time)	residual imputation	1978 (1978 prices)		$X_E + 2,300$ $X_R + 600$
(1984a)	$H/_C, M_{E}/_C, M_{R}/_C$	time-series	f (demand,	dummy	1979	$M_E + 8,000$	$X_E + 4,450$
(1985)	$X_E, \dfrac{X_R}{S_{-E}, S_{-R}}$	/cross-section	relative prices)	variables	(1979 prices)	$M_R\ 0$	$X_R - 1,660$

a EC(8)

b Total visible trade

to EC and non-EC markets, using total EC exports, time, and relative UK/ EC labour costs as explanatory variables. Economical of data as this approach is, it clearly omits one source of variation in exports — namely the demand for and supply of non-EC goods. Thus, if the enlargement of the EC caused both new and original Members to concentrate on each other's markets, FMR would understate the diversion of exports to third markets as both were displaced by the latter's local and non-EC suppliers.

FMR's results suffer from two other problems. First, it is not obvious that their explanatory variables — especially unit costs — were unaffected by accession. Thus the use of the actual values in the *anti-monde* may be misleading. This problem besets every economic, as opposed to merely extrapolative, study, and like everyone else FMR ignore it. Second, FMR impose a range of elasticity values in their *anti-monde* rather than estimate them. This avoids a lot of estimation problems, but leaves one with a range of possible outcomes between which there are no grounds for choosing. For example, the £2,548m increase in M_E quoted in Table 5 comes from a range of £1,089m to £5,546m; the reduction in X_R from a range of $-$£640m to $+$£182m. While the qualitative conclusions are clear — viz. trade creation exceeds diversion for imports, export expansion exceeds export diversion, and the balance of trade in manufactures declines — the ranges are really too large for comfort.

The second of the published quantitative studies is that of Morgan (1980). As only one part of a larger study, Morgan's results for manufactured trade are not described in great detail, but the basic methodology is clear. Distinguishing finished and semi-finished manufactures, Morgan related British imports to demand (non-food consumer spending plus investment for finished goods, industrial production for semis), relative prices, and a variable representing average tariff levels. (It records falls for each set of tariff reductions over 1959–77: Dillon and Kennedy Rounds, EFTA, and accession to the EC.) Applying the estimated price and tariff elasticities to the known tariff reductions entailed by accession, she suggested increases in imports of £500m (finished manufactures) and £250m to £350m (semis). Based explicitly on tariff changes these estimates almost certainly understate the extent of trade creation by missing the non-price components of integration. Furthermore, by considering only total imports of manufactures Morgan is unable to reflect trade diversion.

Morgan's approach to exports was similar to Balassa's (1974) use of *ex post* income elasticities in his study of•European integration. For a series of periods she conducted a constant-shares analysis of UK exports to various markets. This entails calculating what exports would have been in the terminal year of a period if Britain had maintained her initial year shares of each market and expressing actual exports relative to this. The resulting ratio is basically an *ex post* elasticity of demand for exports with respect to market demand rather than income, as in Balassa. Morgan notes that prior to accession these ratios were below one for all markets — reflecting Britain's falling market shares — but that over 1972–76 the ratio for exports to EC (6) was substantially above one. She calculates her *anti-monde* by applying the calculated ratios for the period 1968–72 to the period 1972–76 for exports to EC (6), EFTA, Ireland, Canada, New Zealand and Australia, and then updating it to 1977 taking account of a generally stronger UK export performance in that year. The upshot is an estimated increase in total manufactured exports of £1,075m to £1,125m.

While Morgan's approach has a strong intuitive appeal it is limited in a number of ways. First, it ignores the cross-sectional information available by comparing British performance across markets, even though in her discussion Morgan acknowledges the existence of common influences — namely British competitiveness. Secondly, constant-share analysis is sensitive to the degree and nature of geographical and commodity disaggregation (see Richardson (1971)). Morgan implies that she treats manufactures' less erratic items as a single aggregate, which is very limiting. Thirdly, the use of a single explanatory variable — import demand — is restrictive, especially over a period during which British competitiveness fluctuated so widely.

Daly's (1978) article was the first *ex post* study of trade patterns to be published, but she presented only qualitative results. Mayes (1983a,b) extended her sample and calculated the figures shown in Table 5. Their approach was more agnostic than other researchers'. Mayes, in particular, rehearses the difficulties of measuring accession effects: for example, the confounding effects of the oil price rise, the possibility that demand management and/or the exchange rate were affected by accession, and that the enlargement of the EC affected world prices. From this he concludes that sophisticated model-building is unlikely to yield sufficiently better results than simple extrapolation to warrant the extra effort it requires. Thus he calculates his *anti monde* as a simple continuation of the trend rate of growth of particular ratios over 1963–72.

Out of eight categories of visible trade, six of them manufactures, Mayes finds a significant increase in the EC (6) shares of UK imports for seven — the exception is transport equipment. He estimates the difference in total visible imports from the EC as £5 billion in 1981, of which a significant proportion — about £1.5 billion — is attributable to non-manufactures. For exports, Mayes considers two ratios — the share of the EC (6) in UK exports, $X_E/(X_E + X_R)$, and the UK share of EC (6) imports, $X_E/(X_E + S^*_{EE} + S_{RE})$. From the former he estimates increased exports to the EC of £4.75 billion in 1981, and from the latter £7 billion.[1]

Mayes and Daly's figures cannot be broken down into trade creation and trade diversion, and this limits their usefulness, particularly with respect to welfare judgments. Their commodity disaggregation, on the other hand, is a

[1]These estimates come from Mayes (1983b). Earlier estimates referring to 1980 can be found in Mayes (1983a), but apparently they contain significant errors.

distinct advantage. In the end, however, their exercise stands or falls by its *anti-monde*. While admitting the many and great problems of explaining changes in trade flows, I do not believe that they switch the balance of advantage towards mere trend extrapolation. If economic relationships are not stable through accession, and if additional variables become endogenous, it is implausible to argue that, nonetheless, autonomous time trends will continue roughly unchanged. It is probably true that the marginal returns to increased sophistication in economic modelling diminish, but even if this fact leads a hard-pressed civil servant to prefer trend-based approaches, it should not be a dominant consideration in academic circles. Certainly, it should carry no weight once more sophisticated approaches have been implemented, for then the latter's advantages, even if minor, are available at no extra cost.[2]

The final research programme on measuring accession effects *ex post* is my own, Winters (1983, 1984a, 1985). It offers a preliminary analysis of exports similar to Fetherston, Moore and Rhodes' (1979) and Morgan's (1980), but then develops a rather more sophisticated model which is applied to both exports and imports of manufactures. The latter approach stresses two factors.

First, it shows that, even in the absence of customs unions effects, it is not legitimate to assume that the allocation of a given level of imports over suppliers is independent of the price of, and the demand for, home goods. For example, the allocation of British demand for imported cars between Germany (BMW) and Italy (Fiat) is not independent of the price of British cars (Jaguars). This is proved econometrically by means of a two-stage process. Initially, a very general model of import allocation is estimated, explaining import shares in terms only of the total demand for manufactured imports and the prices of manufactures from each of ten suppliers — five EC (6) partners and five other major industrial countries. This model is considerably more sophisticated and general than the functions used by other commentators, but even so, the second stage of the test shows that its performance can be significantly improved by also making use of information on UK domestic prices for manufactures. Thus the prices of and demand for indigenous manufactures are seen to be essential to explaining the division of imports between partner and non-partner sources, let alone to separating trade diversion and creation. Winters (1984a and 1984b) tests and exploits this result in the context of UK imports of manufactures, while Winters (1985) extends it to imports into five other major OECD countries. It is a considerable strength of the resulting estimates of integration effects that they recognize the importance of home prices in the determination of trade shares.

The second important feature of this work is that it treats the allocation of

[2]In fact Mayes rejects not the possibility that sophisticated modelling could improve significantly upon trend-based estimates, but the belief that existing approaches *have* done so (private correspondence).

expenditure on manufactures over sources in a consistent and rigorous fashion, drawing on a number of results from consumer demand theory. The latter dictates that allocation models should satisfy a number of constraints. The most obvious is that shares in total expenditure should amount to 100 per cent. Equally important is that equi-proportionate changes in all prices and expenditure (which leave *relative* prices and income unchanged) should have no effect on trade shares. Finally, theory also suggests that the effect of a rise in the price of good i on the demand for good j should equal that of a rise in the price of j on the demand for i. These constraints must be imposed in order both to estimate the trade model efficiently and to make its conclusions theoretically consistent. A model which violates them lacks credibility with respect to both its parameter estimates and its predictions of behaviour.

To be, very briefly, more technical, I assume that trade patterns are consistent with the so-called Almost Ideal Demand System (AIDS). For both domestic and various imported supplies, this explains supplier i's share (w_i) of total expenditure on manufactures (E) as a particular function of real expenditure (money expenditure divided by a price index, P) and the prices of all supplies of manufactures, $p_j, j = i \ldots N$. Thus in each year, the share of supplier i may be written

$$w_{it} = \alpha_i + \beta_i \log (E_t/P_t) + \Sigma_j \, \gamma_{ij} \log p_{jt} + u_{it} \qquad (1)$$

where subscript t refers to the year, p_{it} is the average price of sales of manufactures (in year t), by supplier i, P_t is an index of the prices of manufactures from all sources, u_{it} is a stochastic error, α_i, β_i, and γ_{ij} are parameters, and i, j, k $= 1 \ldots N$ all count over suppliers. The various theoretical requirements are imposed by means of linear constraints on the parameters. Total expenditure on manufactures (E) is presumed to be determined prior to its allocation across sources, by a higher stage budgeting process that considers national income and the price indices for the aggregate goods 'manufactures', 'food', 'housing' etc.

In principle, preferential tariff reductions could be incorporated into the AIDS quite simply by altering relative prices. It is preferable, however, to use dummy variables to represent accession, first because accession involved a number of non-price effects and, secondly, because data on the average increase in competitiveness of each supplier's bundle of exports are not available. Thus equations (1) are augmented with terms in $\varepsilon_i D$, where ε_i are coefficients and D takes the value zero until 1971, unity in 1972 (to catch anticipation effects), and (t-1970) in years t $= 1973 \ldots 1979$. This pattern broadly captures the gradual process of integration.

Integration effects on trade with particular countries in 1979 are reported in Table 6. Their substantial size for imports is evident from columns (1) and (2). For every member of 'the Six', over half of actual imports in 1979 is attributable to accession, with imports from Germany alone rising by £3¾ billion. In the remaining rows — which refer to the non-EC countries —

Table 6

'Unadjusted' Integration Effects on UK Manufactured Trade

Trade with	Change in trade due to accession, 1979			
	Imports		Exports	
	£m	as % of actual	£m	as % of actual
France	1934	62	540	25
Belgium-Luxembourg	1745	89	n.c.	
Netherlands	1315	70	n.c.	
W. Germany	3748	69	1611	57
Italy	1332	66	663	55
Sweden	−120	−9	n.c.	
Switzerland	542	21	n.c.	
Japan	722	49	−259	−48
Canada	−232	−44	n.c.	
USA	1186	32	−1249	−44
UK (change in home sales)	−12171	−17	n.a.	

Source: Winters (1984a, 1985)

n.c. not calculated

n.a. not applicable

smaller, but still sizeable, increases in imports are reported. Only Sweden and Canada appear to suffer net trade diversion; for the remaining non-EC suppliers, Switzerland, Japan and the USA, external trade creation appears to outweigh trade diversion. This is plausible because accession reduced UK tariffs on third country imports. Moreover it is sometimes asserted that accession increased non-EC foreign investment in Britain, and it is likely that with Japan and the USA as principal investors, imports of capital and intermediate goods from these countries would have increased.

The most striking result in Table 6, however, is the massive decline in UK sales in its own market — some £12 billion of trade creation.

The figures for external trade creation are surprisingly high, and they raise the possibility that I may be attributing to accession the effects of other secular trends in UK imports. To guard against this, therefore, I adjust the total effects as reported in Table 5. If all the £2 billion of so-called external trade creation were due to secular trends, and would therefore have been observed in the absence of accession, only £10 billion of the decline in UK home sales could be attributed to accession. Furthermore, if similar trends had affected imports from the EC (6) they too would have been about £2 billion higher than our *anti-monde* admits; hence £2 billion should also be trimmed off the estimate of internal trade creation. Overall, therefore, to be on the safe side, Table 5 reports £8 billion of internal trade creation, and no net external trade creation.

The effects of accession on manufactured exports are calculated by applying the import model to each of five major markets for UK manufactures — France, Germany, Italy, Japan and the USA. In each case seven sources of supply are distinguished — the five just listed, the UK, and the rest of the world. As before, homes sales are allowed for in the model of import allocation, systematic theoretical constraints are imposed, and dummy variables are used to represent economic integration. The exercises on the five markets are quite independent; no constraint, implicit or explicit, requires that increases in UK exports to one region should be associated with decreases in exports to another. Thus the conclusion that accession boosted exports to EC countries but curtailed those to elsewhere derives entirely from the data.

The export effects are not as high as those for imports, but are nonetheless quite substantial. Between 25 and 60 per cent of exports to EC countries could be attributed to accession, amounting to around £1.6 billion in the case of Germany. They are partly offset, however, by shortfalls of nearly 50 per cent in exports to non-partner countries — the USA and Japan. The five markets covered accounted for only about 31 per cent of British manufactured exports in 1979, and extending the results to estimate total export effects is rather uncertain. Assume — admittedly optimistically — that exports to Belgium-Luxembourg and the Netherlands increased by the average percentage for France, Germany and Italy; that those to Ireland and Denmark were unaffected; and that 90 per cent of the export displacement occurred in the USA and Japan, because their markets are the most similar to those of 'the Six'. This generates the effects quoted in Table 5 — increases in exports to the EC of £4.5 billion and decreases in those to elsewhere of £1.7 billion.

Although these results are more firmly based in economic theory than are the others quoted in Table 5, they are nevertheless subject to a number of reservations. First, there are obvious problems of aggregation across goods. Not only does this hide interesting results, but it may also bias some of the results. Daly and Mayes offer some disaggregated analysis, and greater detail is available in Shepherd (1983), although the latter does not offer much by way of firm quantification.

Second, there are problems of simultaneity bias. The AIDS presumes that neither total expenditure on manufactures nor any of the prices used depends on the allocation of expenditure over sources. This precludes capturing any terms of trade effects from accession. However, although Petith (1977) has argued that such effects were significant in the original creation of the EC, there is, to my knowledge, no evidence that they were important for manufactures in the case of British accession. The presumption also implies that a country's share of its own market for manufactures has no effect on its prices of, or total expenditure on, manufactures. The effect on prices may safely be ignored, see Winters (1984b), and on expenditure it should be recalled that home sales of manufactures account.

for only around 20 per cent of GNP in Britain.[3]

The most likely danger from simultaneity is that the balance of trade deficit induced by the trade creation led to tighter fiscal policy and/or a lower exchange rate during the 1970s. If so, the estimates above seem likely to understate *anti-monde* imports and hence to overstate integration effects. Even so, however, it is most unlikely that this would seriously undermine the broad conclusions of Table 5.

The exogeneity of expenditure on manufactures also raises difficulties of interpretation as well as of measurement. The model can only adequately capture Meade's 'trade expansion' — the extent to which total consumption rises as consumer prices fall — if the elasticity of demand for the aggregate 'manufactures' is unity. Only then can we legitimately hold that the tariff and consequent price changes leave nominal expenditure unchanged. Otherwise the *anti-monde* will either understate expenditure on imports (for example if prices fell and the elasticity exceeded unity) or overstate it (if prices fell and the elasticity were below unity). My suspicion is that this effect leads to a slight overstatement of *anti-monde* expenditure and thus to an understatement of integration effects.

These reservations obviously reduce the degree of confidence that can be placed on the precise numerical results quoted here. Nonetheless, given their strong theoretical underpinnings, the latter are still probably the most reliable estimates available. Their unavoidable conclusion is that British accession to the EC worsened her trade balance in, and reduced her gross output of, manufactures quite substantially. Even on the most conservative estimate it reduced output by at least £3 billion, about 1.5 per cent of GNP, and the effect could easily have been twice that, see Winters (1985).

The Welfare Consequences of Accession

The natural question following the positive analysis above is whether or not Britain has benefited from accession to Europe. Even assuming that the previous analysis is correct this is a complex question, and the following discussion only scratches the surface of one part of it.

The simplest assertions concerning the welfare effects of accession are of the mercantilist kind — for example, Godley (1980), El Agraa and Jones (1981) and House of Lords (1985). These assume that trade deficits are harmful, because, by reducing demand for domestic output, they reduce domestic income, investment and technical progress, and constrain government policy towards deflation. In general their analysis takes place within a

[3]A restriction of considering manufactures in isolation, however, is that I cannot capture any of the consequences of the adverse shift in the terms of trade of manufactures relative to agriculture. If this raised UK manufacturing costs (via higher wages), my use of actual prices in the *anti-monde* would cause me to under-estimate competitiveness and over-estimate imports in the latter, and thus to under-estimate integration effects.

simple Keynesian macro-economic framework in which unemployment can and does occur. This framework has much to teach us about the contemporary economy, for it is clear that unemployment is very costly, but for several reasons it is not adequate for analysing customs unions.

First, the Keynesian modelling assumption of just a single good is perfectly adequate when one is considering macro-economic changes which affect the prices of all goods roughly equally, for then the composite good theorem may be applied. However, it is quite unable to cope with the gains from specialization when relative prices change, as they do in the face of accession to a customs union.

Second, while it is true that accession caused a deficit in manufactures and that deficits necessarily reduce output in a Keynesian model, it has not been satisfactorily explained why the deficit could not be cured by means other than deflation. To the extent that the exchange rate floated freely in the mid-1970s, the overall current account deficit was determined more by macro-economic and asset market factors than by trade policy. Thus, unless one holds that such factors were themselves influenced by accession, it follows that given an overall current account figure, any increase in the manufactures' deficit due to accession must have been largely offset by changes in other elements of the account. In other words, while accession may have changed the composition of the current account and of output, its effect on the overall level of output would have been relatively minor.[4]

If, on the other hand, the exchange rate were fixed by government action, the current deficit could indeed have been higher with accession than without, but then it could equally well have been reduced by choosing a more appropriate exchange rate target. A frequent objection to devaluation as a response to excess imports is that, to the extent that it works, it reduces real incomes. This takes us immediately to the third problem with the mercantilist analysis: it entirely ignores the fact that people benefit from — experience an increase in real income from — the greater availability of foreign goods. By stressing production and sales above purchase and consumption, mercantilism turns economics on its head, and misses the most important factor in trade policy.

The growth of unemployment since 1973 has obviously had a huge influence on welfare, and there is at least some possibility that, interacting with more fundamental factors such as labour market rigidities, accession has temporarily added to it. It seems misguided to argue, however, either that accession was a major cause of unemployment, or that unemployment is the principal channel through which accession has affected economic welfare.

[4] I am not claiming here that floating exchange rates guarantee current account equilibrium — manifestly they do not, c.f. the USA's current deficit — but just that among the pressures determining the exchange rate and the current balance, trade policy is both relatively unimportant and fairly easily accommodated by changes in the 'underlying equilibrium' exchange rate.

The most common approach to measuring the welfare effects of accession is through the parable of partial equilibrium analysis and consumer and producer surplus. Trade creation is beneficial because high cost domestic supplies are displaced by cheap imports and consumption is expanded by the fall in price (Meade's trade expansion). Trade diversion is costly because it involves the substitution of higher cost products from the partner country for low-cost products from the rest of the world. Figure 1 summarizes the traditional analysis of an importer. Before union, Britain (B) buys from ROW (R) at P_R levying a tariff at rate t, rendering internal prices $P_R(1 + t)$. Domestic absorption is A_0, output Q_0, imports $A_0 - Q_0$ and tariff-revenue area $(C_1 + C_2)$. After union with Europe (E), Britons import from Europe because $P_E < P_R(1 + t)$; internal prices become P_E. Domestic absorption increases to A_1, increasing consumer surplus by $(A + B + C_1 + D)$; domestic production falls to Q_1 reducing producer surplus by D; imports grow to $(A_1 - Q_1)$, but now no tariff revenue is collected, so tariff-revenue is changed by $-(C_1 + C_2)$. The net effect is a welfare change of $(A + B) - C_2$: the gains from trade creation less trade diversion which is equivalent to part of the tariff revenues lost.

Figure 1

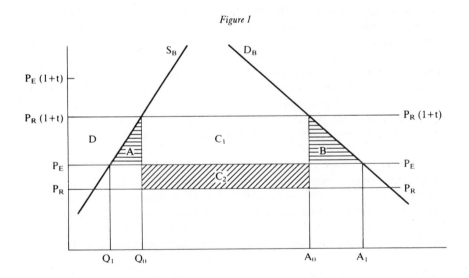

The practical application of this analysis to British accession is complicated because, to my knowledge, there are no existing estimates of the extent to which European prices exceed world prices, especially for aggregates such as manufactures. However, if from the above we know the change in imports $[(Q_0 - Q_1) + (A_1 - A_0)]$ in Figure 1, and if we assume a value of, say, -1.0 for the price elasticity of demand for manufactured imports, we may derive estimates of the change in prices facing consumers; viz. the difference between $P_R(1 + t)$ and P_E. If, then, we accept that there is little trade diversion, and assume that of the £5 billion increase in imports quoted by Mayes (1983b) for 1981, £4.0b is in manufactures, the resulting annual change in welfare is about $+£275m$ — approximately £5 per capita. Added to this there would be some increase in profits and factor rents from the increase in British exports, but overall the static welfare effects appear to be very small.

There are several well-known objections to the procedure just employed. Theoretically the most interesting, although quantitatively not the most significant, is that even when one is solely interested in static welfare gains in a single market, consumer surplus calculations are not the appropriate technique. This is because as one moves along the demand curve, D_B in Figure 1, the marginal utility of money changes, meaning that an extra £1 spending has different welfare significance at the new and the old equilibria (and at every point along the way). Economists have long been aware of this problem, but have only recently provided operational methods of calculating welfare measures, such as compensating and equivalent variation, that are not subject to this objection, e.g. Vartia (1981) and McKenzie and Ulph (forthcoming). (Compensating variation is the increase in income that a consumer requires after a change in prices to allow him just to reattain his former level of welfare; equivalent variation is the increase he would need before the change in prices to allow him to reach the welfare level he actually achieves after the change.)

These new methods become even more critical, when, as in this case, more than one price changes. Implicit in Figure 1 is the assumption of a single homogeneous good, potentially supplied by three producers, but with a single market price. This is plainly wrong for an aggregate such as manufactures where, at the very least, one should recognize that the bundle of goods from France is only imperfectly substitutable for that from Japan. Once we recognize the existence of several, albeit related, markets, we need several diagrams like Figure 1, and the problem arises that a change in one supplier's post-tariff price shifts the demand curves facing the others. Thus, for example, the corners of triangle B no longer lie on the same demand curve. This basically undermines consumer surplus, and although approximations to welfare changes may be derived — e.g. Willig (1976) — none is totally convincing. Fortunately, this is a much less serious difficulty for compensating and equivalent variations, and so the latter offer a better approach to measuring welfare changes.

The calculation of compensating and equivalent variations is generally quite complex, requiring the numerical integration of differential equations. In principle, however, this is not the case in my own work, for the AIDS is based on an explicit expenditure function. This function defines the level of expenditure required to reach a particular level of utility given the vector of prices. Thus we may invert equation (1) to calculate the vector of price changes with equivalent effect to the dummy variables quoted in Table 6 — the 'tariff equivalent' of accession — and then apply these in the AIDS expenditure function. Unfortunately, however, the estimated demand system did not quite satisfy the conditions necessary for integration back to a well-behaved expenditure function — see Winters (1984b), where a slight violation of negativity is described. While this was of little consequence for the estimation of the positive effects of accession — the job that the system was originally designed for — it is important for the estimation of welfare effects. Thus, while the possibility of the direct calculation of a welfare measure reinforces the arguments above for using formal demand systems to explore accession effects, little store can be set by the welfare estimates in this particular case. They imply an equivalent variation to accession of about £45 billion in 1979. While conventional methods almost certainly understate the welfare gains to accession, this estimate clearly overstates them. It does emphasize, however, that the benefits of accession to Britons as users and consumers of manufactures could be substantial enough to outweigh any losses to producers thereof.[5]

Welfare calculations based on compensating and equivalent variations are theoretically more acceptable than those based on consumer surplus, and if they are grounded in systems of demand equations with known and explicit expenditure functions they are not much more demanding computationally. However, both approaches — at least as currently practised — are subject to a number of common limitations even presuming that they are based on accurate positive analysis. For example, they ignore the interactions — in both supply and demand — between manufactures and other sectors of the economy; they ignore any necessary accommodating policy changes; they do not treat the costs of adjustment to trade shocks — notably unemployment — assuming, instead, that factors displaced by trade creation are immediately absorbed back into employment elsewhere in the economy; and they ignore factor mobility between partner countries.[6] While existing studies have occasionally taken account of one or two of these additional factors, it has always been at the cost of greater simplification elsewhere in their models. For example, the neo-mercantilist analysis of unemployment ignores the gains from trade; Miller and Spencer's computable general equilibrium model, which considers inter-sectoral effects, is *ex ante* and thus ignores post-1972 evidence; the optimization model of Aktan (1985) which considers the factor mobility effects of the accession of Greece,

---

[5]Recent research has uncovered a possible means to impose negativity on the AIDS without greatly restricting its responses — Diewert and Wales (1985). The recalculation of these results in this way is an obvious and high priority for future research.

[6]They do, however, take account of economies of scale and dynamic factors in the sectors under study, for, unlike *ex ante* analysis, *ex post* studies observe these factors' effects on the quantity and direction of trade.

Portugal, Spain and Turkey makes no welfare calculations.

Finally, mention should be made of an entirely different approach to measuring the total welfare effects of British accession which utilizes the theory of revealed preferences — Grinols (1984). This asks first what additional income would have been required after accession to allow each Briton to consume his 1972 bundle of goods at post-accession prices. Grinols assumes that all price changes after 1972, except that of oil, were due to accession — a variant, in terms of prices, of residual imputation from a broadly 'no change' *anti-monde*. He finds that positive income transfers would have been necessary — i.e. that accession was costly — in every year except 1979. The second step is to observe that, even if these transfers were made, Britons would not consume their pre-accession bundles, because some change in production and/or consumption would be desirable in order to exploit the price changes induced by accession. The benefits of adjusting production are measured as the value of the change in production since 1972 (after allowing for oil and exogenous growth), at post-accession prices, and those of changing consumption by applying the imputed changes in prices to a simple expenditure function as described above. These effects are similar conceptually to the areas A and B in Figure 1. Both are necessarily positive, but in the British case they are not sufficient to off-set the first change in welfare due to declining terms of trade. Adding in net transfers to EC institutions, Grinols concludes that accession cost Britain about 2 to 3 per cent of GDP over the period 1973–79.

This is a highly original and interesting approach to customs union evaluation, grounding measurement firmly in economic theory. Its drawback is its excessively simple *anti-monde* for prices and production, which, for example, attributes the terms of trade costs of the commodity boom of 1974 and the depreciation of 1976 to accession.

Thus, to date, there has been no convincing or comprehensive estimate of the welfare effects of Britain's accession to the EC. I do not believe that perfection is possible in this or in any other branch of applied welfare economics, but I do believe that greater progress could be made in this particular case. For example, in terms of general equilibrium simulation, Whalley has shown the feasibility of measuring welfare, — e.g. Hamilton and Whalley (1985); Deardorff and Stern (1981) have developed a multi-country multi-commodity model of sufficient detail to capture the main features of integration; and Spencer (1986) has applied such methods to assessing the inter-country distributional aspects of the EC. All these models use simple, but theoretically consistent, functional forms to model trade behaviour, but generalization to more sophisticated specifications would be quite feasible. Moreover, if the functional forms from the simulation models were also used in the estimation of the positive effects of integration, they could be simply slotted back into the simulation models to make the necessary welfare calculations.

CONCLUSION

This article has discussed the main attempts at quantifying the international trade effects, positive and normative, of Britain's accession to the EC. It has argued that there are very substantial technical difficulties to be overcome, but that future research marrying sound data and sensible theory could make significant improvements to our current state of knowledge. In the meantime, the cautious appraisal of existing studies suggests that accession did worsen Britain's trade balance in manufactures, but that far from being costly, the greater availability of foreign manufactures from which this stemmed contributed to economic welfare.

REFERENCES

Aktan, O. H. (1985). "The second enlargement of the European Communities", *European Economic Review*, Vol. 28, pp. 279–308.

Balassa, B. (1974). "Trade Creation and Trade Diversion in the European Common Market: An Appraisal of the Evidence", *Manchester School*, Vol. XLII, pp. 93–135.

Daly, A. E. (1978), "UK Visible Trade and the Common Market", *National Institute Economic Review*, November, pp. 42–54.

Deardorff, A. V. and Stern, R. M. (1981), "A disaggregated model of world production and trade: an estimate of the impact of the Tokyo Round", *Journal of Policy Modelling*, Vol. 3, pp. 127–152.

Diewert, W. E. and Wales, T. J. "Flexible functional forms and global curvature conditions", Discussion Paper 85–19, University of British Colombia.

Fetherston, M., Moore, B. and Rhodes, J. (1979), "EC Membership and UK Trade in Manufactures", *Cambridge Journal of Economics*, Vol. 3, pp. 399–407.

Godley, W. A. H. (1980), "Britain in Europe", *Cambridge Economic Policy Review*, Vol. 6, No. 1, pp. 27–34.

Grinols, E. L. (1984), "A thorn in the lion's paw: has Britain paid too much for Common Market membership", *Journal of International Economics*, Vol. 16, pp. 271–293.

Hamilton, B. and Whalley, J. (1985), "Geographically discriminatory trade arrangements", *Review of Economics and Statistics*, Vol. 67, pp. 446–455.

House of Commons (1984), *The Financial and Economic Consequences of UK Membership of the European Communities: Memoranda*, Treasury and Civil Service Committee, Session 1984–85, Paper 57–II, (HMSO, London).

House of Lords (1983), *Trade Patterns: The United Kingdom's Changing Trade Patterns Subsequent to Membership of the European Community*, Select Committee on the European Communities, 7th Report, Session 1983–84, Paper 41, (HMSO, London).

House of Lords (1985), *Manufacturing Trade*, Report of the Select Committee on Overseas Trade, Vol. III, House of Lords 238–II, (HMSO, London).

Mayes, D. G. (1978), "The Effects of Economic Integration on Trade", *Journal of Common Market Studies*, Vol. XVII, pp. 1–25.

Mayes, D. G. (1983a), "EC trade effects and factor mobility", Chapter 6 of El Agraa, A. M. (ed.), *Britain Within the European Community: The Way Forward*, (MacMillan, London).

Mayes, D. G. (1983b), "Memorandum" in House of Lords (1983), pp. 66–85.

McKenzie, G. and Ulph, D. T. (forthcoming), "An exact welfare measure", *Economic Perspectives*.

Miller, M. H. and Spencer, J. E. (1977), "The static economic effects of the UK joining the EC: a general equilibrium approach", *Review of Economic Studies*, Vol. 44, pp. 71–93.

Morgan, A. D. (1980), "The balance of payments and British membership of the European Community", Chapter 3 of Wallace W. (ed.), *Britain in Europe*, (Heinemann, London), pp. 57–71.

Petith, H. C. (1977), "European integration and the terms of trade", *Economic Journal*, Vol. 87, pp. 262–272.

Richardson, J. D. (1971), "Some sensitivity tests for a 'constant-market-shares' analysis of export growth", *Review of Economics and Statistics*, Vol. 53, pp. 300–304.

Shepherd, G. (1983), "British manufacturing industry and the EC", Chapter 3 of Cohen, C. D. (ed.), *The Common Market After Ten Years*, (Philip Allen, Deddington).

Spencer, J. E. (1986), "Trade liberalization through tariff cuts and the EC: A general equilibrium evaluation", in Srinivasan T. N. and Whalley J. (eds), *General Equilibrium Trade Policy Modelling*, (MIT Press, Cambridge, Mass.).

Vartia, Y. P. (1983), "Efficient methods of measuring welfare change and compensated income in terms of ordinary demand functions", *Econometrica*, Vol. 51, pp. 79–98.

Viner, J. (1950), *The Customs Union Issue*, (Carnegie Endowment for International Peace, New York).

Willig, R. D. (1976), "Consumer surplus without apology", *American Economic Review*, Vol. 66, pp. 589–597.

Winters, L. A. (1983), "Memorandum", in House of Lords (1983), pp. 369–387.

Winters, L. A. (1984a), "British imports of manufactures and the Common Market", *Oxford Economic Papers*, Vol. XXXVI, pp. 103–118.

Winters, L. A. (1984b), "Separability and the specification of foreign trade functions", *Journal of International Economics*, Vol. 17, pp. 239–263.

Winters, L. A. (1985), "Separability and the modelling of international economic integration", *European Economic Review*, Vol. 27, pp. 335–353.

THE SECOND ENLARGEMENT OF THE EUROPEAN COMMUNITIES

Probable Effects on the Members and the New Entrants*

Okan H. AKTAN*

Hacettepe University, Beytepe, Ankara, Turkey

This paper investigates the effects of the second enlargement on the competitive structures of the existing EC members and of four Mediterranean countries: Spain, Portugal, Greece and Turkey. In estimating the probable effects, optimum trade and production structures of the countries concerned were determined with the help of a non-linear optimization model developed by Henderson (1982). The model is extended by incorporating factor movements into the analysis.

1. Introduction

In less than ten years since the First Enlargement of the Community in 1973, with the admission of U.K., Ireland and Denmark to the full membership, the European Communities (EC) are undergoing a second enlargement process with the application of three Mediterranean countries for membership. Greece, being the first country to become an associate member of the European Economic Community in 1962, applied for the full membership status in June 1975 and acceded to the Community on January 1, 1981.

Portugal, after signing a free trade agreement with the EC in May 1972 while remaining in the mini-EFTA, applied for full membership in March 1977. Spain followed Portugal four months later in applying for full membership. Turkey, on the other hand, has been an associate member of the Community since 1963, and has expressed her intention in the Association Agreement to join the Community as a full member, but she feels the need for a longer transition period than the others to prepare her economy to the realities of free competition.

The Second Enlargement of the Community, which is already under way, is likely to have major repercussions on the trade and production structures

*This research was supported by a Ford Foundation grant. The author gratefully acknowledges the many constructive comments of Anne O. Krueger and James M. Henderson. He also thanks Professor Henderson for making available his computer program. The author wishes to thank the Department of Economics, University of Minnesota for its hospitality during his stay as a visiting professor, and the participants of the Trade and Development Workshop of the Department for their valuable discussions and suggestions. This paper was presented at the Ford Foundation — Italian Social Science Council's Southern European Fellowship Conference in March 1982 in Castel Gandolfo, Rome, Italy.

of the participant countries by altering the relative prices of goods, as well as factors, as a result of reduction or elimination of barriers to trade. Furthermore, the participation of the Mediterranean countries to the Community will also initiate changes in the economies of the existing EC countries. Therefore, one has to take all these changes into account in order to draw reasonably valid conclusions from the analysis. That is to say, what is relevant in comparisons is the potential, not actual, economic structures of the countries concerned.

Since enlargement of an existing customs union by admission of new members is likely to alter the relative price structures of all the economies involved, the main concern of the present study is one of determining the optimum trade and production patterns of the countries concerned under a new set of prices, and the resulting changes in the direction of resource allocation. This problem can conveniently be handled by maximizing the country's international value-added subject to observed production functions and factor supply constraints, a model developed and applied by Henderson (1982). This model can be summarized as follows.

2. Structure of the model

Each country is assumed to have $n+1$ sectors, each producing homogenous products:

$1,\ldots,m$ traded goods,

$m+1,\ldots,n$ home-goods,

$n+1$th sector   non-competitive imports.

In classifying the sectors under the 'traded goods' (or 'international goods') and 'non-traded goods' (or 'home-goods') sectors, the conventional approach is followed: Construction, housing — dwelling, public utilities, domestic transportation, banking — insurance, government services and the like are taken as non-traded goods; the rest are the traded goods. Since it is extremely difficult to determine the international prices of those non-traded goods which, in practice, are seen to enter occasionally into international trade (like Turkey's imports of electricity from her Northern neighbours), they are all treated as non-traded, whether they defy the rule or not.

Each country is free to import and export at international prices which are not affected by the trade levels of each country. Physical units of production are defined in such a way that the base-year domestic price for each good equals one. International prices are translated into domestic prices through fixed exchange rates. Factor prices are also measured in domestic currency units, though both factor prices and home good prices reflect international prices.[1]

2.1. Domestic production

Produced intermediate inputs are assumed to be required in fixed proportions for the production of each good as defined by the input–output coefficients. The requirements of non-produced factors, labor and capital, are assumed to be specified by the Cobb–Douglas production functions:

$$X_j = A_j L_j^{\alpha_j} K_j^{(1-\alpha_j)}, \qquad j = 1, \dots, n, \tag{1}$$

where $A_j > 0$, $0 \leq \alpha_j \leq 1$.

The country under consideration has fixed endowments of labor and capital denoted by L^0 and K^0 respectively. Since factors are assumed to move freely between different sectors of the economy, but not between countries the following constraints are imposed:[2]

$$\sum_{j=1}^{n} L_j \leq L^0, \qquad \sum_{j=1}^{n} K_j \leq K^0. \tag{2, 3}$$

It is further assumed that the output level for each traded good cannot be increased or decreased from its base value (X_j^0) by more than 100 δ percent ($0 < \delta < 1$):

$$(1-\delta)X_j^0 \leq X_j \leq (1+\delta)X_j^0, \qquad j = 1, \dots, m. \tag{4}$$

The output constraints, therefore, allow for a relaxation, rather than elimination, of distortions. They provide, at the same time, indirect limits on labor and capital mobility. The limited changes in output are more useful for a consideration of opening up the economies in that they prevent the outcome of complete specialization and, at the same time, allow the more realistic situation of upward sloping supply curves.

2.2. Domestic consumption and home-good outputs

Home-good final consumption levels for a base year, denoted by C_j^0 ($j = m+1, \dots, n$) include all uses other than intermediate input uses, i.e., net trade, final purchases by consumers and governments, investment and inventory

---

[1]This is because factors are paid the values of their marginal products in the production of international goods as well as home goods. As for home goods, inputs used in home goods production have opportunity cost in terms of traded goods production.

[2]These constraints will be relaxed when factor mobility case is introduced into the analysis.

change. In the solution of the model home-goods final consumption levels are treated as constant. Relaxation of the constant-level assumption would substantially complicate the model with little alteration of important results.[3]

The output level for each home-good is determined by its final consumption level (C_j^0) and its use as an intermediate input.

$$X_i \geq C_i^0 + \sum_{j=1}^{n} a_{ij} X_j, \qquad i = m+1, \ldots, n. \tag{5}$$

Solving these $(n-m)$ linear equations for the $(n-m)$ home-good output levels

$$X_i \geq k_i + \sum_{j=1}^{m} \sigma_{ij} X_j, \qquad i = m+1, \ldots, n, \tag{6}$$

where

$$k_i = \sum_{j=m+1}^{n} \mu_{ij} C_j^0, \tag{7}$$

$$\sigma_{ij} = \sum_{h=m+1}^{n} \mu_{ij} a_{hj}. \tag{8}$$

The coefficient μ_{ij} is the quantity of the ith home-good required directly and indirectly to produce one unit of the jth home-good. Here, k_i is a constant giving the gross output of the ith home-good necessary to meet the direct and indirect requirements for the fixed home-good final demands. The coefficient σ_{ij} is the quantity of the ith home-good necessary directly and indirectly to support one unit of output of international good j.

Eqs. (5) and (6) state that the output of each home-good be at least as great as final consumption and production requirements. It can be shown that exact equality holds in equilibrium (see the Khun–Tucker conditions below).

3. Equilibrium properties of the model

An equilibrium solution of the model is determined by maximizing the net international value of a country's production, subject to constraints (1), (2), (3), (4) and (5).

---

[3]The assumption of constant consumption levels for home goods involves the exclusion of positive income effects, and also limits the extent of possible substitution in consumption. This will most likely lead to the underestimation of static resource reallocation gains.

3.1. The international value added

The international value added (IVA) for a country's production can be defined as

$$V = \sum_{j=1}^{m} p_j X_j - \sum_{j=1}^{n} \sum_{i=1}^{m} p_j a_{ij} X_j - \sum_{j=1}^{n} p_{n+1} a_{n+1,j} X_j, \tag{9}$$

which is the international value of the country's traded goods production minus the international value of its traded inputs. Let γ_j be the value of the traded inputs necessary to produce one unit of good j:

$$\gamma_j = \sum_{i=1}^{m} p_i a_{ij} + p_{n+1} a_{n+1,j}, \qquad j=1,\ldots,n$$

and rewrite (9) as

$$V = \sum_{j=1}^{m} p_j X_j - \sum_{j=1}^{n} \gamma_j X_j - \sum_{j=1}^{m} b_j X_j - K, \tag{10}$$

where b_j (see appendix B) is the international value of the traded goods used as inputs directly and indirectly to produce the home goods used as inputs in the production of j:

$$b_j = \sum_{i=m+1}^{n} p_j a_{ji} \sigma_{ij}, \qquad j=1,\ldots,m$$

and K is a constant giving the international value of the traded goods necessary to directly and indirectly support the fixed home goods final demands [see eq. (B.6) in the appendix]:

$$K = \sum_{j=1}^{m} \sum_{i=m+1}^{n} p_j a_{ji} k_i.$$

The constant K has no effect upon the determination of an optimum solution and may be omitted from (10) so that each country is assumed to maximize the direct and indirect IVA from its production of traded goods. In this case the direct and indirect IVA takes the following form:

$$V = \sum_{j=1}^{m} p_j X_j - \sum_{j=1}^{n} \gamma_j X_j - \sum_{j=1}^{m} b_j X_j. \tag{11}$$

Expressing IVA in unit term

$$\hat{z}_j = p_j - \gamma_j - b_j, \qquad j=1,\ldots,m, \tag{12}$$

where $\hat{z}$ is the direct and indirect IVA per unit of j. Direct IVA per unit of j is simply $z = p_j - \gamma_j$. The IVA coefficients are independent of the optimum solutions because the underlying international prices and I/O coefficients are constant.

3.2. The Khun–Tucker conditions

A country desires to select non-negative values for its output and primary input levels that maximize its IVA subject to constraints given by (1), (2), (3), (4) and (5). Form the Lagrange function

$$
Z = \sum_{j=1}^{m} p_j X_j - \sum_{j=1}^{n} \gamma_j X_j + w\left(L^0 - \sum_{j=1}^{n} L_j \right) + c\left(K^0 - \sum_{j=1}^{n} K_j \right)
$$

$$
+ \sum_{j=1}^{n} q_j(A_j L_j^{\alpha_j} K_j^{1-\alpha_j} - X_j) + \sum_{j=1}^{m} u_j[(1+\delta)X_j^0 - X_j] \qquad (13)
$$

$$
+ \sum_{j=1}^{m} v_j[X_j - (1-\delta)X_j] + \sum_{i=m+1}^{n} \pi_i\left(X_i - C_i^0 - \sum_{j=1}^{n} a_{ij}X_j \right),
$$

where the parenthesized constraints have been rewritten so that each is in the form ≥ 0. Since the objective function and constraints of (13) are all concave and the Slater qualification is met, the Khun–Tucker conditions are necessary and sufficient for an optimum. Specifically,

$$
\frac{\partial Z}{\partial X_j} = p_j - \gamma_j - q_j - u_j + v_j - h_j \leq 0, \qquad \frac{\partial Z}{\partial X_j} X_j = 0, \ X_j \geq 0, \ j = 1,\ldots,m, \qquad (14.1)
$$

$$
\frac{\partial Z}{\partial X_j} = \pi_j - \gamma_j - q_j - h_j \leq 0, \qquad \frac{\partial Z}{\partial X_j} X_j = 0, \ X_j \geq 0, \ j = m+1,\ldots,n, \qquad (14.2)
$$

$$
\frac{\partial Z}{\partial L_j} = q_j(MPL_j) - w \leq 0, \qquad \frac{\partial Z}{\partial L_j} L_j = 0, \ L_j \geq 0, \ j = 1,\ldots,n, \qquad (14.3)
$$

$$
\frac{\partial Z}{\partial K_j} = q_j(MPK_j) - c \leq 0, \qquad \frac{\partial Z}{\partial K_j} K_j = 0, \ K_j \geq 0, \ j = 1,\ldots,n, \qquad (14.4)
$$

$$
\frac{\partial Z}{\partial w} = L^0 - \sum_{j=1}^{n} L_j \leq 0, \qquad \frac{\partial Z}{\partial w} w = 0, \ w \geq 0, \qquad (14.5)
$$

$$\frac{\partial Z}{\partial c} = K^0 - \sum_{j=1}^{n} K_j \leqq 0, \qquad \frac{\partial Z}{\partial c} c = 0, \quad c \geqq 0, \qquad (14.6)$$

$$\frac{\partial Z}{\partial q_j} = A_j L_j^{\alpha_j} K_j^{1-\alpha_j} - X_j \geqq 0, \qquad \frac{\partial Z}{\partial q_j} q_j = 0, \quad q_j \geqq 0, \quad j = 1, \ldots, n, \quad (14.7)$$

$$\frac{\partial Z}{\partial u_j} = (1-\delta)X_j - X_j \geqq 0, \qquad \frac{\partial Z}{\partial u_j} u_j = 0, \quad u_j \geqq 0, \quad j = 1, \ldots, m, \quad (14.8)$$

$$\frac{\partial Z}{\partial v_j} = X_j - (1-\delta)X_j \geqq 0, \qquad \frac{\partial Z}{\partial v_j} v_j = 0, \quad v_j \geqq 0, \quad j = 1, \ldots, m, \quad (14.9)$$

$$\frac{\partial Z}{\partial \pi_i} = X_i - C_i^0 - \sum_{j=1}^{n} a_{ij}X_j \geqq 0, \qquad \frac{\partial Z}{\partial \pi_i} \pi_i = 0, \quad \pi_i \geqq 0, \quad i = 1+m, \ldots, n,$$

$$(14.10)$$

where $h_j = \sum_{i=m+1}^{n} \pi_i a_{ij}$ is the direct unit cost in terms of the prices π_i ($i = m + 1, \ldots, n$) of the home good inputs for the production of a unit of good j.

Conditions (14) are necessary and sufficient for optimal solutions. The parameters of the model are defined so that base year outputs provide feasible solutions, and that points in neighbourhoods about these outputs are also feasible.

3.3. Shadow prices and equilibrium conditions

Lagrange multipliers are shadow prices that give the rate at which the maximum value of the objective function would increase per unit increase in the quantity being constrained. Table 1 contains economic interpretations of the shadow prices corresponding to each group of constraints.

Since each traded good is subject to a positive lower limit, and each home good has a positive final demand, either for final consumption or for the production of other goods, all optimal output levels must be positive. Since $X_j > 0$, $\partial Z/\partial X_j = 0$ follows from the condition $(\partial Z/\partial X_j)X_j = 0$, and the first two sets of conditions in (14) are strict equalities in equilibrium. Rearranging

Table 1

Constraint	Shadow price	Definition
(1)	q_j	Optimal DVA per unit of output
(2)	w	Wage per unit of labor
(3)	c	Price per unit of capital service
(4)	u_j	Rent for one more unit of output j
(5)	v_j	Rent for one less unit of output j
(6)	π_i	Price per unit of a home good

terms,

$$p_j = \gamma_j + h_j + q_j + r_j, \qquad j = 1, \ldots, m, \tag{15}$$

$$\pi_j = \gamma_j + h_j + q_j, \qquad j = m+1, \ldots, n, \tag{16}$$

where h_j is the cost of the domestic inputs, $r_j = (u_j - v_j)$ is the rent element, q_j is the optimal domestic value added (DVA) per unit of output:

$$q_j = wl_j + ck_j. \tag{17}$$

Therefore, the price of a traded good equals the sum of the unit costs of its traded inputs (γ_j), its home good inputs (h_j), and its factor inputs (q_j) plus the net unit rent (r_j) arising from its output limits.

The imputed price for a home good (π_j) equals the unit cost of its inputs given by (16).

The eighth set of conditions in (14) states that u_j can be positive only if X_j is at its upper limit, and the ninth set states that v_j can be positive only if X_j is at its lower limit. Consequently, u_j and v_j cannot both be positive for the same good, though both can be zero. In fact, there is at least one marginal good with $r_j = 0$.

Since all primary-factor production functions are Cobb–Douglas, and all outputs are positive, positive amounts of labor and capital will be used in the production of each good. This means that third and fourth sets of (14) are also satisfied as strict equalities with

$$q_j(MPL_j) = w, \qquad j = 1, \ldots, n, \tag{18}$$

$$q_j(MPK_j) = c, \qquad j = 1, \ldots, n, \tag{19}$$

where

$$MPL_j = \partial X_j / \partial L_j = \alpha_j A_j L_j^{(\alpha_j - 1)} K_j^{(1 - \alpha_j)}, \qquad j = 1, \ldots, n$$

and

$$MPK_j = \partial X_j / \partial K_j = (1 - \alpha_j) A_j L_j^{\alpha_j} K_j^{-\alpha_j}, \qquad j = 1, \ldots, n.$$

The marginal products of each factor are always positive for Cobb–Douglas production functions. Therefore, both factors are fully utilized for optimal solutions. Consequently, optimal solutions will be on the transformation surface. Since shadow prices w and c, and marginal productivities are positive, and the partial derivatives of (14.3) and (14.4) equal zero in equilibrium, it follows that the q_js are positive.

The strict equalities in (14.7) and (14.10) will be satisfied in equilibrium since a strict inequality would entail producing and throwing away.

Utilizing (18) and (19) total factor payments for the production of good j are

$$wL_j + cK_j = q_j[\alpha_j(X_j/L_j)]L_j + q_j[(1-\alpha_j)(X_j/K_j)K_j = q_jX_j$$

which equals optimal DVA. Thus, (17) states that the whole of optimal DVA is absorbed by factor payments.

Direct unit DVA for a traded good j differs from the direct unit IVA by the cost of domestic inputs and the rent element:

$$q_j = z_j - h_j - r_j$$

which follows from (15). The q_js are always positive even though the corresponding z_js may be negative. This concept of DVA is relevant only with reference to an optimal solution.

3.4. The cost of distortions

Commodity and factor market distortions prevent a country from obtaining the maximum IVA that would be realized in the absence of such distortions. The difference between observed IVA and the optimum IVA (one obtained from the solutions of the model) provides an overall measure of the costs of distortions (or gains from relaxing distortions).[4]

In measuring the costs of distortions in the present study the following formula, defined by Henderson (1982), is employed:

$$g_j = \frac{z_j}{w\hat{l}_j^* + c\hat{k}_j^*} - 1, \tag{20}$$

where $\hat{l}_j^*$ and $\hat{k}_j^*$ respectively are the optimal direct and indirect labor and capital requirements per unit of output [see the appendix eq. (B.8)], and w and c are the shadow prices of labor and capital. g_j measures the costs of distortions (or gains) relative to the marginal good: g_j is zero for the marginal good, positive for a good with positive rent, and negative for a good with negative rent. This measure gives the number of currency units of IVA obtained per unit of expenditure for domestic factors, valued at shadow prices, in the production of traded goods.

Since the production changes indicated by optimum solutions are constrained by upper and lower limits in the present model g_j reflects the costs

---

[4]Note, however, that these costs (or gains) are static resource allocation costs (gains) of existing distortions (from removal of distortions). Due to its static nature, the model employed here cannot capture the dynamic effects of trade policy changes, such as labor displacement costs and other dynamic adjustment costs.

of distortions in relation to partial relaxation of distortions. The total costs of distortions (or gains) may be substantially understated if the distortions are relaxed completely. Nevertheless, our concern in this study is not so much to obtain the absolute measurement of costs or gains as to determine the likely shifts in the direction of resource allocation. From this point of view, g_j can be used as an indicator of direction of the said shifts when restrictions are relaxed. Therefore, ranking the sectoral production from positive g_js to negative ones will give an indication of potential competitive production structure of the country concerned under freer trade, given the assumptions of the model. Only those sectors with positive g_js will be able to compete in intra-union markets, whereas those with negative ones will require subsidy to survive.

Ranking of sectors for the applicant countries, at the same time, will give some idea as to how competitive or complementary are their economies vis-à-vis the existing EC member economies. If the sectors of those countries with positive g_js overlap to a large extent, it can be inferred that their economies are potentially competitive. If the sectors with positive g_js do not coincide substantially, they can be said to be potentially complementary, and therefore, there will be less scope for change in production and trade structures.

4. Solutions of the model

For the solution of the model the following data and parameters are required:

(1) I/O coefficients a_{ij}.
(2) International prices p_j.
(3) Labor, capital data L^0, K^0.
(4) Cobb–Douglas parameters A_j, α_j.
(5) Base year outputs X_j.
(6) Home good final demands C_i.
(7) Output constraints δ_j.

4.1. Input–output coefficients

The input–output coefficients, a_{ij}s are taken from base-year I/O tables of the countries concerned, and follow the usual I/O definition whereby the domestic price of outputs of each sector equals one.

The input–output data used are as follows:

EEC Countries:	1970 (Ireland: 1969)	44 sectors
Spain:	1975	127 sectors
Portugal:	1974	60 sectors
Greece:	1970	36 sectors
Turkey:	1973	63 sectors

The data of each country are aggregated to provide uniformity in sectoral comparisons. Uniformity in sectoral breakdown is necessitated by the fact that no sectoral comparisons can be made, with any degree of accuracy, between sectors broken down non-uniformly among countries. If, for example, one country has aggregated data for one particular sector and this sector indicates cost disadvantage (i.e., it has a negative 'g' coefficient) under the altered protective system, it cannot be inferred, a priori, that this sector has an overall disadvantage vis-a-vis the same sector of another country which has disaggregated data and shows positive 'g's for some subsectors while negative for others. Aggregation is therefore necessary for the purpose of inter-sectoral comparisons among a group of countries but it, at the same time, disguises the true competitive structure of the sector and tends to reduce the likely gains from re-allocation of resources as indicated by the solutions of the model.[5]

In some instances disaggregation was made possible by the availability of data (as in the case of the existence of more detailed I/O table of the year 1968 for the EC countries). Where data were lacking, aggregation was inevitable.

4.2. International prices

It is most probable that the applicant countries, when they join, will face the prices ruling in the Community. Thus, the EC prices enter into the model as parameters. On the other hand, it might be more interesting to investigate the case where the prices are determined by the lowest-cost producers. This implies that the applicant countries may influence the EC prices. In this case international prices should be employed in order to see where the comparative advantage of each country lies in each line of production.

In the present analysis the latter approach is employed in estimating IVAs and evaluating the resource reallocation effects of the second enlargement.

Let the domestic-currency price of a traded good be denoted by ρ_j and its international price, by p_j

$$\rho_j = (1/R)p_j(1+t_j), \qquad j=1,\ldots,m, \tag{21}$$

where t_j is the tariff rate and R is an exchange rate giving the number of units of domestic currency per dollar. By letting $R=1$ we can measure international prices in domestic currency units. Using the I/O convention of $\rho_j = 1$

$$p_j = 1/(1+t_j), \qquad j=1,\ldots,m. \tag{22}$$

[5]See table 4 and compare the gains for Turkey and Portugal estimated under different degrees of aggregation.

Ideally, implicit tariff rates should be used in (22). The implicit tariff rate provides a measure of divergence between domestic and international prices. It reflects quantitative and other non-quantitative restrictions to trade as well as tariffs. In the absence of implicit rates, nominal rates [for Turkey, calculated by Baysan (1974) and Portugal, calculated by Porto (1976)] or ratio of duty collections to imports (for other countries) were used. The use of such rates introduces an error in so far as they fail to reflect the domestic–international price differences, especially where the use of non-tariff barriers is widespread, However, due to the time constraint, implicit tariff rates could not be calculated for the countries analyzed in this study.

4.3. Labor and capital data

The information on labor and capital was obtained from the I/O data. Wage payments and employer contributions to social security are used to measure labor input, and all other value added except taxes and subsidies is used to measure capital input. This measurement rests on a troublesome assumption that the productivities of laborers are directly proportional to their wage rates. Another problem which arises in this context is that in many countries the income of the self-employed labor in agricultural sector is not taken into account in the measurement of the labor's share in the value added. This shortcoming, as well as protective interventions in factor markets may affect the results systematically, giving a bias to the results obtained in optimal solutions.

The capital data are adjusted in cases in which a capital input is negative. This is a particular problem for sectors that are run with heavy losses and subsidized by the state, such as State Economic Enterprises in Turkey. Comparable data for other sectors are used to make the capital adjustments. In other instances adjustment is required for negative capital input which results from the accounting procedures of the countries concerned.

4.4. Base-year outputs and home-good final demands

The X_j^0s are the base-year gross output levels provided by the input–output tables.

The fixed home-good final demand levels were computed from the I/O data as

$$C_i^0 = X_i^0 - \sum_{j=1}^{n} a_{ij} X_j^0, \qquad i = m+1, \dots, n. \tag{23}$$

These equal total final demands less imports as given by I/O data.

4.5. Output constraints

The coefficient δ in the eq. (4) is arbitrarily set equal to 0.25 to restrict output changes to ± 25 percent. Henderson's findings suggest reasonable variation of δ will not trigger major changes in the solution results [see Henderson (1982)].

4.6. Cobb–Douglas coefficients

On the assumption that α_j is labor's share of base-year DVA in sector j, l_j and k_j, base-year adjusted labor and capital inputs per unit of output, respectively, provide the basis for Cobb–Douglas coefficients.

$$\alpha_j = l_j/(l_j + k_j), \qquad j = 1, \ldots, n. \tag{24}$$

The A_js are determined by dividing the production function (1) by X_j and solving for A_j:

$$A_j = 1/(l_j^{\alpha_j} k_j^{(1-\alpha_j)}), \qquad j = 1, \ldots, n. \tag{25}$$

5. Optimum solutions

Results are presented in table 2. The value-added measure of labor and capital, and the resultant capital–labor ratios are not strictly comparable between countries. Differences result from different rates of remuneration for labor of capital and differences in accounting procedures employed in each country. Column (1) of table 2 contains over-all capital–labor ratios. These ratios are lower in the EC countries than they are in the applicant countries.[6] This seemingly contradictory result, i.e., the relative capital endowments of the EC countries being lower than that of the applicant countries, results from the measurement of labor in efficiency units, and reflects high rate of remuneration of the scarce factor (labor in the Community countries, and capital in the applicant countries).

Base-year capital–labor ratios are compared separately for traded and home goods in columns (2) and (3) of table 2. In Community countries K/L ratios for home goods are higher than that of traded goods. This may be explained by the high level of investments in services in the Community countries. In the applicant countries, home-goods appear to be more labor–intensive. For Turkey, a very high level of K/L ratio is the result of low

---

[6]Though Greece is already a member of the Community, it is treated together with three other applicant countries because it will take time for Greece to feel the full impact of the membership. More important than that, her economy is more similar to three applicant countries than that of the EC countries.

Table 2

Optimum solutions.

	Average K/L ratios			Rates of substitution K/L	Gain in foreign exchange (%)	Gain in traded goods consumption (%)
	All goods	Traded goods	Home goods			
Germany	0.68636	0.67172	0.70499	0.97916	2.1	2.9
France	0.71383	0.57109	0.85743	0.98879	3.1	4.3
Italy	0.76362	0.58234	0.95948	0.96816	4.8	6.4
Netherlands	0.52355	0.61314	0.45951	0.99066	2.7	4.3
Belgium	0.76466	0.64222	0.87638	0.97307	2.6	3.8
Denmark	0.56217	0.45145	0.62864	0.99422	2.5	5.0
Ireland	0.49475	0.56703	0.42665	1.00347	14.0	19.7
U.K.	0.38975	0.37072	0.40672	1.00331	5.0	7.1
Greece	1.65192	2.34363	1.27284	1.04990	3.9	5.7
Portugal	0.94132	1.16563	0.66250	0.98539	3.0	4.3
Spain	0.82627	0.94706	0.73417	0.94565	4.0	4.9
Turkey	1.66383	1.76665	4.76621	1.05761	7.8	5.3

Table 3

Optimum solutions: Change in employment (as percent of total employment).

	Greece	Spain	Portugal	Turkey
Agriculture	−0.57	1.57	2.54	3.87
Other NRB	1.07	−0.09	−0.40	−0.74
Food	0.51	0.43	0.02	0.36
Textile	−0.96	−1.10	−1.38	0.43
Other manufacture	0.89	−1.67	−0.41	−2.74
Home-goods	−0.96	0.86	−0.37	−1.18

wages and accounting procedure employed in the preparation of the I/O tables.

The model is defined so that marginal rate of substitution (MRS) between capital and labor, $-dL_j/dK_j = MPK/MPL$, for the base year equals one for each sector in each country. The optimal rates are given in column (4) of table 2. An optimal rate greater than one means that the wage rate increases more than the price of capital services, which suggests that existing factor market distortions favor use of capital relative to labor. This is the result for two Community countries (Ireland and U.K.) and for two Mediterranean countries (Greece and Turkey).

Implied changes in employment

Table 3 shows the employment changes, implied by shifts from base-year observations to optimum solutions for the four Mediterranean countries. The columns sum to zero since employment totals are the same for the base-years and the optimal solutions.

The optimal solutions indicate agricultural expansion in Spain, Portugal and Turkey, and contraction in Greece.[7] The decline of labor force in agriculture in Greece is offset by expansion of employment in other natural resource based industries, food processing, and other manufactures. A contraction of employment in textile industry is indicated in all applicant countries except Turkey. Optimum solutions also indicate a shift of employment out of manufactures in Spain, Portugal, and Turkey, while employment in the Greek manufacture expands.

6. Factor mobility

The model described above does not take into account the factor movements among countries. Factors were allowed to move only within the boundaries of each country. Formation of a customs union (or participation in an existing one) however, allows for wider freedom of movement of both labor and capital, affecting relative prices, perhaps creating a tendency toward factor-price equalization. Factor mobility is, therefore, likely to alter the optimum production and trade patterns established under restrictions. Thus, competitiveness of each industry is likely to be affected differently by the freedom of movement, depending, among others, on their relative factor intensities.

Factor mobility can be incorporated into the model in various ways. One method is to group all countries together and treat them as a single economic entity, and solve the relevant data for each country simultaneously. Another way, which is adopted in this study, is to assume certain changes in the initial factor endowments of the countries (changes are assumed to result from the factor mobility), and investigate how the resulting changes in relative prices of factors and K/L ratios affect the optimum solutions obtained under factor immobility case.

In introducing the factor mobility, the limits are (arbitrarily) set at 5 percent for labor outmigration and at 10 percent for capital inflow for the applicant countries. The same rates are assumed also for the EC countries, but with factors moving in opposite directions, i.e., capital outflow of 5 percent and labor inflow of 10 percent. The comparative results of the solutions are presented in tables 4 and A.1.[8] The output limits are adjusted by the parameter ξ in such a way as to accommodate changes in endow-

---

[7]A high expansion of agricultural employment in Turkey and a lesser degree in Portugal, indicated by the solutions may, to some extent, be attributed to the measurement difficulties of the agricultural labor force as was mentioned above.

[8]Denmark and Ireland are not included in these calculations due to the lack of data required to affect certain disaggregation.

ments as a consequence of factor mobility:

$$\xi = \frac{(1+\varepsilon)L_0 + (1+\lambda)K_0}{L_0 + K_0}, \tag{26}$$

where ε and λ are percentage changes in labor and capital, respectively.

Table 4 shows the optimum solutions both before and after the factor mobility is introduced. It is seen that when factors are allowed to move gross factor endowment K/L ratios rise for countries exporting labor and importing capital, and relative price of capital falls. Reductions in the price of capital are 19.9 percent for Greece, 13.7 percent for Spain, and 13.2 percent for Portugal. Changes in opposite direction take place in the EC countries, falls in the relative price of labor ranging between 12.6 percent in Belgium and 15.2 percent in Germany.

The gains in foreign exchange earnings and traded goods consumption are seen to have increased considerably when factor mobility is allowed for. The increase in these gains for the Mediterranean countries seem to be plausible, but those for the EC countries are too high. The reason for this may be explained by the differences in factor remunerations in the EC and the applicant countries: the higher wages in the EC countries result in lower overall K/L ratios, and ten percent labor inflow valued at these high wage rates generates a considerable increase in labor while the effect of capital outflow on the total capital endowments remains relatively low. In fact, when labor inflow limit is reduced from ten to five percent (not shown in table 4), it is found that the gains are reduced to levels comparable to those of the applicant countries.

Table A.1 shows the changes which take place after factor mobility is introduced, in competitive structures of the individual industries, competitiveness being measured by the g coefficients. Industries are ranked from the highest value of g to the lowest under factor mobility and compared with the ranking under no-factor mobility case.

It is seen that in Greece and Spain no significant changes in the competitive structure of industries take place when factors are allowed to move. This may be explained by the fact that these two countries are already open to foreign capital, and further inflow of capital will not affect the structure of the industry, given the properties of the model employed in this study.

In Portugal, one marginal sector (Other Non-Metallic Products) and one sector with negative g coefficient (Paper and Paper Products) become competitive under factor mobility. 'Iron and Steel Industry' which had negative g coefficient becomes marginal sector. 'Other Manufactures' sector which was competitive, becomes uncompetitive.

Factor mobility, in general, affects the EC countries favourably, increasing

Table 4

Optimum solutions.[a]

	No factor mobility				Factor mobility[b]			
	L	K	K/L	Δ%	L	K	K/L	Δ%
GREECE								
GFE	—	—	1.09712	—	—	—	1.27035	—
MRS	—	—	0.99281	—	—	—	1.23413	—
P_f	0.83331	0.83934	1.00724	—	0.89776	0.72455	0.80706	−19.9
E_r	—	—	—	3.9	—	—	—	8.7
C_T	—	—	—	5.7	—	—	—	12.8
SPAIN								
GFE	—	—	0.70487	—	—	—	0.81616	—
MRS	—	—	0.99985	—	—	—	1.15687	—
P_f	0.85008	0.85020	1.00014	—	0.91053	0.78706	0.86440	−13.7
E_r	—	—	—	2.9	—	—	—	4.9
C_T	—	—	—	4.2	—	—	—	6.9
PORTUGAL (46 sectors)								
GFE	—	—	0.73031	—	—	—	0.84562	—
MRS	—	—	1.04614	—	—	—	1.20550	—
P_f	0.87608	0.83744	0.95589	—	0.92424	0.76668	0.82952	−13.2
E_r	—	—	—	3.9	—	—	—	5.5
C_T	—	—	—	4.7	—	—	—	6.6
PORTUGAL (23 sectors)								
GFE	—	—	0.72336	—	—	—	0.83758	—
MRS	—	—	1.03261	—	—	—	1.17228	—
P_f	0.81743	0.79162	0.96843	—	0.84659	0.73888	0.87277	−9.9
E_r	—	—	—	2.6	—	—	—	2.1
C_T	—	—	—	3.1	—	—	—	2.5
TURKEY (36 sectors)								
GFE	—	—	1.66383	—	—	—	—	—
MRS	—	—	1.05761	—	—	—	—	—
P_f	1.02895	0.97291	—	—	—	—	—	—
E_r	—	—	—	7.8	—	—	—	—
C_T	—	—	—	5.3	—	—	—	—
TURKEY (24 sectors)								
GFE	—	—	1.51819	—	—	—	1.75791	—
MRS	—	—	1.07835	—	—	—	1.32158	—
P_f	1.02872	0.95398	0.92735	—	1.09867	0.83134	0.75668	−18.4
E_r	—	—	—	4.3	—	—	—	10.2
C_T	—	—	—	4.7	—	—	—	11.3
GERMANY								
GFE	—	—	0.64860	—	—	—	0.56015	—
MRS	—	—	0.98072	—	—	—	0.84273	—·
P_f	0.94413	0.96270	1.01967	—	0.87581	1.02919	1.17513	15.2
E_r	—	—	—	3.1	—	—	—	8.9
C_T	—	—	—	4.2	—	—	—	12.1

Table 4 (continued)

	No factor mobility				Factor mobility[b]			
	L	K	K/L	Δ%	L	K	K/L	Δ%
FRANCE								
GFE	—	—	0.69470	—	—	—	0.59997	—
MRS	—	—	0.98937	—	—	—	0.86904	—
P_f	0.98083	0.99137	1.01075	—	0.92031	1.05900	1.15070	13.8
E_r	—	—	—	3.7	—	—	—	10.9
C_T	—	—	—	5.1	—	—	—	14.9
ITALY								
GFE	—	—	0.74252	—	—	—	0.64127	—
MRS	—	—	0.97560	—	—	—	0.85572	—
P_f	0.89716	0.91960	1.02501	—	0.83518	0.97599	1.16860	14.0
E_r	—	—	—	6.1	—	—	—	12.6
C_T	—	—	—	8.1	—	—	—	16.7
THE NETHERLANDS								
GFE	—	—	0.50055	—	—	—	0.43229	—
MRS	—	—	0.98380	—	—	—	0.85691	—
P_f	0.91677	0.93187	1.01647	—	0.82095	0.95804	1.16699	14.8
E_r	—	—	—	3.2	—	—	—	13.2
C_T	—	—	—	5.1	—	—	—	20.8
BELGIUM								
GFE	—	—	0.72139	—	—	—	0.62302	—
MRS	—	—	0.98157	—	—	—	0.87202	—
P_f	0.92049	0.93777	1.01877	—	0.87839	1.00731	1.14677	12.6
E_r	—	—	—	3.4	—	—	—	10.9
C_T	—	—	—	4.8	—	—	—	15.4
UNITED KINGDOM								
GFE	—	—	0.39002	—	—	—	0.33684	—
MRS	—	—	0.99670	—	—	—	0.87125	—
P_f	1.01780	1.02576	1.00782	—	0.95224	1.09297	1.14779	13.9
E_r	—	—	—	5.2	—	—	—	15.8
C_T	—	—	—	7.4	—	—	—	22.5

[a] GFE = gross factor endowment, MRS = marginal rate of substitution, P_f = factor prices, E_r = foreign exchange earnings, C_T = Traded goods consumption.
[b] For the applicant countries: $-\Delta L = 0.05$, $+\Delta K = 0.10$; for the EC countries: $-\Delta K = 0.05$, $+\Delta L = 0.10$.

the range of their competitive industries. In Germany, Italy, Belgium and the U.K. three industries, in France four, and in the Netherlands six industries become competitive. These industries are presented in a summary form in table 5. As can be seen, there is a large degree of overlapping between the industries which are rendered competitive by the factor mobility. With the exception of 'Office and Data Machines' (in Italy) and 'Other Manufactures' (in the Netherlands) all newly competitive industries have at least one

Table 5

Sectors with improved competitiveness in the EC.

Germany	France	Italy
Other Transport Equip.	Rubber and Plastic Prod.	Metal Products
Paper and Printing	Other Transport Equip.	Office and Data Mach.
Motor Vehicles	Motor Vehicles	Electrical Goods
	Agricul. and Indus. Mach.	
The Netherlands	Belgium	United Kingdom
Leather, Footwear	Metal Products	Other Trans. Equip.
Metal Products	Textile, Clothing	Metal Prods.
Textile, Clothing	Electrical Goods	Electrical Goods
Other Manufactures		Chemicals
Agricul. and Indus. Mach.		
Rubber, Plastic		

counterpart in one or more countries. Only 'Chemicals' show an opposing performance in two countries (in Belgium and the U.K.).

To investigate the influence of factor intensities on the competitive structures of industries, two additional columns are added to the country data in table A.1. The first column indicates the K/L ratios obtained from the no-factor mobility optimum solutions. The second column shows the ranking of industries according to their intensities. These figures, when compared with the next two columns, lend themselves to the following interpretations.

In all the EC countries the most competitive industries are relatively capital intensive ones (with the exception of the 'Tobacco Industry' in Italy, which is highly labor intensive). Again, in all countries, the least competitive industries appear to be labor intensive ones (leaving aside the agricultural based industries). But there are some exceptions: 'Other Manufactures', 'Office and Data Machinery' industries in Germany, 'Products of Cooking' industry in Italy, and 'Chemicals' in the Netherlands, in Belgium and in the U.K. are capital intensive.

This observation is reinforced by the finding that when factor mobility is allowed for, the industries which benefit from these movements, i.e., those which were initially uncompetitive but become competitive, are the ones which are labor intensive (like textiles, other transport equipment, metal products, electrical goods and motor vehicles — as presented in table 5).

Spain's position is close to that of the EC countries in that its most competitive industries are capital intensive (even if the agricultural-based industries are excluded) and the least competitive ones are relatively labor intensive (again except food and dairy products). However, here the similarity ends. The industries benefiting from factor mobility are the ones which are capital intensive. One industry which is improved in competitiveness, but still remaining in the negative range, the chemicals, is highly capital-intensive (K/L: 1.263) and the other which drops from 16th to 19th place in g ranking, electrical goods, is highly labor-intensive (K/L: 0.270).

In Greece the most competitive industries are relatively labor-intensive (K/L ratio ranging between 0.484 and 1.763) except cement production. The least competitive ones are relatively capital intensive (K/L: 1.513–5.716). Two industries which benefit from capital inflow are, as expected, capital intensive. These conclusions reflect the fact that labor is still comparatively cheap in Greece.

In Portugal it is difficult to categorize the competitive industries according to their factor intensities. However, industries benefiting from the factor mobility are capital-intensive ones. 'Paper and Paper Products', 'Other Non-Metallic Products', 'Iron and Steel' are all highly capital-intensive industries. Those losing from the factor mobility are labor-intensive industries like 'Other Manufactures'. 'Ship Building and Repairs', another labor-intensive industry, drops from 11th to 17th place in g ranking.

In Turkey, one previously marginal sector (Agriculture) and two sectors with negative g coefficients ('Non-Metallic Mineral Extraction' and 'Beverages') become competitive under factor mobility. 'Ferrous and Non-Ferrous Ores' sector, which is highly labor-intensive, drops from 14th to 17th in rank.

In conclusion, if the factor movements follow the path sketched in this study, it is likely that the industries which will benefit from this movement will be labor-intensive ones in the EC and capital-intensive ones in the Mediterranean countries. This is likely to increase the competition rather than resulting in complementarity in the Community, especially where the K/L ratios show a reversal between countries. For example 'Other Manufactures' industry is labor-intensive in the Netherlands but in Greece it is capital-intensive. Likewise, 'Paper and Paper Products' industry is labor intensive in Germany, but capital intensive in Portugal. On the whole, freedom of movement of factors and increased competition resulting from the enlargement of the Community is likely to result in more efficient allocation of resources and increased welfare which is indicated by the figures on gains from foreign exchange earnings and traded goods consumption.

7. Concluding remarks

The research described here was intended to investigate the resource reallocation effects of the proposed participation to the Community of four Mediterranean countries (one of which is already a member) on their respective economies, as well as on the existing members of the EC. The solutions of the model indicate that elimination (or reduction) of restrictions on trade is likely to benefit all countries concerned through better allocation of resources. Reduction of barriers to free movement of labor and capital further increases the gains from freer trade. These gains are substantial, considering the limitations imposed on the solutions.

The model employed in this study, however, is a static one. Therefore the optimal solutions indicate only the *static* resource reallocation gains that may result from relaxation of restrictions. Furthermore, adjustment to policy changes is not costless. Ideally, the dynamic costs should also be calculated and set against the benefits. However, the model, with its static character, fails to capture these dynamic costs as well as benefits of dynamic nature. Therefore, an overall evaluation of policy changes cannot be based on the estimates of static gains alone.

A few comments on the methodology employed in the research are in order. Firstly, the model assumes constant returns to scale in production by employing Cobb–Douglas production functions in determining sectoral K/L ratios, and fixed intermediate input coefficients. This, of course, implies constant costs up to a certain output level in each industry where one (or more) constraint(s) becomes binding. With this structure, the model cannot handle the case of falling average costs, which might arise due to scale economies and lengthening of the production runs (which is so important in explaining observed intra-industry trade). Finely disaggregated production structures could be helpful in modeling the case of intra-industry trade. Unfortunately, one hardly finds detailed I/O data. In the present study the number of sectors was restricted to 36 in some cases.

Furthermore, the use of I/O tables with fixed intermediate input coefficients precludes the evaluation of changes which are likely to take place in production functions of a country following its entry in a customs union.

Thirdly, home good final demands were assumed to be constant in the solutions. In fact, elimination of barriers to trade and free movement of factors of production may alter the pattern of consumption through income and substitution effects in all countries concerned, which, by the above assumption, are ignored in this study. It is, however, possible to introduce these changes into the model to give it a more general-equilibrium character, but this would complicate the model unnecessarily while contributing little to what it reveals in its existing form.

As for the assumption employed in the analysis as regards to the free movement of labor affecting the levels of output adversely in the labor-exporting countries, it is not as contradictory as it may seem at first glance in view of the prevailing surplus of labor in these countries. There are at least two reasons why labor out-migration may strain production. First, it is generally the more progressive, more educated, and more skilled people who move across boundaries in search of better opportunities. These laborers, though usually skilled, are willing to be employed in unskilled jobs due to higher wages in the EC countries. Therefore, even if unemployment exists in the labor-exporting countries, there is a time lag involved in filling the jobs vacated by migrants with unskilled ones, during which time production is likely to be affected adversely.

Second, free movement of labor, entailed by integration of markets, will push up wage cost in the applicant countries due to several factors (e.g., harmonization of social laws, unionization, forces working in the direction of factor-price equalization on Stolper–Samuelson lines etc.). It is these effects on wage structure that was intended to be captured in the model by making the labor scarcer, hence, increasing the wage rates in the applicant countries.

International prices are difficult to estimate. Ideally they should be derived through implicit tariff rates. In the absence of such data, average tariff collection rates or nominal tariff rates were used, which are far from being satisfactory measures.

Therefore, more detailed data will undoubtedly increase the accuracy of estimations. That the level of disaggregation, for example, affects the solutions can be observed by comparing two sets of data given for Portugal and Turkey in table 4. Aggregation, by averaging the likely gains and losses, tends to reduce the extent of gains to be achieved by reallocation of productive activities.

The desirability of more detailed data also applies to employment statistics. Breakdown of labor input by skilled and unskilled categories in the solutions will shed more light to the analysis.

Taking into account these considerations and short-comings, the results of this study should be interpreted as indicative of the direction of changes, rather than that of absolute ones.

Appendix A

Table A.1

Optimum solutions

Ranking of competitive $(+g)$ and non-competitive $(-g)$ sectors in the enlarged community.

K/L coef.	Rank		Factor mobility		No factor mobility	
	K/L	g	Sector	g	Rank	g
			SPAIN 1975			
0.701	16	1	Tobacco Prods.	4.534	1	4.578
4.623	27	2	Petroleum, and Prods.	3.940	2	3.740
1.125	20	3	Meat, and Preparation	0.337	3	0.328
0.495	8	4	Radioactive Material	0.168	4	0.189
1.131	21	5	Other Food Prods.	0.164	5	0.157
1.162	22	6	Fer., Non-Fer. Ores, Met.	0.140	6	0.130
0.961	18	7	Non-Met. Min. Extr.	0.103	7	0.100

Table A.1 (continued)

K/L coef.	Rank K/L	Rank g	Factor mobility Sector	g	No factor mobility Rank	No factor mobility g
0.581	13	8	Paper, Printing Prods.	0.061	8	0.075
0.500	9	9	Agricultural Prods.	0.045	9	0.065
0.474	6	10	Timber, Wood Prods.	0.044	10	0.064
0.471	5	11	Other Trans. Equip.	0.037	11	0.058
0.542	12	12	Office, Data Mach.	0.016	12	0.032
0.495	7	13	Other Manufac. Prods.	0.013	13	0.032
1.017	19	14	Fer., Non-Fer. Met. Prods.	0.001	15	0.000
0.506	10	15	Leather, Footwear	0.000	14	0.017
1.263	24	16	Chemical Prods.	−0.025	19	−0.033
0.743	17	17	Non-Met. Min. Prods.	−0.030	17	−0.024
0.611	15	18	Rubber, Plastic Prods.	−0.042	18	−0.031
0.270	2	19	Electrical Goods	−0.049	16	−0.017
0.589	14	20	Textile, Clothing	−0.064	20	−0.052
0.302	4	21	Agricul., Indus. Mach.	−0.091	22	−0.062
0.242	1	22	Coal, Lignite	−0.093	21	−0.057
0.514	11	23	Motor Vehicles	−0.102	23	−0.086
1.231	23	24	Beverages	−0.126	25	−0.133
0.294	3	25	Met. Prods. Exc. Mach.	−0.149	24	−0.121
1.900	26	26	Prods. of Coking	−0.219	26	−0.233
1.475	25	27	Milk, Dairy Prods.	−0.234	27	−0.245
			PORTUGAL 1974			
2.157	40	1	Animal Food	0.525	1	0.470
2.099	39	2	Paper, Pulp	0.210	5	0.172
0.958	28	3	Non-Met. Min. Ext.	0.208	2	0.192
1.093	31	4	Oil, Coal, Met. Min. Ext.	0.198	3	0.177
0.912	26	5	Forestry Prods.	0.166	6	0.152
0.190	8	6	Non-Fer. Met. Prods.	0.147	4	0.175
0.445	10	7	Livestock	0.114	7	0.126
0.504	15	8	Timber, Wood	0.098	8	0.104
1.822	38	9	Edible Oils, Fats	0.081	12	0.051
0.125	4	10	Non-Electrical Mach.	0.066	9	0.102
1.476	33	11	Basic Chem. Prods.	0.066	14	0.041
2.643	44	12	Processed Fruit	0.063	15	0.021
0.127	5	13	Fishery Prods.	0.046	10	0.080
0.518	17	14	Agricultural Prods.	0.038	13	0.045
2.308	43	15	Paper, and Prods.	0.031	20	−0.008
1.496	34	16	Other Non-Met. Prods.	0.028	18	0.000
0.129	7	17	Ship Building, Repair	0.019	11	0.054
0.768	23	18	Electrical Mach.	0.017	16	0.010
2.298	42	19	Iron, Steel	0.000	23	−0.038
0.493	11	20	Printing	−0.020	21	−0.013
0.104	3	21	Other Manufac. Prods.	−0.028	17	0.006
0.507	16	22	Cork	−0.029	22	−0.024
1.275	32	23	Cotton Textiles	−0.039	24	−0.060
0.064	1	24	Footwear	−0.042	19	−0.006
2.169	41	25	Transport Equip.	−0.062	25	−0.096
0.976	29	26	Hard Fibre Textiles	−0.098	28	−0.108
0.715	21	27	Woolen Textiles	−0.103	27	−0.106

Table A.1 (continued)

K/L coef.	Rank K/L	g	Factor mobility Sector	g	No factor mobility Rank	g
0.499	13	28	Clothing	−0.118	31	−0.113
0.494	12	29	Ink, Paint, Varnishes	−0.118	30	−0.113
0.256	9	30	Hides, Tanning	−0.127	29	−0.111
0.129	6	31	Metal Prods.	−0.132	26	−0.104
0.578	19	32	Other Chemical Prods.	−0.132	32	−0.131
0.555	18	33	Furniture, Mattresses	−0.155	33	−0.153
1.514	35	34	Resinous Prods.	−0.155	34	−0.170
0.739	22	35	Glass, and Prods.	−0.194	35	−0.198
0.894	25	36	Rubber Prods.	−0.235	36	−0.243
0.071	2	37	Non-Edible Oils, Fats	−0.291	37	−0.275
1.710	37	38	Cement	−0.303	38	−0.322
1.061	30	39	Petroleum, Coal Prods.	−0.411	39	−0.417
0.651	20	40	Plastic Material	−0.441	40	−0.442
0.883	24	41	Other Food Prods.	−0.463	41	−0.468
3.222	45	42	Meat, and Prods.	−0.506	42	−0.529
1.516	36	43	Beverages	−1.264	43	−1.258
0.952	27	44	Milk, Dairy Prods.	−1.679	44	−1.671
0.503	14	45	Tobacco	−1.703	45	−1.707
			GREECE 1970			
1.403	12	1	Tobacco	0.526	1	0.453
1.617	15	2	Leather Prods.	0.435	2	0.348
1.763	19	3	Food Prods.	0.427	4	0.338
0.940	4	4	Non-Electrical Mach.	0.396	3	0.347
3.864	25	5	Cement	0.325	8	0.214
1.125	7	6	Printing, Publishing	0.321	6	0.261
1.348	11	7	Footwear	0.309	7	0.237
0.484	2	8	Mining, Quarrying	0.293	5	0.289
4.524	26	9	Basic Metal Prods.	0.278	9	0.168
1.570	14	10	Other Chemical Prods.	0.228	10	0.155
1.199	9	11	Metal Prods.	0.191	11	0.136
1.253	10	12	Paper, and Prods.	0.139	12	0.086
0.999	6	13	Const. Mat., Non-Met. Prods.	0.103	14	0.061
0.978	5	14	Rubber Prods.	0.095	15	0.055
1.143	8	15	Electrical Mach.	0.084	16	0.038
0.346	1	16	Transport Equip.	0.050	13	0.062
1.635	16	17	Other Manufac. Prods.	0.007	18	−0.055
1.713	18	18	Basic Chemical Prods.	0.000	19	−0.056
0.496	3	19	Agricultural Prods.	0.000	17	0.000
2.785	23	20	Wood Prods.	−0.018	21	−0.096
1.664	17	21	Textiles	−0.018	20	−0.075
2.157	21	22	Furniture	−0.069	22	−0.137
1.513	13	23	Glass, Glassware	−0.166	23	−0.213
1.802	20	24	Plastic Prods.	−0.176	24	−0.227
2.841	24	25	Beverages	−0.255	25	−0.313
2.174	22	26	Clothing	−0.484	26	−0.522
5.716	27	27	Petroleum Prods.	−2.956	27	−2.764

Table A.1 (continued)

| K/L | Rank | | Factor mobility | | No factor mobility | |
coef.	K/L	g	Sector	g	Rank	g
			TURKEY 1974			
1.867	15	1	Other Food Prods.	0.829	1	0.709
0.583	4	2	Other Manufactures	0.716	2	0.643
2.333	19	3	Tobacco	0.335	3	0.237
2.345	20	4	Meat, and Prods.	0.188	4	0.091
0.565	3	5	Agricultural Prods.	0.009	5	0.000
0.781	7	6	Non-Met. Mineral Extrac.	0.005	6	−0.032
0.830	9	7	Beverages	0.000	8	−0.046
0.816	8	8	Textile, Clothing	−0.005	7	−0.050
1.488	11	9	Non-Electrical Mach.	−0.015	9	−0.072
3.021	22	10	Leather, Footwear	−0.147	11	−0.217
0.666	6	11	Non-Met. Mineral Prods.	−0.165	10	−0.201
2.184	18	12	Agricultural Mach.	−0.175	12	−0.237
1.593	13	13	Chemicals	−0.276	13	−0.322
1.548	12	14	Wood, Furniture	−0.295	15	−0.339
1.648	14	15	Motor Vehicles	−0.315	16	−0.359
12.533	23	16	Petroleum, Coal Prods.	−0.319	18	−0.395
0.249	1	17	Fer., Non-Fer. Ores	−0.349	14	−0.339
0.249	2	18	Coal Mining	−0.370	17	−0.360
1.943	17	19	Electrical Mach.	−0.427	19	−0.466
1.073	10	20	Paper, and Prods.	−0.483	20	−0.509
1.925	16	21	Fer., Non-Fer. Met. Prods.	−0.572	22	−0.602
0.642	5	22	Other Transport Equip.	−0.580	21	−0.587
2.599	21	23	Rubber, Plastic	−0.902	23	−0.909
			GERMANY 1970			
2.516	26	1	Fer., Non-Fer. Met., Ores	15.627	1	15.463
0.904	20	2	Petroleum, and Prods.	1.762	2	1.734
0.763	17	3	Non-Met. Min. Ext.	1.437	3	1.403
0.511	9	4	Non-Met. Min. Prods.	1.425	4	1.372
2.178	25	5	Tobacco Prods.	0.916	5	0.940
0.677	14	6	Fer., Non-Fer. Met. Prods.	0.165	6	0.146
1.032	22	7	Other Food Prods.	0.104	7	0.098
0.666	13	8	Timber, Wood Prods.	0.102	8	0.083
0.456	6	9	Leather, Footwear	0.072	10	0.044
0.436	5	10	Textile, Clothing	0.065	13	0.035
0.725	16	11	Chemical Prods.	0.056	11	0.041
0.778	18	12	Coal, Lignite	0.051	12	0.038
1.314	24	13	Meat, and Prep.	0.050	9	0.050
0.070	1	14	Other Transport Equip.	0.040	19	−0.019
0.552	10	15	Rubber, Plastic Prods.	0.033	14	0.010
0.422	4	16	Metal Prods. exc. Mach.	0.030	16	0.000
0.588	11	17	Prods. of Coking	0.029	15	0.009
0.868	19	18	Paper, Printing	0.001	17	−0.008
0.481	7	19	Motor Vehicles	0.000	20	−0.026
0.716	15	20	Other Manufactures	−0.003	18	−0.018
0.177	2	21	Electrical Goods	−0.006	23	−0.051
0.601	12	22	Office, Data Mach.	−0.015	21	−0.035
0.397	3	23	Agri., Indust. Mach.	−0.018	22	−0.049
1.005	21	24	Milk, Dairy Prods.	−0.080	24	−0.086
1.265	23	25	Beverages	−0.160	25	−0.159
0.490	8	26	Agricul., Forestry	−0.164	26	−0.186

Okan H. Aktan

Table A.1 (continued)

K/L coef.	Rank K/L	Rank g	Factor mobility Sector	g	No factor mobility Rank	No factor mobility g
			FRANCE 1970			
0.410	13	1	Fer., Non-Fer. Ores, Met.	37.709	1	36.814
0.415	14	2	Tobacco Prods.	3.671	2	3.590
0.961	24	3	Petroleum, and Prods.	1.955	3	1.952
0.748	22	4	Non-Met. Min. Ext.	1.371	4	1.354
0.601	21	5	Non-Met. Min. Prods.	1.267	5	1.241
0.516	18	6	Meat, and Prep.	0.653	6	0.631
2.536	26	7	Beverages	0.280	7	0.308
0.375	10	8	Leather, Footwear	0.160	9	0.133
1.281	25	9	Other Food Prods.	0.134	8	0.142
0.445	15	10	Timber, Wood Prods.	0.120	10	0.099
0.525	19	11	Fer., Non-Fer. Met. Prods.	0.104	11	0.089
0.259	5	12	Electrical Goods	0.078	12	0.045
0.323	8	13	Met. Prods. exc. Mach.	0.057	14	0.028
0.450	16	14	Paper, Printing	0.050	13	0.032
0.382	11	15	Textile, Clothing	0.047	15	0.023
0.293	6	16	Other Manufactures	0.029	16	0.000
0.323	7	17	Rubber, Plastic Prods.	0.013	17	−0.014
0.206	2	18	Other Transport Equip.	0.010	18	−0.024
0.206	1	19	Motor Vehicles	0.005	20	−0.029
0.328	9	20	Agri., Indust. Mach.	0.000	19	−0.027
0.386	12	21	Office, Data Mach.	−0.025	21	−0.048
0.495	17	22	Agricul., Forestry	−0.041	22	−0.060
0.588	20	23	Chemical Prods.	−0.050	23	−0.062
0.805	23	24	Milk, Dairy Prods.	−0.101	24	−0.105
0.226	3	25	Coal, Lignite	−0.137	26	−0.167
0.226	4	26	Prods. of Coking	−0.138	25	−0.168
			ITALY 1970			
0.285	7	1	Fer., Non-Fer., Ores, Met.	73.786	1	70.864
0.081	1	2	Tobacco Prods.	14.613	2	13.755
1.665	26	3	Petroleum, and Prods.	3.749	3	3.778
0.640	18	4	Non-Met. Min. Prods.	1.820	4	1.772
0.405	10	5	Non-Met. Min. Ext.	1.389	5	1.320
0.814	22	6	Milk, Dairy Prods.	0.528	6	0.511
0.577	17	7	Fer., Non-Fer. Met. Prods.	0.171	7	0.151
0.709	19	8	Other Food Prods.	0.152	8	0.136
0.483	12	9	Chemical Prods.	0.147	9	0.121
0.524	15	10	Other Manufactures	0.111	11	0.086
0.505	14	11	Rubber, Plastic Prods.	0.098	13	0.073
0.454	11	12	Paper, Printing Prods.	0.097	14	0.070
1.010	24	13	Timber, Wood Prods.	0.096	10	0.090
0.774	20	14	Leather, Footwear	0.089	12	0.075
0.252	5	15	Coal, Lignite	0.087	16	0.043
1.134	25	16	Meat, and Prep.	0.061	15	0.057
0.545	16	17	Textile, Clothing	0.051	17	0.029
0.152	3	18	Motor Vehicles	0.048	18	0.000
0.375	9	19	Met. Prods. exc. Mach.	0.019	19	−0.011
0.369	8	20	Office, Data Mach.	0.019	20	−0.012
0.242	4	21	Electrical Goods	0.000	21	−0.039
0.271	6	22	Agricul., Indus. Mach.	−0.021	22	−0.055
0.088	2	23	Other Transport Equip.	−0.064	23	−0.112
0.488	13	24	Agricul. Forestry	−0.212	24	−0.231
0.793	21	25	Beverages	−0.300	25	−0.308
0.989	23	26	Prods. of Coking	−2.384	26	−2.374

Table A.1 (continued)

K/L coef.	Rank K/L	Rank g	Factor mobility Sector	g	No factor mobility Rank	No factor mobility g
			THE NETHERLANDS 1970			
0.570	15	1	Non-Met. Min. Ext.	3.734	1	3.456
0.614	17	2	Tobacco Prods.	1.789	2	1.630
0.925	20	3	Non-Met. Min. Prods.	0.824	3	0.738
4.111	24	4	Petroleum, and Prods.	0.660	4	0.647
0.492	11	5	Agricul., Forestry	0.138	6	0.067
0.474	10	6	Motor Vehicles	0.137	7	0.065
0.416	8	7	Timber, Wood Prods.	0.122	9	0.047
0.672	19	8	Other Food Prods.	0.120	8	0.058
1.196	23	9	Beverages	0.109	5	0.067
0.345	5	10	Paper, Printing Prods.	0.076	11	0.000
0.152	1	11	Leather, Footwear	0.070	13	−0.020
1.136	22	12	Fer., Non-Fer. Met. Prods.	0.068	10	0.024
0.392	6	13	Met. Prods. exc. Mach.	0.056	12	−0.016
0.175	2	14	Textile, Clothing	0.027	15	−0.057
0.517	13	15	Other Manufactures	0.020	14	−0.042
0.399	7	16	Agri., Indust. Mach.	0.011	16	−0.058
0.452	9	17	Rubber, Plastic Prods.	0.000	18	−0.065
0.642	18	18	Milk, Dairy Prods.	−0.004	17	−0.060
0.288	4	19	Other Trans. Equip.	−0.022	20	−0.095
1.071	21	20	Chemical Prods.	−0.048	19	−0.088
0.594	16	21	Electrical Goods	−0.054	21	−0.108
0.495	12	22	Office, Data Mach.	−0.079	22	−0.136
0.228	3	23	Coal, Lignite	−0.091	23	−0.163
0.521	14	24	Meat, and Prep.	−0.168	24	−0.219
			BELGIUM 1970			
1.569	24	1	Petroleum, and Prods.	5.843	1	5.999
0.563	17	2	Non-Met. Min. Ext.	3.149	2	3.139
0.501	16	3	Non-Met. Min. Prods.	0.706	3	0.700
0.410	10	4	Tobacco Prods.	0.614	4	0.601
0.587	18	5	Milk, Dairy Prods.	0.400	5	0.399
0.115	3	6	Other Trans. Equip.	0.137	8	0.104
0.394	7	7	Motor Vehicles	0.132	7	0.122
0.443	12	8	Prods. of Coking	0.127	6	0.126
0.357	4	9	Paper, Printing Prods.	0.055	9	0.043
0.462	13	10	Other Manufactures	0.036	10	0.030
0.739	20	11	Fer., Non-Fer. Met. Prods.	0.023	11	0.028
0.366	5	12	Leather, Footwear	0.013	16	0.002
0.849	22	13	Timber, Wood Prods.	0.011	12	0.019
0.439	11	14	Rubber, Plastic Prods.	0.009	15	0.002
0.377	6	15	Met. Prods. exc. Mach.	0.005	18	−0.006
0.396	8	16	Textile, Clothing	0.003	19	−0.006
0.399	9	17	Electrical Goods	0.002	20	−0.009
0.861	23	18	Other Food Prods.	0.000	14	0.008
0.772	21	19	Chemical Prods.	−0.006	17	0.000
3.859	25	20	Meat, and Prep.	−0.021	13	0.017
0.001	1	21	Office, Data Mach.	−0.024	22	−0.055
0.488	14	22	Agri. Indus. Mach.	−0.047	21	−0.052
0.491	15	23	Agricul. Forestry	−0.130	23	−0.134
0.065	2	24	Coal, Lignite	−0.254	24	−0.279
0.720	19	25	Beverages	−0.426	25	−0.424

Okan H. Aktan

Table A.1 (continued)

K/L coef.	Rank K/L	Rank g	Factor mobility Sector	g	No factor mobility Rank	No factor mobility g
			UNITED KINGDOM 1970			
1.088	23	1	Fer., Non-Fer. Ores, Met.	125.906	1	125.541
1.459	25	2	Petroleum, and Prods.	7.529	2	7.523
1.117	24	3	Tobacco Prods.	6.318	3	6.262
0.237	11	4	Non-Met. Min. Prods.	3.314	4	3.156
2.075	26	5	Beverages	1.593	5	1.609
0.332	18	6	Non-Met. Min. Ext.	0.931	6	0.871
0.325	15	7	Other Manufactures	0.468	7	0.420
0.192	4	8	Leather, Footwear	0.285	8	0.232
0.199	5	9	Textile, Clothing	0.154	10	0.108
0.329	17	10	Other Food Prods.	0.152	9	0.116
0.217	9	11	Timber, Wood Prods.	0.143	11	0.098
0.644	21	12	Prods. of Coking	0.105	12	0.083
0.347	19	13	Paper, Printing Prods.	0.101	13	0.067
0.210	6	14	Fer., Non-Fer. Met. Prods.	0.098	14	0.058
0.292	13	15	Milk, Dairy Prods.	0.089	15	0.053
0.037	1	16	Other Trans. Equip.	0.056	19	−0.003
0.051	2	17	Motor Vehicles	0.056	17	0.001
0.118	3	18	Coal, Lignite	0.053	16	0.002
0.216	8	19	Met. Prods. exc. Mach.	0.040	18	0.000
0.236	10	20	Electrical Goods	0.029	20	−0.011
0.655	22	21	Chemical Prods.	0.000	21	−0.018
0.300	14	22	Meat, and Prep.	−0.005	22	−0.037
0.326	16	23	Rubber, Plastic Prods.	−0.015	23	−0.047
0.215	7	24	Office, Data Mach.	−0.020	24	−0.059
0.242	12	25	Agri., Indus. Mach.	−0.058	25	−0.093
0.496	20	26	Agricul., Forestry	−0.103	26	−0.125

Appendix B: Mathematical properties of the model

In this appendix derivation of some of the equations used in the text is given.

B.1. The input–output balance equation is

$$X = AX + C, \tag{B.1}$$

where X and C are n-component row vectors of output and final consumption levels respectively, and A is an $(n \times n)$ matrix of input–output coefficients with typical element a_{ij}. Partitioning (B.1) into international and home good blocks,

$$\begin{pmatrix} X_T \\ X_H \end{pmatrix} = \begin{bmatrix} A_{TT} & A_{TH} \\ A_{HT} & A_{HH} \end{bmatrix} \begin{pmatrix} X_T \\ X_H \end{pmatrix} + \begin{pmatrix} C_T \\ C_H \end{pmatrix}, \tag{B.2}$$

where the subscript T designates the m international goods and the subscript H designates the $(n-m)$ home goods. By block multiplication

$$X_T = A_{TT}X_T + A_{TH}X_H + C_T,$$
$$X_H = A_{HT}X_T + A_{HH}X_H + C_H. \tag{B.3}$$

Solving (A.3) for home goods outputs,

$$X_H = (I - A_{HH})^{-1}A_{HT}X_T + (I - A_{HH})^{-1}C_H \tag{B.4}$$

which is the same as eq. (6) in the text. The coefficient k_i is the ith element of the matrix product $(I - A_{HH})^{-1}C_H$, and σ_{ij} is an element of the $[(m-n) \times m]$ matrix product $(I - A_{HH})^{-1}A_{HT}$. The coefficient μ_{ij} is an element of the home goods inverse matrix $(I - A_{HH})^{-1}$.

B.2. Rewriting eq. (9) in matrix terms

$$V = P_T X_T - \Gamma_T X_T - \Gamma_H X_H, \tag{B.5}$$

where P_T is an m component row vector of international prices, and Γ_T and Γ_H are row vectors containing the γ coefficients for international and home goods respectively. Substituting for X_H from (B.4)

$$V = [P_T - \Gamma_T - \Gamma_H (I - A_{HH})^{-1}A_{HT}]X_T - \Gamma_H (I - A_{HH})^{-1}C_H \tag{B.6}$$

which is the same as (10). The square bracketed term on the right is an m component vector of the $\hat{z}_j$ coefficients, and K equals the second term on the right. The b_j are given by the vector $\Gamma_H (I - A_{HH})^{-1}A_{HT}$.

B.3. Let L_T^* and L_H^* be vectors of labor services per unit of output coefficients that correspond to an optimal solution. Let W denote total labor service use so that

$$W = L_T^*H_T + L_H^*X_H. \tag{B.7}$$

Substituting from (B.4),

$$W = [L_T^* + L_H^*(I - A_{HH})^{-1}A_{HT}]X_T + L_H^*(I - A_{HH})^{-1}C_H. \tag{B.8}$$

The square bracketed term on the right is a vector of the $\hat{l}_j^*$ used in (20). The second term on the right is the quantity of labor service used to support the home goods final demands. A similar derivation is applicable for capital service coefficients.

References

Baysan, T., 1974, Economic implications of Turkey's entry into the common market, Ph.D. dissertation (University of Minnesota, Minneapolis, MN).

Henderson, James M., 1982, Optimal factor allocations for thirteen countries, in: A.O. Krueger, ed., Trade and employment in developing countries, 2: Factor supply and substitution (University of Chicago Press, Chicago, IL).

Porto, M., 1976, Tariff structure and tariff policy in Portugal, thesis submitted for a B.Phil. degree in economics (University of Oxford, Oxford).

Statistical Documents

EUROSTAT, 1978, Input-output tables, The nine and the community, Special series 9 (Luxembourg).

Instituto de Estudios de Planificacion, 1975, Tablas input-output de la economia Espanola, 1970 (Madrid).

Fondo para la Investigacion Economica y Social de la Confederacion Espanola de Cajas de Ahorros, 1979, La estructura productiva Espanola, Tablas input-output de 1975 y analisis de las interdependencias de la economia Espanola (Madrid).

Ministry of Coordination – National Account Service, Centre of Planning and Economic Research, 1978, Input-output table of the Greek economy, 1970 (Athens).

Grupo de Estudos Basicos de Economia Industrial (GEBEI), 1978, Sistema de matrices (60 × 60), 1979 (Lisbon).

State Institute of Statistics, 1973, Inter-industry transactions matrix of Turkey (Ankara).

The Effect of Trade on Plant Size

Jürgen Müller and Nicholas Owen
with the assistance of Ursula Schulz

1. INTRODUCTION

The fact that a country, region, or town can improve the material living standards of its citizens through trade has been recognized for centuries, for trade is simply the geographical dimension of the phenomenon which drives all economies—specialization. How these material benefits can be calculated in a convincing way, in general, or in regard to a particular component of trade is the main question which concerns this study of some German manufacturing industries.

When tariffs, quotas, and other barriers to international trade are removed, we would expect trade to expand due to the substitution of imports from lower-cost partners for higher-cost domestic production. The most extensive literature on these effects relates to the European Community, covering mainly the period from the Community's formation to 1970 or thereabouts. Many of the earlier studies were predictive in nature: that is, they estimated the extent to which the removal of internal tariffs within the Community (and of changes in tariffs on imports from Third Countries implied by the adoption by all members of the Common external tariff) would affect trade, using the knowledge then available of the sensitivity of trade to price changes. They could not reflect any progress which the Community was able to achieve in reducing non-tariff barriers. As more statistics on Community trade became available, it was natural that studies on this theme should attempt to compare the actual trade patterns with the hypothetical pattern which would have occurred in the absence of the Community—the so called 'anti-monde'.

Reviewing this literature, Mayes (1978) was able to conclude that 'it is clear after such a wealth of research that the bounds of magnitude have been established for the effects of EC-integration on trade [in manufactures] . . . the range for 1970 is approximately $8 billion to $15 billion' (p. 20). A component of this additional trade represented trade diversion—switching from non-Community suppliers to Community suppliers as a result of the preference accorded to the latter. To some extent the misallocation of resources associated with this diversion was offset by the benefits of external trade creation attributable to the fact that the Community's common external tariffs were on the whole lower than some members' pre-Community tariffs. But the bulk of the additional trade represented internal trade creation—the substitution of imports from

Community partners in place of domestic production. A consensus view is that trade creation in 1970 accounted for around $10 billion of the additional trade, a figure equivalent to 30 per cent of the $33 billion intra-Community trade in manufactures for that year.

This conclusion is an important step, but it does not tell us how important these increases in trade are, in terms of their economic benefits. The levels of tariffs which were imposed prior to the Community's formation are not a reliable guide because one cannot infer, from a tariff alone the magnitude of the domestic industry's response to its removal. At one extreme, there may be no response. The removal of the tariff causes substitution of foreign for domestic products. At the other extreme, the domestic industry might respond to the threat of imports by improving its efficiency, reducing its unit costs by the full extent of the tariff. In this case, imports would hardly increase at all, but the efficiency gains would be substantial and lasting. We need a linkage which relates trade flows to industrial performance if we are to comment on the significance of trade creation effects.

The approach adopted below follows a line of analysis developed by Scherer *et al.* (1975) and Owen (1976 and 1983), namely, an industry-based statistical analysis which has been shown to be capable of establishing the size and direction of the effects of trade on industrial structure, and vice-verse, taking into account economies of scale. Although these were identified by Meade (1955) as being central to the analysis of trade, their significance has not been fully explored. This approach ignores macro-economic phenomena, such as changes in the terms of trade resulting from the development of trade. It makes no attempt to trace the linkages through the German economy of any of the changes in industrial structures which may be identified.

2. THE ANALYTICAL FRAMEWORK

How do industries respond to the development of international trade? Trade offers, at the same time, threats and opportunities—the threat of extinction in the face of superior competitors permitted unrestricted access to the domestic market and the opportunity to expand into new markets. Most individuals would make efforts to improve their performance if faced with such a widening in the structure of incentives and penalties. It would be surprising if companies, or indeed any organization, did not do likewise. There is no need for a sophisticated economic theory to be able to understand the connection between the exposure to foreign competition and improved performance.

The form which this response may take is not intuitively obvious; still less is the way in which its value can be measured. What is 'performance'? How is it to be measured? Productivity looks a plausible candidate, except that trade itself moderates the prices which producers can charge. A producer who previously registered a substantial value-added per employee, or per DM of capital invested, in a cosy, profitable, and protected domestic market might have to perform better in open competition just to sustain this performance.

In this study we have decided to address the question of performance in an indirect way, by considering *changes in industries' structures*. Most manufacturing processes are subject to economies of scale. For any technology there is a minimum efficient technical scale (METS) which exhausts these economies. The higher the responsiveness of cost with respect to scale, i.e. the faster the cost curve falls, the larger will be the gains from specialization. The more closely an industry's representative plant size approaches this METS, the lower the industry's unit costs will be. An index of the representative plant size provides one reliable and visible index of an industry's performance. Not only are an industry's plant sizes ascertainable, but so too are the parameters of economies of scale—the unit cost gradient and the METS at which unit cost ceases to decline. There are, of course, other sources of inefficiency which are unrelated to sub-optimal plant size—working practices for example; but it would be surprising to find that an industry which organized its resources into configurations of plants which approached METS in size proved deficient in these other respects too.

Although we use plant size as the basic measure of scale we also consider the firm rather than the plant as the relevant dimension in industries such as cars, tractors, and trucks, which embrace several stages of production. We have to recognize, too, that scale is not always a crucial factor in business. Higher-quality products may have secured a market niche for themselves, which allows them to be produced in smaller plants at higher costs. Consequently, different size-classes of plants producing a similar product coexist side by side and survive quite profitably, each serving some subset of the market to which its special attributes are best adapted.

There is therefore, in principle, also a trade-off between greater product variety and cost minimization for a given production technology. But this technology is not a fixed constraint. It is open to the management to design their way around it, by building into their product components with a high degree of commonality (the 'Baukasten' principle, or 'Meccano set' approach). Plant size and lot size can interact. A manufacturer who moves to higher total volume while at the same time designing a greater commonality of components, will succeed in *compounding* their effects to achieve a greater effective increase in scale than might be indicated by the increase in plant size alone.

The pioneering study of the factors which determine industrial structures was that by Scherer and colleagues (1975). The most significant results which emerge from Scherer's study are, first, that *domestic* market size had an important effect on plant sizes; this factor helped to explain why American plants were larger than the European plants in general, and larger than Germany's plants in particular. Second, and linked to this first result, was the finding that the enlargement of an industry's market through *trade* allowed the scale of an industry's typical operating units to increase. These effects were not found to be offset by imports: import penetration did not cause plant size to shrink (even though the number of plants may be reduced). These two findings, taken together, suggest that the expansion of German trade has pulled up the size of the representative plant in German industries, the more so in industries which participated actively in this trade, and less so in industries which, for one reason or another, participated in trade to only a marginal degree. Trade and structural change are likely to be closely linked in those industries in which the domestic market, measured in terms of METS plants it can support, is small.

Domestic market size itself should be conducive to METS operation: if each producer is content to retain his accustomed share of the domestic market, and looks for market growth to provide room for new capacity, for a given growth in the market there is more room for efficient-sized increments of capacity, if the market size is larger. Scherer *et al.* (1975, p. 93) showed that the trade-off between carrying excess capacity when new plants are first introduced and achieving lower unit costs through economies of scale will tend to favour large plants when the absolute size of the market is larger, given an independently determined growth rate of demand and willingness on the part of the producer to accept his accustomed share of the market.

This approach is sound as far as it goes; that is, if one accepts the assumption that producers are typically passive with respect to market shares, both in the domestic market and neighbouring markets. Some industry leaders have been governed by a 'spheres of influence' mentality which inhibits them from invading neighbouring markets for fear of provoking retaliation which would disturb the equilibrium in their domestic market. But we are not convinced that this typifies European business, for if it did, how could intra-EC trade in manufacturers have grown as fast as it did? The 'spheres of influence' mentality is a manifestation of oligopolistic behaviour, and would therefore be expected to be associated with high industrial concentration of ownership. If it were a powerful inhibiting factor one would expect to find that intra-EC trade was lower in relation to manufacturing output in those industries where industrial concentration was highest. Owen (1983, p. 99) found that the reverse was the case: that intra-EC trade for most manufacturing industries was positively (though weakly) related to industrial concentration. Thus, except in industries dominated by nationalistic public purchasing behaviour, which severely inhibits trade, we would not expect to find producers motivated only by a desire to retain their market shares. We therefore thought it relevant to consider, as a theroetic underpinning to this study, the economics of aggressive business behaviour as a means of finding room for larger and more economic plants.

An approach of this kind has been developed by Owen (1983) which takes as its starting point the familiar observation that in most industries, plants of different sizes, and hence of different unit costs, coexist within the same industry. Clearly, there are limits to the extent to which aggressive producers are prepared to reduce prices and drive out smaller, high-cost competitors, in order to find room for METS plants. Those limits are determined by the temporary losses which would be incurred in that period in which the smaller, less efficient producers resist this pressure. If these losses outweigh the eventual gains in profit associated with larger market shares and lower unit costs, the aggressive producer will hold back. But what is of particular interest to us in this study is the way in which the opening up of the Community and other markets for German producers may change the balance of argument in favour of more aggressive behaviour on the part of leading German producers. International trade accelerates structural change because it allows industry leaders a greater range of profitable opportunities to displace high-cost producers at home *and* abroad. If the expansionist producer was confined to its own domestic market and was looking to find room for a particular increment of capacity it would have to calculate the price reduction necessary to drive out competitors who occupied market shares needed for new increment of capacity. The larger the increment, the larger the price reductions. The least efficient producers in the industry, living at the margin of existence, could be expected to retire, once their capacity had exhausted its useful life, in response to quite modest reductions in price. More efficient producers would withdraw only if the price reduction was substantial. The advantage of exporting in this context is that the aggressive producer need not reduce price by the more substantial amount necessary to drive out the moderately efficient domestic producer. Supposing similar cost structures abroad, neighbouring markets will provide sufficient high-cost 'targets' which, together with those in the domestic industry, can provide sufficient market space for an increment of low cost capacity achieved with the minimal reduction in price.

This approach forms our expectations about structural change. We expect to find that the leading producers in those German manufacturing industries which expanded through exporting will increase their share of the domestic market through the elimination of smaller German producers. We would be prepared to attribute some part of the structural change of the German industry to the expansion of German exports since, as has been explained above, it is the economics of expanding on two fronts at once which is so much more favourable than expanding at the expense of domestic producers alone. This proposition is supported by an interesting finding of the Scherer study. Scherer *et al.* (1975) found that the representative plant size in an industry (measured in relation to the METS for the manufacturing technology concerned) responded very sensitively to the export performance of the industry: 'Of special interest are the high multiplicative export elasticities, suggesting that if exports increase from say 10 to 20 percent of domestic production, the average observed size of the Top 50 percent plant rises by approximately 35 percent' (p. 120). This increase could not have been accounted for by increased export sales by themselves even if the largest plant possible had been constructed for this purpose alone. The sensitivity of the change in representative plant size to export performance could only have been accounted for by the *displacement* of smaller plants in the exporter's own industry, taking place at the same time as the drive towards export markets.

The converse of Scherer's market size argument is that those German industries which have been exposed to increasing import penetration have less room to built efficient plants. But there may be dynamic effects which offset the loss of efficiency due to smaller plants. Producers in industries affected by imports are unlikely to stand idly by, observing the elimination of their fellow competitors, for how could they be sure that it was not their turn next? Import penetration must improve performance among the *survivors*, which may include structural changes in the direction of larger, more efficient plants. It may have the reverse effect—encouraging German producers to exploit their comparative advantage, produce higher-quality products, in smaller plants.

In summary, the benefits which Germany has derived from trade in general but in particular from intra-Community trade need therefore to be calculated in (at least) two dimensions: the reallocation of her resources away from industries in which Germany suffers a comparative disadvantage and towards those industries in which she enjoys a comparative advantage (e.g. away from textiles towards engineering); and also on the basis of reallocation of resources *within* industries, away from smaller, less-efficient plants towards larger, more-efficient plants, in a process by which the leading producers in export-oriented industries find room for larger, low-cost capacity.

We are not attributing all structural changes to trade. Far from it; we recognize, for example, that in some industries, such as footwear, the METS is so small in relation to the size of the domestic market that it is easily achievable without trade at all. Eastman and Stykolt (1967) suggested that if the size of the domestic market exceeds the METS by a factor of 15 or more, trade would be unlikely to have an effect on industry structure.

With these qualifications in mind, we investigated a simplified version of Scherer's model applied to Germany alone. We undertook the following steps:

1. Considered the manufacturing technology in each of 12 industries (see Table 3), to discover the METS necessary to exploit the available economies of scale (and how it may have changed with the advent of new technologies), and second, the rate at which unit costs fall as small

increases, i.e. the scale penalty associated with lower than METS output.

2. Examined the evolution of the plant size structure of each industry over the period 1960 to 1980. Attention focused on the representative plant size, measured in this study as the average size of the largest plants which account for 50 per cent of an industry's output—the cumulative average plant size (CAPS).

3. Considered the development of international trade to assess whether, and to what extent, there appears to be an association between this development and changes in the industries' structures.

4. Where such changes can be identified, the studies attempt to estimate the resource savings involved on the basis of the unit cost gradients estimated at stage (1) above.

The sample of industries chosen was a small one, but embraced a variety of industries: new and old industries, capital- and labour-intensive sectors, and consumer and producer goods. In all of the industries covered, trade played a role, but trade patterns varied significantly between the various industries. Space considerations do not allow us to report the findings of the industry studies in detail here, but the results of an analysis of the sample as a whole are of interest.

3. STATISTICAL RESULTS

We attempted to explain representative plant sizes in our sample, as a proportion of METS, in terms of four variables:

1. Domestic market size (C):
    Consumption of the product in question, divided by the METS for the industry concerned.

2. Cost Gradient (k):
    The cost penalty at one-third METS.

3. Exports (X):
    1 + Exports/production.

4. Imports (M):
    1 − Imports/consumption.

Like Scherer, we considered a multiplicative relationship between the variables:

$$\frac{Representative\ plant\ size}{\text{METS}} = A \ \frac{C^{\alpha}}{\text{METS}} \ k^{\beta} \ \left(1 + \frac{X}{P}\right)^{\gamma} \ \left(1 - \frac{M}{C}\right)^{\delta}$$

Our interest would focus mainly on whether the trade variables (3) and (4) and the scale variable (2) have had a statistically significant effect on plant sizes, how large these effects have been, and to what time lags they might be subject. We analysed the structures of 20 German industries in 1965, by combining Scherer's German sample of 12 industries with others. We also analysed the structures of 12 German industries in 1980.

1965 Results

The results of our regressions appear in Table 1. (We lagged the export, import and demand variables, just as Scherer did, by two years on the assumption that plant size needs time to adjust and cope with a growth in market size.) Market size (regression 1) was by itself able to explain over half the variations in plant size among the 20 industries in 1965 as measured in the adjusted R^2.

TABLE 1. *Regression results: plant size and trade, 1965 (dependent variable: average plant size/METS; 20 industries, all variables in logarithmic form)*

Regression	Constant term	$\dfrac{\text{Consumption}}{\text{METS}}$	Cost gradient	$1 + \dfrac{\text{Exports}}{\text{Production}}$	$1 - \dfrac{\text{Imports}}{\text{Consumption}}$	$\bar{R}^2$
1	−0.54	0.41**				0.55
		(4.97)				
2	−0.84	0.48**		3.68*		0.66
		(6.18)		(2.51)		
3	−0.50	0.56**	0.50	2.36	0.21	0.63
		(5.70)	(1.80)	(1.53)	(0.14)	
4	−0.22	0.60**	0.43	1.44	1.84	0.86
		(6.31)	(1.34)	(1.13)	(0.82)	

t ratios in parentheses.
* Significant at 5 per cent level.
** Significant at 1 per cent level.

Regression 2 suggests that exports were a statistically significant factor, which explained a further 10 per cent, but regression 3 is unable to distinguish the contribution of exports from those of cost gradient and imports.

The unit cost gradient was moderately significant, and in the expected direction; the steeper the cost gradient, the closer were representative plants to their industries' METS value.

In 1963, trade was not very pronounced in this larger sample; it is interesting, nonetheless, to see signs that exports were already influencing plant size in 1965, and that Scherer's results for 6 countries and 12 industries are reflected in the results for Germany alone on the basis of 20 industries.

Equation 4 reports the results for the sample of only the 12 industries reported in the case studies (without the additional industries from the Scherer sample). The coefficients of the smaller sample are very similar, except for the increase in the import coefficient. The positive import coefficient surprised us; we had actually expected on the basis of the industry studies that imports, too, would encourage relative plant size.

That does not seem to be the case. We shall come back to this question in the discussion of the 1980 results.

1980 Results

In moving to 1980 we had to address the question of technological change and its effect on METS: should plant size and market size be deflated by updated METS estimates? Should we assume that industries adjust to technological change automatically, irrespective of changes in markets or in trade, or would it be fairer to judge the effect of these factors against 1965–vintage METS estimates? The problem is that we were dealing with a moving target, and it is not even clear what kind of target it is. Are we dealing with objective changes in technology, or with changes in business leaders' perceptions of what these technologies imply for efficient plant size?

In only one industry, television sets, was there a significant change in manufacturing technology within the period. In other industries the change was more gradual or nonexistent. In petrochemicals for example, 500,000 tons were already accepted as the METS in the 1960s, and have not been increased since. Automated techniques have probably raised METS in some industries, e.g. vehicle building and white goods. We have therefore adjusted the 1965 METS figures in a conservative way as our preferred approach: the only significant changes relate to television manufacture, in which automatic techniques were introduced after 1965, and combine harvesters, where the METS was adjusted downwards to reflect the fact that, in terms of work content, a 1980–vintage machine was equivalent to two or more 1965 machines. In Table 2 the regressions 1 and 2 are based on

TABLE 2. *Regression results: plant size and trade, 1980 (dependent variable: average plant size/METS; 12 industries, all variables in logarithmic form)*[a]

Regression structure	Constant term	$\frac{\text{Consumption}}{\text{METS}}$	Cost gradient	$1 + \frac{\text{Exports}}{\text{Production}}$	$1 - \frac{\text{Imports}}{\text{Consumption}}$	$\bar{R}^2$
1 1980/1976	−2.448	0.699** (5.19)	−0.245 (0.60)	4.43* (2.26)	2.04** (4.71)	0.80
2 1980/1978	−2.844	0.694** (6.01)	−0.431 (1.15)	4.52* (2.43)	2.26** (5.06)	0.83
3 1980/1976[b]	−0.301	0.641** (6.43)	−0.320 (1.07)	5.94** (4.10)	1.29** (5.07)	0.81
4 1980/1978[b]	−3.48	0.594** (6.16)	−0.330 (1.08)	6.58** (3.89)	1.21** (5.01)	0.79

[a] Average plant size/METS and cost gradient are recorded in 1980; the other variables are recorded in the earlier year mentioned
[b] Using 1965 METS estimates.
** Significantly different from zero at 1 per cent level.
* Significantly different from zero at 5 per cent level
t ratios in parentheses.

TABLE 3. *METS Values and scale gradients for the 12 industries*

	METS values 1965	METS values 1980	Conservative METS values 1980	Scale gradient
Polyethylene	0.5 mt	0.5 mt	0.5 mt	0.190
Polypropylene	0.5 mt	0.5 mt	0.5 mt	0.190
PVC	0.5 mt	0.5 mt	0.5 mt	0.190
Leather shoes (in pairs)	1.0 m	1.0 m	1.0 m	0.015
Refrigerators and freezers	0.5 m	1.2 m	0.8 m	0.065
Washing machines	0.8 m	0.8 m	0.8 m	0.075
Combine harvesters	50 th	50 th	20 th	0.100
Antifriction bearings	800 n	800 n	800 n	0.100
Television sets				
Black and white	0.03 m	1.2 m	1.0 m	0.120
colour		1.2 m	1.0 m	0.120
Tractors	0.125 m	0.250 m	0.125 m	0.120
Trucks	0.125 m	0.250 m	0.125 m	0.120
Cars	1.0 m	2.0 m	1.0 m	0.150

Key: N = number of employers; mt = million tones; th = thousand; m = million units.

1980 METS estimates; regressions 3 and 4 are based on 'conservative' 1980 METS estimates, very similar to 1965 estimates (see Table 3).

The 1980 results are more decisive than those for 1965. The explanatory power of the model (as measured by the adjusted R^2) has increased to 80 per cent. The statistical significance of both the export and the import variables is greater than in the 1965 results; also their coefficients are larger. The export coefficient is between 4 and 6; the import coefficient is between 1 and 2.2. Exports exert a powerful positive effect on plant size as expected; imports tend to depress plant size, contrary to our initial expectations.

The direction of the effect of imports seems to suggest that the market-reducing effect on plant size dominates the competitive pressure which imports exert on management to reduce costs, by, among other means, building larger plants. But the down-sizing of plants in response to imports may conceal important product shifts. The German white goods industry, for example, was pushed 'up-market' by the import threat posed by cheap Italian products and encouraged to produce higher-quality products for particular segments of European markets. This strategy involved smaller volumes per plant, accounting for the negative relationship between imports and plant size. METS can only be achieved in mass markets. Germany's comparative advantage does not lie in those segments. Trade benefits Germany because it offers premium quality producers (Daimler–Benz, Miele, Porsche) opportunities to achieve volumes which, though well short of METS, could not be achieved within the German market alone.

In the 1980 sample the negative scale coefficient is not statistically significant. Its persistent negative sign is puzzling, when we recall that the coefficient for the 1965 parameter was positive, as expected.

The economic significance of the results

To assess the economic significance of the results, consider the following conceptual experiment. Let us suppose that the trade flows in these German industries were, in aggregate, the same in 1978 as they were in 1963, in relation to German production and consumption levels. That is to say, suppose that aggregate exports in these industries had remained at 23 per cent of aggregate production, instead of growing to 45 per cent; and that aggregate imports had remained at 9 per cent of aggregate consumption, instead of growing to 31 per cent. How much larger was the actual average plant size in the sample in 1980 than it would have been in this hypothetical alternative? And how much more efficient were these industries, due to the exploitation of economies of scale, as a consequence?

We have already indicated reasons for preferring regressions (3) and (4) in Table 2. In regression (4), plant size responds to changes in trade patterns by the factor $(1 + X/P)^{6.58} (1 - M/C)^{1.21}$, assuming that consumption remains unaffected by changes in trade patterns.[1] On this basis, the changes in trade patterns between 1963 and 1978 boosted the average plant size in the sample by over 100%.[2]

The impact of this plant size effect on efficiency can be calculated from the average unit cost–plant size relationship in the sample. Unit costs at one-third METS were on average 14.3 per cent higher than at the METS itself. A doubling of plant size implies a reduction in unit cost of 8 per cent.[3] This conceptual experiment implies an increase in trade equivalent to 40 per cent of 1978 production. The efficiency gains were therefore equivalent to 20 per cent of the increment of trade which stimulated them.

4. CONCLUSIONS

There have been many studies which have analysed the growth in trade, and its causes, but very few which have attempted to assess the economic significance of this growth in trade. This study has addressed this question by looking at the effects of trade on the structures of 12 German manufacturing industries. It suggests that the growing participation of

---

[1] This assumption is not strictly correct, but is accurate enough for this purpose. Consumption is largely determined by GDP, which is unlikely to be significantly affected by changes in the structure and performance of such a small sample of industries (for manufacturing as a whole it would be otherwise). Moreover, the demands of the sample industries are not highly interrelated, with the exception of the petrochemical sectors.

[2] $1 + X/P$ was 1.23 in 1963, 1.466 in 1978 and $1 - M/C$ was 0.914 in 1963, 0.693 in 1978

$$\left(\frac{1.446}{1.23} \right)^{6.58} \left(\frac{0.693}{0.914} \right)^{1.21} = 2.07.$$

[3] This figure of 14.3 per cent implies a cost function: unit cost $= k \times$ plant size $^{-0.122}$. Doubling plant size has a cost effect $=$ antilog $(-0.122 \log 2) = 0.92$.

these industries in international trade between 1963 and 1978 had a significant effect on their representative plant size. It is difficult to disentangle the effects of trade and of technological change in a sample as small as this, but it seems possible that the growth in trade had the effect of doubling plant size between 1963 and 1978. The economies of scale in these industries were such that a scale effect of this order implies a unit cost reduction in the sample of 8 per cent. The efficiency gains were equivalent to 20 per cent of the increment of trade which was responsible for these structural changes.

REFERENCES

EASTMAN, H. C. and STYKOLT, (1967) *The Tariff and Competition in Canada.* New York.
MAYES, D. (1978) 'The effects of economic integration on trade', *Journal of Common Market Studies*, pp. 1–25.
MEADE, J. E. (1955) *The Theory of Customs Unions*, Amsterdam.
OWEN, N. (1976) 'Scale economies within the EEC', *European Economic Review*, 7 pp. 143–163.
OWEN, N. (1983) *Economies of Scale, Competitiveness and Trade Patterns within the European Community.* Oxford.
SCHERER, F. M., BECKENSTEIN, A., KAUFER, E. and MURPHY, R. D. (1975) *The Economics of Multi-Plant Operation: An International Comparison Study*, Cambridge, USA.

THE DETERMINANTS OF INTRA-EUROPEAN TRADE IN MANUFACTURED GOODS

Bela BALASSA*

Johns Hopkins University, Baltimore, MD 21218, USA

Luc BAUWENS*

G.R.E.Q.E.-E.H.E.S.S., 13002 Marseille, France

The determinants of intra-European trade in manufactured goods are examined using three models. The first model tests whether inter-industry specialization between pairs of countries can be explained in terms of inter-industry differences in factor intensities and inter-country differences in factor endowments. The second model tests the effects of country and industry characteristics in the extent of intra-industry specialization. The third model combines the first two to analyse the determinants of bilateral gross trade in individual industries. The empirical results support the specific hypotheses put forward to specify the models.

1. Introduction

The authors set out to examine the factors determining intra-European trade in manufactured goods in the framework of alternative models. The first model is designed to explain the pattern of *net trade* (exports less imports or net exports) between pairs of countries in terms of inter-industry differences in factor intensities and inter-country differences in factor endowments. The second model investigates the effects of country characteristics and industry characteristics in the extent of intra-industry specialization between pairs of countries. Finally, the third model combines the first two to analyse the determinants of *gross trade* between pairs of countries in

*Bela Balassa is Professor of Political Economy at the Johns Hopkins University and Consultant to the World Bank; Luc Bauwens is at the Ecole des Hautes Etudes en Sciences Sociales and was a Researcher at the World Bank. The authors gratefully acknoweldge the financial support of the World Bank and the Belgium 'Collège Interuniversitaire en Management' in the preparation of the paper. The preliminary version of the paper was presented at the 'Quatrièmes Journées de Microéconomie Appliquée held in Louvain-la-Neuve, Belgium on June 4–5, 1987. The authors are thankful to Professor Bernard Lassudrie-Duchène for his helpful comments. However, they alone are responsible for the opinions expressed in the paper that should not be interpreted to reflect the views of the World Bank.

0014–2921/88/$3.50 © 1988, Elsevier Science Publishers B.V. (North-Holland)

individual industries. While net trade is affected by comparative advantage, gross trade is also influenced by the extent of intra-industry specialization, which increases exports as well as imports in bilateral trade.

The investigation covers altogether 152 product categories in the manufacturing sector as defined by the United States Standard Industrial Classification (SIC), with the exclusion of natural resource products whose manufacture is importantly affected by the availability of natural resources in a particular country.[1] The classification scheme has been established by merging 4-digit SIC categories in cases when the economic characteristics of particular products have been judged to be very similar.[2]

Sections 2 and 3 of the paper describe the hypotheses to be tested in regard to inter-industry and intra-industry specialization among European countries and report the empirical results for each. Section 4 tests these hypotheses in the framework of a model that combines the determinants of inter-industry and intra-industry specialization. Sector 5 presents the conclusions and indicates the policy implications of the findings.

2. The determinants of inter-industry specialization

This paper tests the hypothesis that, in bilateral trade among European countries, relative capital abundance is associated with the net exports of capital intensive commodities. It thus involves defining comparative advantage with respect to industry and country characteristics. Industry (product) characteristics refer to factor intensities, expressed as the value of physical capital per worker (p_i) and the value of human capital per worker (h_i). In turn, country characteristics refer to the endowments of physical capital (G_j) and human capital (H_j), expressed in per capita terms.

2.1. Specification

The estimating equation can be specified utilizing a two-stage procedure. In the first stage, the normalized net exports of product i from country j to country k (NNX_{jki})[3] are regressed on physical (p_i) and human (h_i) capital intensities as in (1).[4] This is done for each pair of countries j and k, such

---

[1] The investigation excludes foods and beverages (SIC 20), tobacco (SIC 21), non-ferrous metals (SIC 333), as well as several 4-digit categories covering textile waste, preserved wood, saw mill products, prefabricated wood, veneer and plywood, wood pulp, dyeing and tanning extracts, fertilizers, adhesives and gelatin, carbon black, petroleum refining and products, asbestos and asphalt products, cement and concrete; lime, gypsum products, cut stone products, and lapidary work. It also excludes ordnance (SIC 19), for which comparable trade data are not available.

[2] The principal criteria have been high substitution elasticities in production and in consumption.

[3] Net exports of commodity i from country j to country k are normalized by dividing with the sum of exports and imports of commodity i in trade between countries j and k.

[4] In the following discussion, we do not introduce residuals in the equations. For a discussion of the estimation method and alternative specifications, see Balassa and Bauwens (1985).

that $j > k$. In the second stage, the estimated coefficients, β^p_{jk} and β^h_{jk} are regressed, respectively, on the relative physical and human capital endowments of country j with respect to country k as in (2.1) and (2.2).

$$NNX_{jki} = \alpha_{jk} + \beta^p_{jk} \ln p_i + \beta^h_{jk} \ln h_i \tag{1}$$

$$\beta^p_{jk} = a^p + b^p \ln \frac{G_j}{G_k}, \tag{2.1}$$

$$\beta^h_{jk} = a^h + b^h \ln \frac{H_j}{H_k}. \tag{2.2}$$

Substituting the right hand sides of these last two equations into the first yields eq. (3) that can be estimated in one step. The explanatory variables $\ln(G_j/G_k)\ln p_i$ and $\ln(H_j/H_k)\ln h_i$ are interaction terms between the relative endowment of j with respect to k in a given factor, and the intensity of use of this factor in the production of product i. In turn, the coefficients of $\ln p_i$ and $\ln h_i$ can be interpreted as the constants of the second stage equations.

$$NNX_{jki} = \alpha_{jk} + a^p \ln p_i + a^h \ln h_i + b^p \ln \frac{G_j}{G_k} \ln p_i + b^h \ln \frac{H_j}{H_k} \ln h_i. \tag{3}$$

Eq. (3) has been expressed in linear terms. For purposes of estimation, use has been made of a non-linear function as in (4), where $\gamma' z_{jki}$ stands for the right-hand side of (3). This has been derived from the logistic function $y = 1/(1 + \exp - t)$, where $0 \le y \le 1$, utilizing the transformation $x = 2y - 1$. Thus,

$$-1 \le x = [2/(1 + \exp - t)] - 1 = (1 - \exp - t)/(1 + \exp - t) \le 1.$$

$$NNX_{jki} = \frac{1 - \exp - (\gamma' z_{jki})}{1 + \exp - (\gamma' z_{jki})} + \varepsilon_{jki}. \tag{4}$$

Estimation by non-linear least squares has the advantage of limiting the predicted values of the dependent variable to the range $(-1, +1)$, which is the range of the actual values of this variable. Also, it it not necessary to include the country specific intercepts α_{jk}, the estimation of which would be costly and difficult as there are 639 such terms.

2.2. Data

Data on the capital stock, employment, value added, and wages used in calculating physical and human capital intensities originate from the U.S.

Census of Manufacturing and are averages for the years 1969 and 1970. Data on unskilled wages for the same period have been taken from the *Monthly Labor Review*, published by the U.S. Bureau of Statistics; they pertain to the 2-digit industry group, thus involving the assumption that unskilled wages are the same within each 2-digit group.

Capital intensity has been defined in terms of stocks as well as flows. In the first case, physical capital intensity has been equated to the value of the capital stock per worker while human capital intensity has been derived as the discounted value of the difference between the average wage and the unskilled wage using a 10 percent discount rate. In the second case, physical capital intensity has been defined as non-wage value added per worker and human capital intensity as the difference between the average wage and the unskilled wage.

The trade data used in the investigation relate to 1971. They have been obtained from the GATT tapes. The commodity classification scheme employed has required the use of trade data down to the 5 digit level. In a few cases when 5-digit data were not available, they have been estimated from the 4-digit data on the basis of the worldwide composition of trade.

The sum of gross fixed investment over the seventeen year period between 1954 and 1970, estimated in constant prices and converted into U.S. dollars at 1967 exchange rates, has been used as a proxy for physical capital endowment for the countries concerned. Investment values have been assumed to depreciate at a rate of 4 percent a year, reflecting the obsolescence of capital, with capital equipment assumed to have a useful life of 17 years. The relevant information has been obtained from the World Bank economic and social data base, and the estimates have been expressed in per capita terms.

The Harbison–Myers index of education has been used as a proxy for human capital. The index is derived as the secondary school enrollment rate plus five times the University enrollment rate, both calculated in their respective age cohorts. It is a flow measure and estimates pertaining to 1965 have been utilized as an indicator of a country's general educational level, and thus its human capital base, in 1971.

2.3. Empirical results

Table 1 reports the estimates for bilateral trade among European countries, obtained by the use of stock and flow measures of capital in columns (1) and (2), respectively. In the estimated equations, the regression coefficients of the interaction terms involving relative capital endowment and factor intensity variables have the expected sign, indicating that the relative factor intensity of trade is positively correlated with relative factor endowments. These coefficients are statistically significant at the 1 percent level; the other coefficients of the regression equations are significant at least at the 5 percent level. Finally, the (adjusted) coefficient of determination is 0.74.

3. The determinants of intra-industry specialization

The hypothesis is tested that in bilateral trade among European countries, the extent of intra-industry trade defined as the share of intra-industry trade in total trade is affected by country and industry characteristics. The relevant hypothesis are stated below following a description of the statistical methodology.

3.1. Specification

The index of intra-industry trade, IIT_{jki}, is defined in (5), where X^e_{jki} and M^e_{jki} stand for the adjusted exports and imports of industry i in trade between countries j and k while X_{jki} and M_{jki} denote the corresponding unadjusted flows. The formula makes adjustment for imbalance in total trade between countries j and k, when X_{jk} and M_{jk} represent the total exports and imports of country j in trade with country k.[5] The index takes values from 0 to 1 as the extent of intra-industry trade increases.

$$IIT_{jki} = 1 - \frac{|X^e_{jki} - M^e_{jki}|}{X^e_{jki} + M^e_{jki}} = 1 - \frac{\left|\dfrac{X_{jki}}{X_{jk}} - \dfrac{M_{jki}}{M_{jk}}\right|}{\dfrac{X_{jki}}{X_{jk}} + \dfrac{M_{jki}}{M_{jk}}}, \tag{5}$$

In the regression equations explaining inter-country and inter-industry differences in the extent of intra-industry trade, IIT_{jki} is used as the dependent variable. In turn, the explanatory variables include the country characteristics and the industry characteristics described below.

Various considerations are relevant to the choice of the functional form utilized in the estimation. To begin with, a linear or loglinear equation may give estimated values that lie outside the 0 to 1 range. While a logistic function does not have this shortcoming, its logit tranformation[6] cannot handle values of 0 and 1. At the same time, although values of 1 (representing the complete intra-industry specialization) do not occur in the sample, values of 0 (representing complete inter-industry specialization) are of importance.

[5] While Aquino (1978) made adjustment for the imbalance in trade in manufactured goods, the present study follows Balassa (1979) in adjusting for the imbalance in total trade, so as to allow for inter-industry specialization between primary and manufactured goods that is of particular importance in trade between developed and developing countries. As suggested by Lassudrie-Duchène in his comments on the paper, there are also other possible methods of adjustment.

[6] $\ln(IIT_{jki}/1 - IIT_{jki}) = \beta' Z_{jki} + u_{jki}.$

In trade among all the countries concerned, there are potentially 23,256 observations.[7] IIT_{jki} is, however, not defined in 3,409 cases, because $X_{jki} = M_{jki} = 0$; i.e., no trade takes place in a particular industry category between two particular countries. Among the remaining 19,847 observations, 5,339 (27 percent) are equal to 0, because either X_{jki} or M_{jki} is zero; i.e., there is complete inter-industry specialization.

Given the importance of the zero observations, a logistic function is a better specification, since it can handle such observations. We have thus estimated (6), by non-linear least squares, where Z_{jki} is the vector of the explanatory variables, β is the vector of the regression coefficients, and ε_{jki} is a random disturbance term. The specification involves decomposing $\beta' Z_{jki}$ as shown in (7), where C refers to country characteristics and I to industry characteristics.

$$IIT_{jki} = \frac{1}{1 + \exp - \beta' Z_{jki}} + \varepsilon_{jki}. \tag{6}$$

$$\beta' Z_{jki} = \beta_0 + \beta^{C'} Z_{jk}^C + \beta^{I'} Z_i. \tag{7}$$

While none of the individual terms in (7) includes both the country and the industry dimensions of the variation of the dependent variable IIT_{jki}, they are both incorporated in the entire function. This means that the effects of country characteristics on the index of intra-industry specialization are assumed to be invariant across industries and the effects of industry characteristics on the index of intra-industry specialization are assumed to be invariant across country pairs.

3.2. Country characteristics

In examining trade in differentiated products, Linder advanced the proposition that 'the more similar the demand structures of two countries, the more intensive, potentially, is the trade between these two countries' (1961, p. 94). He further argued that while 'a whole array of forces influences the demand structure of a country ... the level of average income is the most important single factor and that it has, in fact, a dominating influence on the

---

[7]There are 18 countries trading in 152 commodity categories, but we eliminate one-half of the observations since $IIT_{jki} = IIT_{kji}$. In order of decreasing per capita GNP in 1971, the countries are Switzerland, Sweden, Denmark, Germany, Norway, France, Belgium, Netherlands, Finland, Austria, United Kingdom, Italy, Ireland, Spain, Greece, Portugal, Yugoslavia and Turkey.

structure of demand [so that] similarity of average income levels could be used as an index of similarity of demand structures' (ibid). The converse of this proposition is that 'per capita incomes differences are a potential obstacle to trade... . When per capita income differences reach a certain magnitude, trade can only take place in certain qualitatively homogeneous products' (ibid, p. 98).

In utilizing a model where intra-industry trade occurs in differentiated manufactured goods produced under economies of scale, Helpman subsequently provided proof of the proposition that, in the case when the home country has a lower (or equal) capital-labor ratio than the foreign country and factor prices are equalized, 'if we reallocate the world's labor and capital stock in a way which increases the foreign country's capital–labor ratio and reduces the home country's capital–labor ratio without disturbing commodity prices and factor rewards, then the share of intra-industry trade ... will decline' (1981, p. 325). Now, 'since the higher the capital–labor ratio the higher is income per capita (in a cross country comparison), this raises the hypothesis that a country's share of bilateral intra-industry trade is negatively correlated with the absolute difference in bilateral incomes per capita' (ibid., p. 337).

Helpman also provided proof of the proposition that, in two countries that have the same capital–labor ratio, 'a redistribution of resources which preserves each country's initial capital–labor ratio increases the volume of trade if it reduces the inequality in country size, and it reduces the volume of trade if it increases the inequality in country size. The volume of trade is largest when both countries are of equal size' (ibid., p. 327). On the assumptions made, the entire increase in trade takes the form of intra-industry trade. Correspondingly, one may hypothesize that the extent of intra-industry trade between any two countries will be negatively correlated with differences in their size.

The two propositions were combined by Dixit and Norman who showed that 'if the two countries are of similar size, and have no clear comparative advantage across industries, then we will see the predominant pattern of trade as one of intra-industry trade' (1980, p. 288). Comparative advantage is defined in terms of differences in factor endowments, for which per capita income differences may again be used as a proxy.

Linder further suggested that 'the higher the per capita income, the higher will be the degree of quality characterizing the demand structure as a whole' (1961, p. 99), when higher product quality is embodied in 'more complex, elaborated, refined or luxurious' (ibid.) products. As these products tend to be differentiated, the extent of intra-industry trade between any two countries is expected to be greater, the higher is their (average) per capita income.

Finally, Lancaster showed that, owing to economies of scale, the equilibrium number of differentiated manufactured products will be the greater, the larger is the size of the market[8] (1980, p. 158). Correspondingly, it may be hypothesized that the extent of intra-industry trade between any two countries will be positively correlated with their (average) size.

We have considered various hypotheses linking the level of per capita incomes and country size, as well as inter-country differences thereof, to the extent of intra-industry trade. According to these hypotheses, the extent of intra-industry trade is expected to be positively correlated with the average per capita income and the average size of the two countries and negatively correlated with inter-country differences in per capita incomes and in country size.

While the hypotheses have originally been formulated in a two-country model, in the present case they are tested in a multi-country model. At the same time, it should be recognized that empirical testing has not permitted introducing some of the restrictive assumptions made by the authors in developing their hypotheses.

In testing the stated hypotheses, per capita income is represented by GNP per head and country size by GNP.[9] But, rather than taking absolute values of inter-country differences in per capita incomes and size, use is made of a relative inequality measure that takes values between 0 and 1. This measure is superior to utilizing the values of the differences, which are affected by the absolute magnitudes of the particular country characteristics in the different countries. The relative inequality measures is shown in (8), where w refers to the ratio of a particular country characteristic in country j to the sum of this characteristic in country j and partner country k.

$$INEQ = 1 + [(w)\ln(w) + (1-w)\ln(1-w)]/\ln 2. \tag{8}$$

The next question concerns the introduction of transportation costs. In models of intra-industry trade, such as that of Krugman (1979), transportation costs will reduce the volume of such trade. However, the literature does not provide us with a presumption that intra-industry trade will thereby be affected relatively more (or less) than inter-industry trade. Such a presumption may be established if information flows are introduced.

There is no need to provide information on the characteristics of

---

[8] As Lancaster notes, this result will not obtain if economies of scale are derived from a homogeneous production function of constant degree.

[9] While the domestic consumption of manufactured goods would have been a more appropriate measure of the size of domestic market for these products, the necessary data are not available for some countries and are subject to considerable error in regard to others. At the same time, from available information it appears that the consumption of manufactured goods and the gross national products are highly correlated.

standardized (non-differentiated) products, such as copper metal, steel ingots, and caustic soda, which have uniform specifications across the world and hence their trade is determined largely by relative costs, giving rise to inter-industry specilization. However, there is need for information on the characteristics of differentiated products, such as machinery, transport equipment, and consumer goods, which are subject to intra-industry trade.

It can be assumed that the availability of information decreases, and its cost increases, with distance. Correspondingly, it may be hypothesized that the extent of intra-industry trade between any two countries will be negatively correlated with the distance between them. Distance is measured in miles between the centers of geographical gravity for each pair of countries.

The existence of common borders will also contribute to information flows. Furthermore, as Grubel and Lloyd suggested, in countries sharing a common border, intra-industry trade may occur 'in products which are functionally homogeneous but differentiated by location' (1975, p. 5). Thus, it may be hypothesized that the extent of intra-industry trade will be greater between countries that share a common border than between countries which do not have common borders.

The separate introduction of distance and border variables permits testing the hypothesis that common borders have economic significance for intra-industry trade beyond that of distance. In the econometric investigation, the existence of common borders is represented by a dummy variable, which takes the value of 1 when the two countries share a common border and is 0 otherwise.

In a model incorporating specific capital and constant returns to scale, Falvey found that the volume of intra-industry trade will vary inversely with the level of tariffs and of trade restrictions in general (1981, p. 505). But, again, the question is if tariffs will affect intra-industry trade relatively more than inter-industry trade. Balassa (1977) suggested that such would be the case in the event of trade liberalization in general and economic integration in particular. This is because adjustments to reductions in trade barriers would occur largely through rationalizing operations and changing the product composition of individual industries, with national product differentiation contributing to intra-industry trade.

The same author showed that trade liberalization (1977) and economic integration in the framework of the EEC and EFTA (1966, 1975) were in fact accompanied by increases in the extent of intra-industry trade among the countries in question. In the present investigation, the hypotheses are tested that the extent of intra-industry trade between any two countries is negatively correlated with the average level of their trade restrictions and positively correlated with participation in integration schemes.

Estimates of tariff levels are not available for a number of countries and the tariff equivalent of quantitative import restrictions is not known with any confidence for others. Correspondingly, an indicator of trade orientation is used to measure the extent of trade restrictions.[10]

Dummy variables are included to represent participation in the European Common Market (EEC) and the European Free Trade Association (EFTA). Familiarity with each other's products may also contribute to intra-industry trade between particular countries. As common language breeds familiarity, it can be hypothesized that the existence of a common language will increase the extent of intra-industry trade between any two countries. This hypothesis is tested in regard to English, French, Spanish, German, Portuguese, and Scandinavian languages.

3.3. Industry characteristics

Linder (1961) and Drèze (1960) were the first to emphasize the importance of product differentiation in international trade. In the theoretical models of Krugman (1979), Lancaster (1980) and Helpman (1981), product differentiation is taken to be a precondition on intra-industry specialization.

Following Caves (1981) and Toh (1982), the Hufbauer (1970) measures of product differentiation (the coefficient of variation of export unit values) is employed in the present study. Furthermore, a marketing cost variable introduced by Caves (1981), which measures the share of marketing costs (other than purchased advertising) in total costs in each industry, is also introduced in the equation as a measure of product differentiation.

Theorists of intra-industry trade hold that economies of scale are a sine qua non of intra-industry specialization; in the absence of scale economies, all product varieties could be produced domestically and no intra-industry trade would take place. Various indicators were employed as proxies for economies of scale in empirical investigations of intra-industry trade. Hufbauer regressed value added per man on firm size, measured in terms of employment; Loertscher and Wolter (1980) used average value added per establishment; Caves (1981) divided minimum plant size by a measure of the cost disadvantages of small firms; and Lundberg (1982) utilized the share of labor force in firms having more than 500 workers for this purpose.

All these measures relate costs to plant size. This is not the relevant consideration, however, regarding economies of scale in industries producing differentiated products, which are characterized by horizontal and vertical

---

[10] In the absence of data on the height of trade barriers in a number of countries, the indicator of trade orientation for bilateral trade used in the present study is the sum of the percentage deviations between actual and hypothetical per capita exports. Hypothetical values have been derived from a regression equation incorporating per capita incomes, population, the ratio of mineral exports to GNP, and distance from foreign markets as explanatory variables. [For a detailed explanation and the estimating equation actually employed, see Balassa and Bauwens (1987)].

specialization.[11] The former involves lessening product variety in individual plants while the latter entails producing parts, components, and accessories of a particular product in different plants. Now, vertical and horizontal specialization may involve reducing – rather than increasing – plant size.

Correspondingly, the above measures of economies of scale reflect the relative importance of product standardization and are hence expected to be negatively correlated with the extent of intra-industry trade.[12] In the present investigation, Caves' measure is used. This involves dividing the ratio of the average size of the largest plants in U.S. industry, accounting for approximately one-half of industry shipments, to total industry shipment, by the ratio of value added per worker in the smaller plants, again accounting for one-half of industry shipments, to value added per worker in the larger plants.

Product standardization is further related to the extent of industrial concentration; ceteris paribus, the possibilities for concentration can be expected to decline with the differentiation of the product. It may thus be hypothesized that intra-industry trade will be negatively associated with industrial concentration. This hypothesis is tested by utilizing the internationally adjusted concentration ratio introduced by Toh (1982), which is derived by dividing the traditional concentration ratio (the share of the largest four firms in the industry's output) by the share of imports in the industry's output.

Finally, offshore assembly provisions may lead to increased intra-industry specialization by encouraging the international division of the production process, involving vertical specialization. Correspondingly, a positive correlation is hypothesized between offshore assembly and the extent of intra-industry trade. In the present investigation, the offshore assembly variable is defined as the share of imports exempted from duties under offshore assembly provisions in total U.S. imports.

3.4. Empirical results

The results reported in column (3) of table 1 support the hypotheses that have been put forward. As expected, the extent of intra-industry trade is positively correlated with average per capita incomes (AY/P), average country size (AY), trade orientation (ATO), and the existence of a common border ($BORDER$), and it is negatively correlated with income inequality ($INEQY/P$), inequality in country size ($INEQY$), and distance (D). All the variables are highly significant statistically. The EEC, EFTA, and the

---

[11]These concepts were first introduced in Balassa (1967). As Lassudrie-Duchène suggested in his comments on the paper, horizontal specialization may relate to final as well as to intermediate products while vertical specialization occurs in intermediate products.

[12]Caves also expects a negative sign for this variable on the grounds that extensive scale economies would confine production to a few locations. This notion again pertains to standardized rather than to differentiated products.

Table 1

Explanation of trade in manufactured goods among European countries (estimated coefficients, with t-values in parentheses).[a]

	(1)		(2)		(3)		(4)	
Constant	−0.600	(13.10)	−0.739	(14.88)	0.594	(3.00)	15.848	(49.21)
ln G_j/G_k ln p_i	0.219	(23.13)	0.234	(22.50	−	−	0.339	(34.29)
ln H_j/H_k ln k_i	0.118	(8.82)	0.115	(8.61)	−	−	0.183	(9.99)
ln AY/P	−	−	−	−	0.761	(16.97)	2.361	(41.57)
$INEQY/P$	−	−	−	−	−0.923	(8.10)	−1.109	(9.48)
ln AY	−	−	−	−	0.286	(10.86)	2.569	(62.10)
$INEQY$	−	−	−	−	−1.156	(18.98)	−2.876	(28.26)
ATO	−	−	−	−	0.698	(11.35)	1.479	(16.04)
ln D	−	−	−	−	−0.265	(11.96)	−1.349	(34.33)
$BORDER$	−	−	−	−	0.321	(9.86)	0.725	(11.35)
EEC	−	−	−	−	0.074	(1.84)	0.511	(6.09)
$EFTA$	−	−	−	−	0.177	(5.65)	1.897	(35.55)
$ENGLISH$	−	−	−	−	0.832	(8.10)	2.132	(9.78)
$FRENCH$	−	−	−	−	0.483	(4.57)	0.114	(0.53)
$GERMAN$	−	−	−	−	0.293	(4.70)	0.491	(3.69)
$SCAND.$	−	−	−	−	0.102	(1.93)	0.584	(5.62)
PD	−	−	−	−	0.316	(10.08)	0.766	(14.59)
MKT	−	−	−	−	2.127	(4.91)	14.290	(19.62)
$ECSC$	−	−	−	−	−2.341	(6.05)	−11.567	(19.64)
$IACR$	−	−	−	−	−1.364	(7.91)	−7.632	(31.05)
OAP	−	−	−	−	0.133	(2.31)	−	−
ln p_i	−0.051	(2.77)	0.045	(2.05)	−	−	−	−
ln h_i	0.245	(14.71)	0.228	(13.74)	−	−	−	−
R^2	0.74	−	0.74	−	0.58	−	−	−
$\hat{\sigma}$	0.37	−	0.37	−	0.28	−	3.51	−
N	21,585	−	21,585	−	19,847	−	46,512	−

[a] (1) logistic estimates of eq. (3), using the stock measure of physical and human capital (p_i and h_i),
(2) as (1), but using the flow measure of p_i and h_i,
(3) estimates of eq. (6),
(4) estimates of the Tobit model (12).
Sources: see text.

common language dummy variables have also the expected positive sign and are highly significant statistically, except that the EEC and Scandinavian variables are significant only at the 10 percent level.

Among industry characteristics, the Hufbauer measure of product differentiation (PD) has the expected positive sign and it is highly significant statistically. This is also the case for the marketing variable (MKT), leading to the conclusion that intra-industry trade increases with the degree of product differentiation.

The economies of scale ($ECSC$) and the industrial concentration ($IACR$) variables are negatively correlated with the extent of intra-industry trade and are highly significant statistically. Again, the results correspond to expectations as the variables are considered to be indicators of product standardization. Finally, the offshore assembly variable (OAP) has the expected positive sign and it is significant statistically at the 5 percent level.

4. The determinants of inter-industry and intra-industry specialization combined

4.1. Specification

Having tested hypotheses pertaining to inter-industry and to intra-industry specialization separately, we next test these hypotheses jointly in the framework of a model that combines the determinants of inter-industry and intra-industry specialization. This is done by the use of eq. (9) that incorporates the two sets of variables affecting the exports of product i from country j to country k, denoted by X_{jki}.[13] The dependent variable is measured in logarithms, in order to ensure the positivity of predicted trade flows.

$$\ln X_{jki} = \beta_0 + \beta^{e'} Z^e_{jki} + \beta^{a'} Z^a_{jki} + u_{jki}. \tag{9}$$

In the equation, Z^e_{jki} denotes the vector of variables affecting inter-industry trade, i.e., the interaction terms between the relative factor endowments and factor intensities described in section 2.[14] By definition, these interaction terms are anti-symmetrical with respect to the country indices ($Z^e_{jki} = -Z^e_{kji}$). In turn, Z^a_{jki} is the symmetrical vector of variables influencing intra-industry trade ($Z^a_{jki} = Z^a_{kji}$).

Eqs. (10) and (11) can be derived from eq. (9) and the properties of the explanatory variables stated previously (assuming $u_{jki} = 0$).

$$\tfrac{1}{2}(\ln X_{jki} + \ln X_{kji}) = \beta_0 + \beta^{a'} Z^a_{jki}. \tag{10}$$

$$\tfrac{1}{2}(\ln X_{jki} - \ln X_{kji}) = \beta^{e'} Z^e_{jki}. \tag{11}$$

Eq. (10) shows that the geometric mean of X_{jki} and X_{kji}, which is a measure of gross trade between countries j and k in product i, depends on the variables affecting intra-industry trae but is independent of the variables influencing inter-industry trade. In turn, eq. (11) shows that the ratio of X_{jki} to X_{kji}, which is a measure of discrepancy between exports and imports,

---

[13] Country indices j and k take values from 1 to 18 for $j \neq k$. Since imports of country j from country k are equal to exports of k to j, there is no need to introduce imports in a separate equation.

[14] The variables $\ln p_i$ and $\ln h_i$ are not included in eq. (9), although they were included in estimating eq. (3). In the latter case, the coefficients of these variables are the constants of eqs. (2), which means that they are essentially adjustment terms for the level of the β coefficients. Such an adjustment is not required in the case of eq. (9). Also, $\ln p_i$ and $\ln h_i$ would influence gross trade in the same way as do the variables affecting intra-industry trade in eq. (10) below, but would not influence net trade as the interaction terms in eq. (11).

hence of net trade, depends on the interaction terms representing the comparative advantage of countries j and k in regard to product i, but it is independent of the variables affecting intra-industry trade.

There are large numbers of zero observations; there are further observations near to zero. Correspondingly, use has been made of the Tobit estimation procedure that involves transforming (9) into (12). In (12) it is assumed that the disturbances u_{jki} are independent, and each of them has a normal distribution with mean 0 and variance σ^2.

$$\ln X_{jki} = \beta_0 + \beta' Z_{jki} + u_{jki} \quad \text{if} \quad \beta_0 + \beta' Z_{jki} + u_{jki} \geq \ln 0.1$$

$$= \ln 0.1 \qquad\qquad \text{if} \quad \beta_0 + \beta' Z_{jki} + u_{jki} < \ln 0.1, \tag{12}$$

with $Z'_{jki} = (Z^{e'}_{jki} Z^{a'}_{jki})$ and $\beta' = (\beta^{e'} \beta^{a'})$.

Under this formulation, unobserved trade flows (including those with a value less than \$0.1 million) are assumed to be generated in the same way as the observed flows, but since they are not observed, all we know about them is that the event $\beta_0 + \beta' Z_{jki} + u_{jki} < \ln 0.1$ has occurred. Given the normality assumption on u_{jki}, the probability of this event is a function of the parameters to be estimated (β and σ^2). Hence, the knowledge of the values of the explanatory variables corresponding to the unobserved flows provides information on the parameters. The observed trade flows and the corresponding values of the explanatory variables provide information on the parameters as in the usual regression model. These two sets of information are combined in the likelihood function [Amemiya (1984)] shown in (13).

$$L = \prod_0 \Phi[\sigma^{-1}(\ln 0.1 - \beta_0 - \beta' Z_{jki})] \prod_1 \sigma^{-1} \phi[\sigma^{-1}(\ln X_{jki} - \beta_0 - \beta' Z_{jki}], \tag{13}$$

where $\prod_0$ ($\prod_1$) denotes that the product is taken over all trade flows less than 0.1 (greater than or equal to 0.1). $\Phi(y) = (2\pi)^{-1/2} \int_{-\infty}^{y} \exp - \frac{1}{2} t^2 \, dt$, i.e., the standard normal distribution, $\phi(y) = (2\pi)^{-1/2} \exp - \frac{1}{2} y^2$, i.e., the standard normal density. Estimation has been done by the maximum likelihood procedure.[15]

4.2. Empirical results

Column (4) of table 1 reports the results obtained by estimating eq. (12). It is apparent that apart from the French language variable, all the stated hypotheses relating to inter-industry as well as intra-industry trade are

---

[15] The authors thank Gordon Hughes of Edinburgh University for providing his maximum likelihood package (MLPACK). A quasi-Newton method has been used with an analytic gradient while the asymptotic covariance matrix of the parameters has been estimated by evaluating analytically minus the inverse of the Hessian at the maximum likelihood estimate.

confirmed by the results. This includes also the EEC variable and the Scandinavian language variable, which are statistically significant at the 1 percent level in the present specification.

The results provide support to the Heckscher–Ohlin theory of international specialization, inasmuch as the relative factor intensity of trade is shown to be positively correlated with relative factor endowments; the more capital (labor) abundant is country j relative to country k, the more capital (labor) intensive will be its exports to that country. As shown by the positive signs of the coefficients of the interaction terms $\ln G_j/G_k \ln p_i$ and $\ln H_j/H_k \ln h_i$, this conclusion applies equally well to physical and to human capital.

The results further confirm the hypotheses put forward by various authors concerning the effects of country characteristics on intra-industry trade. Thus, they show that trade flows between any two countries are the greater (a) the smaller are differences in their per capita incomes ($INEQY/P$) and in their country size ($INEQY$), and (b) the higher their average per capita income (AY/P), and their average size (AY).

The results also indicate that trade between any two countries is negatively correlated with geographical distance (D) between them whereas the existence of common borders ($BORDER$) tends to increase the extent of such trade. High trade orientation (ATO) provides further impetus to bilateral trade.

It is further apparent that economic integration contributes to trade among the participating countries. This conclusion applies equally well to the European Common Market (EEC) and the European Free Trade Association (EFTA). Similar results are obtained in regard to language and cultural groups. Thus, members of these groups tend to trade more with each other than with non-members. This is shown by the positive signs of the regression coefficients for the English, German, and Scandinavian language and cultural groups all of which are highly significant statistically although this is not the case for the French language and cultural group.

Among industry characteristics, both measures of product differentiation – price dispersion (PD) and marketing cost share (MKT) – are positively correlated with trade as it was hypothesized. In turn, the expected negative correlation is obtained in regard to variables representing product standardization, including plant economies of scale ($ECSC$) and industrial concentration ($IACR$). Finally, offshore assembly provisions (OAP) contribute positively to international trade flows as expected.

5. Conclusions

This paper has examined the determinants of international trade in manufactured goods among European countries. It has considered the impact on bilateral trade in individual industries of factors affecting inter-industry specialization, intra-industry specialization, as well as the two together.

The empirical results support the hypotheses put forward in the paper. To begin with, it is apparent that the relative capital intensity of exports is positively correlated with relative capital abundance. This conclusion applies equally well to physical and to human capital.

While factors determining comparative advantage explain inter-industry specialization, or unidirectional trade, a variety of country characteristics and industry characteristics contribute to intra-industry specialization, or mutual trade among pairs of countries. To begin with, the results show that trade between any two countries is positively correlated with their average per capita income and country size and negatively correlated with inter-country differences in these variables. Furthermore, distance is a barrier to trade whereas the existence of common borders has the opposite effect. High trade barriers also hinder bilateral trade while participation in integration schemes as well as common language and culture promote trade among European countries. Finally, product differentiation tends to increase and product standardization reduce intra-industry, and hence total trade, and offshore assembly has a positive impact on intra-industry trade.

The results may be interpreted to indicate the gains European countries may obtain from international specialization in general and from economic integration in particular. They should thus provide incentives for overall trade liberalization, as well as for the completion of the European integration process.

References

Amemiya, Takeshi, 1984, Tobit models: A survey, Journal of Econometrics, Annals, no. 1, 3–61.

Aquino, Antonio, 1978, Intra-industry trade and inter-industry specialization as concurrent sources of international trade in manufactures, Weltwirtschaftliches Archiv 114, no. 2, 175–196.

Balassa, Bela, 1966, Tariff reductions and trade in manufactures among industrial countries, American Economic Review 56, no. 3, 466–473.

Balassa, Bela, 1967, Trade liberalization among identical countries: Objectives and alternatives, ch. 5 (McGraw-Hill for the Council on Foreign Relations, New York).

Balassa, Bela, 1975, European economic integration (North-Holland, Amsterdam).

Balassa, Bela, 1977, Effects of commercial policy on international trade, the location of production, and factor movements, in: Bertil Ohlin, Per-Ove Hesselborn and Per Magnus Wijkman, eds., The international allocation of economic activity (Macmillan, London) 230–258.

Balassa, Bela, 1979, Intra-industry trade and the integration of developing countries in the world economy, in: Herbert Giersch, ed., On the economics of intra-industry trade (Mohr, Tubingen) 245–270.

Balassa, Bela, 1986, The determinants of intra-industry specialization in United States trade, Oxford Economic Papers 38, no. 2, 220–233.

Balassa, Bela and Luc Bauwens, 1985, Comparative advantage in manufactured goods in a multi-country, multi-industry and multi-factor model, in: Theo Peeters, Peter Praet and Paul Reding, eds., International trade and exchange rates in the late eighties (North-Holland, Amsterdam) 31–52.

Balassa, Bela and Luc Bauwens, 1987, Intra-industry specialization in a multi-country, multi-industry framework, Economic Journal 97, 923–939.

Caves, Richard E., 1981, Intra-industry trade and market structure in the industrial countries, Oxford Economic Papers 33, no. 2, 203–223.

Dixit, Avinash K. and Victor Norman, 1980, Theory of international trade (Nisbet, Welwyn and Cambridge University Press, Cambridge).

Drèze, Jacques, 1960, Quelques réflexions sereines sur l'adaptation de l'industrie belge au Marché Commun, Comptes rendus des Travaux de la Société Royal d'Economie Politique de Belgique, no. 275.

Falvey, Rodney F, 1981, Commercial policy and intra-industry trade, Journal of International Economics 11, no. 4, 495–512.

Grubel, Herbert G. and P.J. Lloyd, 1975, Intra-industry trade (Macmillan, London).

Helpman, Elhanan, 1981, International trade in the presence of product differentiation, economies of scale and monopolistic competition: A Chamberlin–Heckscher–Ohlin approach, Journal of International Economics 11, no. 3, 305–340.

Hufbauer, G.C., 1970, The impact of national characteristics and technology on the commodity composition of trade in manufactured goods, in: Raymond Vernon, ed., The technological factor in international trade (National Bureau of Economic Research, New York) 145–231.

Krugman, Paul R., 1979, Scale economies, product differentiation, and the pattern of trade, American Economic Review 70, no. 5, Dec., 950–959.

Lancaster, Kelvin, 1980, Intra-industry trade under perfect monopolistic competition, Journal of International Economics 10, no. 2, 151–175.

Linder, Burenstam Staffan, 1961, An essay on trade and transportation (Wiley, New York).

Loertscher, Rudolf and Frank Wolter, 1980, Determinants of intra-industry trade: Among countries and across industries, Weltwirtschaftliches Archiv 116, no. 2, 280–292.

Lundberg, Lars, 1982, Intra-industry trade: The case of Sweden, Weltwirtschaftliches Archiv 118, no. 2, 303–316.

Toh, Kiertisak, 1982, A cross-section analysis of intra-industry trade in U.S. manufacturing industries, Weltwirtschaftliches Archiv 118, no. 2, 282–301.

INTERNATIONAL TRADE AND INTEGRATION OF THE EUROPEAN COMMUNITY

An Econometric Analysis*

Alexis JACQUEMIN

Université Catholique de Louvain, B-1348 Louvain-la-Neuve, Belgium

André SAPIR

Université Libre de Bruxelles, B-1050 Brussels, Belgium

The paper contributes to the policy debate on European integration by analyzing intra-Community trade and studying the structural determinants of European competitiveness. Four types of explanatory factors of intra-EC trade are distinguished: (1) factors related to inter-industry trade; (2) factors pertaining to intra-industry trade; (3) factors which reflect natural and policy-induced barriers to trade; and (4) factors reflecting supply constraints. Distinction is drawn between two contrasting factors that favor intra-area trade: those that foster economic welfare and those that hinder a more efficient world division of labor.

1. Introduction

The creation of a large common market has always been, ever since the Treaty of Rome was signed thirty years ago, the keystone of the European edifice. The rationale for transforming national markets into a single market is that it tends to improve European specialization and efficiency as well as intensify competition, and, thereby, increase trade, and foster economic welfare.

During its first fifteen years, the European Community (EC) witnessed a

*This paper is partly based on a report prepared for the Centre for European Policy Studies (CEPS) and funded by the Commission of the European Communities. Neither institution bears any responsibility for the content of the paper. The authors are grateful to Massimo Cingolani and Jean-François Lebrun for extensive assistance. Simon Erlich and staff members of the Commission also provided help with the data. An earlier version was presented at the CEFI Conference on Imperfect Competition and International Trade in Aix-en-Provence, at Erasmus University in Rotterdam, at the Second Annual Congress of the European Economic Association in Copenhagen and at the Institute for International Economic Studies in Stockholm Comments by the audiences and by Bela Balassa, Herbert Glejser, Philippe Goybet and Frank Wolter are gratefully acknowledged.

rapid expansion of intra-area trade as a result of dismantling all tariffs and quantitative restrictions among the member countries. The expansion of trade was accompanied by rapid economic growth in the Community.[1]

Since 1973 Europe has undergone a prolonged period of slow growth and high unemployment. At the same time there has been a slowdown in intra-area trade. This trend has recently been documented by Jacquemin and Sapir (1988) who use the ratio of intra-Community imports to total (i.e., intra- and extra-Community) imports as an index of intra-Community trade. They show that two sub-periods can be distinguished in the evolution of intra-EC trade in manufactured goods for the Community of Ten. The first one, starting in 1958, is characterized by a steady increase in the share of intra-Community imports reaching a peak of 61 percent in 1972. The second period, starting in 1973, indicates a more irregular tendency: stagnation around 60–61 percent between 1973 and 1979, followed by a decline in 1980 with a further stagnation thereafter at around 58 percent. The slowdown in intra-Community trade becomes far more striking when the new member-countries (especially the United Kingdom) are excluded.

There are two broad categories of factors which may account for the deceleration of intra-Community trade. One includes macroeconomic, short-term factors such as exchange rate variability or misalignment. The second category reflects a structural, long-term weakness possibly associated with the failure to complete the process of European integration.[2] In view of the success of the European Monetary System (EMS) at stabilizing exchange rates and the positive impact on intra-EMS trade [De Grauwe (1987)], the burden of explaining the relative slowdown in intra-EC trade falls heavily on structural factors.

The Community's loss of momentum has prompted efforts by the European Commission to adopt structural measures for completing the internal market. The aim is to eliminate, by the end of 1992, all physical, fiscal, and technical barriers among the twelve member countries in order to give new impetus to trade and revitalize economic growth.

The purpose of this paper is to contribute to the policy debate on European integration by analyzing intra-Community trade and studying the structural determinants of European competitiveness. Distinction will be drawn between two contrasting factors that favor intra-area trade: those that foster economic welfare and those that hinder a more efficient world division of labor. The study relies on a new databank allowing, for the first time, to

---

[1] See, for instance, Balassa (1975), Owen (1983) and Pelkmans (1986).

[2] For a recent discussion of the role of industrial structure on trade performance, see Lawrence (1987) who, on the basis of a 22-sector analysis, argues that '[s]tructure is unlikely to explain the differences [among the main OECD countries] in industrial performance' (p. 360). However, in a comment Jacquemin has pointed to the need to examine industrial characteristics and performance in more disaggregate fashion in order to draw proper inference.

conduct research on European industry at a rather disaggregated level that distinguishes over one hundred sectors.

2. Theoretical background for explaining intra-EC trade

In the existing theoretical literature there is no general argument resulting in the prediction of a distinct impact by trade factors according to whether they are related to trade of an intra- or extra-Community origin. The purpose of this section is to provide a simplified framework allowing such a distinction. The explanation rests on modern trade theory which predicts intra-industry trade in differentiated manufactured products between similar countries and inter-industry trade between countries with different factor endowments or technologies.

Divide the world into two regions, the European Community and the rest of the world. The EC can be viewed as a set of countries with relatively similar factor endowments and technologies. In turn, the rest of the world can be subdivided into two regions called North and South which comprise of the non-EC industrialized countries and the developing nations, respectively. The European Community and North share similar factor endowments and technologies which generally differ from those of South.

The prediction about the direction of trade depends upon whether a given manufactured good is either homogeneous, produced under constant returns to scale or differentiated, produced under increasing returns to scale. Trade between the European Community and South will be primarily inter-industry trade of goods belonging to the former category: a given Community member will tend to import homogenous goods from South rather than from EC partners if they use intensively factors of production which are abundant in South. On the other hand, trade between the European Community and North will be primarily intra-industry trade in differentiated/increasing-returns products: a given Community member will tend to import differentiated goods from North rather than from EC partners if it enjoys some competitive advantage.

Within this framework, four types of explanatory factors of intra-EC trade can be distinguished: (1) factors related to inter-industry trade; (2) factors pertaining to intra-industry trade; (3) factors which reflect natural and policy-induced barriers to trade; and (4) factors reflecting supply constraints.

As regards the determinants of *inter-industry trade*, the neo-factor proportion extensions of the Heckscher–Ohlin theory are well known. In particular, the production factor constituted by capital has been broken down into two components: human capital and physical capital. Moreover, in the Ricardian perspective, an effort has been made to introduce several aspects of technological advantage in explaining the pattern of trade. To the extent that Europe possesses relatively advanced technologies and large stocks of capital, it can be expected to enjoy a comparative advantage in high-tech and capital-intensive industries.

Concerning the determinants of *intra-industry trade*, theoretical elements are based on the roles of product differentiation and economies of scale. There is a tendency for increasing-returns industries, other things equal, to locate in the largest markets and export to other markets.[3] To the extent that the degree of European integration is similar to that of other industrialized countries, European industry will not be handicapped in realizing economies of scale. But if European markets are fragmented so that firms are constrained to operate at suboptimal plant size a disadvantage will appear.

The existence of product differentiation (which is especially found in consumer products) implies monopolistic competition which, from the consumer's viewpoint, may correspond to a demand for variety in products. As far as a country's range of potential imports of manufactured goods is determined by its internal demand [Linder (1961)], countries with similar demand structure will trade more with each other. Intra-EC trade would then be promoted if, indeed, European countries exhibit a greater similarity of demand among themselves than vis-à-vis the other industrialized countries. However it must be noted that this potential effect will be realized only if European producers are able to respond to a common pattern of European preferences over the spectrum of differentiated products.

Because of the strict assumptions behind the two main strands of trade theory, no unambiguously correct and conclusive test of these theories has been formulated and applied so far. 'Instead there have been piecemeal improvements in the empirical applications of trade theories' [Deardorff (1984, p. 469)]. These applications, however, have fostered a consensus on the economic factors contributing most to the understanding of international trade. The purpose here is to identify those factors that are able to explain the relative intensity of intra-EC imports of an intra- as well as inter-industry nature.

The third type of factor which is expected to influence EC imports of Community origin are the barriers to international trade. An obvious natural barrier is transport costs which are expected to positively influence trade between neighbours. Most barriers, however, are artificial, in the form of regulations and institutions. Some of these can protect the entire European market, as in the case of the common external tariff. Others, such as national public procurement policies, can favor individual countries or specific industries within a given country, therefore affecting intra-Community imports as well as imports of extra-Community origin. It is worth pointing out here that a large number of these barriers could be eliminated by harmonizing and integrating markets. However, other types of strategic

[3] See Krugman (1980).

actions which also result in changes detrimental to international trading conditions are deemed by governments to be their sovereign right. This type of barrier probably necessitates recourse to various forms of cooperation among states to preclude the damaging effects of a non-cooperative solution.

The final type of factor concerns the ability of suppliers to respond to the dynamics of international demand. In line with previous studies [for instance, Buigues and Goybet (1985)], one may wonder whether European corporations have been able to exploit rapidly growing product markets.

In the light of the previous distinctions, it is useful to point out the possible welfare implications of an empirical analysis of the determinants of EC imports of Community origin. In the 1960s several studies were made of the relative importance of *trade-creation* and *trade-diversion* effects resulting from the formation of the European Common Market. The main result was the strong predominance of trade creation.[4]

This issue has been raised again in the current context. But the question today is: what are the factors, at the inter- and intra-industry level, which positively influence EC imports of Community origin, and which can be viewed as expressing European competitiveness leading to sustained trade creation, and what are the factors which correspond to trade diversion? Once this question can be answered, it will be possible to indicate the characteristics of European industry which could and should be reinforced and those which have to disappear over time.

3. Empirical analysis

In this section we present an econometric study intended to account for the levels of the share of intra-EC imports in total imports for the 'big Four' member states (i.e., France, the FRG, Italy, and the UK) in 1973 and 1983. As already indicated in the previous section, the explanatory factors can be divided into four groups:

inter-industry trade determinants (human capital, physical capital, technology);
intra-industry trade determinants (economies of scale and degree of product differentiation);
barriers to trade (transport costs, tariffs, Common Agricultural Policy, public procurement); and
ability to supply rapidly growing demands.

On the basis of the previous considerations, the determinants of the intra-Community trade index can be measured as follows.

[4]See, for example, Kreinin (1974) and Balassa (1975).

The *human capital* variable is expressed by the reciprocal of the share of non-qualified employment in total employment in industry.

The *physical capital* variable is measured using per capita value added.

The *technological factor* is measured by the ratio between R&D staff and total staff.

As regards *economies of scale*, we have used British data on the output achieved in each industry by the largest plants, which account for 50% of total output.

Product differentiation is captured by a dummy variable which takes the value 1 for consumer goods and the value 0 otherwise.

Transport costs are measured by the reciprocal of the price per kilo of Belgian imports.

To measure the *common external tariff* we used the observed tariff which corresponds to the amount collected by Belgian customs divided by the value of extra-Community imports.

The role played by the *Common Agricultural Policy* is expressed by a dummy variable which takes the value 1 for the agro-business sectors and 0 for the other sectors.

One variable has been used with reference to barriers within the EC: *public procurement*. This is calculated on the basis of two-digit national input–output tables by the ratio between sales to the public sector and total sales.[5]

The rate of growth of consumption on OECD countries is used to identify *areas of fast growing world demand*.

Lastly, a dummy variable has been introduced for sector 461 (sawing and processing wood) which is characterized in all countries and for both 1973 and 1983 by an atypically low share of intra-EC imports.[6]

Our regression analysis covers all of the observations available ($n=361$), which are obtained by pooling the observations for each of the 'big Four' countries. This pooling was rendered necessary by the fact that certain structural variables were missing for some industries in some countries.[7] In order to retain the possibility of specific effects produced by the late entry of the UK, as suggested in the introduction, we have introduced a national dummy variable for the *United Kingdom*. This variable takes the value 1 if the observation belongs to the U.K. and 0 otherwise.

Two ordinary-least-squares (OLS) regressions, one for 1973 and one for

[5]The absence of three-digit input–output tables made it necessary to assume a uniform behaviour within two-digit industries.

[6]This is explained by the fact that this industry is based on a natural resource which is scarce in the EC.

[7]If the intention had been to carry out regressions by country on a sample covering the same variables and the same sectors, the number of observations per country would have been less than 20.

1983, have been carried out in order to be able to compare the possible changes of effect exercised by the explanatory variables on *the share of imports of Community origin in EC imports*. A semi-logarithmic specification has been adopted, expressing the view that the explanatory variables exercise a decreasing marginal effect.[8]

Given that the dependent variable is bounded by the values of 0 and 1, and could yield biased coefficient estimates, a logit transformation has also been made, as well as the corresponding adjustment for the expected heteroscedasticity of the residuals. Having multiplied the dependent variable m and the explanatory variables by the adjustment factor, $\sqrt{\hat{m}(1-\hat{m})}$, we have used weighted least squares to estimate our equation.[9]

The results of the regressions appear in table 1. A pair of OLS equations is presented for 1973 and 1983 (eqs. I and II), along with a parallel pair of logit eqs. (III and IV).

These regressions show a similar pattern in the years 1973 and 1983. For both years the summary statistics (R^2 and F ratio) are relatively high, and the effects of most variables are consistent with our expectations.[10] According to the OLS estimations, intensive human capital and skilled labour, substantial physical capital, and high R&D activity are all conducive to a high level of intra-Community imports in relation to imports of extra-Community origin.

In contrast, intra-Community trade is not the preferred option in fast expanding industrial sectors, confirming previous studies by the Commission of the EC. Economies of scale also have a negative impact, suggesting that, given the still fragmented Common Market, firms belonging to other large integrated industrialized countries are more able to exploit the scale advantages.

The EC also has a handicap in the domain of consumer goods, which can be considered to be systematically less standarized than intermediate goods and more dependent on efficacious non-price policies.

The common external tariff plays its anticipated part in assisting intra-Community trade. Its impact in terms of welfare does not, however, have the same positive connotation as that of R&D. It appears that in 1983 this protectionist effect is reinforced in the case of the agro-business sectors, which in all probability reflects the effective role played, in terms of diversion of trade, by the Common Agricultural Policy.

Transport costs constitute another barrier to trade. In industries where

---

[8] A double-log specification gives similar results to those obtained with the semi-log form.

[9] To obtain $\hat{m}$, m has been regressed on the same set of independent variables as in the OLS regression.

[10] An inspection of the correlation matrix does not reveal a strong collinearity problem. The matrix is available upon request.

Table 1
Regression analysis of determinants of the share of intra-EEC imports.[a]

	Ordinary least squares		Logit	
	1973 I	1983 II	1973 III	1983 IV
Constant	55.375	46.568	0.703	−0.164
	(3.61)	(3.20)	(0.84)	(−0.22)
Human capital	3.304	6.138	0.202	0.288
	(1.43)	(2.80)	(1.58)	(2.64)
Physical capital	9.970	13.610	0.462	0.669
	(2.40)	(3.46)	(2.03)	(3.37)
R&D	2.419	2.641	0.140	0.131
	(2.90)	(3.35)	(3.06)	(3.35)
Economies of scale	−1.692	−1.552	−0.070	−0.070
	(−1.73)	(−1.68)	(−1.30)	(−1.52)
Product differentiation	1.570	−4.456	0.132	−0.170
	(0.61)	(−1.83)	(0.94)	(−1.43)
Transportation costs	3.235	2.750	0.193	0.145
	(4.73)	(4.25)	(4.95)	(4.34)
Common external tariff	2.436	2.254	0.126	0.112
	(3.64)	(3.56)	(3.47)	(3.53)
Common agric. policy	−4.051	10.015	−0.110	0.581
	(−1.09)	(2.84)	(−0.54)	(3.28)
Public procurement	−2.278	−2.097	−0.094	−0.090
	(−2.50)	(−2.43)	(−1.85)	(−2.09)
Demand growth	−1.196	−2.367	−0.092	−0.133
	(−0.64)	(−1.35)	(−0.90)	(−1.53)
Sector 461	−48.139	−41.267	−3.448	−2.586
	(−4.82)	(−4.36)	(−3.50)	(−2.96)
United Kingdom	−19.370	−6.937	−1.052	−0.329
	(−6.76)	(−2.56)	(−6.78)	(−2.44)
R^2 (adjusted)	0.339	0.312	0.265	0.258
F	16.353	14.604	11.801	11.454

[a]Figures in brackets are *t*-statistics.

these costs are substantial, intra-Community trade is helped by the geographical proximity of the member states.

As regards national public procurement, the following explanation seems to account for the negative effect observed. These purchases centre mainly on activities such as telecommunications and transport where national producers are systematically favoured. If it proves essential to have recourse to the external market, extra-Community partners are given preference. It would appear that not only are national public procurement policies unfavourable to intra-Community trade, but also that they systematically encourage imports from the rest of the world.

Finally, as suggested in the introduction, the United Kingdom has a systematically inferior amount of trade with the Community.

In order to compare our results in 1973 and 1983 we have computed the beta-coefficients corresponding to the OLS estimates.[11] As regards barriers to trade, it is interesting to contrast the stable effect produced by the common external tariff with the impact of the CAP – non-significant in 1973 but positive and highly significant in 1983. The successive enlargements of the EC seem to have boosted the dissuasive effect of the Common Agricultural Policy.

Another characteristic of the 1973 and 1983 results are the increased positive effect of the R&D efforts as well as of the human and physical capital. By contrast a handicap has appeared in the consumer goods sectors.

Finally, the difference between the United Kingdom and the other three 'big' countries has been strongly reduced between 1973 and 1983. This confirms, in the context of a multivariate analysis, the convergence phenomenon identified in Jacquemin and Sapir (1988).

These results are, on the whole, confirmed when using the logit transformation. However, the negative effects of scale economies and demand growth are less significant.

Table 2

Beta-coefficients corresponding to the ordinary least squares estimates.

	1973	1983
Human capital	0.081	0.153
Physical capital	0.145	0.201
R&D	0.176	0.204
Economies of scale	−0.082	−0.085
Product differentiation	0.036	−0.118
Transportation costs	0.276	0.272
Common external tariff	0.185	0.187
Common agric. policy	−0.072	0.196
Public procurement	−0.133	−0.137
Demand growth	−0.032	−0.074
Sector 461	−0.226	−0.203
United Kingdom	−0.373	−0.145

4. Conclusions

This study is the first analysis of intra-EC trade made at a relatively disaggregated industrial level. Our work has been hampered by the absence

[11] These coefficients are obtained by multiplying the OLS estimates by the ratio of the standard deviations of the dependent and independent variables.

or poor quality of European standardizing for some data, especially concerning production and several structural variables. It is hoped that this research will encourage the indispensable setting up of more complete, homogenous information. In spite of those limitations, a set of conclusions can be derived from the study. We have seen that the EC countries are becoming increasingly involved in a process of world-wide division of labour at the expense of European integration, which is making time.

Our multiple regression analysis has enabled an initial identification of a set of variables which tend, other things being equal, to be conducive or detrimental to intra-Community imports in comparison with imports from the rest of the world. This analysis has been done for the years 1973 and 1983.

According to their probable effects in terms of Community welfare, two types of variables can be distinguished. Some, such as Research and Development and human capital, are conducive to intra-Community trade and enable better 'resistance' to imports of extra-Community origin on the basis of assets reflecting genuine competitive advantages and, therefore, trade creation. Other variables, intended to capture the common external tariff and agro-business policy, while also being conducive to intra-Community trade, probably promote it at the expense of greater integration into world competitiveness and the international division of labour, thus implying trade diversion. Just as the influence of the first type of variables could well be strengthened through various Community policies, such as cooperation in R&D and the accumulation of human capital, so the part played by the second type should be considered makeshift, destined to be gradually phased out. This suggests that it is no doubt necessary to resist the temptation to create a sort of 'generalized Community preference' designed to defend intra-EC trade systematically by various measures resulting in the checking of the progress of world free trade. But it is also necessary to beware of a pure 'laissez-faire, laissez-passer' approach, which would ignore the importance, for the common interest, of strategic behaviour patterns in the formation and dynamics of competitive advantages.

References

Balassa, B., 1975, Trade creation and trade diversion in the European Common Market: An appraisal of the evidence, in: B. Balassa, ed., European economic integration (North-Holland, Amsterdam).

Buigues, P. and P. Goybet, 1985, Competitiveness of European industry: Situation to date, European Economy, Sept.

Deardorff, A., 1984, Testing trade theories and predicting trade flows, in: R. Jones and P. Kenen, eds., Handbook of international economics, Vol. I (North-Holland, Amsterdam).

De Grauwe, P., 1987, International trade and economic growth in the European monetary system, European Economic Review, Feb./March.

Jacquemin, A. and A. Sapir, 1988, European integration or world integration?, Weltwirtschaftliches Archiv, 127–139.

Kreinin, M., 1974, Trade relations of the EEC; An empirical investigation (Praeger, New York).

Krugman, P., 1980, Scale economies, product differentiation, and the pattern of trade, American Economic Review 950–959.

Lawrence, R.Z., 1987, Trade performance as a constraint on European growth, in: R.Z. Lawrence and C.L. Schultz, eds., Barriers to European growth; a transatlantic view (Brookings, Washington, D.C.).

Linder, S.B., 1961, An essay on trade transformation (Wiley, New York).

Owen, N., 1983, Economies of scale, competitiveness, and trade patterns within the European Community (Clarendon Press, Oxford).

Pelkmans, J., 1986, The competitiveness of European industry and the internal market, Paper presented at the EIASM Seminar on Competitiveness of European Industry, Brussels, 27–28 Feb.

Geographically Discriminatory Trade Arrangements

Bob Hamilton and John Whalley*

Abstract—An eight-region numerical general equilibrium model of global trade is used to investigate the impacts of various geographically discriminatory trade policy arrangements (GDAs) on regional trade and welfare. Results suggest that the important factors determining gains and losses in any GDA are such issues as whether initial levels of protection are asymmetric, the relative sizes of participating regions, and the pattern of trade between participating and non-participating countries. Results also appear to confirm the implication of Wonnacott and Wonnacott (1981) that the gain from reducing a partner's tariff is typically a more important consideration in evaluating potential benefits from a customs union, than the traditional concerns of trade creation and trade diversion.

I. INTRODUCTION

Current concerns among trade policy-makers over geographically discriminatory trade arrangements (GDAs) reflect a number of different factors. One is that many commentators on trade policy matters are now taking an increasingly pessimistic view on the future of multilateralism under the GATT. Another is the increasing discussion of geographically discriminatory arrangements as instruments of trade policy.

These raise a number of important issues. Is it true that trading regions can improve on current multilateral GATT arrangements through bilateral or other GDAs? If so, what form are regional groupings likely to take if there is further fragmentation in the GATT, and how do the competing interests of the major industrialized countries come into play in determining what could happen? Should the GATT continue to operate on its present multilateral basis involving (effectively) only developed countries, and how can developing countries be brought into this trade liberalization process?

In this paper a numerical eight-region general equilibrium model of world trade is used[1] to evaluate the impacts on both global and regional trade and welfare of alternative GDAs. The results presented bear on

Received for publication May 15, 1984. Revision accepted for publication December 20, 1984.

* University of Western Ontario.

We are grateful to seminar groups at the National Bureau of Economic Research and Western Ontario for helpful comments. We wish to acknowledge financial support from SSHRC, Ottawa.

[1] This is an extension of earlier four- and seven-region models due to Brown and Whalley (1980), and Whalley (1985).

these questions, but are also relevant to theoretical debates on the customs union issue. A recent paper by Wonnacott and Wonnacott (1981) implicitly argues that much of the previous customs union literature[2] may have neglected a significant factor in both explaining customs union formation and analyzing gains and losses to individual countries. They suggest that the major reason any country participates in a customs union is to penetrate the partner's market, and the main source of increased penetration (and the main benefit from participation) comes from the reduction of the partner tariff. Wonnacott and Wonnacott emphasize that in most cases where customs unions are involved, negotiators concentrate almost exclusively on the reduction of the partner tariff.

Our results suggest that in any particular GDA it is usually relatively easy to identify the main considerations in determining both the total size of the joint gain and its division between regions. Whether any individual country gains or loses, for instance, is most heavily influenced by the initial level of protection in the partner country. Traditional trade creation/trade diversion effects come surprisingly low on the list.

II. A GENERAL EQUILIBRIUM MODEL OF WORLD TRADE

The eight-region numerical general equilibrium model of world trade used to analyze impacts of GDAs is based on earlier four- and seven-region global trade modelling efforts in which the second author has been involved. The description here is kept brief since the main focus is on results and the model is described elsewhere; see Whalley (1985).

The model is most easily thought of as a numerical analogue of a Heckscher-Ohlin trade model, with the two departures from pure Heckscher-Ohlin form that demand production function parameters differ across regions, and that products are heterogeneous across regions rather than homogeneous. The model incorporates eight trading regions: the United States, the EEC, Japan, Canada, Other Developed, New Industrialized (NICs), and Less Developed Countries (LDC's). The size of these regions in the model reflects their relative U.S. dollar GNP for 1977 in the World Bank Atlas.[3]

The model incorporates six products produced in each region: 1. Agriculture and Food; 2. Mineral Products and Extractive Ores; 3. Energy Products (including oil); 4. Non-mechanical Manufacturing; 5. Machinery and Transport Equipment (including vehicles); and 6. Construction, Services, and Other Non-traded Goods. Each of the first five goods are internationally traded, with an assumed heterogeneity by region prevailing across production sources. The sixth commodity is nontraded for all regions.

The same commodity classification is used for trade, domestic production

---

[2] See, for example, Viner (1950), Lipsey (1957), Johnson (1965) and Berglas (1979).
[3] See the discussion in Whalley (1985).

and final demands, with an approximate concordance adopted between the different classification systems appearing in the basic data used to parameterize the model. Problems of data availability for all regions, plus the dimensions involved in obtaining a general equilibrium solution for an eight-region model, limit the model to 6 products and 8 regions; 48 products in total.

The assumption of product heterogeneity by region (the so-called 'Armington' assumption) implies that products are differentiated on the basis of geographical point of production as well as by physical character-istics. Similar products are imperfect substitutes in both demand and production, i.e., Japanese manufactures are treated as qualitatively different products from U.S. or EEC manufactures. This treatment is used both to accommodate the statistical phenomenon of cross-hauling in international trade data, and to exclude specialization in production occurring as a behavioral response in the model.[4] This structure also enables empirically based import demand elasticities to be incorporated into the model specification.

Explicit demand functions for each region are derived from hierarchical CES/LES preference functions, and CES production functions are used.[5] Producers maximize profits and competitive forces operate such that in equilibrium all supernormal profits are competed away. Trade in newly produced investment goods (investment flows), interest and dividends, and foreign aid also enter the model, with the latter two being treated as income transfers between regions.

The model examines international trade equilibria, where demands equal supplies for all products, and in each region a zero-profit condition is satisfied for each industry, representing the absence of supernormal profits. In equilibrium, a zero external sector balance condition (including investment flows, dividends, interest and transfers) holds for each region.

Production and demand patterns in each of the regions revolve around the domestic and world price systems. For each product the market price is taken to be the price at point of production. Sellers receive these prices, purchasers (of both intermediate and final products) pay these prices gross of tariffs, NTB tariff equivalents, and domestic taxes. No transportion costs are considered.

An important feature of the model is the structure of substitution possibilities on both the demand and production sides, as represented by the CES and CES/LES functions. The elasticities of substitution in these

---

[4] In some of the earlier numerical general equilibrium models where homogeneous products were assumed, large production responses were encountered even for cases where the change in trade policies was quite small. This reflected the limited curvature of production surfaces in these models. The use of the Armington assumption on the demand side removes extremes of specialization from the model.

[5] It is important to note that constant rather than increasing returns to scale production functions are used. This issue as it relates to numerical general equilibrium modelling is discussed in Harris (1984) and Whalley (1984).

functions determine price elasticities of goods and factor demands. Because of the product heterogeneity assumption, these elasticities also control import and export demand elasticities for each region.

In production, each industry has a CES value-added production function which specifies substitution possibilities between the primary factor inputs, capital and labor services. No technical change is incorporated, and both factor inputs are assumed immobile between regions. In addition, each industry uses the outputs of other industries (both domestic and imported) as inputs in its own production process. Substitution between intermediate products is incorporated, while fixed coefficients in terms of composite goods are assumed.

Each fixed coefficient requirement is specified in terms of a composite good, which itself is represented by a nested CES function, with elements of the composite (i.e., products identified by geographical point of production) entering as arguments. Substitution occurs between comparable domestic and composite imported commodities at the top level of nesting, with further substitution taking place between import types differentiated by location of production.

On the demand side, final demand functions are used for each region, derived from nested CES/LES utility functions. A hierarchy of substitution possibilities is used, involving similar products imported from the various regions and composites of imports across sources and comparable domestic products. Use of these nested functions enables empirical estimates of price and income elasticities in world trade to be incorporated into the model. These values guide parameter choice for elasticity values in the nested CES functions (i.e., between similar products subscripted by location of production). The LES features allow income elasticities in import demand functions to differ from unity.

Since each region generates demands from utility maximization, the market demand functions in the model satisfy Walras' Law, i.e., that at any set of prices the total value of demands equals the total value of incomes. The incomes of regions are derived from the sale of primary factor endowments, plus transfers received (including foreign aid).

The model incorporates tariffs and non-tariff barriers (NTBs) in ad valorem equivalent form, along with domestic tax policies. Other domestic distortions, such as those in labor and capital markets, are ignored. Impacts of various GDAs can be considered by computing equilibria associated with alternative policy regimes.

The procedures used in applying the model are summarized in Whalley (1985). A worldwide general equilibrium constructed from 1977 data is assumed in the presence of existing trade policies in all regions. The model is calibrated to this data set through a procedure which determines parameter values for the model functions consistent with this equilibrium observation. Counterfactual analysis then proceeds for any specified policy change. A counterfactual equilibrium for a policy or other change is found using a Newton method involving an estimate of the Jacobian matrix of excess factor demands and government budget imbalances.

This calibration procedure first involves constructing a data set for a given year in a form which is consistent with the equilibrium solution concept of the model; a 'benchmark equilibrium data set.' Once assembled, parameter values for equations can be directly calculated from the equilibrium conditions using the calibration procedure described in Mansur and Whalley (1984). Since the model specification must be capable of reproducing the benchmark data as an equilibrium solution, this calibration procedure requires more information than contained in the benchmark equilibrium data set when CES/LES functional forms are used. This is met by specifying elasticities of substitution and minimum requirements in the functional forms. Once these are chosen, demand functions are solved for share parameters consistent with both equilibrium prices and quantities. On the supply side, cost functions are similarly solved for share and unit parameters consistent with equilibrium prices and input use by industry.

As might be expected, the values chosen for substitution elasticities have a substantial impact on the results produced by the model, and so a central case model specification is adopted around which sensitivity analysis can be performed. Given the present focus on effects of changes in trade policies, an especially important set of parameters are the substitution elasticities which determine trade elasticities. Import price elasticities for developed countries in the model reflect the Stern, Francis, and Schumacher (1976) compendium of trade elasticities, and estimates for developing countries are due to Khan (1974). Estimates for the United States, EEC, and Japan by Stone (1979) provide detailed estimates by product, and are approximately consistent with the values used in the model. The low values (in absolute terms) of import price elasticities produced by these and other studies have been extensively commented on in the literature. In the present model these produce significant terms of trade effects under alternative GDAs, and their role should thus be highlighted.

III. RESULTS

We consider a number of bilateral trade arrangements each involving various combinations of the regions identified in the model. Counterfactual equilibria under these alternative policy regimes are computed and compared to the 1977 benchmark equilibrium. We focus on the annual welfare effects by region as measured by Hicksian equivalent variations in 1977 billions of dollars, and on regional terms of trade effects. We initially concentrate on free trade areas to abstract from the terms of trade effects which may accompany the adoption of common external protection.

In table 1 results are reported for a series of two-region free trade areas, each involving the United States. This series of free trade areas is

TABLE 1. *Results for a Series of Bilaterial Free Trade Areas (FTAs) Involving the U.S. (all protection bilaterally removed)*

	US–EEC FTA	US–Japan FTA	US–Canada FTA	US–Other Dev. FTA	US–NIC FTA	US–LDC FTA
A. *Annual Welfare Impacts (EVs in $billions, 1977)*						
US	5.1	2.8	0.6	2.0	8.1	8.0
EEC	0.7	0.0	–0.2	–0.9	–0.4	–1.0
Japan	0.2	1.2	–0.1	–0.1	–0.4	–0.3
Canada	–0.4	–0.3	1.3	0.0	0.2	0.0
Other Dev.	–2.6	–1.5	0.0	0.5	0.0	0.5
OPEC	0.1	0.0	0.0	0.0	–0.1	–0.5
NIC	–0.9	–0.5	–0.2	0.0	–2.9	0.6
LDC	–1.8	–1.2	–0.1	–0.2	0.0	–0.2
B. *Terms of Trade Impacts (% change, positive indicates improvement)*						
US	2.5	1.4	0.0	0.7	3.4	3.6
EEC	–0.3	0.0	–0.1	–0.4	–0.1	–0.5
Japan	0.2	0.1	–0.1	0.0	–0.4	–0.2
Canada	–0.8	–0.6	0.7	–0.1	0.2	–0.2
Other Dev.	–1.2	–0.7	0.0	–0.2	0.0	0.2
OPEC	0.2	0.1	0.1	0.1	–0.1	0.2
NIC	–0.6	–0.4	–0.1	0.0	–6.4	0.3
LDC	–1.0	–0.7	0.0	–0.1	–0.1	–4.6

somewhat arbitrarily chosen from the many combinations of regions which can be considered with the model. Although all protection is bilaterally removed in these cases, we have also considered comparable cases in which we eliminate only tariffs. These are not reported due to space constraints.

In the U.S.–EEC case, the United States receives a welfare gain, the EEC a somewhat smaller gain, while most other regions lose. The terms of trade effects are positive for the United States, and small negative for the EEC. The single most important factor determining the outcome in this particular case is differences in the initial levels of protection in the United States and the EEC, particularly the higher non-tariff barriers on agricultural products in the EEC. The terms of trade effects are explained primarily by the U.S. penetration of EEC markets as the EEC removes its agricultural NTBs against the United States.[6] A comparable pattern occurs in the U.S.–Japanese case, where significant gains also occur for the United States, with smaller gains for Japan and a small terms of trade improvement. Again, the asymmetries in initial levels of protection,

---

[6] In other results for a U.S.–EEC free trade area (not reported here) where only tariffs are removed and agricultural NTBs remain unchanged, the terms of trade effect for the EEC becomes positive.

particularly in the NTBs, are a dominant factor in determining the outcome.

In the U.S.–Canadian case, most of the gains go to Canada since Canada is a small region relative to the United States. This accords with the intuition that the relative size of regions can also be a dominant factor in determining the division of gains from a free trade arrangement. The United States gains in this case because of the removal of non-tariff barriers in Canada; where tarrifs alone are eliminated bilaterally, the United States loses.

In the U.S.–Other Developed case, once again, asymmetries in the initial levels of protection are the dominant consideration in determining who gains and who loses. The Other Developed region includes the smaller GATT members (e.g., Australia, New Zealand, Austria) who have higher levels of protection than larger countries such as the United States. In the two final cases in table 1, involving free trade between the United States and NICs and the United States and LDCs, the importance of these asymmetries in the initial levels of protection becomes even clearer. In these cases both the NICs and LDCs, which are sharply more protectionist than the United States, have a significant terms of trade loss, and the United States a marked term of trade gain.

In each of these cases the United States experiences gains of varying sizes. However, rather than trade creation/trade diversion effects being the important consideration, the initial levels of protection in the regions participating in the free trade arrangement, and differences in relative sizes of regions, principally determine gains and losses.

In table 2 further free trade areas are evaluated. In the EEC–Japanese case, where the initial levels of protection are more symmetric than in the U.S. cases, both the EEC and Japan gain, with a slightly larger terms of trade improvement for Japan.

Results for a 'Northern' free trade area (table 2, column 2) provide some insight on the issue of whether or not countries gain more from multilateral rather than bilateral arrangements. In this case, all five participants in the free trade arrangement improve their welfare by the free trade arrangement. Only the Other Developed suffers a terms of trade deterioration, although they still receive a welfare gain due to the consumption effects associated with the free trade area. The gains to all other participating regions are large. For the United States, the $5 billion gain is dominated only by a free trade arrangement with the EEC. The $9.5 billion gain to the EEC compares to a $0.7 billion gain from a free trade arrangement with the United States. The Japanese gain of $2 billion compares to a $1.2 billion gain from a free trade area with the United States, and Canada also gains more than it would from a free trade arrangement with the United States.

These results suggest that a major effect of the GATT is an improvement in the terms of trade of developed countries with NICs and LDCs. GATT

TABLE 2. *Welfare Results from Further Free Trade Areas (all protection removed within FTA)*

	EEC–Japan FTA	'Northern' FTA (US, EEC, Japan, Canada, Other Dev.) Other Dev.)	'Southern' FTA (NIC, LDC)
A. *Annual Welfare Impacts (EVs in $billions 1977)*			
US	–0.3	5.0	0.0
EEC	0.8	9.5	–0.2
Japan	1.0	2.0	–0.2
Canada	–0.0	2.4	0.1
Other Dev.	–0.7	0.3	–0.1
OPEC	0.0	–0.8	–0.0
NIC	–0.4	–4.8	–0.1
LDC	–0.6	–9.6	3.7
B. *Terms of Trade Impacts (% change, positive indicates improvement)*			
US	–0.2	1.4	–0.0
EEC	0.3	2.8	–0.1
Japan	0.8	0.1	–0.2
Canada	–0.1	2.5	0.1
Other Dev.	–0.3	–1.6	–0.1
OPEC	–0.1	–0.6	–0.1
NIC	–0.2	–3.2	–1.4
LDC	–0.3	–5.1	1.4

trade liberalization stimulates trade in manufactured products among developed countries, and developed countries improve their terms of trade with exporters of agricultural products and raw materials (LDCs).

The final column of table 2 examines a Southern free trade area between NICs and LDCs. In this case, NICs participating in the free trade area suffer a welfare loss. NICs are a significant importer of raw materials and agricultural products from LDCs, while LDC imports from NICs are much smaller, LDCs increase their penetration of NIC markets more than NICs increase their access to LDC markets. This result emphasizes that a third consideration, the initial pattern of trade between the participating regions, can also be crucial in determining results, as well as asymmetries in initial levels of protection or size of regions.

In table 3, we examine the U.S.–Canadian case in more detail, emphasizing the importance of factors beyond trade creation and trade diversion in determining regional gains or losses from GDAs. The first column reports the same U.S.–Canadian free trade arrangements as considered in table 1, the abolition of all protection. The second column reports results of abolition of only tariffs. As already mentioned, the United States suffers both a terms of trade and welfare loss in this case. Subsequent columns investigate the impacts of using alternative common levels of external protection in the GDA, on regional gains or losses.

TABLE 3. *Further Investigation of U.S.–Canadian Trade Arrangements*

	US–Canada FTA[a] All Protection	US–Canada FTA Tariffs Only	US–Canada CU[b]–Tariffs–Common Tariff US Rates	US–Canada CU–All Protection–Common Protection US Rates	US–Canada CU–Tariffs–Common Tariff Canadian Rates	US–Canada CU–All Protection–Common Protection Canadian Rates	US–Canada CU–All Protection–Common External Protection–10%	US–Canada CU–All Protection–Common External Protection–20%	US–Canada CU–All Protection–Common External Protection–30%
A. Annual Welfare Impacts (EVs in $billions, 1977)									
US	0.6	-0.6	-0.7	0.4	1.6	2.8	0.0	8.2	14.9
EEC	-0.2	-0.1	0.0	0.1	-1.2	-1.3	1.0	-1.9	-4.5
Japan	-0.1	-0.1	-0.0	-0.1	-0.8	-0.9	-0.2	-1.9	-3.3
Canada	1.3	1.1	1.0	1.1	1.1	1.3	1.1	1.9	2.4
Other Dev.	0.0	0.0	0.1	0.0	-0.4	-0.4	0.4	-0.2	-0.7
OPEC	0.0	0.0	0.0	0.0	-0.0	-0.1	-2.0	-4.7	-7.1
NIC	-0.2	-0.0	0.0	0.0	-0.4	-0.5	3.1	0.8	-1.2
LDC	-0.1	0.0	-0.0	-0.2	-0.0	-0.2	2.3	1.5	1.3
B. Terms of Trade Impacts (% change, positive indicates improvement)									
US	0.0	-0.4	-0.5	-0.1	1.0	1.5	-0.9	4.5	9.6
EEC	-0.1	-0.1	0.0	0.1	-0.5	-0.5	0.4	-0.8	-1.9
Japan	-0.1	-0.1	-0.1	-0.1	-0.9	-0.9	-0.3	-1.9	-3.3
Canada	0.7	1.8	1.4	-0.1	1.8	0.7	-0.1	1.6	3.1
Other Dev.	0.0	0.0	0.0	-0.0	-0.1	-0.2	0.1	-0.1	-0.3
OPEC	0.1	0.0	0.0	0.0	0.1	0.1	-1.4	-2.8	-4.3
NIC	-0.1	-0.0	0.0	0.0	-0.2	-0.3	2.0	0.5	-0.9
LDC	0.0	0.0	0.0	-0.0	-0.1	-0.1	1.4	0.9	0.3

[a] FTA = Free Trade Area.
[b] CU = Customs Union.

In the U.S.–Canada customs union case, where only tariffs are eliminated and the common tariff is set at U.S. rates, welfare effects are comparable to the free trade arrangement with tariffs only. However, where the common protection is set at Canadian levels, a sharp gain accrues to the United States with a larger gain to Canada. These results occur because when U.S. protection is raised to Canadian levels, Canada (being the relatively smaller country) gains from the higher protection in the United States, and further penetrates the U.S. market. In the all protection case, setting common external protection at either U.S. or Canadian levels also makes a major difference to the size of gains or losses. A terms of trade deterioration occurs for the United States with common protection set at Canadian rates.

The final three columns emphasize how the level of common external protection in a customs union can sharply affect the size of regional gains or losses. Varying common external protection between 10% and 30% increases the welfare gain to the United States from a customs union with Canada in the all protection case from $0 to $14 billion, with the latter case resulting in a terms of trade improvement of nearly 10%. The impact of the level of common external protection on the terms of trade for Canada also shows through in these cases.

We conclude from this table that the usual focus in the customs union literature on trade creation and trade diversion effects not only neglects the important issue of the initial level of partner protection, but also neglects the potential for a joint terms of trade improvement through common external protection. This in turn suggests that while the threat to multilateralism in the GATT from bilateral free trade arrangements may be small, the threat from groups of countries breaking away and forming customs unions who then exploit common external protection for a terms of trade gain may be more pronounced.

Table 4 reports impacts on trade flows for the US–EEC bilateral free trade arrangement considered earlier, and reveals some of the difficulties in separately identifying trade creation and trade diversion effects from GDAs. This table emphasizes the differences between general equilibrium calculations of the effects of GDAs in which all effects, including terms of trade changes, are captured, and the partial equilibrium analyses in theoretical literature which abstract from terms of trade effects. In the U.S.–EEC free trade area case, for example, there is an increase in imports by the United States from the EEC of approximately $6 billion. However, because of the trade balance condition, the import change column for the EEC is completed by a series of negatives, and the column for the United States by a series of positives. Because of the change in relative price it becomes difficult to separately identify the trade creation and trade diversion effects from these numbers alone.

An understandable concern with the approach used here is that the particular numerical specification in the model may be crucial for results.

TABLE 4. *Impacts of Geographical Discriminatory Arrangements on Trade Flows (changes in trade flows in 1977 $ billions)*

US–EEC Free Trade Area (All Protection)

Exporting Region	US	EEC	Japan	Importing Region Canada Dev.	Other	OPEC	NIC	LDC
US	0.0	9.7	–0.4	–0.4	–0.7	–0.4	–0.5	–0.6
EEC	5.8	0.0	0.1	0.1	–0.6	0.3	0.1	–0.0
Japan	0.6	–0.2	0.0	0.0	–0.2	–0.0	–0.0	–0.2
Canada	0.7	–0.5	–0.0	0.0	–0.0	–0.0	–0.0	–0.0
Other Dev.	0.8	–2.1	0.3	0.1	0.0	0.2	0.1	0.1
OPEC	0.8	–0.4	–0.0	0.0	–0.2	0.0	–0.1	–0.2
NIC	0.7	–0.9	0.0	0.0	–0.1	0.0	0.0	–0.0
LDC	0.7	–1.2	0.2	0.0	–0.0	0.2	0.0	0.0

This issue is investigated in table 5. In these sensitivity analyses, we focus on the U.S.–EEC free trade area case from table 1, and vary elasticities from the values used in the central case specification of the model. Central case welfare and terms of trade results from table 1 are given in the final column on the right-hand side of the table.

Varying elasticities of substitution for import types from the central case values (in the neighborhood of 1) between 1.5 and 5 for all products in all regions sharply increases the welfare gains and terms of trade improvements which accrue to the EEC and the United States. This occurs because the key margin of substitution in a free trade area is between the geographically subscripted products. The larger is this elasticity, the larger the substitution effect in favor of partners in the free trade arrangement.

On the other hand, varying the elasticity of substitution between composite imports and domestic products can change results the other way. If the elasticity of substitution between domestic and imported products is set at 0.75, the terms of trade improvement for the EEC in the central case changes to a terms of trade deterioration. The terms of trade improvement for the United States is larger in this case because in the central case the import price elasticity in the United States is larger than in the EEC. The use of a common 0.75 value thus removes the effect of the difference across regions.

When the elasticity of substitution between domestic products and import composites is raised, terms of trade effects become more negative for the EEC and smaller for the United States because of the change in the relative elasticities between composites of imports and domestic products, and import types. Under changes in import income elasticities, results are relatively unaffected, confirming that the key parameters affecting results in GDAs are those producing the substitution effects between products subscripted by region, rather than income effects.

TABLE 5. Sensitivity Analysis for U.S.–EEC Free Trade (All Protection)[a]

	Elasticity of Substitution between Import Types Set at 5.0 All Regions	Elasticity of Substitution between Import Types Set at 5.0 All Regions	Elasticity of Substitution Between Domestic Products and Imports Set at 0.75 All Regions	Elasticity of Substitution between Domestic Products and Imports Set at 1.5 All Regions	Elasticity of Substitution between Domestic Products and Imports Set at 3.0 All Regions	Import Income Elasticity = 0.9 for Regions 1–6, 1.1 for Regions 7, 8	Import Income Elasticity = 0.75 for Regions 1–6, 1.25 Regions 7, 8	Import Income Elasticity 1.5 for All Regions	Central Case
A. Annual Welfare Impacts (EV's in $billions, 1977)									
US	9.2	12.5	9.6	5.8	3.3	5.2	5.1	4.8	5.1
EEC	2.6	3.3	-0.2	-0.8	-0.5	0.9	1.3	0.4	0.7
Japan	0.1	0.2	-0.4	0.0	0.6	0.2	0.2	0.1	0.2
Canada	-1.4	-2.1	-1.7	-0.4	0.4	-0.4	-0.4	-0.4	-0.4
Other Dev.	-5.2	-6.9	-3.5	-1.4	-0.1	-2.7	-2.8	-2.3	-2.6
OPEC	-0.4	-0.8	0.1	-0.1	-0.0	0.1	0.1	0.1	0.1
NIC	-2.7	-4.2	-2.3	-0.7	1.0	-0.8	-0.7	-0.7	-0.9
LDC	-3.9	-5.3	-2.8	-1.3	0.6	-1.7	-1.6	-2.8	-1.8
TOTAL	-1.7	-3.2	-1.3	1.2	5.3	0.7	1.4	-1.0	1.0
B. Terms of Trade Effects (% change, positive indicates improvement)									
US	4.5	5.9	5.5	3.0	1.2	2.5	2.3	2.6	2.5
EEC	0.8	1.4	-0.5	-1.1	-1.5	-0.3	-0.3	-0.1	-0.3
Japan	0.1	0.2	-0.4	0.1	0.6	0.3	0.3	0.1	0.2
Canada	-3.0	-4.3	-3.5	-0.8	0.5	-0.8	-0.7	-1.0	-0.8
Other Dev.	-2.3	-2.9	-1.6	-0.6	0.0	-1.1	-1.1	-1.3	-1.2
OPEC	-0.2	-0.6	0.4	0.3	0.3	0.2	0.2	0.2	0.2
NIC	-1.7	-2.5	-1.7	-0.4	0.5	-0.6	-0.6	-0.7	-0.6
LDC	-2.2	-3.0	-1.8	-0.7	0.2	-1.0	-1.0	-1.0	-1.0

[a] The elasticity configuration used in the central case is as follows:
Substitution elasticity between import types is 1.5 for all countries.
Substitution elasticity between domestic and imported products for Regions 1–8 are 1.66, 0.9, 0.78, 1.02, 0.89, 1.38, 1.28.
Unit income elasticities in demands in all regions.

IV. CONCLUSION

In this paper an eight-region numerical general equilibrium model of global trade is used to investigate the impacts of various geographically discriminatory trade policy arrangements (GDAs) on regional trade and welfare. Our analysis is motivated both by the policy concern that pressures for regional fragmentation of existing multilateral trade arrangements are growing, and recent debates in the customs union literature as to the significance of various factors in determining the outcome in any particular union.

Results suggest that the important factors determining gains and losses in any GDA are such issues as whether initial levels of protection are asymmetric, the relative size of participating regions, and the pattern of trade between participating and non-participating countries, rather than the trade creation/trade diversion issues usually emphasized in theoretical literature. Results also suggest that while the incentives to engage in bilateral free trade areas rather than to participate in multilateral negotiations (such as the GATT) may be small, use of common external protection by participants better off compared to wider multilateral arrangements. Finally, results appear to confirm the implication of the recent paper by Wonnacott (1981) that the gain from reducing a partner's tariff is typically a much more important consideration in evaluating potential benefits from a customs union, than the traditional concerns of trade creation and trade diversion.

REFERENCES

Berglas, Eitan, 'Preferential Trading Theory: The *n* Commodity Case,' *Journal of Political Economy* 87 (Dec. 1979), 913–931.
Brown, Fred, and John Whalley, 'General Equilibrium Evaluations of Tariff-Cutting Proposals in the Tokyo Round and Comparisons with more Extensive Liberalisation of World Trade,' *Economic Journal* 90 (Dec. 1980), 838–866.
Harris, R. G. (with the assistance of David Cox), *Trade, Industrial Policy, and Canadian Manufacturing*, Ontario Economic Council (1984).
Johnson, Harry G., 'An Economic Theory of Protectionism, Tariff Bargaining and the Formation of Customs Unions,' *Journal of Political Economy* 73 (June 1965), 256–283.
Khan, Mohsin S., 'Import and Export Demand in Developing Countries,' *IMF Staff Papers* (Nov. 1974), 678–693.
Lipsey, Robert G., 'Trade Diversion and Welfare,' *Economica* 24 (Feb. 1957), 40–46.
Mansur, A., and John Whalley, 'Numerical Specification of Applied General Equilibrium Models: Estimation, Calibration and Data,' in H. Scarf and J. Shoven (eds.), *Applied General Equilibrium Analysis* (New York: Cambridge University Press, 1984).

Stern, R. M., J. Francis and B. Schumacher, *Price Elasticities in International Trade: An Annotated Bibliography* (New York: Macmillan Publishing Co. for the Trade Policy Research Centre, 1976).

Stone, Joe A., 'Price Elasticities of Demand for Imports and Exports: Industry Estimates for the U.S., the EEC, and Japan,' this REVIEW 61 (May 1979), 306–312.

Viner, J., *The Customs Union Issue*, Carnegie Endowment for International Peace (1950).

Whalley, John, 'Trade, Industrial Policy, and Canadian Manufacturing,' review article of a monograph by Richard Harris, *Canadian Journal of Economics* 18 (May 1984), 386–398.

——, *Trade Liberalization Among Major World Trading Areas* (Cambridge, MA: MIT Press, 1985).

Wonnacott, Paul, and Ron Wonnacott, 'Is Unilateral Tariff Reduction Preferable to a Customs Union? The Curious Case of the Missing Foreign Tariffs,' *American Economic Review* 71 (Sept. 1981), 704–714.

The Community's Industrial Competitiveness and International Trade in Manufactured Products

P. Buigues and Ph. Goybet

1. INTRODUCTION

This paper examines the European Community's trading performance since the first oil shock, sets out the main findings of that examination and, finally, indicates broadly the directions in which international trade is likely to develop, as well as the new challenges for the European Community. The analysis is based exclusively on manufactured products, i.e. on the focal point of international trade. Manufactured products account for 85 per cent of all trade in goods and goods for some 78 per cent of all trade in goods and services.

The approach adopted is based on one established fact. Since 1973, despite sluggish economic growth, demand for a small number of industrial products has remained buoyant, with growth rates akin to those of the 1960s. The great success achieved by some industrialized countries, in particular Japan, stems from the fact that they have been particularly adept at adapting to structural changes in world demand. The more flexible and innovative they have become, the better they have been able to adjust to these structural changes, redirecting, in step with those changes, their means of production to the growth sectors of the economy.

TRENDS IN WORLD DEMAND

On the basis of a breakdown of industry into 14 branches it is possible to compare and classify those branches in terms of the rate of growth of domestic demand over the period 1972–85 (Table 1). The definition of demand used here for each of the three major areas (Europe, United States, and Japan) is a conventional one: domestic demand = share of domestic output intended for the home market + imports. Defined in this way, domestic demand (or apparent consumption) is a much broader concept than final domestic demand, since it also includes intermediate consumption. Three categories of branches will be applied systematically:

The views expressed are those of the authors, who are employees of the Commission of the European Communities, and remain their sole responsibility and not that of the Commission and its services.

TABLE 1. *Trends in domestic demand by industrial branch in the Community, the United States and Japan, in volume terms. Average annual rate of growth over the period 1972–85 (percentages)*

	EUR7	USA	Japan
Strong-demand sectors	*5.0*	*5.2*	*14.3*
Office and data processing equipment	9.0	6.5	7.2
Electrical and electronic equipment and supplies	3.5	7.2	20.7
Chemicals and pharmaceuticals	5.3	2.3	9.9
Moderate-demand sectors	*1.2*	*2.8*	*3.1*
Rubber and plastics	2.8	5.4	2.0
Transport equipment	1.7	2.7	5.2
Food, beverages, and tobacco	1.2	0.4	0.0
Paper pulp, packaging, and printing	1.6	2.9	2.7
Industrial and agricultural machinery	−0.1	5.6	5.6
Weak-demand sectors	*−0.3*	*0.5*	*2.4*
Metal goods	−0.5	−0.4	3.4
Miscellaneous industrial goods	−0.6	2.1	1.9
Ferrous and non-ferrous minerals and metals	+0.6	−1.8	2.0
Textiles, leather and clothing	−0.2	2.0	2.2
Non-metallic minerals (construction materials)	+0.1	1.7	1.1

Source: Volimex, Commission services.
Note: The sectors are divided between those in which demand between 1972 and 1985 in OECD countries increased by more than 5 per cent (strong demand), those in which demand increased by around 3 per cent (moderate demand) and those in which demand increased by less than 2 per cent (weak demand).

Strong-demand sectors

The branches included in this category are by far the least affected by the cyclical fluctuations observed in the industrialized economies. Such is the case, for example, with the information technology, office equipment, and precision instruments branch, where the average annual rate of growth has remained practically unchanged since the beginning of the 1970s. It is interesting to note, moreover, that information technology needs have grown more rapidly in Europe (9 per cent per year) than in the United States and Japan (6.5 per cent and 7.2 per cent per year respectively). European firms in this sector have therefore invested heavily in new plant and machinery, the problem being to know whether supply has managed to keep pace with this sharp increase in demand.

Electrical engineering (electrical equipment, heavy electrical plant) and electronics (consumer electronics, telecommunications equipment) present a somewhat different picture. Growth in Europe (3.5 per cent per year) lags a long way behind that in Japan (20.7 per cent per year). However, a closer analysis of the trends in world demand shows that demand for electronic components is continuing to expand rapidly, while heavy electrical plant is experiencing some contraction in demand.

In the chemical sector a similar production differentiation phenomenon is evident. While pharmaceuticals have been spared by the crisis, the petrochemical industry as a whole has suffered the backlash of higher oil prices. Emphasis must be laid here on the buoyant growth in the Community chemicals market in contrast to the United States market.

A feature common to this group of products for which there is very strong demand is their very pronounced new-technology content. This group of industries on its own accounts for over 50 per cent of R&D spending, whereas it represents about 25 per cent of value-added.

Moderate-demand sectors

This grouping comprises sectors that differ a great deal both in terms of their role in the productive system and as regards type of customer. It includes plant and machinery for the productive system, and demand for such equipment is heavily dependent on the trend of gross fixed capital formation in industry: industrial and agricultural machinery. The scale of the investment problem facing European countries is clearly illustrated by the differences in the growth rate of demand between Europe (−0.1 per cent per year), the United States and Japan (5.6 per cent per year).

This grouping also includes the agri-food, drink, and tobacco industries, which are directly dependent on private consumption. Growth in this area has been modest (around 1 per cent per year) but has followed a very steady trend over time, having been hardly affected by the crises. The situation is similar in the case of paper pulp, packaging, and printing, and in that of rubber and plastics.

A more detailed disaggregation would be needed for the transport equipment sector. Shipbuilding, for example, has been severely hit by the crisis, while aerospace emerged in much better shape. Lastly, demand for cars, which plays a considerable part in European industry, has not returned to the growth levels recorded in the 1970s, when households were buying for the first time. Demand for cars is now slackening, and is often confined to replacement purchases, particularly in the United States.

Weak-demand sectors
(growth of less than 1 per cent per year on average over the long term)

This category includes a number of traditional sub-groups. Demand in the textile, leather, and clothing industries contracted in volume terms in Europe between 1973 and 1985. This sector is characterized by a very sluggish growth rate trend and by a quite marked sensitivity to economic recessions. In many respects the situation in the steel and metal goods sectors is quite similar to that in the textile industry, although both sectors displayed greater sensitivity to economic crises. The markets downstream (motor vehicles, building and construction) are now 'replacement' markets, indicating that, here too, the growth prospects for demand in the medium term should show little, if any, change from the trends observed over the past ten years.

Finally, the building materials and non-metallic minerals sector is largely dependent on developments in construction and public works. This explains why demand remained flat over the period under review.

The sectoral classification of individual countries in some cases diverges quite significantly. Overall, the strong-demand sectors showed an appreciably more rapid rate of growth in Japan than in the other countries. The moderate-demand and weak-demand sectors, however, show a similar pattern. The rate of growth of demand in each sector should therefore be compared with that of industry as a whole for each of the economic areas in question, and the classification made is justified on that basis.

THE PART PLAYED BY IMPORTS IN DOMESTIC DEMAND

A country's domestic demand is met either by domestic production or by imports. In a market economy, consumers choose between domestic and foreign products according to a number of criteria, principal among which are price, quality and technology. Taking industrial products as a whole, the Community's dependence on imports increased over the period 1973–85 (by 4.5 percentage points in 12 years). The situation in the United States is similar (Table 2). In both of these areas (Europe and the United States) domestic output accounts for little under 90 per cent of domestic demand, with imports accounting for the remainder. The penetration rate trends for Japan, on the other hand, clearly indicate the extent to which the Japanese economy is a closed economy. Over the 12 years the rate of penetration of foreign products on the Japanese market remained remarkably stable (at

TABLE 2. *Penetration rates. Proportion of domestic demand accounted for by imports (as percentages)*

	1973	1979	1980	1981	1982	1983	1984	1985	Difference 1979–73	Difference 1985–79
Total industry										
EUR7	8.7	10.4	11.1	11.3	11.4	11.9	13.1	13.1	+1.7	+2.7
USA	6.3	8.7	9.3	9.5	9.6	10.0	11.7	12.3	+2.4	+3.6
Japan	4.9	5.1	5.2	4.9	5.2	4.9	5.1	4.8	+0.2	−0.3
Strong demand										
EUR7	10.0	13.0	14.1	15.9	16.7	17.4	19.5	19.9	+3.0	+6.9
USA	6.3	9.3	9.8	10.2	10.7	12.2	14.6	15.0	+3.0	+5.8
Japan	4.2	5.1	4.9	4.7	5.1	4.9	5.1	4.9	+0.9	−0.2
Moderate demand										
EUR7	7.1	7.7	8.1	8.6	8.5	8.7	9.6	9.7	+0.6	+2.0
USA	5.9	7.7	8.3	8.3	8.2	8.3	9.5	10.3	+1.9	+2.6
Japan	4.0	4.3	4.6	4.3	4.2	4.3	4.3	4.1	+0.3	−0.2
Weak demand										
EUR7	10.0	12.5	13.4	12.4	12.4	13.1	13.9	13.8	+2.4	+1.3
USA	6.9	9.8	10.3	10.8	11.3	11.4	13.4	13.9	+2.9	+4.1
Japan	5.8	5.7	5.9	5.4	6.0	5.6	5.8	5.4	−0.1	−0.3

Source: Volimex, Commission of the European Communities.

around 5 per cent). The existence of non-tariff barriers in Japan in part explains this very difficult situation for Japan's competitors. Despite the fact that the level of penetration of foreign products in the United States in 1973 was similar to that in Japan (+ 6.3 per cent in the United States and + 4.9 per cent in Japan), that rate had increased to 12.3 per cent in the United States by 1985, compared with only 4.8 per cent in Japan.

1. The overall increase in the penetration rate in the Community conceals widely differing situations according to the activity sector in question: relative stagnation of the penetration rate in the weak-demand sectors and a sharp rise in that rate in strong-demand sectors. The Community shows an increasing propensity to import high-tech. and strong-demand products, whereas in the traditional branches, where demand is weak, the Community is proving increasingly successful in warding off extra-Community imports: in 12 years the penetration rate in the strong-demand sectors thus increased by almost 10 percentage points, whereas in the weak-demand sectors the rate increased by only 3 percentage points. In Japan, by contrast, there is no appreciable difference between the penetration rates for the different sectors.

2. In the early 1970s the United States was in a similar situation to Japan as regards openness to foreign products, with the level of import penetration running at around 5 per cent. The United States market, however, has gradually opened up to imports of foreign products, particularly in the strong-demand sectors where, in 1985, imports accounted for more than 15 per cent of domestic demand. This opening-up of the United States market accelerated further between 1982 and 1985 with the rise of the dollar. However, this opening-up of the United States domestic market has brought little benefit to European companies. The share of the United States domestic market taken by European imports remained virtually unchanged for 10 years and stood at approximately 2.5 per cent of domestic demand in 1985, irrespective of the sectors in question (strong demand, moderate demand, or weak demand). Community industrial exports to the United States market therefore expanded at much the same rate as United States domestic demand. In the strong-demand sectors, however, the share of United States domestic demand taken by non-Community imports increased from 4.8 per cent in 1973 to 12.2 per cent in 1985. In the weak-demand sectors too, the growth of extra-Community imports into the United States was very strong, rising from 5.2 per cent in 1973 to 11.2 per cent in 1985. It is thus mainly non-European, and in particular Japanese, exports which have benefited from the opening-up of the United States market.

3. In the case of Japan, Community products account for less than 1 per cent of domestic demand for manufactured products, whatever sector is considered. Only two branches have recorded a penetration rate in

excess of 10 per cent in Japan: steel products, and office and data-processing equipment. However, the companies benefiting from the relative openness of the Japanese market in these branches are not European companies.

A marked differentiation between intra- and extra-Community trade

A comparison between intra- and extra-Community trade yields a number of new findings (Table 3). In certain branches intra-Community imports have increased more rapidly than extra-Community imports. This is particularly true of food products, beverages, and tobacco, i.e. a sector in which the common agricultural policy has favoured intra-Community trade. These results confirm the conclusions of the study made by Jacquemin and Sapir (1988). It is also clear that Community imports are gaining at the expense of non-Community imports in such highly human and real capital-intensive industries as chemicals, paper, and steel.

TABLE 3. *Comparison of intra- and extra-Community import trends (1979–86)*

Branches in which intra-Community imports increased more rapidly than extra-Community imports		Branches in which intra-Community imports increased less rapidly than extra-Community exports	
Food, beverages, and tobacco	+2.6	Office and data-processing equipment	−7.0
Chemicals and pharmaceuticals	+0.3	Electrical and electronic equipment	−6.0
Paper	+0.3	Industrial machinery	−3.1
Steel	+0.1	Motor vehicles, aeronautics, other transport equipment	−2.2
Metal goods	0.0	Textiles, leather, and clothing	−1.2
		Rubber and plastics	−0.3

The figures represent the differences between the intra-Community penetration rates and the extra-Community penetration rates between 1979 and 1986

Source: Volimex, Commission services.

By contrast, in product branches with a high technological content (such as office machinery, data-processing, electrical equipment, and electronics), extra-Community imports have increased more rapidly than intra-Community imports. This also applies to industrial machinery and transport equipment. Thus, in branches which involved public procurement (telecommunications, aeronautics, and electronics), the external markets used are predominantly non-Community markets. However, the completion of the large internal market could alter some of the recent developments noted. The removal of non-tariff barriers, in particular technical standards and the opening-up of public procurement, should give an appreciable boost to intra-Community trade in these branches.

Origin of imports differs widely according to nature of products

The OECD countries amount for two-thirds of the Community's imports of manufactured products (Table 4). However, in the strong-demand sectors the United States and Japan play a dominant role (54 per cent of the total), but their importance decreases significantly in the moderate-demand sectors (37.3 per cent of the total) and becomes almost marginal in the weak-demand sectors (10.2 per cent of the total). The pattern of technological dependence characteristic of strong-demand products is very evident here.

The newly industrialized countries of southern Asia are beginning to play a part in the strong-demand sectors (6.1 per cent of the total) and they are playing an important role in the weak-demand sectors, where they have now overtaken the United States (9.2 per cent) compared with 7.6 per cent). Finally, the eastern European countries have a genuine presence only in the weak-demand sectors. Imports from all the OPEC countries are clearly underestimated here, since no account is taken of imports of energy products. Over the long term, structural changes in the origin of Community imports are occurring to varying degrees according to changes in relative exchange rates and the improved competitiveness of certain areas.

TABLE 4. *Structure and geographical breakdown of the Community's industrial imports in 1986*

	Total industry	Strong demand	Moderate demand	Weak demand
OECD	67.7	78.5	76.8	47.4
USA	19.9	31.3	20.4	7.6
Japan	14.5	22.6	16.9	3.6
Rest of OECD (including EFTA)	33.3	24.6	39.5	36.2
Eastern European countries	4.8	2.7	3.5	8.4
Developing countries, of which	18.9	11.4	14.5	31.2
Southeast Asia	6.1	6.7	2.3	9.2
Africa (excluding OPEC)	2.9	0.4	2.3	6.3
OPEC	1.4	0.9	1.3	2.0
Latin America	4.6	1.3	6.6	6.1
Rest of the world	8.6	7.4	5.2	13.0
Total	100%	100%	100%	100%

Source: Volimex.

A comparison between the structure and geographical breakdown of United States and Community imports is of particular interest. (Table 5). The appreciable role played by Japan is immediately apparent: 26.7 per cent of the United States total imports of industrial products, compared with only 14.5 per cent for European Community imports. An analysis of the type of imports from these two areas (European Community and

TABLE 5. *Structure and geographical breakdown of the United States imports in 1986 (value – percentage of total)*

	Total industry	Strong demand	Moderate demand	Weak demand
OECD	71.0	68.3	88.4	47.5
Japan	26.7	37.7	31.4	9.2
EUR12	22.2	18.9	25.3	20.6
Rest of OECD (including EFTA)	22.1	11.7	31.7	17.7
Eastern European countries	0.4	0.5	0.3	0.7
Developing countries, of which:	20.6	23.8	8.5	35.6
Southeast Asia	6.8	7.6	5.0	8.9
Africa (excl. OPEC)	9.9	14.5	2.5	16.4
OPEC	1.0	0.4	0.3	2.6
Latin America	0.6	0.3	0.2	1.7
Rest of the World	8.0	7.4	2.8	16.2
Total	100%	100%	100%	100%

Source: Volimex.

Japan) is particularly revealing: while Japan plays a dominant role in the strong-demand sectors (37.7 per cent of imports), its contribution diminishes appreciably in the weak-demand sectors (9.2 per cent). The Community's share of United States imports is, by contrast, particularly high in the moderate-demand sectors (25.3 per cent of the total); its share diminishes appreciably in the strong-demand sectors (18.9 per cent of the total). To sum up, the pattern of events on the United States market seems to be that European industry is gradually concentrating on products which are less elaborate, which are less susceptible to competition from Japan and the new producing countries of Southeast Asia but which suffer from weak growth in demand. It is revealing to note that in 1986 the proportion of United States imports accounted for by the countries of Southeast Asia already stood at 14.5 per cent, as opposed to only 18.9 per cent for the Community countries.

THE RESPONSE OF COMMUNITY EXPORTERS

An appreciable increase in the proportion of output exported

In parallel with the increasing share of Community domestic demand taken by foreign products, particularly high-tech. and strong-demand products, there was a very sharp rise throughout the period 1972–85 in the proportion of Community industrial output being exported. (Table 6.) In 1985, manufacturing firms in the Community exported 17.4 per cent of their output to the rest of the world, compared with 7.7 per cent in the United States and 14.6 per cent in Japan.

In all cases the strong-demand sectors are those in which the proportion

TABLE 6. *Proportion of output exported, in value terms (1985)*

	Total industry	Strong demand	Moderate demand	Weak demand
EUR7	17.4	24.9	15.7	14.9
USA	7.7	13.0	7.4	3.4
Japan	14.6	19.3	18.6	6.9

Source: Sectoral databank, Volimex.

of output exported is highest, which clearly confirms that these sectors are the most open to international competition. For all categories of industrial products the value of the exported output is higher in Europe than in the other economic areas, apart from the moderate-demand sector, where the proportion of output exported by Japan is higher than that in the Community; this is, of course, explained by exports of Japanese cars. At first sight the Community's export performance is satisfactory. The proportion of output exported increased from 11.4 per cent in 1973 to 14.2 per cent in 1978 and to 17.4 per cent in 1985. This encouraging export performance is all the more significant in that the figures for output exported relate only to trade with countries outside the Community. If exports to their member states were also included, the percentage proportions of Community output exported would be virtually doubled.

The situation in the United States is markedly different. The share of United States industrial output exported peaked at 10.1 per cent in 1980. Between 1980 and 1985 the proportion of output exported steadily declined and fell to 7.7 per cent in 1985, a level similar to that reached in the early 1970s. This trend is explained, firstly, by the rapid growth of domestic demand, which led US companies to concentrate on their home market rather than on exports. Secondly, the steady appreciation of the dollar against the currencies of the United States competitors up to 1985 brought about a slow but steady contraction of United States export growth.

In the case of Japan the growth in the proportion of output exported has been spectacular over the long term. Between 1973 and 1985 the share of output exported increased by 6.1 percentage points, although the corresponding increase recorded in the European Community is comparable (+6 percentage points between 1973 and 1985). A more detailed sectoral breakdown shows that Japanese output in certain sectors has a very considerable bias towards export markets, which account for 41.2 per cent of output in the transport equipment sector, for 36.7 per cent of output in the data-processing and office equipment sector, and for 25 per cent of output in the industrial machinery sector.

A reduction in market shares in value terms up to 1985

This favourable picture for the Community must, however, be qualified by

TABLE 7. *Market shares in value terms. Exports of a given country or area to the rest of the world/exports of all OECD countries to the rest of the world (percentages)*

	1973	1979	1980	1981	1982	1983	1984	1985	1986	Difference 1979–73	Difference 1986–79
Total industry											
CEE[a]	26.8	27.0	27.0	26.4	26.6	26.0	25.2	25.6	26.3	+0.2	−0.7
USA	15.4	15.3	16.2	17.8	17.2	16.5	16.6	16.0	13.9	−0.1	−1.4
Japan	10.5	11.4	12.3	15.0	14.6	15.6	16.9	16.8	16.8	+0.9	+5.4
Strong demand											
CEE[a]	28.0	27.4	26.9	25.6	25.8	25.2	24.0	24.9	25.6	−0.6	−1.8
USA	17.5	18.1	19.1	20.6	20.9	20.1	20.7	19.3	17.0	+0.6	−1.1
Japan	12.4	13.1	14.1	17.2	16.5	18.5	20.6	20.2	20.8	+0.7	+7.6
Moderate demand											
CEE[a]	27.0	26.7	27.5	26.3	26.3	25.3	24.3	24.3	25.2	−0.3	−1.5
USA	18.7	17.7	18.1	20.3	19.1	18.2	18.0	17.9	15.1	−1.0	−2.6
Japan	9.2	10.9	12.2	14.7	14.0	15.0	16.4	16.5	16.8	+1.7	+5.9
Weak demand											
CEE[a]	25.5	27.2	26.6	27.6	28.1	28.3	28.5	29.2	29.4	+1.7	+2.2
USA	8.9	8.8	10.5	10.3	9.4	8.8	8.5	7.8	7.0	−0.1	−1.8
Japan	10.9	10.5	10.9	13.3	13.5	12.9	13.0	12.4	10.9	−0.4	+0.4

Source: Volimex, DG II.
[a] In the case of the Community, only extra-Community exports are included.

the analysis of market share trends in value terms. Increases in the proportion of output exported lead to an actual increase in market share in value terms only if Community exports grow more rapidly than those of its trading partners. It is clear that this growing tendency for production to be export-biased has been accompanied by a steady decline in the market shares held by the European Community throughout the world.

The analysis of market shares in value terms set out in Table 7 makes it possible to measure the trend of a given area's exports to the rest of the world compared with the total exports of all OECD countries to the rest of the world.

Overall, the Community saw its share of manufactured product markets fall steadily between 1979 and 1984 (−2 percentage points of market share). The situation began to improve in 1984 and the Community regained 1 percentage point of market share in 2 years. This pattern of events applied to all the sectors in question: strong-, weak- and moderate-demand sectors. However, over the long term (between 1973 and 1986) the Community lost 2.4 percentage points of market share in the strong-demand sectors, 1.8 percentage points in the moderate-demand sectors, and gained 3.9 percentage points in the weak-demand sectors!

Following a good year in 1981, the United States steadily lost market share up to 1986 (almost 4 percentage points in 5 years). This deterioration applied to all industrial products: between 1981 and 1986 there was a loss of 3.6 percentage points in respect of strong-demand products and a loss of 5.2 percentage points in respect of moderate-demand products.

In the case of Japan, market shares grew between 1979 and 1984 (by 5.5 percentage points in 5 years). Since 1984, Japan's share of the market in industrial products has marked time at a high level of approximately 17 per cent. Over the long term (1979–86), the weak-demand sectors were the only ones in which Japan's market share marked time; in the case of the strong-demand sectors its market share gain was 8.3 percentage points.

As market shares in value terms are calculated on the basis of exports measured in dollar terms, the relative exchange-rate movements of any given currency play an important part in the trends recorded. It is therefore appropriate to complete this analysis of market shares in value terms with figures showing export trends in volume terms (see Table 8). Viewed from this angle the European Community's performance lies half-way between that of the United States and that of Japan. The United States is clearly the major loser of export market shares, since the 1986 its exports were down on those in 1980 in volume terms (–14 per cent between 1980 and 1986). It is also interesting to note the performance of Japanese industry in the strong-demand sectors: it increased its exports by almost 84 per cent in 6 years in volume terms, compared with a figure of only 32 per cent for the European Community. Japan also shows the widest differences between the rates of export growth in the strong-demand sectors and those in the weak-demand sectors—proof of Japan's structural adjustment to constantly changing world demand.

TABLE 8. *Exports to the rest of the world in volume terms: 1986 index (1980 = 100)*

	Total industry	Strong demand	Moderate demand	Weak demand
EUR7	116.2	131.7	109.6	112.9
USA	86.5	99.7	87.2	61.4
Japan	131.8	183.9	116.8	93.5

Source: Sectoral databank, Volimex.

Unfavourable pattern of export specialization

When viewed from a more detailed sectoral angle, the pattern of Community industry's external trade specialization is worrying. On the one hand the degree of export specialization in the Community is low in the case of strong-demand and moderate-demand products: its specialization coefficient is appreciably below 1 in the case of electrical and electronic equipment, and data-processing and automated office equipment. On the other hand, there is a high degree of specialization in products for which demand has marked time or has declined: metal goods, leather, footwear, non-metallic minerals.

The patterns of specialization in the United States and Japan contrast

TABLE 9. *Export specialization in 1986 and change compared with 1973*

EUR10[a]	Level 1986		Variation[b] 1986-73	USA	Level 1986		Variation[b] 1986-73	Japan	Level 1986		Variation[b] 1986-73
1. Miscellaneous industrial products	WD	1.7	-0.0	1. Transport equipment	MD	2.6	-0.2	1. Electrical equipment and electronics	SD	1.9	+0.2
2. Leather, footware	SD	1.4	+0.2	2. Information technology, precision and office equipment	SD	1.6	+0.2	2. Motor vehicles	MD	1.7	+0.7
3. Metal goods	WD	1.3	+0.2	3. Industrial machinery	MD	1.1	-0.1	3. Information technology, precision and office equipment	SD	1.5	+0.1
4. Industrial machinery	MD	1.3	0.0	4. Electrical equipment and electronics	SD	1.1	+0.0	4. Transport equipment	MD	1.1	-1.5
5. Non-metallic minerals	WD	1.2	+0.2	5. Chemicals	SD	1.1	+0.0	5. Steel and metal ores	WD	1.0	-0.4
6. Chemicals	SD	1.2	+0.0	6. Food products	MD	1.1	-0.0	6. Industrial machinery	MD	0.9	+0.3
7. Textiles, clothing	WD	1.1	+0.2	7. Paper and packaging	MD	0.9	-0.0	7. Rubber and plastics	MD	0.7	-0.2
8. Food products	MD	1.0	+0.1	8. Motor vehicles	MD	0.8	-0.3	8. Metal goods	WD	0.7	-0.4
9. Rubber and plastics	MD	1.0	-0.1	9. Rubber and plastics	MD	0.8	-0.0	9. Non-metallic minerals	WD	0.6	-0.1
10. Steel and metal ores	WD	0.9	+0.1	10. Metal goods	WD	0.6	+0.0	10. Miscellaneous industrial products	WD	0.6	-0.2
11. Electrical equipment and electronics	SD	0.9	-0.1	11. Non-metallic minerals	WD	0.6	+0.0	11. Textiles, clothing	WS	0.5	-0.6
12. Transport equipment	MD	0.9	+0.1	12. Miscellaneous industrial products	MD	0.6	-0.0	12. Chemicals	SD	0.5	-0.2
13. Motor vehicles	MD	0.8	-0.3	13. Steel and metallic ores	WD	0.5	-0.0	13. Leather, footwear	WD	0.2	-0.3
14. Information technology, precision and office equipment	SD	0.7	-0.1	14. Textiles and clothing	WD	0.4	+0.0	14. Paper, packaging	MD	0.2	-0.0
15. Paper, packaging	MD	0.6	+0.1	15. Leather, footwear	WD	0.3	+0.1	15. Food products	MD	0.1	-0.1
Strong demand	(SD) 1.0		-0.1	Strong demand	(SD) 1.2		+0.1	Strong demand	(SD) 1.2		+0.1
Moderate demand	(MD)1.0		-0.1	Moderate demand	(MD)1.1		-0.1	Moderate demand	(MD)1.0		+0.1
Weak demand	(WD)1.0		+0.2	Weak demand	(WD)0.5		-0.1	Weak demand	(WD)0.7		-0.4

[a] Extra-Community trade for the Community of Ten.
[b] Change: difference in specialization between 1983 and 1972

NB: Export specialization=

$$\text{Export specialization} = \frac{\text{Exports in a sector in one country}}{\text{total exports of that country}} // \frac{\text{Total exports of that sector for the OECD area}}{\text{total OECD exports}}$$

Source: Volimex, DG II.

sharply with that in the Community, since their economies are highly specialized in the strong-demand and moderate-demand sectors.

In Japan in particular, the specialization coefficients are especially high in the electrical, electronic, data-processing, and office equipment sectors. The same applies, of course, to transport equipment. If the trends of the specialization coefficients over the period 1973–86 are analysed, it can be seen that the coefficients in the strong-demand sectors have fallen in the European Community. By contrast, Japan is continually increasing its export specialization in strong-demand sectors, with the exception of chemicals. Contrary to its counterparts in other countries, the Japanese chemical industry accounts for only a small and declining proportion of Japan's exports, which is largely explained by the rise in energy prices in a country without any resources of that kind.

The sectoral classification in the United States is also largely in keeping with the movements in world demand. The degree of United States export specialization is high for strong-demand products (automated office and data-processing equipment, electrical and electronic equipment, chemicals) and low for products in least demand (steel, textiles, leather and clothing). Thus, despite the United States steady market losses between 1981 and 1986, the export specialization of Unites States industry is still structurally favourable. A detailed analysis of the trend of market shares by product (Table 10) clearly confirms this initial diagnosis.

The Community is rapidly losing ground in the case of electrical and electronic equipment (−3.7 percentage points), cars (−3 percentages

TABLE 10. *Gains and losses of export market shares over the period 1979–86 Gains (+) and losses (−) of Community market shares vis-à-vis third countries over the period 1979–86[a] (in descending order)*

Branch	Loss	Branch	Gain
Electrical equipment and supplies	−3.7	Leather and footwear	+6.8
Motor vehicles	−3.0	Timber, furniture	+5.1
Rubber and plastic	−2.3	Textiles and clothing	+4.0
Other transport equipment	−2.1	Non-metallic minerals and products based on them	+2.8
Other industrial products	−1.7	Paper, printing	+1.7
Office and data-processing equipment, precision and similar instruments	−1.6	Chemicals	+1.5
Metal products excluding machinery and transport equipment	−1.2	Ferrous and non-ferrous metals other than fertile and fissile materials	+1.3
Industrial and agricultural machinery	−0.5	Food products, beverages and tobacco-based products	+0.7

[a] Market share is defined as EUR10 exports to the rest of the world compared with exports by OECD countries to the rest of the world.
Source: Volimex, Commission services

points) and office and data-processing equipment (−1.6 percentage points). These are all product sectors in which demand is strong, or in which there is investment growth. By contrast, the Community has gained market shares in such sectors as leather and footwear (+6.8 percentage points), timber and furniture (+5.1 percentage points), i.e. product sectors in which competition from the newly industrialized countries is strongest. In these sectors, where demand is declining or marking time, any gain in export volume is clearly made at the expense of a competing country and ultimately contributes less to industrial growth. The chemical and pharmaceutical sectors, in which Community industry continues to play a major role, are exceptions. The Community productive system has thus concentrated its export gains on weak-demand products.

A poor geographical spread of extra-Community exports

The geographical breakdown of Community exports to third countries in part determines the Community's chosen specialization in products for which demand is marking time. Thus, while Japan accounted for 14.5 per cent of the Community's imports of manufactured products in 1986, only 3.2 per cent of the Community's exports went to the Japanese market in the same year. By contrast, the developing countries account for 18.9 per cent of the Community's imports and for more than 30 per cent of its exports. Only the newly industrialized countries of Southeast Asia are in a similar position to Japan (accounting for 6 per cent of our imports but for only 3.5 per cent of our exports). Thus, by directing a steadily increasing proportion of their exports to non-industrialized countries, the Community

TABLE 11. *Structure and geographical breakdown of the European Community's exports in 1986 (in value terms – as percentage of total)*

Partner	Total industry	Strong demand	Moderate demand	Weak demand
OECD, of which	55.9	51.0	56.1	61.5
USA	20.8	15.8	24.1	21.5
Japan	3.2	3.7	2.8	3.4
Other OECD	31.9	31.5	29.2	36.6
East European countries	5.5	5.7	4.9	6.3
Developing countries, of which:	30.1	30.0	32.1	26.9
Southern Asia	3.5	4.6	2.9	3.3
Latin America	4.4	4.9	5.0	2.9
Africa (excluding (OPEC)	4.5	4.5	5.2	3.3
OPEC	10.6	9.9	11.7	9.6
Rest of the world	8.5	13.4	7.0	5.3
Total	100%	100%	100%	100%

Source: Volimex.

countries are managing to continue to export a large share of what they produce; however, the goods exported to those areas do not have the same technology content. It is clear that in the field of strong-demand and high-technology products, demand for the industrialized countries (Japan and the United States) is not of the same kind as that in newly industrialization countries.

The Community is thus beset by a whole series of weaknesses: products in least demand account for a greater proportion of exports than in Japan or the United States. It exports less to Japan than the United States does, and less to the United States than does Japan. Community exports to the developing countries, in particular OPEC countries, account for a high proportion of its sales abroad, making it very dependent on income movements in those countries. By contrast, its presence in the newly industrialized countries, especially those in Southeast Asia and Latin America, the expanding Third World markets, is still very limited. In Latin America it lags well behind the United States, while in Southeast Asia it is easily outstripped by Japan.

The Community market is better protected than the major export markets

In general, however, Community firms have performed better on the Community market than an third country markets. The Community countries' share of their own domestic Community market stood at 72.1 per cent in 1986, i.e. 1 percentage point more than in 1973 and roughly the same as in 1979.

The general pattern of strengths and weaknesses in terms of market share is roughly comparable on the Community and non-Community markets. In some sectors the Community is in a strong position on both the Community market and the major export markets: food, leather, skins, footwear, textiles, and clothing. In strong-demand sectors, such as electrical, electronic, office and data-processing equipment, European firms are in a weak position on both the Community and non-Community markets.

However, the trends observed at sectoral level on the two markets are different. The better performance of Community firms on their own Community market can be seen at a more detailed sectoral level (Table 12). Thus, in the electrical and electronic sector, the Community countries lost 8 percentage points in 7 years (1979–85), whereas the loss ·on the Community market was only 4.1 percentage points. A similar trend can be observed in the case of office and data-processing equipment (−4.3 percentage points on third country markets compared with −0.4 of a percentage point on the Community market) and in that of cars (−8.4 percentage points on third country markets compared with −1.6 percentage points on the Community market).

TABLE 12. *Market shares on the Community and third country markets (1986)* *(as percentages)*

Community market	1986/79[a]	Non-Community market	1986/79[b]
Food products	89.0 +3.0	Leather, skins, footwear	75.4 +7.9
Leather, skins, footwear	84.7 +2.5	Textiles, clothing	60.3 +5.4
Non-metallic mineral	82.9 +4.0	Food products	57.8 +2.7
Textiles, clothing	82.4 +0.6	Chemicals	55.5 +2.2
Rubber and plastics	82.2 −1.2	Non-metallic minerals	55.4 +3.4
Motor vehicles	80.7 −1.6	Metal goods	54.0 +0.2
Metal goods	80.2 +4.0	Rubber and plastics	49.5 −4.8
Metallic minerals	78.5 +6.0	Agricultural and industrial	48.9 −0.5
Chemicals, pharmaceuticals	76.5 −0.5	machinery	
Agricultural and industrial	66.8 −3.8	Metallic minerals	42.1 +2.3
machinery		Timber, furniture	37.4 +5.8
Timber and furniture	61.1 +7.9	Electrical and electronic	35.0 −8.0
Electric and electronic	60.4 −4.1	equipment	
equipment		Office and data-processing	32.4 −4.3
Office and data-processing	53.9 −0.4	equipment	
equipment		Transport equipment	30.4 −3.2
Other transport equipment	51.8 +1.6	Motor vehicles	28.6 −8.4
Paper and printing	51.7 +5.5	Paper and printing	27.1 +2.5

[a] Market share difference between 1979 and 1986.
Source: Volimex.

CONCLUSIONS

1. For the Community, the future consolidation of growth depends on the capacity of European supply to adapt to structural changes in world demand. Against a background of slackening economic growth the average annual rate of growth of demand for a small number of industrial products has held steady at more than 5 per cent in volume terms: office and data-processing equipment, electrical and electronic equipment, chemical and pharmaceutical products.
2. The Community is showing an ever-increasing propensity to import strong-demand products which also have a high technology content. In 12 years the penetration rate increased by almost 10 percentage points in those sectors, whereas in the weak-demand sectors the penetration rate increased by only 3 percentage points. It is true that the United States market has also steadily opened up to imports of foreign products, the rise in the dollar having accelerated that process between 1982 and 1985. On the United States market, however, all sectors have been affected in an equivalent manner by this growth in imports. Furthermore, this opening-up of the United States domestic market has had little or no beneficial effect on European firms, since our share of that market has marked time at around 2.5 per cent. In the case of Japan, finally, the proportion of domestic demand accounted for by imports has remained at the same level over the past 15 years.

3. Parallel with these developments, intra-Community trade has increased less rapidly than extra-Community imports in the most buoyant sectors: office and data processing equipment (−7 per cent per year) and electrical and electronic equipment (−6 per cent per year). Only products connected with the common agricultural policy constitute a clear exception to this trend (a difference of +2.6 per cent per year between intra- and extra-Community imports).

4. Faced with the increasing opening-up of the Community market to imports, European firms have exported a growing proportion of their output to non-Community markets. In 1985, European firms exported 17.4 per cent of their output, as opposed to 7.7 per cent for the United States and 14.6 per cent for Japan.

5. However, this increasing tendency for output to be exported has been accompanied by a steady reduction in the market shares held by member states throughout the world. This development has been accompanied by an unfavourable structural effect: a fall of 2.4 percentage points in market shares in strong-demand sectors between 1973 and 1986, compared with a gain of 3.9 percentage points in market shares in weak-demand sectors of the same period. Japan, by contrast, has increased its market shares by 8.3 percentage points in the strong-demand sectors, compared with a no-change situation in the weak-demand sectors.

6. An examination of export trends in volume terms completes the analysis of market shares in value terms. This clearly shows the considerable decline of United States industry, which, in six years (between 1980 and 1986), saw its exports fall by almost 15 per cent in volume terms. Over the same period, Community exports increased by 16 per cent, compared with almost 32 per cent for Japanese exports.

7. The geographical breakdown of Community exports to non-Community countries reflects its specialization choices. Thus, while Japan accounted for 14.5 per cent of the Community's imports of manufactured products in 1986, it accounted for only 3.2 per cent of the Community's exports for the same year. The developing countries, by contrast, accounted for 18.9 per cent of the Community's imports and for more than 30 per cent of its exports.

8. Happily for European firms, the Community market remains more protected than its major export markets, and this is true even of the strong-demand sectors. In the electrical and electronic equipment sector, market share losses on the Community market amounted to 4.1 percentage points over a period of 7 years (1979–86) compared with a loss of 8 percentage points on non-Community markets.

9. Japanese industry is characterized by its strong degree of adaptation to the evolution of international demand. Relying on the development of their exports, firms in the high-technology sectors increased their output spectacularly, thus helping to reduce their production costs,

growth of their value-added and the creation of employment. In the case of other sectors faced with a less buoyant level of demand, their record has proven more modest even though systematically superior to that of their main trading partners.

American industry has been less dependent on export markets and has adapted itself to the moderate growth rate of its internal market. Since the beginning of the 1980s, faced with foreign import penetration which increased even more rapidly until 1985 as a result of the overvaluation of the dollar, American firms would appear to have regained control over the growth of their productivity. Industrial sectors in total benefited from the phase of recovery whose effects become noticeable during the course of the recent improvement of their trade balance.

The Community, which is particularly open to import penetration, has likewise tried to improve its competitive position through enhancement of its productivity. Over the long term, the Community has recorded productivity increases slightly above those of the United States, though at the cost of a sharp contraction in employment levels. Despite a more sustained growth in industrial value added in the sectors experiencing a strong level of demand, the Community has not apparently overcome those structural handicaps which affect its industrial performances. The volume of its production of high technology remains inadequate, which explains to a large extent its loss of market share and the acceleration in the rate of penetration of third-country products.

REFERENCES

Buigues, P. and Goybet, Ph. (1985) 'Competitiveness of European industry. Situation to date', *European Economy*, September.
CEPII (1983) 'Economie mondiale: la montée des tensions', *Economica*, Paris.
Commission of the European Communities (1986) 'The improvement in the Community's competitiveness and industrial structures'. Document Collection, Brussels.
Jacquemin, A. and Sapir, A. (1988), 'European integration or world integration?' *Weltwirtschaftliches Archiv, Review of World Economics*, Band 124.

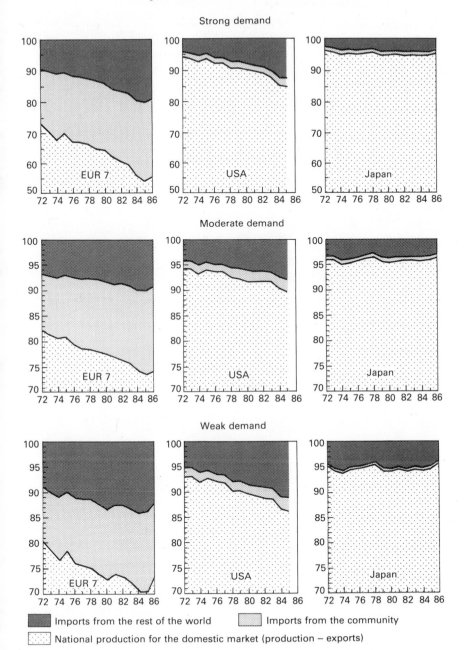

Strong demand

Moderate demand

Weak demand

■ Imports from the rest of the world   ▨ Imports from the community

░ National production for the domestic market (production – exports)

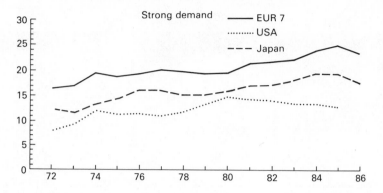

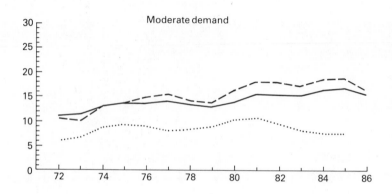

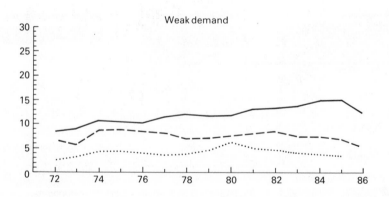

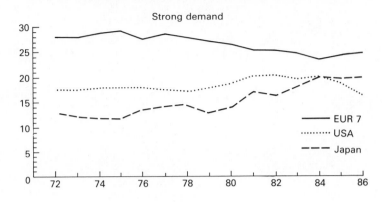

Strong demand

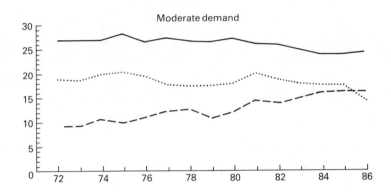

Moderate demand

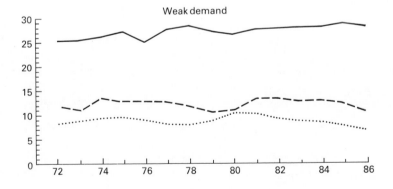

Weak demand

PART III

Policy Issues for the Economics of 1992

ROBERT Z. LAWRENCE
CHARLES L. SCHULTZE

Barriers to European Growth: Overview

AFTER the initial reconstruction from the damage of the Second World War, Europe experienced twenty-five years of unparalleled economic performance. Labor productivity grew at a rate more than three times its average in the previous eighty years. Investment was extraordinarily high, and new technology was introduced into the production process at a very rapid rate. Yet the labor force adjusted smoothly; unemployment stayed year after year at very low levels. And while inflation occasionally became a problem, for the most part it was kept under control.

In the early 1970s, however, Europe's economic performance began to deteriorate on almost every count: GNP growth, productivity, unemployment, and inflation. Although performance also deteriorated elsewhere in the industrial world, the difference was that in Europe unemployment kept on rising all through the 1970s and early 1980s not with a cyclical rhythm but monotonically. Indeed, unemployment accelerated its upward move after 1980. By 1986 unemployment among the European members of the OECD stood at over 11 percent, 2 percentage points higher than it had been at the height of the 1982 recession, and 4 percentage points higher than it was in the United States. Explanations for the problems are complex and policy prescriptions contradictory. But both Left and Right agree that Europe faces a serious economic problem, even if its precise nature and the appropriate remedies remain hotly debated.[1]

1. The prevailing view is captured by the titles of studies such as Andrea Boltho, ed., *The European Economy: Growth and Crisis* (Oxford University Press, 1982); Ralf Dahrendorf, ed., *Europe's Economy in Crisis* (Holmes and Meier, 1982); Kenneth Dyson and Stephen Wilks, eds., *Industrial Crisis: A Comparative Study of the State and Industry* (St. Martin's Press, 1983); "Europe's Technology Gap," *Economist* (November 24, 1984), pp. 93–98; Assar Lindbeck, "What Is Wrong with the West European Economies?" *World Economy*, vol. 8 (June 1985), pp. 153–70; and Peter Gourevitch and others, *Unions and Economic Crisis: Britain, West Germany and Sweden* (London: Allen and Unwin, 1984).

From an American perspective Europe's central economic problem has been its failure to provide sufficient jobs for its labor force. The growth of output per worker has slowed, but it has also slowed in Japan and the United States, and at the present time output per worker seems to be growing more than twice as fast in Europe as in the United States. What improves productivity growth eases the problem of excessive real wages and makes it possible to pursue expansionary policies further than would otherwise be the case. And so we are concerned with both efficiency and resource utilization, but our main attention is still focused on the latter.

This volume presents an American viewpoint on the causes of and possible remedies for Europe's economic problems. It contains papers by American economists on various aspects of the European economy that were initially presented at a conference held at the Brookings Institution in October 1986. There they were subjected to critical evaluation and discussion by a number of European economists and policymakers. The evaluations and summaries of the discussions are included along with each of the papers.

This overview chapter starts with a capsule description of the major hypotheses—partly conflicting, partly complementary—that have been prominently put forward in Europe to explain its economic difficulties. Next it summarizes the findings of each of our authors and synthesizes from their results and from the discussions at the conference an overall assessment of the causes of Europe's economic difficulties, in particular its high unemployment. It closes with some recommendations for economic policy.

Alternative Diagnoses

Our reading of the economic literature suggests that analysts have concentrated on four strands of causation, intertwined in different ways, to explain Europe's current predicament: impediments to growth resulting from shifts in structural growth patterns, the debilitating effects of the welfare state, inappropriate prices in the aggregate supply function, and the interaction of exogenous shocks and macroeconomic policies. In what follows we provide a flavor of each as seen by its advocates. Counterarguments follow later.

The Changed Structure of Growth

The forces behind postwar European growth have run their course: since 1973 there has been a sea change in the nature of growth, one that European institutions are ill-equipped to deal with.[2]

European expansion in the 1950s and 1960s reflected unusually favorable conditions in the markets for factors of production. Indeed, as Angus Maddison has shown, the growth rates achieved in this period were far higher than those in Europe's historical experience.[3] An abundant supply of workers streaming into industry from agriculture and from neighboring countries to the east and south kept wages in check. Oil discoveries in the Middle East and the dominance of certain major oil companies (the so-called seven sisters) ensured secure supplies of cheap energy. U.S. technologies enabled the relatively backward European economies to realize rapid improvements in productivity. Rising real incomes enlarged markets at home, while the removal of trade barriers through the actions of the European Community (EC), the European Free Trade Association, and the various multilateral trade rounds, along with improvements in communications, opened up markets abroad. For several European nations, undervalued currencies contributed to export-led growth. Secure in their expectations of cheap production inputs and growing markets, European entrepreneurs invested heavily with funds supplied by high domestic savings rates and, after 1958 when European currency convertibility revived international capital markets, supplemented by foreign borrowing.

Growth followed traditional patterns. Immediately after World War II it was concentrated in infrastructure, construction, and such basic industries as steel and chemicals; later it extended into transportation equipment, machinery, and consumer electronics. Industrial policies strengthened and enlarged firms to exploit economies of scale and to make them competitive with American counterparts. Except in the United Kingdom, success was widespread. Economic strategies ranging

2. See Business Round Table Ad Hoc Task Force, "Job Creation: The United States and European Experience, Analysis of the Issues of Economic Growth and Job Generation," staff working paper (Washington, D.C.: Business Round Table, December 12, 1984).

3. By contrast, growth rates in the United States were only about 20 percent higher than those in its historical experience; see Angus Maddison, "Growth and Slowdown in Advanced Capitalist Economies: Techniques of Quantitative Assessment," *Journal of Economic Literature*, vol. 25 (June 1987), pp. 649–98.

from the social market economy in Germany to the *dirigiste* approach of France all seemed to work.

But in the early 1970s conditions changed. The movement of labor from the farms to the cities had run its course, while immigration from southern Europe was bringing with it considerable social problems. The baby boom generation entered the labor market with rising expectations and weaker commitments to the work ethic. Labor relations deteriorated, and labor militancy increased. In 1973 OPEC ushered in what was to be a decade of expensive and insecure energy supplies. Exchange rates adjusted to raise European labor costs toward parity with those of its foreign competitors. Former growth sectors of the economy—standardized manufactured products such as steel, automobiles, and ships—experienced sluggish demand and increasing competition from Japan and the newly industrialized countries of Asia.[4] Unfortunately, Europe had specialized in these medium-technology products. In the information industries that were becoming the locus of global industrial growth European firms performed poorly.[5]

The European economies had exhausted the benefits of relative backwardness, and they now experienced problems in graduating from a catch-up economy to one on the frontier of technology. In a catch-up economy the avenues of growth are known, and government, management, and labor can follow fairly set formulas to achieve given results. But at the frontier, flexibility and the capacity to cope with uncertainty and risk are crucial. Europe has failed to adapt its management systems, labor relations, capital market institutions, and government policies to those of a postindustrial economy.

Competitiveness at the frontier depends on innovation rather than the adoption and adaptation of existing technologies. The commercial exploitation of new technologies hinges not simply on committing resources to research and development (in which Europe far outspends Japan) but on the close collaboration between scientific institutions and industry (which Europe does poorly).

The new modes of production call for reallocation of labor within

4. See for example, Robert B. McKersie, *Job Losses in Major Industries: Manpower Strategy Responses* (Paris: OECD, 1983).

5. See "Europe's Technology Gap." See also Pari Patel and Keith Pavitt, "Measuring Europe's Technological Performance," draft for a chapter in Henry Ergas, ed., *A European Future in High Technology?* (Brussels: CEPS, forthcoming); and OECD, *Industry in Transition: Experience of the 1970s and Prospects for the 1980s* (Paris: OECD, 1983).

companies and across the economy. Old work rules must be abolished, even though Europe's strong unions resist such changes. Workers must have general training to adapt to new tasks, and European education, which has encouraged apprenticeships that provide specific skills, must adapt. The labor force must also be able to move easily to where the jobs are. The United States and Japan have successfully reallocated their labor forces, the former by relying principally on the market, the latter by shifting workers within firms. But heavy sales taxes on European housing, cultural traditions, slow-moving large corporations, and poorly functioning labor markets inhibit such reallocation.

Small firms and entrepreneurs will have to take a greater part in the new European economy. Entrepreneurs willing to take large risks must be encouraged and financed and the entry of new businesses facilitated. This change of attitude will not be easy. Harsh bankruptcy laws like those in Germany induce excessively conservative decisions. New firms, which cannot rely on capital from earnings or from banks on the basis of long-standing relationships, must be able to raise equity in active venture capital and over-the-counter markets. But with the exception of the United Kingdom, these options remain relatively undeveloped in Europe. The European policy of creating large "national champion" industries has badly misfired, the market power conferred on them having shielded them from new rivals and the pressures to leave declining industries. Competitive pressures must be allowed to force innovation and adaptation.[6]

Employment must grow in business services, finance, communications, and retail trade, but in many European sectors, state monopolies and regulation inhibit new business ventures. In addition, firms must strive to create markets of continental size: the fixed costs of R&D in the development of telecommunications, for example, are so great that only through access to a large market with common standards can firms sustain them. But the uncommon market, in which each nation seeks to advance its own national champions in pursuit of a "diversified production base," precludes the emergence of companies with genuinely European strategies.[7] Indeed, with a few exceptions, only the American

6. See Paul A. Geroski and Alexis Jacquemin, "Corporate Competitiveness in Europe," *Economic Policy*, no. 1 (November 1985), pp. 169–218.

7. As noted in Geoffrey Shepherd, François Duchêne, and Christopher Saunders, eds., *Europe's Industries: Public and Private Strategies for Change* (Cornell University Press, 1983), Western Europe's larger countries are in the worst of all worlds. Their

and Japanese multinationals have pan-European strategies. As the *Economist* notes, "Testing and certification requirements, differing standards, border delays and restraints on trade in services all take their toll on trade between EEC countries."[8]

Above all, these structural changes have major political consequences for the distribution of social power; the beneficiaries of the old order must yield to the new. Unions and regions wedded to the old industries must give way to accommodate the interests of new firms and labor force entrants. In the 1950s and 1960s, growth was built without the need for clearing away the old order and outmoded industrial capacity: that had been accomplished by the war. And employing new entrants such as refugees and displaced farmers was relatively easy. But the growth patterns of the 1980s and beyond will require reallocating productive factors from activities in which they are entrenched and comfortable. Inducing displaced industrial workers into the service sector is considerably more difficult.

The inadequate adjustment of its industry has reduced Europe's ability to compete in global markets. Domestic demand and supply are increasingly mismatched. Domestic expansion spills abroad, with little effect on the home economy. Poor trade performance has in turn damaged the industrial base and severely reduced employment opportunities in industry.

The Excessive Role of the State

A different, although not necessarily contradictory, view attributes Europe's economic problems to the rapid growth and large size of the welfare state. Over the course of the postwar period, European nations vastly increased their commitments not simply to maintain full employment but to maintain employment in specific regions, firms, and even jobs. They sought not simply to provide basic benefits for the poor but to provide broad support for housing, education, day care, and retirement for the middle class. Such traditional regulatory objectives as safety on the job were expanded to ensure worker participation in management

---

home markets are too small, but their illustrious histories provide them with pretensions to be full-range producers.

8. "Europe's Technology Gap," p. 95. See also Commission of the European Communities, "Completing the Internal Market," white paper from the Commission to the European Council (Brussels, June 1985).

decisionmaking and government oversight of plant closures and layoffs. Because market forces often seemed unfair or inadequate states began to allocate credit, encourage mergers, and nurture national champion firms, eventually becoming full-fledged entrepreneurs operating state-owned industries responsible for a wide range of products. And they aimed not simply to redistribute income through the tax system but to do so indirectly by minimum wage legislation, agricultural support programs, and price controls. In its efforts to ensure economic security, the welfare state advanced to the point that it stifled initiative, stimulated waste, and curtailed growth.[9]

As a result of excessive state intervention the link between achievement and reward has been severed. Failing firms are bailed out by subsidies, nationalizations, and trade protection; failing workers by employment subsidies, extensive unemployment and disability benefits, and training programs.[10] Disability and sickness benefits are available without adequate proof of illness.[11] At the same time, confiscatory marginal tax rates penalize successful entrepreneurs and productive workers.[12] State intervention also burdens employers. Firms are reluctant to hire new workers because of the difficulties of firing them if they do not work out, and they are reluctant to take on part-time workers because of distortions from social security taxes. They also hesitate to expand beyond certain levels because they then become susceptible to costly administrative requirements.

The taxes, transfer payments, and minimum wage legislations of the welfare state have also meant that wages and prices do not reflect supply and demand. Despite increased unemployment among younger workers in Sweden, the United Kingdom, and France, wages for youth relative

9. See, for example, Theodore Geiger, *Welfare and Efficiency: Their Interactions in Western Europe and Implications for International Economic Relations* (Washington, D.C.: National Planning Association, 1978); Per-Martin Meyerson, *Eurosclerosis: The Case of Sweden* (Stockholm: Federation of Swedish Industries, 1985); Herbert Giersch, ed., *Reassessing the Role of Government in the Mixed Economy: Symposium 1982* (Tubingen: J. C. B. Mohr, 1983); and Herbert Giersch, "Eurosclerosis," Kiel Discussion Papers 112 (Kiel Institute for World Economics, October 1985).

10. See OECD, *High Unemployment: A Challenge for Income Support Policies* (Paris: OECD, 1984).

11. According to Herbert Giersch, in Germany 70 percent of sick days are taken on Monday or Friday and only 4 percent on Wednesdays. See "Eurosclerosis," p. 8.

12. In 1983, for Europe as a whole, a single-earner married couple with two children and the income of an average production worker paid the equivalent of 42.5 percent of its income in taxes and had a marginal tax rate of 59 percent. See OECD, *Structural Adjustment and Economic Performance: Synthesis Report* (Paris: OECD, 1987), p. 14.

to those of adults rose substantially between the mid-1960s and the early 1980s because of collective bargaining practices and legislated youth-specific minimum wage rates (which in Germany, however, have remained fairly constant).[13] The availability of free health care, day care, and other benefits encourages waste, as allocation occurs through rationing rather than by marginal cost-pricing. Political pressures instead of rates of return determine the allocation of capital. Regulatory and other political pressures stifle competition. Government procurement discriminates not only against foreign firms but also against those too small to be perceived as potential national champions. Restrictions on business hours prevent the expansion of specialized retail stores. State-controlled transportation services use cross-subsidization to drive up the prices of services that are actually cheap in order to subsidize the prices of those that are not.

Coincident with the expansion of government commitments has come the expansion of systems to deliver the benefits and increases in taxes to pay for them. As a result, public spending has taken an ever-larger share of gross national product.[14] The increased tax burdens have rapidly raised marginal tax rates, damaging incentives to work harder and earn more. And the European political systems have promised more than they can pay for, sacrificing the future for the present.[15] Despite significant reductions in public investment, government deficits have burgeoned; increased taxes have financed only part of the spending spree.[16]

The explosion in state spending in the 1970s has given way to painful attempts at retrenchment in the 1980s, and European governments have been unwilling to add to the deficits to reflate their economies. Thus in addition to inhibiting microeconomic adjustments, large structural deficits have prevented the use of countercyclical fiscal policies.

13. See *OECD Employment Outlook* (Paris: OECD, September 1984), chap. 5, for an excellent treatment of this question.

14. See Peter Saunders and Friedrich Klau, *OECD Economic Studies: The Role of the Public Sector,* no. 4 (Spring 1985, *special issue*), p. 12.

15. On promises see, for example, "The Burden Imposed by Social Security Contributions since the Beginning of the Seventies," *Monthly Report of the Deutsche Bundesbank,* vol. 38 (January 1986), pp. 16–23; on sacrificing the future, see Michel Albert and James Ball, *Toward European Economic Recovery in the 1980s: Report to the European Parliament,* Georgetown University, Center for Strategic and International Studies, Washington Papers 109 (Praeger, 1984), esp. pp. 8–20.

16. See for example, Michael Emerson, "The European Stagflation Disease in International Perspective and Some Possible Therapy," in Emerson, ed., *Europe's Stagflation* (Oxford University Press, 1984), pp. 195–228.

Aggregate Supply Imbalances

The third source of current European economic problems stems from distortions in aggregate supply relationships. Real wages and profits do not reflect what is appropriate ·to full employment,[17] and aggregate demand policies have contributed to the insensitivity of wages to unemployment.

First, the battle over income shares in the late 1960s sent real wages soaring to levels incompatible with a return to previous employment levels. Shortly thereafter the economies of Europe, like those throughout the world, were afflicted with a series of unfavorable, price-raising supply shocks, the oil price increases in 1974 and 1979–80, and a sharp slowdown in productivity growth. Some argue that to these shocks should be added the loss of competitiveness to Far Eastern nations. As a consequence, the path of real wages that was consistent with the maintenance of high employment fell to a lower level and grew more slowly. But the real wages paid to workers did not adjust accordingly. Instead, wages increased at the expense of profits. Consequently, investment slumped, and what investment there was attempted to save labor expense rather than expand capacity. As capacity stagnated, a shortage of capital coexisted with an excess supply of labor. The full use of capital corresponded to higher and higher levels of unemployment. This situation implied that efforts to restore full employment would result in more inflation. The natural rate of unemployment had shifted upward secularly because real wages were high and because of an inadequate capital stock.[18]

17. See Jacques Artus, "The Disequilibrium Real Wage Rate Hypothesis: An Empirical Evaluation," and Leslie Lipschitz and Susan M. Schadler, "Relative Prices, Real Wages, and Macroeconomic Policies: Some Evidence from Manufacturing in Japan and the United Kingdom," *International Monetary Fund Staff Papers*, vol. 31 (June 1984), pp. 249–302, 303–38; Jeffrey D. Sachs, "Real Wages and Unemployment in the OECD Countries," *Brookings Papers on Economic Activity, 1:1983*, pp. 255–304; and Dennis Grubb, Richard Jackman, and Richard Layard, "Wage Rigidity and Unemployment in OECD Countries," *European Economic Review*, vol. 21 (March–April 1983), pp. 11–39.

A more skeptical view is to be found in Robert J. Gordon, "Wage-Price Dynamics and the Natural Rate of Unemployment in Eight Large Industrialized Nations," paper presented to OECD Workshop on Price Dynamics and Economic Policy (September 1984).

18. For a discussion of the relationship between capacity utilization and unemployment, see Friedrich Klau and Axel Mittelstadt, "Labour Market Flexibility and External Price Shocks," Working Paper 24 (Paris: OECD, September 1985).

Aggregate Demand Policies and the Response to Shocks

A fourth view assigns an important part of the blame for Europe's unemployment problem to deficient aggregate demand, caused principally by macroeconomic policies that remained too restrictive for too long and exacerbated by weakness in the private demand for investment goods.

To stem the inflationary consequences for their own economies of the two OPEC price hikes and the Reagan administration's economic program, European monetary authorities were compelled to follow tight policies.[19] While some attempted to avoid such contractions (for example, Sweden's bridging policies after the 1973–74 oil shock and François Mitterrand's expansionary program in the early 1980s), the strong interdependence of the European economies rendered such strategies impotent. In principle, fiscal policies might have been used to offset some of the contractionary impulses in the 1980s, but structural deficits prevented their use.

The aggregate demand shocks left a serious and persistent legacy. They damaged the ability of labor markets to function and destroyed investor confidence. Displaced workers became discouraged and their skills outmoded. They have been disenfranchised from their unions, which no longer take account of their employment opportunities when pressing for higher wages.

European investors have also been affected. Before the 1970s they assumed that growth could be sustained. In 1974, however, they learned how vulnerable growth was to sudden inflationary shocks. The slump damaged their confidence and contributed to the fall in investment. Moreover, much of Europe's productive capacity had been constructed on the assumption of much faster growth. Only when such capacity was utilized would investment recover. The interaction of the destruction of investor confidence and the slump in aggregate demand created a cumulative process of recession. Declining profit margins typify cyclical declines; with sufficient demand stimulus these profit margins would

19. See especially, James Tobin, "Unemployment in the 1980s: Macroeconomic Diagnosis and Prescription," in Andrew Pierre, ed., *Unemployment and Growth in the Western Economies* (New York: Council on Foreign Relations, 1984), pp. 79–112; and Andrea Boltho, "Economic Policy and Performance in Europe since the Second Oil Shock," in Emerson, ed., *Europe's Stagflation*, pp. 10–32.

recover. Declining productivity growth is also primarily the result of the aggregate demand shock.[20]

Policymakers in Europe refuse to pursue more expansive policies for some combination of three reasons—all of them unwarranted according to those who argue that a Keynesian expansion would work. First, policymakers believe that excessive real wage aspirations and structural rigidities would convert demand stimulus not principally into additional output but into higher inflation. Second, having spent the better part of the past six years reducing their budget deficits, with varying degrees of success, they (and apparently their voters) are reluctant to reverse course. And third, there is a widespread belief that only export-led growth generated by the rest of the world appears an acceptable means of reestablishing growth. In particular, this concern is so strong in the key German economy that policymakers seem to believe it impossible to raise aggregate demand sufficiently to absorb the excess supply of labor, and those nations more willing to expand cannot do so without German expansion because their exchange rates will depreciate.

Interactions

Independently, none of these four strands adequately explains Europe's economic problems, but together they interact to create circles of stagnation. For example, the exhaustion of old growth opportunities should have occurred gradually; it is difficult to explain how, on their own, structural changes have caused the sudden erosion in European growth and the rise in unemployment observed after 1973. Again, the constraints presented by the growth of the welfare state would not have been binding if the nature of structural change had not shifted or if aggregate growth in demand had been sustained. The commitment to particular employment opportunities remained relatively inexpensive as long as growth followed predictable and stable patterns; but when structural change required deemphasizing politically powerful heavy industries, commitments to maintain jobs in these sectors became extremely expensive. Similarly, the welfare state could afford generous unemployment benefits as long as unemployment remained low, and

20. See John F. Helliwell, Peter H. Sturm, and Gerard Salou, "International Comparison of the Sources of Productivity Slowdown, 1973–82," *European Economic Review*, vol. 28 (June–July 1985), pp. 157–91.

could pay for annual increases in living standards as long as rapid productivity growth continued.

But when the supply shocks of the 1970s hit the European economies and when the nature of structural change shifted, government spending exploded. This led to increased taxes, which further raised labor costs and discouraged investment. The declines in productivity growth and the deterioration in terms of trade and competitiveness made the process of wage determination yield inappropriate factor prices—an outcome reinforced by the provisions of the welfare state. Inappropriate factor prices in turn implied that efforts to stimulate aggregate demand became increasingly inflationary, inducing the need for much tighter aggregate demand policies.

Sluggish demand also induced a conservative and pessimistic view of structural change. Workers accustomed to changing jobs in an environment of excess demand found that layoffs meant long spells of unemployment. Accordingly, unions became more rigid in demanding limits on layoffs. Because innovation, too, depended on strong demand, productivity growth slowed in the sluggish environment. Thus the four strands can be interwoven almost without limit, and the complex interrelationships of the problems suggest that growth cannot be restored unless all four are attacked simultaneously—hence the despair sometimes termed Europessimism.

Some Conceptual Issues

In the first paper in this volume Paul Krugman sets out to provide an analytical framework within which to examine the issues involved. He identifies the most important European problem as the rise in unemployment since 1973 and observes that while excessively high real wages are the mechanism that has brought it about, this fact does not explain the underlying causes. The paper raises questions about the explanations for European unemployment and the policy prescriptions advocated to reduce it.

Krugman considers a variant of the argument that the rise in unemployment has been primarily caused by the very nature of the structural change that has occurred. Although he discusses the claim of those made uneasy by technological innovation that accelerating automation (labor-saving technology) and expanding trade with developing countries have dramatically reduced labor demand at any given wage rate, he rejects this view because it is inconsistent with the data. If technological change is highly labor-saving, labor demand should be reduced; but output per employed worker should rise and profits should increase as a share of value added. In fact, however, 'output per employed worker has not accelerated in Europe (labor productivity growth has decelerated) and the share of production costs attributable to labor has increased.

The persistence of unemployment over the medium run cannot, Krugman argues, be ascribed simply to insufficient aggregate demand. To be sure, there is insufficient demand for labor at existing wage rates, but the reason is that European policymakers are prevented from increasing aggregate demand by the fear of rekindling inflation. The primary problem thus lies on the supply side, in the increase of the unemployment rate associated with stable inflation. The trade-off between inflation and unemployment has clearly worsened. Inflation rates in the mid-1980s are similar to those of the 1960s, but unemployment is now much higher.

Krugman feels that explanations blaming the market-stifling impact of the welfare state, so-called Eurosclerosis, offer some important insights. Restrictions that discourage the firing of employees may account for the particularly high proportions of long-term and youth unemployment. But other aspects of this explanation are troublesome. He argues that, in principle, the net effect of such restrictions on employment at any given real wage is ambiguous: restrictions impede flows both in and out of unemployment. And the timing of the European slowdown seems inconsistent with the view that the welfare state brought on Eurosclerosis: the welfare state was already highly developed in the 1960s. Why did a social system that seemed to work extremely well in the 1960s become increasingly ineffective thereafter? Krugman quotes Assar Lindbeck's view that the deterioration in adjustment capabilities brought about by the welfare state had long been occurring but only revealed itself in the face of the shocks of the 1970s.

Krugman also raises some issues about the empirical relevance of studies of real wages. Simply comparing the growth of real wages with that of labor productivity, he cautions, may provide misleading estimates of the extent of disequilibrium. Labor productivity is not independent of real wages since changes in real wages induce the substitution of capital for labor. Similarly, shifts in income shares between labor and capital may be misleading indicators of the extent to which wages are excessive.

Such shifts could be the result of an equilibrium when production functions or technological change have particular characteristics. Krugman concludes that we should be skeptical of even the most sophisticated econometric estimates of the appropriate real wage.

He also considers the argument that the shocks of the 1970s led to unemployment, which in turn raised the nonaccelerating inflation rate of unemployment (NAIRU)—the so-called hysteresis explanation. Hysteresis can result if slow growth reduces capital formation, thereby lowering the marginal product of labor compatible with any given level of employment. It can also occur if the economy writes off workers who have been unemployed too long, either because they lose skills and become discouraged, as Layard and Nickell emphasize, or because they become disenfranchised from the wage-setting process, as the insider-outsider models predict. Krugman observes that perhaps generous unemployment and government support for unions contributes to the hysteresis process. But, he asks, if European unions worry only about insiders, why was Europe able to increase employment in the 1960s?

Although he is skeptical of technotrade pessimism as an explanation for Europe's rising unemployment, Krugman notes that one response to it could be to accept stagnant employment, and to take labor demand as given and ration work instead of trying to improve the functioning of labor markets or reducing real wages. But he points out that this solution may keep output unnecessarily low. An alternative approach would reduce wages, so as to increase employment, and offset the distributional impact by profit sharing or by redistribution through the tax system.

Krugman is also skeptical of prescriptions to raise aggregate demand to reduce unemployment rates to their previous levels. He suggests that virtually all economists believe the European NAIRU has shifted upward. Indeed, he observes that the aspirations of European policymakers, even those left of center, to achieve fuller employment have become very limited. If the root cause of the change in NAIRU is overexpansion of the welfare state, he cautions, increasing demand will simply lead to inflation. The appropriate solution is to make the economy more flexible, presumably by scaling back welfare state benefits. He notes, however, that with the exception of the government of Margaret Thatcher, no government has summoned the political will to undertake such measures on a large scale. Krugman therefore considers second-best options such as subsidizing employment, removing the social security financing burden from labor costs, and tying wages more closely to profits.

However, he cautions that such measures may not succeed if those who are employed have no interest in allowing the unemployed to obtain work. Krugman draws on the work of Jeffrey Sachs to argue that in the face of hysteresis unemployment can be reduced only by permanently increasing inflation and inflation reduced only by increasing unemployment.

These pessimistic considerations suggest that new policy tools must be developed—selective job creation might be an example. And despite their poor track record, incomes policies may be worth trying. Krugman notes that the previous hysteresis of the 1930s was only ended by the Second World War. A dramatic change in policy regimes seems called for.

Findings of This Study

We found it useful to distill from the public debate and the economic literature four broad hypotheses about the sources of Europe's economic slowdown and the obstacles to its future growth. Paul Krugman's discussion of analytical issues considers variants of these hypotheses. But to use additional empirical evidence and economic analysis to separate fact from fancy and unsupported assumption from reasoned judgment, we found it necessary to organize the remainder of the investigation somewhat differently. The other studies in this book develop the implications of each hypothesis for six major aspects of the European economies, and then, within each area, confront the implications of the various hypotheses with the data and the analysis.

The first of these areas is the *performance of labor markets*. Each of the hypotheses implies something about labor markets. And two of the four—the damage done by excessive real wages and insufficient demand—have to be evaluated principally through an analysis of labor markets. The papers by Gary Burtless, Robert Flanagan, and Charles Schultze are concerned with the labor market.

The second area of analysis, in the paper by Robert Lawrence, is the *performance of firms and industries in international markets*. Lawrence seeks to determine whether European industries are afflicted with inadequate competitiveness characterized especially by a sluggish response to changes in international markets. .

The *performance of financial markets* is the subject of Robert Aliber's paper. How efficiently and cost effectively did European financial markets allocate funds from savers to investors? Did poor performance in financial markets lead to less saving, to less investment, to misallocated investment?

These investigations of labor markets, product markets, and financial markets share a common concern with the causes of Europe's slower growth and higher unemployment. They seek to identify current barriers to faster growth and higher employment by asking why growth slowed and unemployment rose in the first place. The next three areas of investigation are concerned with various macroeconomic features of the European economies, partly because they have been blamed by some as the cause of Europe's slower growth but more importantly because even if they are not responsible, they may nevertheless be obstacles to better performance in the future.

Therefore the fourth area of investigation, *government budget and fiscal policies,* is taken up by Paul Courant. While Courant deals with the proposition that excessive levels of taxation and spending by European countries have dulled initiative and reduced investment and so been an important cause of sluggish growth, his principal concern is fiscal policy. In particular he investigates the issue of whether fiscal policy in any or all of the European countries is so constrained that it cannot be used as an expansionary measure, even granted the existence of room for some demand stimulus.

The next subject area is closely related, and in his paper on *national saving and investment* Charles Schultze considers three questions. What has happened over the past twenty years to national rates of saving and investment (public and private) and what has caused the changes? Are current rates of private investment sufficient, from a supply-side standpoint, to support a reasonable growth of economic potential in the major European countries? To what extent would an expansion of aggregate demand relative to potential GNP increase national saving and investment rates?

Finally, Richard Cooper investigates *potential constraints on growth from the balance of payments.* When any one European country expands relative to the others, its imports rise relative to exports. To the extent it cannot attract an inflow of foreign capital, the resulting current account deficit will depreciate its currency. How important is the balance-of-payments constraint? How necessary is it that any pan-European expansion be jointly coordinated among all individual European countries?

The European economy is vast, complex, and diverse. To investigate the economy of each country in detail would require a study of much greater scope than is feasible here. Accordingly, although they draw on the experience of other countries, these papers focus primarily on the three largest: France, Germany, and the United Kingdom. In addition, they consider Sweden to gain insight into a smaller country and one that does not belong to the European Community. And a few papers consider still other countries.

The pages that follow summarize and then attempt to integrate the findings of the authors. They present findings about specific problems, offer some policy recommendations, and necessarily leave some unresolved puzzles. In addition, as will gradually become evident, several very general themes emerge. First, the evidence and the analyses will not support the conclusion that any one of the four hypothesized elements is the dominant cause of Europe's slow growth and high unemployment. The sources of the problem are manifold, not monolithic, and involve both cyclical and structural elements. Second, some although by no means all of Europe's worsened economic performance—with respect to such indicators as productivity growth, unemployment, investment, and profitability—is not so much a sign of deeply rooted economic problems as the result of an inevitable return to normality from an earlier performance that was outstanding but unsustainable. Third, the evidence fails to support a number of specific factors that have been widely cited as responsible for Europe's slower growth. Fourth, the major structural sources of Europe's problems appear to be concentrated in its labor markets. The authors could not trace any substantial part of Europe's economic growth problems to inefficiencies in its financial markets, a lack of industrial flexibility, or a failure to be competitive.

Performance of Labor Markets

Classified very broadly there are four potential sources of the great increase and sustained high level of European unemployment: the Keynesian problem of deficient aggregate demand; the neoclassical problem of rigid wage aspirations that failed to adjust sufficiently to the supply shocks and reduced productivity growth of recent years; structural maladjustments in labor markets, including work disincentives from overly generous unemployment insurance systems, that interfered with the efficient allocation of labor supplies to labor demands; and the phenomenon of *hysteresis*—that as unemployment rose and remained high, it lost some or all of its capacity to moderate wage increases.[21]

UNEMPLOYMENT COMPENSATION. Two sets of observations have given rise to the belief that the relatively generous unemployment insurance systems of most European countries have created work disincentives that have caused rising unemployment. First, virtually all microeconomic studies of the subject have concluded that both the level of unemployment benefits relative to the wage of employed workers and the length of time benefits are available increase the average length of unemployment. Second, the United States, with a much less generous compensation system than is found in European countries, has suffered a much smaller rise in unemployment; and much of the difference in unemployment experience is due to the substantially shorter duration of unemployment in the United States.

Gary Burtless starts his assessment of unemployment compensation systems in Germany, France, the United Kingdom, and Sweden with an analytical description of their major characteristics. Because the systems differ significantly, he develops a set of comparable indexes along a limited number of dimensions. In brief, he finds that all the European systems are more generous than those in the United States along the two most important dimensions: the replacement ratio—the average ratio of benefits to prior wages—and the length of time benefits are available. He also finds that, measured by average expenditures per unemployed worker, the systems in Sweden and France have become more generous since the 1970s, the system in Germany less generous (after 1975), and that in the United Kingdom gradually more generous until the mid-1970s and slightly less so thereafter.

Burtless quickly disposes of the naive argument that the generosity and substantial growth of unemployment insurance in European countries relative to the United States explains the difference in unemployment behavior between the two. In the 1960s the unemployment rate in the United States was much higher than in Europe, while unemployment compensation was much less liberal. Europe's unemployment compensation systems were relatively generous long before its unemployment started to grow. Moreover, among European countries themselves there is no relationship between changes in the liberality of benefits and

---

21. *Hysteresis* is a technical term that, when applied to any economic variable—such as exports or unemployment—means that when the variable rises (falls), it will create conditions that tend to keep it high (low).

changes in unemployment. The system become more generous in the past ten to fifteen years both in France, where unemployment rose sharply, and in Sweden, where unemployment rose very little. The worst increase in joblessness has occurred in the United Kingdom, where the overall generosity of the compensation system has probably decreased since 1975.

A more sophisticated argument proposes that when major shocks from either the demand or supply side drive up unemployment, high levels of jobless pay reduce workers' incentives to adjust, lengthen the average duration of unemployment, and thus contribute to the overall rise in the unemployment rate. Burtless notes that almost without exception the published studies have found statistically significant relationships between the duration of unemployment and the level of benefits available. Burtless argues, however, that the effect of unemployment depends on the state of the labor market. In a tight labor market, where the number of vacancies is high relative to the number of unemployed, generous jobless benefits will indeed induce the unemployed to search longer, which will cause the average duration of both unemployment and vacancies to rise and the unemployment rate to increase. But in a relatively loose labor market, where vacancies are not so plentiful, any job turned down by an unemployed person getting benefits will be snapped up by someone without such benefits. The composition of the unemployed will change—more of them will be drawing benefits—but neither the average duration nor the overall rate of unemployment will be substantially affected. Ironically, making compensation more generous may increase unemployment when it is low but is not likely to add much to unemployment when it is at the levels it has been in Europe for some time now. Moreover, using data from Britain and the United States, Burtless shows that even if effects derived from microeconomic studies are applied to the overall duration of unemployment, the changes in the generosity of the British system relative to that in the United States would account for only a tiny fraction of the rise in U.K. unemployment relative to that in the United States in recent years.

Burtless concludes that liberal unemployment compensation may have slowed the reemployment of jobless workers in France, the United Kingdom, and Germany, but the effect is too minor to have constituted a significant contribution to increased unemployment in those countries.

STRUCTURAL PROBLEMS IN LABOR MARKETS. Robert Flanagan starts with the observation—based on a number of earlier studies, and supported in Charles Schultze's paper on wages in this volume—that the rise in European unemployment has been greater than can be explained either by low aggregate demand or by excessively high wage growth. Excluding, for the moment, the existence of hysteresis phenomena, this observation implies that for one reason or another structural problems in European labor markets interfere with the smooth balancing of labor demands and supplies.

Increased structural problems in European labor markets are directly evidenced by the fact that Beveridge curves have shifted upward. (The curve plots the inverse relationship between unemployment and unfilled job vacancies. In a tight labor market unemployment is low while unfilled vacancies are high; in a loose market the opposite is true.) An increase in unemployment due to deficient aggregate demand and an increase due to excessive real wages share the common characteristic that they lead to movements along a given Beveridge curve because employers have fewer jobs to offer while the number of workers without jobs increases. A rise in structural maladjustments, however, causes an upward shift of the curve. When adjustment is poor, large numbers of unemployed exist simultaneously with large numbers of unfilled jobs.

Flanagan marshalls evidence to show that many explanations offered to account for the growth of structural unemployment in Europe are either invalid or, if valid, not very important quantitatively. One proposed explanation, for example, asserts a growing mismatch between the skills and locations of unemployed workers and skill requirements and locations of potential new jobs. This mismatch could have arisen because the pace of industrial change increased while European labor market institutions adjusted inefficiently and sluggishly. Or it could be that European labor markets became more inefficient because of the spread of job protection laws or restrictive union agreements or the increasing rigidity and compression of relative wages.

Flanagan finds that the interindustry dispersion of employment growth rates (a measure of the pace of structural change) did rise in the 1960s and early 1970s but declined in the second half of the 1970s and, except for the United Kingdom, into the 1980s. On this measure, therefore, the pace of structural change slowed rather than quickened. Flanagan also finds that the growing ratio of vacancies to the number of unemployed in many European countries was spread among all industries and regions. Thus whatever the reason for the upward shift of the Beveridge curve,

Flanagan concludes structural failures of European labor markets did not stem from an accelerated pace of structural change, nor did they show up as a skewed mismatch between labor surpluses in certain declining industries and regions and excess labor demands in other industries and regions.[22]

Decreasing worker mobility in Europe is also often cited as responsible for structural maladjustments and higher unemployment. In turn this lack of mobility is sometimes attributed to the marked compression of relative wages, which presumably reduces the incentives for workers to change jobs. Flanagan finds that European mobility did decrease, but it also decreased substantially in Sweden and the United States, where, of course, unemployment behaved quite differently. Further, he presents evidence that the causation goes the other way—lower demand for labor and higher unemployment in Europe reduced workers' willingness to leave one job to try for another. An empirical analysis of mobility in France suggests that relative wage compression did decrease mobility but that most of the reduction was caused by the decline in labor demand. Flanagan also argues that the effect of European job protection laws may have been less to raise the level of unemployment than to concentrate its incidence among "outsiders"—young people, women, new entrants.

Thus Flanagan finds only limited evidence for barriers to growth on the supply side of labor markets. But he does observe some striking characteristics of the rise in unemployment that leads him to suggest an alternative explanation. He himself finds (or cites the work of other authors) that in France, Germany, and the United Kingdom, for any given vacancy rate, there has been a decline in the rate at which people leave unemployment but no increase in the rate at which people move into unemployment. That is, the upward shift in the Beveridge curve— higher unemployment at any given vacancy rate—is associated not with a greater propensity of workers to lose jobs but is accounted for by longer durations of unemployment and a smaller probability of finding a job for those who are unemployed.

Gary Burtless, as we saw, found no evidence that the longer duration of joblessness arose because more generous unemployment compensation made workers choosier about the jobs they were willing to take. That increased duration must therefore have arisen because firms became

22. While this story is widely correct in the 1970s, there did appear to be some growth in industrial, but not regional, mismatches between workers and jobs in 1981 and 1982 (when Flanagan's data ends).

choosier about hiring workers. Flanagan associates this increased unwillingness to hire with the growing compression of European intrafirm wage differentials. Employers want willing and qualified workers who will stay with the job. Turnover is costly, and stability of the work force improves productivity. Screening applicants to determine if they will stay with the firm and remain productive is costly, however, and even when done well is highly imperfect. Paying low wages to new workers but providing generous wage increments with seniority thus establishes a self-screening mechanism. By initially accepting low wages, workers in effect post a bond that they will stay with the firm and perform effectively. But Flanagan offers evidence that solidaristic wage policies—at least in Sweden, France, and Italy—have substantially reduced these intrafirm wage differentials. Moreover, while job protection measures, formal and informal, may not have played a large direct role in raising unemployment, they may have made it more difficult for employers to use trial-and-error methods of selecting employees. All of this, according to Flanagan, has effectively raised the cost of hiring and has made firms more reluctant to take on new workers. The result has been similar to an increase in labor costs, but an increase confined to new employees. At the margin, firms are reluctant both to hire new outside workers and to fire valued insiders. The consequence, says Flanagan, is an increase in the duration of unemployment, a concentration of unemployment among inexperienced outsiders,[23] and a reduced willingness on the part of firms to respond to changes in the market environment whenever those changes require a more rapid pace of new hiring and firing.

REAL WAGES AND REAL WAGE ASPIRATIONS. Perhaps the most widely held view about the cause of Europe's high unemployment is that it stems from excessively high and downwardly rigid real wages. They first got out of line in the late 1960s when, as already noted, there was a virtual explosion of European wages. The gap between real wages and what the economy could pay while still maintaining full employment got further out of line in the years that followed, when oil prices rose sharply and productivity growth fell, while the path of real wages did not adjust downward accordingly. Reacting to the excessive wages, firms reduced

23. In Germany, for example, Flanagan finds that, controlling for the vacancy rate, there has been a decline in the probability of men but not women being fired, while the declining probability that an unemployed person will find a job has been more heavily concentrated among women than men.

output and produced that output with more capital-intensive methods.[24] An extensively used measure of the extent of the real wage excess is the "wage gap," the cumulative excess of the growth of real product wages over the cyclically adjusted growth in productivity since some base period, usually the mid-1960s. An equivalent measure is the growth in labor's share of income (again, adjusted to remove the effects of cyclical changes in productivity).

Until recently most of the discussion about wage gaps centered on manufacturing. Using data from the Commission of the European Communities that allocates self-employment income between wages and return to capital, Charles Schultze calculates wage gaps for the total nonfarm business sector in the United States, the United Kingdom, Germany, France, and Italy. He finds that in Germany, Italy, and the United Kingdom positive wage gaps did appear in the 1970s but have subsequently disappeared (in the United States they have remained very low). In France and Italy, however, a wage gap emerged in the business sector as a whole in the 1970s. It subsequently diminished in both countries but remains at a substantial level in France. In the manufacturing sector, wage gaps opened up in all countries in the 1970s, but except in Germany, where the gap remains large, and to a lesser extent in the United States, the gaps have disappeared.[25]

More fundamentally, Schultze argues that observing the actual course of real wages will not be a useful guide to the role of excess wage aspirations in causing unemployment. In the context of the ongoing or expected rate of inflation, employers bargaining formally or informally with their employees set nominal wages presumably designed to produce some desired real wage. But these real wage aspirations are not the same

24. If firms' marginal cost curves slope upward and if in the long run prices are set equal to or proportional to marginal costs, then a rise in unemployment, whatever its cause, will ultimately be associated with a growth in real wages relative to what they would have been at full employment. Thus the effect on unemployment of a rise in the Beveridge curve could be offset by a sufficient decline in real wage aspirations. But we have reserved the term "excess real wages" to refer to the more limited hypothesis that real wage aspirations first rose autonomously in the late 1960s and then got further out of line when they failed to adjust downward to the falling productivity growth and the oil price increases of the 1970s.

25. Robert Gordon has also developed wage gap measures for the total economy aggregated across eleven European countries and finds that the real wage gap rises only very slightly between 1973 and 1975 and then declines almost continuously to a value, in 1984, well below the 1973 level. See Robert J. Gordon, "Productivity, Wages, and Prices Inside and Outside of Manufacturing in the U.S., Japan, and Europe"(Cambridge, Mass.: National Bureau of Economic Research, November 1986).

thing as real wage outcomes. If, for example, the rate of productivity growth falls and other supply shocks occur, while the growth of real wage aspirations does not moderate, inflation will begin to rise, and cannot be halted without a higher unemployment rate. The nonaccelerating inflation rate of unemployment (NAIRU) will have increased. Macroeconomic policy may initially tolerate escalating inflation but will not accept it in the long run: restrictive policies will eventually be introduced to halt the rise. Actual unemployment will then increase to meet the NAIRU, and—since the monetary authorities will probably want to reverse some of the initial rise in inflation—may rise above the NAIRU. In broad outline this is what happened in Europe during the 1970s and early 1980s. As Stephen Nickell points out in his comment on Gary Burtless's paper, if, in the short and medium run, employers set prices by applying a constant markup to standard unit costs, the path of real wages would adjust to the lower path of trend productivity growth. No real wage gap, as conventionally calculated, would be observed. Yet excess wage aspirations would have been the underlying cause of the rise in unemployment.

In the long run as well, real wage outcomes may not tell anything about whether real wage aspirations have been excessive. If the elasticity of substitution in the production function is less than one—and a number of studies suggest that in manufacturing, at least, it is—then in the normal course of economic development real wages will rise faster than trend productivity, even when there is full employment. Schultze also argues that adjustments in real exchange rates can alter the competitive environment and demand elasticity facing monopolistically competitive domestic firms, alter their markups over marginal costs, and thus change real wages without necessarily leading to a rise in unemployment.

WAGE DETERMINATION IN EUROPE AND THE UNITED STATES. Since real wage aspirations, and not ex post real wages, are the relevant exogenous variable that interacts with other economic variables and economic policy to determine employment, Schultze turns to an analysis of the determinants of wages. He develops and fits augmented Phillips curve equations for the total nonfarm business sectors in the United States, Germany, France, Italy, and the United Kingdom. These equations have the following special characteristics. First, the unemployment rate is not used to measure excess labor demand or supply. Since the Beveridge curves have shifted upward significantly in Europe and to a lesser extent in the United States, the level of unemployment associated with zero excess labor demand has risen, so that use of the unemployment rate to measure excess demand or supply will give misleading results. On grounds that the trend of output would tend to reflect long-term changes in NAIRU, Schultze uses the deviation of actual from trend output (the gap) as a measure of excess labor demand and supply.[26]

Second, Schultze posits that the upward path of workers' wage norms or aspirations, which employers take into account in setting wages, does not adjust quickly or automatically to changes in productivity growth or other supply considerations but that eventually it will. Wage norms may also shift exogenously, as appears to be the case during the wage explosion of the late 1960s. An increase in the pace at which wage norms are rising relative to productivity growth will accelerate inflation and set in motion the process described earlier. Schultze allows for changes in wage aspirations through shifts in the constant of his wage equations. He finds evidence that wage norms did shift upward in the four European countries at the end of the 1960s. After 1973 productivity growth declined, increasing still further the gap between wage aspirations and the capability of the European economies to meet those aspirations while simultaneously providing high employment. The NAIRU rose, as did unemployment and inflation. By the early 1980s, in response to restrictive macroeconomic policies, actual unemployment had risen above the NAIRU and inflation declined. Finally, in the early 1980s wage norms or aspirations did appear to be declining.

From these wage equations and estimates of the current trend level of productivity growth Schultze calculates the natural rates of output— the level of the gap at which inflation will not rise or accelerate above its current rate—and finds that in Germany, France, and Italy actual output was some 2 to 3 percent below the natural level in 1985. In the United Kingdom, however, the equations imply that output in 1985 was somewhat above the level at which inflation should begin rising.

Through Okun's law equations, which relate the level of the gap to the level of unemployment, estimates of the 1985 natural rate of output were translated into estimates of the NAIRU. These are given below for

26. From 1976 on, Schultze extends the previous trend of output with movements in the capital stock adjusted to take account of a long-term upward drift in the capital-output ratio. This is a very conservative measure of the gap. The growth of the capital stock has slowed sharply since the 1970s, and some of that slowdown may have reflected not only increases in the NAIRU but also a Keynesian deficiency of effective demand. To that extent the gap measure understates the degree of economic slack.

Robert Z. Lawrence and Charles L. Schultze

Germany, France, and Italy under both the standardized definition of unemployment used by the OECD and that used by the United States. (Italian actual unemployment, under the OECD definition, is for 1985.)

	OECD definition			U.S. definition (BLS)		
	Germany	France	Italy	Germany	France	Italy
NAIRU	6.5	9.2	9.9	6.0	9.5	5.7
Actual (1986)	8.3	10.3	10.5	7.6	10.7	6.2

From the wage equations Schultze also estimates how much of the rise in the NAIRU since the late 1960s is due to excess wage aspirations. These are measured as the algebraic sum of three components: the rise in aspirations in the late 1960s, plus the decline in the trend rate of productivity growth after 1983, less the decline in wage aspirations in the early 1980s. The results suggest that in the four European countries most of the net rise in the NAIRU between the late 1960s and the mid-1980s was not due to excess wage aspirations but either to hysteresis effects or to upward shifts in the Beveridge curve reflecting structural problems in labor markets.

In Germany and the United Kingdom, the two countries where the relevant data are available, regressions of the unemployment rate on the vacancy rate provide strong direct evidence for upward shifts in the Beveridge curve, shifts that were particularly large in the United Kingdom. Rising Beveridge curves in turn may reflect structural changes in labor markets. They may also reflect hysteresis to the extent that the phenomenon arises either from an obsolescence of the skills of unemployed workers or from the increasing concentration of unemployment among young or inexperienced outsiders.

If hysteresis phenomena are important, a rise in unemployment will only temporarily exert a moderating influence on wages. The standard statistical test for hysteresis, therefore, is to see whether a lagged unemployment term in a standard wage equation has a significant positive coefficient to offset the negative coefficient on current unemployment. Schultze finds that for Germany, Italy, and the United Kingdom there are indeed significant positive coefficients on lagged unemployment, ones almost as large as the initial coefficient. But he and his discussant Charles Bean argue that given the virtually monotonic rise in European unemployment over the past twelve to fifteen years, the positive coefficient on lagged unemployment may simply be reflecting the effect of a rising NAIRU. Under circumstances that have prevailed in Europe, it is impossible statistically to distinguish the two phenomena. Nevertheless, Schultze argues that on the weight of the evidence developed or cited by Flanagan, it is impossible to believe that the huge apparent upward shift of the Beveridge curve in the United Kingdom could have stemmed solely from structural changes in the demand for labor among regions, industries, or occupations. In a much weaker way the same can be said of the other three countries. By elimination, therefore, hysteresis may be playing a role in sustaining employment at high levels in the United Kingdom, and, with less certainty, in other European countries.

Product Markets and Trade Performance

Pessimism about Europe's international trade performance has become widespread. Trade is seen not only as a major constraint on expansion but also as the source of deindustrialization. Robert Lawrence questions some of these views. Using a system of trade equations to determine the foreign and domestic growth rates compatible with balanced trade at unchanged terms of trade, he finds that Sweden, France and Germany can keep trade balanced while matching 3 percent GNP growth rates in the rest of the OECD. Without an increase in its oil exports, however, the United Kingdom will be able to grow at no more than half that rate.

Lawrence also finds that real devaluations are usually effective in improving trade balances, but his estimates of import and export price elasticities tend to be low. Devaluation is thus no panacea. European countries are so open that even if trade flows are fairly price elastic, the terms-of-trade costs of output growth more rapid than the rest of OECD could be considerable. Each 1 percent rise in British GDP for example, increases imports by 2 percent. Thus even if British exports and imports both had unitary price elasticities, the change in the terms of trade needed to keep trade balanced in the face of a 1 percent rise in growth above the warranted rate would reduce real income by 0.5 percent. In the short run, individual European countries may borrow readily, but over the medium term they will only be able to deviate from the growth rates of their trading partners by undergoing considerable changes in their terms of trade. The external linkages will keep most European countries growing at similar rates.

Lawrence uses his equation system to account for the trade perfor-

mance of his four sample countries. He argues that the rise in oil prices
rather than a fundamental deterioration in manufacturing competitiveness (see the remarks by Armin Gutowski) was primarily responsible
for the German current account deficit in 1979 and 1980. He also finds
that in 1986, starting from a very large trade surplus, Germany had room
to grow more rapidly than its trading partners without reducing its
current account surplus below its historic average.

The real depreciation experienced by Sweden since the mid-1970s
was required not to offset an erosion in manufacturing performance but
to compensate for the service costs of increased international indebtedness and higher oil import bills. In the absence of such shocks in the
future, Sweden should be able to grow at its long-run potential rate
without shifting its terms of trade.

Despite French alarm in the early 1980s about the need to reconquer
its domestic market, Lawrence finds that higher oil prices were the major
source of the deteriorating French trade balance. His analysis, however,
does point to problems in French export behavior after 1980. In particular, manufactured goods exports have performed poorly despite real
devaluations, increased profit margins, and excess capacity.

The external performance of the United Kingdom has been poor
throughout the period. In the absence of its oil bonanza the United
Kingdom would require considerable real depreciation if it were to match
the growth rate of its trading partners. Moreover, manufacturing competitiveness has been severely eroded over the past fifteen years in a
manner that cannot be neatly explained by its price competitiveness.

Lawrence's paper calls into question the argument that the peculiar
nature of the structural changes after 1973 damaged European competitiveness and adversely affected growth. It has been alleged that in several
European countries supply and demand became increasingly mismatched, which would presumably have increased marginal import
propensities. But in his tests on Germany and France, Lawrence finds
no change in the response of imports to domestic demand growth, either
before or after 1974. Nor have exports seemed to respond differently to
global demand. He does, however, find a small increase in import
propensities in the United Kingdom.

Europeans have attributed the declining share of manufacturing
employment to poor trade performance. Lawrence emphasizes that,
particularly since 1980 but with the notable exception of the United
Kingdom, trade has actually exerted a positive influence on the share of

the industrial sector. Weak domestic demand associated with slow overall growth and particularly poor investment has been the major reason for the fall in manufacturing employment. Lawrence also finds that patterns of domestic use rather than trade performance (that is, competition with developing countries) are the dominant reason for the shrinkage in low-technology industries. The restoration of demand rather than increased competitiveness is the key to sustaining manufacturing growth.

It is difficult to confirm arguments linking poor European trade performance with the extent of structural change or the mix of products produced or traded. The structure of European employment and industry changed as much in the decade before 1973 as it did in the decade following. The composition of production is remarkably similar between major European economies and those of the United States and Japan. And the trade structure of the United Kingdom resembles that of Germany and the United States. The degree of structural change is not clearly related to performance. While the product structure of Japanese manufacturing changed the most, the second largest shifts took place in the United Kingdom. Germany achieved its strong trade performance despite the smallest structural shifts in industry. The data also fail to demonstrate a clear association between rates of new business formation and industrial growth and trade performance. The United Kingdom has the highest rates of firms entering the marketplace.

Lawrence notes that France, the European country with the most distinctive industrial policies, actually has the least distinctive trade structure. The industrial composition of its manufactured exports is highly correlated with the composition of its imports. He also argues that shifts in François Mitterrand's industrial policies have either been caused by or resulted in a marked deterioration in French manufacturing export performance.

Lawrence questions the notion that improvements in high-technology competitiveness are essential if trade performance is not to constrain European growth. He notes that in Sweden and France high-technology exports actually increased more rapidly than imports between 1970 and 1983. Although the growth of German high-technology imports has exceeded exports, Germany retained a considerable surplus in such trade in 1983. A continuation of these trends, Lawrence demonstrates, is unlikely to pose a serious threat to German trade performance in the medium term.

Performance of Financial Markets

The inadequate nature of European financial institutions has been perceived as a structural problem limiting European growth. The focus in Robert Aliber's paper is to determine whether the sluggishness of business investment in Europe is better explained by the high cost of capital to European firms or by the low level of anticipated profitability of investment in Europe. Aliber presents evidence that the performance of European financial markets has not been an important reason for sluggish growth. While the shortcomings of European financial market arrangements may have raised interest rates, these effects have been overshadowed by the complication of higher levels of saving and the lower levels of anticipated profitability on new European investment. Using data on direct foreign investment by American and European firms, Aliber argues that those headquartered in Western Europe have a cost-of-capital advantage over American firms. These firms could have invested more domestically if the domestic market had appeared more profitable, but they did not do so despite their cost-of-capital advantage.

Aliber's paper systematically analyzes the determinants of the cost of capital. Savings rates have been higher in Europe than in the United States, and real interest rates on government securities in Europe have been lower. Potentially, the costs of financial intermediation could offset these lower real rates in the cost of capital to corporate borrowers: limited competition between banks and the failure to fully realize economies of scale because of the national segmentation of markets could increase the difference between the returns obtained by investors and the costs paid by borrowers. In addition, the illiquidity of European markets and limited information about borrowers could induce investors to demand a large spread between the interest rates charged nongovernmental borrowers and those charged governmental borrowers.

In exploring these possibilities Aliber notes that European and American banks pay investors similar rates when they compete in Eurocurrency and bond markets. He also points out that since large borrowers and large investors can choose between offshore and domestic markets, the wedges between interest rates paid and interest rates received by these borrowers and investors in domestic markets cannot differ substantially from those in offshore markets. Similarly, competition keeps the costs of raising money from banks and from markets closely linked for large borrowers. The coexistence of these sources of funds implies that for large participants unhindered by capital controls competition limits the room for large differences among countries in the size of intermediate wedges. Aliber cautions that smaller borrowers and investors may have greater difficulty using offshore markets and could face larger wedges. Indeed, transaction costs of buying securities differ across national markets for small investors. But Aliber finds that these are not large enough to offset the advantage of lower European real interest rates.

Aliber's explicit examination does not indicate that the costs of intermediation of bank finance (the ratios of operating costs to assets) are higher in Europe than the United States. His data on the ratio of equity prices to book value suggest lower costs of capital in Germany than in the United States, while in other European countries, with the exception of the Netherlands, equity capital costs seem similar to those in the United States.

Investor expectations of the higher profitability of investments in the United States have been borne out. Aliber finds that by 1985 manufacturing rates of return in the United States were considerably higher than they were in Western Europe.

Performance of Budget and Fiscal Policy

At the risk of ignoring some important differences of timing and emphasis, one can say that the various European governments have exhibited a common pattern of fiscal policy. During the 1970s and the early 1980s government expenditures as a share of GDP rose substantially. In the past few years that trend has been halted and, in some countries at least, marginally reversed. Until 1979 or 1980 revenues did not keep pace; deficits in most countries became quite large. Since then, in virtually all countries fiscal policy has become restrictive; budget deficits have been reduced and, after cyclical adjustments, many countries have achieved a structural budget surplus. From the standpoint of fiscal policy the swing toward restrictive practices has been both pervasive and substantial and has been pursued in the face of rapidly mounting unemployment. As of the middle of 1987 there is little sign that any European government will relax these policies.

Paul Courant's chapter on budget and fiscal policy analyzes these trends for Germany, France, Sweden, and the United Kingdom, and then frames one central question: given some economic slack in these countries (with the possible exception of Sweden) and considering that they have made marked progress in consolidating their budget deficits, why are the governments unwilling to relax fiscal policy as a means of generating additional growth in aggregate demand?

Courant considers several reasons. The first is the problem of "solvency." The governments of Western Europe do not have to worry about solvency in the sense of being unable to pay their bills, but they do have to assume they cannot pursue policies that lead to an indefinitely continuing rise in the ratio of government debt to GNP. Hence if the continuation of current budget policies implies a rising ratio of government debt to GNP, taxes will eventually have to be raised or expenditures reduced to ensure solvency. Governments whose budgets are at or near the margin where solvency, so defined, is in doubt will naturally be reluctant to relax fiscal policy to stimulate their economies, since the relaxation cannot be sustained and will eventually require tax increases.

Because interest on the public debt is a component of budget expenditures, the higher the interest rates and the higher the ratio of debt to GNP, the larger the surplus of revenues will have to be to ensure solvency. The lower the expected growth rate of GNP, the smaller the tolerable growth of debt, and the larger the revenue requirement for solvency. But Courant's examination of the current budget positions of Germany, France, Sweden, and the United Kingdom finds that, even when conservative assumptions about interest rates and growth rates are used, the problems of solvency are not a constraint on expansionary fiscal policy.[27]

A second and more serious constraint on relaxing fiscal policy is the problem of long-run "crowding out." National saving as a share of GDP fell substantially over the past two decades in all four countries. Some of the decline is cyclical, but even when corrections are made, the decline remains significant. Most of it can be accounted for by a fall in government saving as budget surpluses turned into deficits while investment outlays declined. In the United Kingdom during the early 1970s and in Sweden from 1978 to 1982, foreign borrowing made it possible to

27. There is a dark spot in this rosy picture. In Germany, and to a lesser extent in France and the United Kingdom, the effect of demographic changes on the social security systems will generate increases in the ratios of government debt to GNP over the next twenty-five years, assuming no changes in the budget policy. And in the United Kingdom, North Sea oil revenues will eventually run out. But, Courant argues, the necessary corrections in future budgets—because of the higher debt-GNP ratio—will not have to be significant.

sustain domestic investment temporarily in the face of a decline in national saving. But over the period as a whole declining government saving led to lower domestic investment.

On the basis of this analysis Courant concludes that even though some demand stimulus may be warranted—again, Sweden aside—a permanent increase in the fiscal deficit would lower even further the already low levels of domestic investment. Would a temporary fiscal stimulus then be effective, and if effective, would it be useful? Courant argues that just as fiscal stringency in recent years reduced output, fiscal expansion could be expected to raise it. But would the effects of temporary stimulus disappear once it was withdrawn? Would the economy be left no better off in the long run and with a higher level of government debt? Courant suggests that the answers depend on the extent to which hysteresis is present.

If hysteresis is at work, high unemployment would tend to perpetuate itself by creating conditions in the labor market that are unfavorable for economic expansion. By the same token, however, an initial increase in demand, with its attendant fall in unemployment, could create the more favorable labor market conditions that would make it possible for unemployment to stay lower. According to Courant, the state of economic knowledge is not sufficient to determine whether a temporary fiscal stimulus could set in motion this benign chain of events and produce a permanent improvement in the economy. But if the judgment were made that labor market hysteresis does indeed describe a real phenomenon, that would greatly strengthen the case in favor of expansive fiscal action.

Courant also points out that government investment has plummeted. To the extent that public investment opportunities with decent rates of return are available, a temporary stimulus concentrated in such expenditures would match the resultant increase in government spending with an increase in productive assets, so that even if the fiscal effects of such a stimulus did wear off, national wealth would have been permanently increased with the use of national resources that would otherwise have lain idle.

Turning from fiscal policy, Courant examines the effects on investment of taxing capital income in the four countries. While the effective tax rates on capital income are substantial in each, they have not risen in the past several decades and in some countries have declined. It is difficult, therefore, to blame taxes for the fall in domestic investment.

Moreover, empirical studies suggest that tax policy is not very effective at inducing investment.

Courant does note, however, that in each country capital income is taxed differently, depending on the type of asset, the kind of owner, and the means of financing. These differences are enormous and introduce substantial distortions into the economic structure. Although recent literature suggests that the measurable improvement in national output from eliminating these distortions may not be huge, Courant argues that in this situation the direction of the effect is unambiguous. Tax reforms aimed at reducing these distortions would clearly make the economies of Europe more efficient and responsive to consumer preferences.

Saving and Investment

In his second paper Charles Schultze looks further at the decline in national rates of saving and investment examined by Courant. Covering Germany, France, Italy, and the United Kingdom, Schultze suggests that the fall in investment as a share of GNP since the 1960s is not the result of a crowding-out process, whereby declining national saving drove up interest rates and thereby discouraged investment, but rather proceeded independently of the fall in saving and indeed may have caused it.

According to Schultze, the 1950s and 1960s were a period of disequilibrium and catch-up. The best available technology was far ahead of what was incorporated in Europe's capital plant, although management and workers were perfectly capable of operating on the frontier of innovation. The profits to be earned from investing in this new technology were large relative to the cost of capital, and this induced a heavy volume of investment. But as the capital stock grew rapidly, the output-capital ratio fell, and profitability gradually declined. For the business sector as a whole, in France and Italy the fall in profitability was exacerbated by declining profit margins. But in other countries, decreasing profitability was chiefly associated with a deterioration in the output-capital ratio. As profitability declined so did investment. And, after 1980, the accelerator effects of the sharp reduction in output growth came to play an important role. As one side effect of the steadily falling output-capital ratios that characterized most European countries over the past several decades, a higher investment share of GDP is now required to produce any given rate of growth in the capital stock.

It is quite probable that the fall in investment demand during the 1970s, as it weakened the growth in aggregate demand, called forth from governments a more relaxed fiscal policy, which was principally responsible for the decline in national saving. For Germany, France, Italy, and the United Kingdom, Schultze estimates the private business investment that would be required, from a supply-side standpoint, to provide a growth of economic potential large enough to absorb the projected growth in the labor force and to generate productivity gains roughly in line with the current trend. He finds that the current level of investment in all four countries is below the "required" level, but not by a large amount.

Schultze calculates that if in the next several years France and Germany grew about 1 percent faster than their long-term potential and Italy about 0.75 percent faster—which would be possible without inflationary pressures if calculations of the NAIRUs in Schultze's paper on real wages are roughly correct—the resulting improvement in profitability and the accelerator effect of reducing the gap would increase investment demand enough to make the growth of the business capital stock roughly consistent, on the supply side, with the estimated growth of potential business GDP.

Schultze also finds that the cyclical sensitivity of national saving, principally through cyclical variations in the budget deficit, is substantial. He estimates that a catch-up increase in output of the magnitude suggested earlier would raise the national saving rate in Germany and France by roughly enough to match the increase in required investment. Partly because of the modest size of the catch-up allowed for Italy in the above scenario, its saving rate would still remain a little below the required level.

Finally, Schultze points out that the German current account surplus will shrink in the next several years. The surplus was 4 percent of GDP in 1986; if it levels off at 1.5 percent of GDP, that, together with a catch-up, would provide room both for the needed expansion of domestic investment and for a deficit-raising fiscal stimulus.

Constraints on Growth from Balance of Payments

The consequences of expansionary demand policies for balance of payments have been said to represent a major constraint on stimulative aggregate demand policies in economies as open as those in Europe.

Richard Cooper challenges this view. He argues that now, in contrast to the immediate postwar period when exchange rates were fixed and international borrowing capacities limited, the external constraint is unimportant. European economies now enjoy widespread opportunities for international borrowing. In addition, they have greater flexibility to adjust their exchange rates.

Cooper presents six case studies in which severe external constraints allegedly limited growth. In late 1976 the United Kingdom arranged a loan and an adjustment program from the International Monetary Fund. This arrangement did not, Cooper argues, result from a fundamental impairment of Britain's creditworthiness, but was actually used by Chancellor Denis Healey to generate external support and pressure for a policy that was controversial domestically. Nor were the problems experienced by Italy, when it borrowed from the IMF in 1977, related to a failure in its economic policies. Instead, capital outflows were driven by the political crisis associated with the increasing popularity of the Communist party. In addition, like Britain, Italy found it helpful to use the disciplinary pressure of the IMF in implementing such domestic policies as the reform of methods for adjusting wages to inflation, which were highly controversial.

Despite weakness in the German economy, in early 1981 the Bundesbank tightened monetary policy in response to a perceived critical deterioration in the balance of payments. But Cooper finds that these measures were self-imposed rather than compelled by an externally imposed constraint on German policy. Germany was quite able to finance its current account deficit by private foreign borrowing—indeed capital inflows responded promptly to increased German interest rates. But German concerns about rising public debt and the desire to be a net exporter of capital induced policies to lower fiscal and current account deficits.

The speculative run on the French franc in 1983 prompted the Mitterrand government to accompany currency devaluation with fiscal austerity and official restraints on wages and prices. Cooper points out that the government's nationalization policies had caused unusually large amounts of capital flight. Nonetheless, he notes that in 1983 commercial banks remained eager to lend to France. He argues, therefore, that French policy was dictated by domestic constraints—an economy actually close to full employment; the desire to remain in the European monetary system; and a concern about the conditions associated with the buildup in foreign debt.

Cooper cites the success of Swedish devaluation policies in the early 1980s as an example of the ability of a small open European economy (that is willing to absorb the inflation and tolerate a deterioration in its terms of trade) to use improved competitiveness to expand in the face of sluggish global demand. He concludes from his case studies that unlike developing countries, European countries were in no case denied access to external credit. Instead, domestic policymakers' desires to change economic strategies were the principal reason for policy choices. Cooper also cites evidence indicating considerable autonomy in setting interest rates exists in major European economies, although he cautions that interest and exchange rates may not be adjusted independently.

Any European country that wants to expand can do so, he concludes. If it runs a current account deficit by expanding, it can permit its currency to depreciate to eliminate the deficit. Alternatively, by an appropriate policy mix—for example, expanding fiscal policy and tightening monetary policy—it can increase activity without currency depreciation because the higher interest rates associated with such a mix will induce sufficient external borrowing to cover the current account deficit. Openness in an economy thus creates new opportunities as well as imposing new constraints. Real currency depreciation is a means of stimulating domestic output and employment not available in a closed economy; appreciation is an additional tool for reducing inflation; and the ability to borrow abroad permits a divergence between spending and production decisions. Cooper cautions, however, that not all countries can exercise such options simultaneously.

While arguing that European economies can act independently, Cooper also points to the benefits of coordinated actions. Expanding together with trading partners will result in smaller current account deficits than expanding alone. This reduces the need for foreign borrowing or depreciation. In most European economies fiscal expansion, even when accompanied by accommodating monetary policy, will not be very effective under fixed exchange rates. Simulation exercises indicate that much of the impact leaks abroad. Fiscal multipliers can, however, be increased through collective action.

Cooper cautions, though, that coordinated action is difficult to implement. Small countries often find it comfortable to await actions from their larger trading partners, and most countries seem to prefer export-led rather than domestically generated growth. Moreover, collective error could be more damaging than independent and partly offsetting national actions.

Additional Reflections on Market Rigidities

Reflection on the papers and comments in this volume, especially those dealing with the labor market, suggests several additional lines of thought about the sources of European unemployment. The first has to do with the possibility of hysteresis-like phenomena in the Beveridge curve. The second involves the possibility that some of the recent declines in real wages relative to productivity may, paradoxically, reflect a worsening of the aggregate supply curve.

HYSTERESIS IN THE BEVERIDGE CURVE? There is one important development that, in varying degrees, characterizes the labor markets of all the large European countries. It is recognized recurrently in Robert Flanagan's paper and in other sources, and it contrasts strongly with labor market developments in the United States. European workers simply move less frequently among firms and into and out of unemployment than was formerly the case and than is now the case in the United States. As Flanagan notes, any lessening of demand for labor, even if unaccompanied by increased labor market rigidities, will tend to reduce mobility. When vacancies are few, workers are less likely to quit to look for a better job. Fewer jobs to be filled means less hiring as well as fewer separations. But in Europe labor mobility appears to have decreased even after the decline in labor demand is taken into account. Flanagan presents evidence for this in the case of France. He also shows that, after controlling for vacancies, the flow out of unemployment into employment in Germany has decreased. Firms are reluctant to hire because hiring has become more costly and because firing has become more difficult. Thus even though vacancy rates are low—reflecting the lack of demand for labor—they are still significantly higher relative to unemployment than earlier relationships would have suggested. And while employers find the various job protection laws costly, they are, says Flanagan, anxious to hold onto their increasingly valued insiders. Germany, Italy, and the United Kingdom have thus experienced sizable declines in both the rate of hiring and the rate of separations, in contrast to the United States, where both increased even as unemployment drifted upward.[28] John Martin, in his comment on Flanagan, presents data showing that the proportion of jobs held for less than two years has fallen, while the proportion held for ten years or more has risen. In 1982,

---

28. *OECD Economic Outlook*, no. 36 (December 1984), pp. 56–57.

when the overall unemployment rate in the United States was higher than in Europe, only 17 percent of the unemployed in the United States had been out of work for a year or more, compared with 45 to 65 percent in Germany, France, and the United Kingdom.

These developments reflect a European labor market that has become increasingly rigid and is characterized by institutional devices and other forces that seek to lock insiders into current jobs and protect their wages while freezing out new entrants and those who have lost their jobs. But these developments may themselves be the products of a long period of slow growth and high unemployment. When unemployment continues to rise and employment falls or stagnates for a long time, the resulting environment breeds protective responses among workers and in the political arena that yield the phenomena noted.

High unemployment may feed on itself in another way. Changes in the international competitive environment and in technology continue throughout a period of high unemployment. The economy does gradually adjust, but it adjusts to the mix of output and employment that goes with slow growth and declining employment, not to the mix that would accompany higher growth and full employment. As a consequence, the longer unemployment lasts and the smaller the turnover rate among the unemployed, the wider the gap between the skills and locations of the unemployed and the potential requirements of a high-employment economy. The actual mismatch may be modest, but the potential mismatch can be much larger. When vacancies do begin to rise, the economy moves along a more unfavorable Beveridge curve. And, of course, a similar sequence of events produces an aggregate level and a composition of industrial capacity inadequate to a high-employment economy. The latter problem can be overcome by vigorous investment, but it limits the pace of any recovery.

Thus in the sense that a long period of rising unemployment itself begins to produce rigidities and imbalances in labor markets, there exists another kind of hysteresis—a hysteresis of the Beveridge curve.

THE MEANING OF RECENT REAL WAGE MODERATION: A PESSIMISTIC HYPOTHESIS. According to Flanagan, the combination of compression in pay scales within firms and institutional and legal constraints on layoffs raises the cost of both hiring and firing. And as Jacques Drèze points out in his comments on Paul Krugman's paper, the more such costs increase, the more hiring decisions become akin to long-term investment decisions: uncertainty about future demand and labor costs increases the risk premium on expansion. In Drèze's words, "It is precisely because anticipation regarding demand and labor cost remains guarded and uncertain that European firms today are investment shy and hiring shy."

In analytical terms the consequences of the increase in the fixed costs of hiring workers and increased uncertainty is not merely to raise the cost of labor but to steepen the slope of the aggregate supply curve. Because of their greater reluctance to take on added inputs, firms meet an increase in aggregate demand less with a rise in output and more with an increase in markups. Charles Schultze's wage equations suggest that, in the short and medium run at least, the rise in prices is not fully captured by higher wage demands in the next round. Thus, ex post, real wages fall relative to productivity. But the moderation does not generate more employment. If this is true, greater rigidity in the labor market can combine with an increase in uncertainty about the future to reduce the output and employment gains that could be achieved without renewing inflationary pressures.

DOES AUSTERITY BREED FLEXIBILITY? With perhaps a few exceptions neither the papers in this volume nor other research studies suggest that the long period of restrictive macroeconomic policies, slow growth, and high unemployment in Europe has resulted in substantial progress toward more flexible labor markets in Europe. Some of the macroeconomic evidence on mobility and job turnover is a few years out of date, but as far as it goes none implies movement toward more mobility. When we were able to formulate Beveridge curves, none showed any evidence of shifting down. With respect to government actions toward liberalizing the economy there have been more promises than results. For the EC as a whole, government spending as a share of GNP has continued to rise: in 1985 it was 6 percentage points higher than in 1980. And as the 1987 OECD economic survey of Germany diplomatically put it, "So far, Government action in the field of deregulation has been modest. . . ."[29] In an environment of high unemployment and stagnant employment opportunities, it is hardly surprising that governments consider the immediate and tangible costs of economic liberalization in terms of greater job insecurity as outweighing their longer-term and intangible benefits, however much larger those benefits are.

The Schultze wage equations show some evidence of a downward shift in wage aspirations that may have been produced by the sustained

29. *OECD Economic Surveys, 1986–87: Germany* (Paris: OECD, 1987), p. 58.

period of high unemployment. But insofar as rigidities in the labor market are concerned, while we are not confident of our ability to assign causality and are even less confident about prescribing specific cures, we think it demonstrable that a strategy of slow growth and sustained austerity has not reduced them.

A Summary of Conclusions

The papers in this volume, we believe, help narrow the choices among explanations for Europe's unemployment problems and among policy recommendations to deal with them. First, the contributors have presented evidence that heavily discounts the importance of some explanations given for Europe's problems. Whatever the difficulties caused by the large size and growth of European welfare states, we could not find evidence that their generous unemployment compensation schemes were a major cause of the rise in unemployment. Similarly, while Paul Courant argues strongly in favor of reforming the taxation of capital income, he does not find that current European tax systems have played a significant role in the reduction of European investment that has occurred over the past twenty years. The evidence brought to bear directly and by citation in the papers by Robert Flanagan and Robert Lawrence does not support the view that Europe was confronted with an increased pace of change in the structure of the labor demand or in its international competitive environment. Paul Krugman rejects the argument that automation and trade with developing countries have caused rising unemployment. Robert Aliber finds that Europe was not penalized during the period by relatively high real interest rates or inefficient and costly financial markets. Paul Courant concludes that the reluctance of European governments to adopt more expansionary fiscal policies cannot be rationalized on grounds of endangering solvency. And finally, Richard Cooper argues that any one government could, if it wished, expand domestic demand and find the means of financing the accompanying trade deficit without a serious deterioration in its exchange rate. (Lawrence points out, however, that while this may be true in the short run, it is not in the long run.)

Not only can certain explanations be discounted but the relative importance of others can be roughly assessed. In Germany, France, and Italy the actual unemployment rate is now above the NAIRU—there is room to expand aggregate demand without running into serious inflationary problems. But the Keynesian component of the unemployment problem is not very large. And in the United Kingdom, however, we could find no evidence that wage inflation has recently been behaving in a way that would indicate a natural rate of unemployment below the actual rate. In Germany, France, Italy, and the United Kingdom the component of unemployment due to the explosion of real wage aspirations in the late 1960s and the subsequent failure of aspirations to adjust fully downward as productivity growth slackened in the 1970s is no longer large.

Most of the rise in unemployment stems, we believe, from two sources with unknown relative importance: hysteresis effects in the determination of wages (especially in the United Kingdom but possibly in other countries) and increasing structural rigidities in European labor markets, characterized by a reduction of labor force flows among firms, industries, and regions and into and out of unemployment. Decreased mobility was reflected in a rising Beveridge curve, which might itself be partly hysteretic in nature. That is, Europe's sustained experience with high and rising unemployment may have led to protective mechanisms and rigidities that helped perpetuate the unemployment.

That we do not ascribe an important part of Europe's current unemployment to a continuing failure of real wage aspirations to adjust downward in the face of the supply shocks of the 1970s does not imply that real wage moderation is unimportant. Even if rigidities and immobilities in the labor market persist, reductions in real wage aspirations relative to productivity growth can help offset the consequences of those rigidities and make possible higher employment. Moreover, to the extent that real wages fail to moderate further, or do so sluggishly, removing impediments to rapid adjustment in product markets could help raise employment by increasing efficiency and productivity, thereby raising the warranted real wage.

While moderation in real wage aspirations is important, it must be accompanied by appropriately expansive economic policies to be effective. Sometimes the arguments in favor of real wage moderation seem to suggest that the principal gain will be to induce the use of more labor-intensive means of production, thus generating additional employment without any increase in output. In fact, the room for expanding employment, with constant output, through a change in the ratio of wages to capital costs is likely to be limited.[30] A large employment increase will require a large output increase. The major advantage from lower real wage aspirations is not principally that they would induce more labor-intensive means of production but that they would increase the rate at which aggregate demand and output could expand without inflationary consequences. Wage moderation will permit but does not itself generate that expansion. For that, complementary macroeconomic policies of expansion are required.

Strategies for the Future

One possible strategy for dealing with unemployment can be rejected out of hand. That would be to accept today's high unemployment and current rigidities in the labor market as inevitable and to search for the best ways of living with the situation—through sharing jobs, for example. For reasons given below this approach is not only premature but potentially dangerous.

On the basis of the conclusions the contributors to this volume have reached and the judgments made earlier, we urge a two-pronged strategy. First, structural reform in both labor and product markets must be a central component of any programs to reduce unemployment. Neither our authors nor we have developed a list of targets for legislative and institutional reform. But they are numerous. There are institutional barriers to greater wage flexibility and mobility such as the legal arrangements in Germany by which union agreements can be made mandatory on nonunion firms and workers. And although Robert Flanagan argues that the impact of European job protection laws on employment has been exaggerated, they do exist and they do raise the cost and the risks of hiring. Easing the burden of these laws is a bit like tax reform—attempts to measure the quantitative result often suggest the magnitudes are small, but they are unambiguously in the right direction.

30. On the standard Cobb-Douglas and competitive pricing assumptions (with the capital-income share labeled α,) the real wage elasticity of employment, assuming output is allowed to vary while the stock of capital remains fixed, is $1/\alpha$. With a typical value for α of 0.30, the elasticity is 3.3. But if output is fixed and capital is allowed to vary, the elasticity is not $1/\alpha$ but α, which is only one-eleventh as great. See James Tobin, "Comment," and Martin Neil Baily's comments in "General Discussion" of Robert M. Coen and Bert G. Hickman, "Keynesian and Classical Unemployment in Four Countries," *BPEA*, *1:1987*, pp. 198–205, 206.

Removal of barriers to the flow of goods, services, people, and ideas within and among European countries could indirectly alleviate unemployment by raising the warranted real wage and inducing more investment.[31] And since competitive forces can be brought to bear by movements in goods and services as well as by movements in factors of production, the liberalization of inter-European trade, especially in services, would be an indirect means for unemployed outsiders to exert pressure on the insider labor market. As for specific decisions needed to meet the target for a "boundary-free" common market by 1992, removing the barriers to a free flow of services within Europe, dismantling the formal and informal barriers to trade that have grown up in specific industries such as textiles, automobiles, and semiconductors, and opening up public procurement to international competition represent some of the steps that should be taken.[32] On the domestic front, continuing the recent progress in reducing industrial subsidies and pursuing meaningful deregulation, especially in transportation, communications, and finance, would—as in the United States—not only improve efficiency but increase wage flexibility in a number of key industries.

Tax reform, especially to reduce distortions in the tax treatment of different kinds of investment and to reduce marginal effective tax rates on investment income, while producing no bonanza, would also improve efficiency and again indirectly help employment by raising the warranted real wage. Most important, the kinds of reform needed involve process— improving the efficiency and speed with which resource flows adjust to changes in the economic environment. What should be avoided are government attempts to impose through subsidies, regulation, or investments in national champions a specific set of outcomes and a specific industrial structure.

Second, the structural reforms should be coupled with the introduction of more expansive macroeconomic policies designed to raise the growth of GDP for several years significantly above the growth of long-term potential. The bulk of recent research, including the relevant parts of this study, conclude that there is some economic slack in most European

31. For a catalog of the barriers that still exist within Europe, see Commission of the European Communities, "Completing the Internal Market."

32. General government purchases of goods and services amounted to 9 percent of European (EC) GDP in 1985. Commission of the European Communities, "Annual Economic Report, 1986–1987," communication from the Commission to the European Council (Brussels, October 1986), p. 127.

countries. Some of the current unemployment would effectively be absorbed by a higher level of aggregate demand without substantial inflationary consequences.

If our argument for more expansive policy rested solely on this ground, however, we would have little to say to European policymakers that they have not heard—and ignored—many times before. The case for a carefully administered dose of expansion rests on two additional grounds. First, we think the balance of the evidence favors the proposition that sustained high unemployment loses some of its force to moderate real wage aspirations—the corollary of which is that an expansion in aggregate demand will have more unemployment-lowering and less inflation-raising consequences than predicted by the standard analysis. Even more important, perhaps, we are convinced that structural improvements in labor markets are much more likely to occur when an economy is expanding than in the current environment of highly restrictive policy and slow growth. However necessary the recent restrictive policies may have been to reduce inflation and to moderate real wage aspirations, there is little evidence they have improved the flexibility and adaptability of the European economies. Indeed, our discussion of the possible hysteretic component to labor market rigidities suggests that slow growth may have made matters worse.

European unemployment has lost some of its force to moderate wages, and it may be exacerbating labor market rigidities. To some extent high unemployment creates the conditions for its own perpetuation. If so, an initial successful effort to lower unemployment could pay multiple dividends and help turn a vicious circle into a virtuous one through its effect in improving the structural characteristics of Europe's labor markets.

The argument that hysteretic components have contributed significantly to unemployment is admittedly speculative. Several participants in this study offered reasons why, in the context of monotonically rising unemployment, hysteresis in wage determination could not be demonstrated from time series data. And our argument for the existence of a hysteretic component to labor market immobility has been inferred from bits and pieces of evidence. But the existence of some Keynesian slack—even if modest—provides insurance. Stimulative action to expand aggregate demand and produce an initial reduction in unemployment, taken one step at a time, should not increase inflation unduly even if our twin conclusions about hysteresis are wrong. The effect of the recent and prospective reduction in the U.S. trade deficit, by creating additional slack in Europe, adds still more insurance.

The approach outlined here meets the basic difficulty identified by Paul Courant that a permanent fiscal stimulus runs the danger of crowding out sorely needed business investment, while a temporary stimulus may give only temporary results. If structural reforms are put in motion simultaneously, and if we are right that lower unemployment will itself help reduce rigidities, then the improved growth prospects on the supply side would induce higher investment and raise the growth of private demand.

Though Richard Cooper has argued that any of the major countries of Europe could finance the balance-of-payments consequences of a unilateral speed-up in growth, the chances of achieving a sustained improvement would be far greater if these countries acted together. While countries can for a time secure financing for a current account deficit, they are unlikely to be able to continue indefinitely. They could, of course, offset the tendency for current accounts to deteriorate by currency depreciation, but they would be better off if expansion by their trading partners allowed them to avoid the effects of depreciation on their price levels and terms of trade.

As Europe's strongest economy, Germany has a key role to play in the expansion. In mid-1987 Germany remains far within its external and internal constraints. Robert Lawrence argues that despite the appreciation of the deutsche mark through mid-1987, Germany could grow 1 percent a year faster than the OECD for three years without driving its current account into deficit. Charles Schultze's conservative estimates put German unemployment at almost 2 percent above the level at which inflation will accelerate, before allowing for the possibility of hysteresis.

The alternative to this mixed strategy of stimulating demand and encouraging structural. reform is to continue the present neoclassical and conservative policy of steady-as-you-go. Our fundamental objection to such an approach is only partly that it eschews stimulating demand while we recommend it. The objection also arises from other sources. The conservative view holds that rigidities and inflexibilities in labor and other markets will only be wrung out by persistent discipline and that expansionary macroeconomic policies at the present time would relax that discipline before the cure was affected. But we believe the prospects for structural reform through liberalizing markets and increasing the mobility of resources will be much more favorable—politically and economically—in an environment of growing output and employment.

It is, in the best of circumstances, difficult to convince people that the indirect and long-term benefits from reducing protective barriers outweigh what they perceive as an immediate and direct threat to job security. That difficulty, we think, rises and falls in direct proportion to the growth in overall job opportunities. In the past ten years, liberalizing measures seem to have been much easier to promote in the U.S. environment of job growth than in the European environment of job stagnation. The discipline of the last six or seven years has indeed moderated wage aspirations and brought down inflation in Europe, but there is little evidence to suggest discipline has improved the adaptability and flexibility of European labor markets or permitted the large-scale enactment of liberalizing laws.

A steady-as-you-go policy poses another danger. Recession and supply shocks have not been banished from the world economy. Can we be confident that the liberal political and economic institutions of Europe would come unscathed through a recession or new supply shocks, given the current European unemployment rate of more than 11 percent? Moreover, the attitude that avoids on principle any role for expansionary macroeconomic policies may carry over from an environment of 2.5 percent growth in demand—where the policy is at least debatably appropriate—to an environment of much slower growth, where by any standards the policy is harmful. In the transition period when the U.S. trade deficit is likely to be falling sharply, such a policy could ratchet unemployment upward even more.

A Final Observation

Throughout the conference at which the papers in this volume were presented, one caveat was reiterated by both American and European participants: a large and inherently irreducible uncertainty attaches to any quantitative estimate either of the natural rate of unemployment or the real wage gap. Economists cannot and should not expect to convince policymakers to alter their views or to adapt new policies on the basis of such estimates. We are fully aware of that. But neither does the uncertainty about measurements of the natural rate or the wage gap warrant continuation of a conservative, steady-as-you-go policy. In either case one takes a not insignificant risk of being wrong. It is the likelihood of a positive relationship between employment growth and a reduction of rigidities that is at the core of our preference for a policy combining expansionary macroeconomic policies with structural reform.

Industrial change, barriers to mobility, and European industrial policy

Paul A. Geroski

University of Southampton

and

Alexis Jacquemin

University of Louvain-la-Neuve, Belgium

1. Introduction

Within the European Community, there is now a widespread feeling of industrial crisis. In contrast to the prosperous 1950s and 1960s, the 1970s and 1980s have seen sluggish growth and a series of major shocks to which European economies have adjusted only slowly. In this paper, we evaluate the design of industrial policy within this context. Our theme is that industrial policy can and should be used to encourage and direct change in industrial markets. Drawing both on recent developments in the economic theory of industrial organization and on a growing body of empirical evidence, we emphasize not only the market failures which prevent free markets attaining static efficiency but also the longer run importance of dynamic incentives in a changing world. In our view, industrial policy should be designed not to specify and enforce particular *outcomes* but to alter market *processes* by attacking the rigidities which impede both the force of market selection external to the firm, and the pressures for change from within the firm.

Our discussion is in two main parts. In Section 2 we contrast the policy problems of the 1960s with those of the 1970s and 1980s, in part to show why a change in industrial policy was needed, and in part to stress how market rigidities have become the key problem which industrial policy must tackle. Section 3, the main part of the paper, investigates these rigidities, particularly those arising from entry and exit barriers

* We are grateful to our discussants, John Vickers and Tony Venables, for useful observations on an earlier draft, to the Economic Policy Panel for a stimulating discussion, and to the editors. The usual disclaimer applies.

and their manipulation through strategic behaviour by private agents and by governments. By referring to the emerging high tech industry and the mature steel industry, we illustrate how the preoccupation of policy has shifted from large size and scale economies to the promotion of innovation and change. In the final section, we draw out the implications of our analysis and offer our conclusions.

2. The current policy problem

2.1. The inheritance from the 1960s

In the 1960s European industrial policy sought to exploit the link between size and competitiveness which was widely believed to exist. Epitomized in Servan-Schreiber's *The American Challenge,* policy aimed to create European super-firms to compete with the US giants, and to break down intra-Community trade barriers to enable these super-firms to have access to a sufficiently large internal market to enjoy the scale economies of large output which were assumed to exist.

This strategy involved a surprising tolerance of the adverse consequences of highly concentrated market structures. Textbook welfare analysis suggests that any efficiency gains from large size must be set against the welfare cost of a larger deadweight burden of monopoly, arising because price is driven above the marginal cost of producing the good. In practice, policy makers concluded that the gains were likely to exceed the costs for three reasons. First, scale economies were widely believed to be large and ubiquitous, enabling potentially large cost reductions throughout the economy. Second, a series of empirical investigations, originating with Harberger's famous 1954 study, had concluded that the deadweight burden of monopoly was small. Finally, it was widely believed that the integration of the European market would allow the new super-firms to realize the desired scale economies without undue concentration and market power. Hence policy makers found it easy to draw up the balance: the gains from larger firms outweighed their costs, and policy was geared to fostering such firms.

This meant a green light for mergers which transformed the corporate economy of Europe in the 1960s. With the exception of petroleum, the largest European firms are now of comparable size with the largest in the United States, though interestingly both are significantly larger than those in Japan. For example, the ten largest European firms plus the five largest US firms have total sales approximately equal to the top one hundred Japanese firms. Unlike the United States, however, the European merger boom was predominantly one of horizontal merger between competing firms in the same industry, as Table 1 makes clear.

Table 1. Merger activity in five European nations

Country	Period	Coverage	Number of Mergers	Percentage Horizontal	Vertical	Other
Sweden	1946–69	Mining and Manufacturing	1,800	79.8	7.6	12.6
France	1950–72	Manufacturing and Distrib.	565	48.3	24.7	27.0
W. Germany	1970–77	All	2,091	72.3	15.2	12.5
UK	1965–77	All	1,562	74.0	4.0	21.0
Netherlands	1958–70	Manufacturing	1,021	62.4	11.6	26.0

Source: Mueller (1980).

Table 2. The effect of mergers on concentration in the UK

Industry	10 Firm concentration Ratio (%) 1954	1965	% Change due to mergers
Food	62.1	80.5	70.1
Drink	40.8	87.2	76.3
Chemicals	80.6	86.4	31.2
Metal manufacture	58.7	74.3	107.1
Electrical Engineering	60.4	81.2	105.8
Vehicles	57.2	85.8	70.6
Textiles	55.9	74.2	127.8
Paper and publishing	63.6	78.1	111.1
Miscellaneous	58.3	65.6	95.9

Source: Cowling *et al.* (1980).

As a consequence, the concentration of European industry increased markedly. Between 1953 and 1970, the share of net UK manufacturing output supplied by the hundred largest firms rose from 27% to 40% (Hannah and Kay, 1977); similar results occurred in France, Germany, Sweden and the Netherlands (see e.g. Müller, 1976). For Europe as a whole, the sales of the 50 largest European firms as a percentage of gross industrial output increased from 15% in 1965 to 25% in 1976 (Locksley and Ward, 1979). Although mergers were not the sole cause of increased concentration, they were the most important, as Table 2 suggests.

2.2. Did the 1960s policy work?

Four strands of evidence suggest that, with hindsight, the 1960s industrial policy was somewhat misconceived. The first two strands indicate that the trade-off between the efficiency gains from scale economies

Table 3. Estimated optimal plant scales in the Common Market, 1968

Article	Type	Optimal plant scale as % of EEC output
Shoes	leather, simple	0.2–0.3
Woollen carpets	machine made, tufted	5.0–6.0
Beer	Pilsener, bottled	0.1–0.15
Cars (assembly)	standard passenger	1.5–5.0
Steel drums	55 A.G.	6.0–7.0
Refrigerators	simple, small	9.0–10.0
Washing machines	simple, small	10.0–11.0
Steel	ingots	3.5–4.5
Nitrogenous fertilizers		6.0–7.0

Source: Jacquemin and de Jong (1977).

Table 4. Number of plants of minimum optimal size compatible with domestic consumption

Industry	USA	UK	France	Sweden	W. Germany
Shoes	523	165	128	23	197
Construction	452	57	57	10	52
Cement	59	17	22	4	29
Petroleum	52	9	8	3	10
Steel	39	7	6	2	10
Cigarettes	15	3	2	0.3	3
Refrigerators	7	1	2	0.5	3

Source: Jacquemin and de Jong (1977).

and the welfare costs of increased concentration was much less favourable than originally believed. The evidence in Scherer (1980) and in Tables 3 and 4 above suggest that scale economies are by no means as ubiquitous or as large as originally believed.[1] Similarly, comparing international competitiveness in Britain, Germany, and the United States, Prais (1981) found that productivity differences are explained much less by differences in the size of establishments than by differences in labour relations, training, and the availability of skilled workers. We can do no better than endorse his conclusion: 'It perhaps deserves emphasis that manufacturing industry, even in the most efficient of modern economies, to a large extent proceeds with plants of only moderate size.' (Prais, 1981, p. 270). This view is reinforced by direct

---

[1] Tables 3 and 4 refer to the size of an individual plant. Mergers create not only larger plants but multi-plant enterprises. Scherer (1975) discusses multi-plant economies for twelve industries in a number of countries, and concludes they were rather modest.

Table 5. Strikes by establishment size in the UK, 1971–73

Plant size (number of employees)	% Of plants with strikes	Working days lost per 1000 employees	Workers involved per 1,000 employees	
			directly	indirectly
11–24	0.2	15	1.5	0.1
25–99	1.0	72	7.3	2.6
100–199	2.9	155	18.1	1.3
200–499	6.1	329	34.2	4.8
500–999	14.3	719	72.6	19.9
1,000–1,999	25.2	1,128	95.6	30.6
2,000–4,999	44.0	2,075	152.6	77.6
5,000 or more	75.8	3,708	314.2	322.5

Sources: Churnside and Creigh (1981) and Prais (1981).

studies of the efficiency gains from mergers which have generally shown that these were often disappointing. Perhaps the most comprehensive investigation, by Cowling and his associates (1980), concludes that efficiency was rarely increased by merger and sometimes actually declined after a merger.

In retrospect, not only were the potential efficiency gains from mergers overestimated, but also it seems that the original Harberger estimates of the monopoly costs may have been seriously underestimated. Although the correct way to measure the deadweight loss remains the subject of some controversy, estimates as high as 7% of GDP have been produced by Cowling and Mueller (1978) for the UK and by Jenny and Weber (1983) for France. Even if we regard these as an upper bound, we believe that the welfare cost considerably exceeds the orders of magnitude (less than 1% of GDP) on which policy decisions in the 1960s were taken.

In reassessing early European industrial policy, we can now go beyond the observation that the assumed trade-off between scale economies and welfare cost was too optimistic. Two further conclusions have emerged from subsequent empirical research. First, large establishments tend to induce considerable problems in industrial relations. Working conditions tend to be authoritarian and regimented, leading to worker alienation. Table 5 shows that strikes tend to grow exponentially with plant size. Other symptoms may include higher quits, absenteeism, and other non-strike forms of industrial action, all of which tend to increase with plant size. These additional costs can easily out-

Table 6. The distribution of R&D expenditure and innovation by firm size in the UK

Employees in firm	Gross R&D expenditure £m, 1975	Number of innovations 1970–79
1–99	—	157
100–499	18.6	201
500–999	21.8	86
1,000–4,999	90.4	167
5,000–9,999	107.3	80
10,000 or more	971.8	612

Source: Pavitt *et al.* (1985).

weigh the modest efficiency gains accruing from the potential for scale economies.

The final strand of evidence concerns the dynamic efficiency of large firms. Standard estimates of the cost of monopoly are often dismissed on the Schumpeterian grounds that any static welfare costs will be outweighed by dynamic gains arising from the fact that large firms innovate more than do small or medium sized firms. The evidence on this subject is incomplete, but what we now have does not provide impressive support for the Schumpeterian view. (A good survey of this research can be found in Kamien and Schwartz (1982); European studies can be found in Jacquemin and de Jong (1977)). Table 6 shows that many innovations originate in firms with *less* than 1,000 employees, despite their much smaller share of R&D expenditures. It is of course difficult to judge the importance of innovations, and this may vary with firm size. In smaller firms, design activities are important relative to development activities, and such firms may innovate primarily in machinery and instruments where their contribution is large. In larger firms, the R&D function tends to be more formalized. Nevertheless, whilst Table 6 and similar evidence confirms that large firms are most responsible for expenditure on R&D, it is much harder to demonstrate that larger firm size in any way contributes to greater innovation.

Together, these four strands of evidence suggest that the industrial policy of the 1960s may have been ill-conceived. The new super-firms did not give rise to a new competitive efficiency in Europe. Indeed, by creating a group of firms with sufficient market power to be considerably sheltered from the forces of market selection, the policy may have left Europe with a population of sleepy industrial giants who were ill-equipped to meet the challenge of the 1970s and 1980s.

2.3. The problems of the 1970s and 1980s

We have argued that the *size* of European firms was perceived as the policy issue of the 1960s. In spite of continuing claims for more European mergers, size should no longer be a European preoccupation in our view. Previous policy has already eliminated most of the transatlantic size differential, and in any case we have argued that the benefits of large firms had been substantially overestimated. More recent concern has been with the severity of the shocks buffeting the European economy, and with its sluggishness in responding to them. On the one hand, there have been substantial changes in the real price of raw materials (most notably energy) whilst, on the other hand, there have been considerable changes in comparative advantage (for example in steel and shipbuilding) caused in part by the rise of the newly industrialized countries. There have also been rapid technological advances in some industries (electronics, biotechnology), shifts in consumer demand caused for example by demographic shifts, and substantial reversals in government policy at both macroeconomic and microeconomic levels.

It is frequently asserted that European economies are slow to adjust compared, say, with the United States. If true, this suggests that European economies will be vulnerable to the shocks described above. Certainly, there is considerable *prima facie* evidence for this claim. European unemployment has increased markedly, yet wage structures seem rigid and labour mobility low. The average age of manufacturing capital in Europe exceeds that in the United States and Japan, and has considerably worsened over the last decade, thus increasing Europe's technological obsolescence, (Cette and Jolly, 1984). The level of European investment has fallen and its composition is not encouraging. For example, the relative position of high tech industries has deteriorated during 1970–85. The share of total EC exports accounted for by such goods has increased by less than 1% while their share in EC imports has risen by over 2%. This is in marked contrast to the rapid expansion of these industries in the United States and Japan. Data collected by the European Commission (1983) suggest that European exports are increasingly medium tech goods in which the major competitors will be the newly industrialized countries.

Two particular examples of inflexibility have been isolated by recent research. Encaoua *et al.* (1983) have shown that Britain and (to a rather lesser extent) Sweden are far less price flexible than the United States and Canada, let alone Japan. A more detailed examination of sectoral variations in price flexibility shows that it is firms in highly concentrated industries protected from import competition which are slowest to adjust to cost and demand changes (Encaoua and Geroski, 1984).

Perhaps more worrying is the poor innovation record of European countries, especially in the high technology areas which we discuss in more detail later in the paper. Ergas (1984) pinpoints new firm creation as a major factor in explaining the superior US performance in this area. In part this reflects a difference in government procurement policies and financial support for R&D. In the United States, small high-tech firms sell as much as half their output to the federal government and benefit from extensive R&D support to new firms. In contrast, public procurement in Europe is channelled primarily through a small number of large national suppliers. These arguments suggest that industrial policy should focus not on the attainment of large size but rather on the dynamic performance which is fostered by entry and mobility within industries.

2.4. Policy implications for the 1970s and 1980s

We have argued that the problems of the 1970s and 1980s have arisen from the sluggish response of the European economies to the shocks which occurred during this period. If this diagnosis is correct, the major aim of industrial policy must be to increase mobility and speed up adjustment.

Essentially, there are two ways in which this objective might be achieved. First, governments could try to anticipate changes, predict future developments, and make decisions about where resources should be invested for future growth. In short, the public sector might try to lead the private sector through a more or less explicit planning procedure. In practice, this type of policy often takes the form of 'picking winners', predicting the emergence of 'sunrise' sectors, and charting the rationalization of 'sunset' sectors.

Alternatively, industrial policy can try to provide a framework in which private sector flexibility is encouraged and adjustment to shocks is facilitated. Rather than attempting to make centralized decisions, this latter approach seeks to affect the process of private decentralised decision making by providing incentives for more rapid adjustment and by attacking the barriers which impede change. The distinction between the two policy approaches is analogous to that between substantive and procedural rationality. In the planning approach, the concern is to make the right choice; in the infrastructure approach, the concern is to ensure that private agents and markets make choices in the right way.

Our concern here is with an industrial policy of the second kind. While European civil servants are often highly qualified, the informational requirement for a successful implementation of the first type of policy is enormous. Thus we believe that industrial policy should build on the market mechanism, but seek to remove the obstacles which impede the smooth and efficient working of that mechanism. To understand how such an industrial policy should be framed, it is essential to discuss in more detail the way such markets presently work. Since we have already documented the effect of earlier industrial policy in leaving Europe with a population of super-firms, we focus our attention on the operation of such oligopolistic markets and seek to bring to bear some of the insights of recent developments in the economics of imperfectly competitive markets. In so doing, we shall stress the role of barriers to mobility and their variation across different industries.

3. Flexibility and adjustment in markets

Initially, we examine the role that entry plays in market competition, emphasising the link between entry and innovation. Then we discuss entry barriers which may be innately structural, or may be created by the strategic actions of individual firms or by governments. We proceed to a similar discussion of exit barriers. Together, entry and exit barriers can seriously impede the incentives and pressures of market selection. To illustrate these ideas, we examine two case studies in more depth: the emerging semi-conductor industry and the declining steel industry. Finally, having argued that these barriers may severely weaken the competitive pressures external to the large firm, we consider whether the internal dynamics of large corporations can provide a substitute pressure for selection and change.

3.1. The role of entry and mobility

Entry is both a disciplinary and an innovatory force. As a discipline, entry acts to bid away excess profits and drive industrial structure towards cost minimizing configurations. As a force for innovation, entry operates by throwing up new ideas embodied in the particular challenges of individual entrants to which incumbent firms must respond.[2] Hence, unduly high entry barriers and intra-industry mobility barriers will not only weaken disciplinary forces but will also reduce innovation.

---

[2] Standard economic theory focuses almost exclusively on entry as a discipline, as in the theory of contestable markets (Baumol *et al.*, 1982). In such a context, von Weizsäcker (1980) and Demsetz (1982) have argued that 'too much' entry may occur, so that some entry barriers may be desirable. In our view, this objection is weakened when one also recognizes the role of entry in stimulating innovation.

Since so much of economic theory emphasizes the role of entry as a discipline, perhaps we should elaborate the role of entry in the generation and diffusion of innovations. This may occur in several ways. First, entrants may not use genuinely new ideas but merely make use of already known but as yet unadopted methods. Should the entry challenge succeed, incumbents will face additional pressure to adopt this innovation more rapidly than would otherwise have been the case. Alternatively, the entrant may introduce a new process as the basis of its entry challenge. In this case, the incumbent may be forced to adopt the innovation or to respond with a counter-innovation. In any of these circumstances, entry is likely to stimulate innovation.

Many examples of this phenomenon have been documented. Shaw and Sutton (1976) cite the UK dry cleaning industry as an example in which entry spurred the adoption of previously known, but unutilized, techniques. The innovation concerned a technology which favoured the operation of small shops with on-site cleaning and self-service, coin-operated, dry cleaning. Rapid entry in the 1950s and 1960s forced incumbents to respond by converting from factory-based cleaning to on-site cleaning, a move they had been resisting for over a decade. Kaplinsky (1983) documents the second type of entry, based on a genuinely new technique, for the computer aided design (CAD) industry, where entry by new firms in 1969–74 led to the rapid diffusion of such services in the United States in the electronics industry. The success of these firms and the growing penetration of CAD into manufacturing eventually prompted a predatory takeover of CAD suppliers by the incumbent firms, such as General Electric, whose structure and operation was affected as a result. The UK potato crisp industry illustrates the third type of response, in which the incumbent makes a counter-innovation. Here the entry by Golden Wonder was based on new packaging techniques, continuous frying coolers, and a marketing switch from consumption in pubs towards direct sales for home consumption (Bevan, 1974). The incumbent, Smiths, responded to this extension of the market (which doubled in five years) with the proliferation of a wide variety of new product flavours.

As a final example of the effect of entry on innovation, we consider the computer industry. Brock (1975) distinguishes two types of entry strategy employed in this industry. Imitative entry (expansion through compatibility) develops a product line compatible with an existing line but offered for a lower price, a strategy which is vulnerable to a price war or to a redesign of the incumbent's existing product range. Of three examples he considers (the UNIVAC SS80 targetted against the IBM 650, the Honeywell H-200 against IBM's 1401, and the RCA Spectra 70 against IBM's 360/30), only Honeywell made this strategy successful, challenging IBM at a time when IBM was unable to respond quickly with a new product. In contrast, innovative entry (expansion through technical advance) is designed to open up new product markets and here the primary risk is to avoid duplication by incumbent rivals. Successful challenges (Control Data's 6600, Burroughs' multi-processing innovations, and the work of Digital Computers with mini-computers) pushed technical advance throughout the industry, but so did unsuccessful challenges (Philco's large scale transistor computer, and GE's time sharing innovations). The key to success or failure of entry challenges seems to have been whether or not the incumbent IBM could reply quickly with a matching innovation. Of 21 major innovations examined by Brock in this industry, only six could be credited to IBM. Indeed, each of the three generations of computers was ushered in by an entry challenge. In general, IBM played a 'fast second' strategy of replying quickly with matched innovations whenever they were threatened by new products and/or entrants. Since it is far from obvious that, unchallenged, IBM would have introduced such innovations as quickly or extensively as they did, much of this induced innovation must be attributed to the effects of entry. Despite IBM's long dominance of this industry, it has not been allowed to become a sleepy giant because it has been continually forced to face competitive entry challenges.

Why should entry spur innovation in the ways described above? From the point of view of an incumbent with an established method of doing business, the profitability of current operations represents an opportunity cost. In the absence of an entry threat, an incumbent will innovate only if the *increase* in profits offsets the investment involved. Entrants, by contrast, have no such prior commitment and so consider whether the *whole* of the profits outweigh the cost of the investment.[3] This insight simultaneously explains why entrants may be first to adopt new methods and why, when thus threatened by an entrant, incumbents may be quick to adopt the innovation to defend their existing profits.

Of course the effects of entry on innovation can be exaggerated. Much entry (particularly by very small firms) is purely imitative (so-

[3] This is the essence of the argument of Arrow (1962), who uses it to conclude that a competitive industry (with no pre-innovation profitability) is more likely to innovate than a monopoly. A consequence of this structure of incentives is that 'too little' investment in innovation is likely to be done by incumbents, a result not inconsistent with the findings of Mansfield *et al.* (1977) who found (for a sample of 17 innovations) a median social rate of return of 56% compared to a private one of 25% (the former exceeded the latter in 13 cases). This argument is also consistent with the finding that many R&D projects undertaken by large incumbents are of short term nature, aimed at modest advances, and have a high rate of obsolescence (e.g. Schott, 1976).

called 'me-too' entry), and entry barriers in many industries protect incumbents from all but the most substantive innovative challenges. Innovative entry is likely to be most important during the early stages of the product life cycle. Gort and Klepper (1982) study the historical development of 46 products. Their results suggest that early stages of product development are characterised by substantial entry, with many of the new innovations being brought in by entrants. After a time, net entry is zero, though both gross entry and exit are still occurring. Then there is a rationalization induced by selection amongst the various innovations, and exit occurs, as winners of the initial race consolidate and eliminate weaker rivals. The winners gradually develop a knowledge of the fundamental features of the industry demand and technology which form the basis of entry barriers against latecomers. Such innovations as do occur are largely internal to the industry and eventually the remaining incumbents are protected by substantial entry barriers, at which point all fundamental change ceases.

The potential importance of entry in stimulating innovation is perhaps best illustrated by an example where its effects have not materialized. One example of such a situation is that of the US steel industry, which has long been protected by substantial entry barriers, and has enjoyed a co-ordinated pricing scheme which has kept the industry fairly profitable. Leading firms have been notoriously slow in adopting even well known, profitable innovations (for example, blast oxygen furnaces and continuous casting methods), succumbing only after much smaller domestic rivals (or more importantly, imports) threatened their position.

We have argued that the pace of innovation is likely to depend closely on the threat of entry. In computers, there have been a vigorous stream of entry challenges. In steel, the pressure from entrants has been much weaker. This suggests that to understand the reasons for sluggish innovation in Europe, and the potential role for a modern European industrial policy, we have to examine entry barriers in more detail. To that task we now turn.

3.2. Structural barriers to entry

Mobility barriers are anything which impede the ability of firms to enter or leave an industry, or to move from one segment of an industry to another. They can be grouped into two classes which we prefer to call 'structural' and 'behavioural' (this corresponds to the distinction between 'innocent' and 'strategic' barriers introduced by Salop, (1979)). Structural barriers arise from basic characteristics of the industry such as technology and demand. They are, in principle, exogenous to the firm, and can lead to market structures which are 'naturally' imperfect, and where only a limited number of firms can make profits in the industry. By contrast, behavioural barriers arise from the strategies adopted by incumbent firms in the market. They include the post-entry response of incumbents to entry challenges, and any pre-entry activity designed to enhance the structural difficulties entrants face.

In his pioneering study, Bain (1956) identified three sources of structural entry barriers: product differentiation, absolute cost advantages, and scale economies. Product differentiation poses difficulties for entrants because prior purchases of the incumbent's brand are sunk investments by consumers (Schmalensee, 1982). When product characteristics cannot be easily evaluated by inspection, and differ in unusual and complex ways, the opportunity cost to a consumer of trying a new brand with uncertain attributes may be high. Absolute cost advantages arise whenever the entrant has a higher unit cost curve than the incumbent as, for example, when the incumbent enjoys superior access to technology, location, or factor markets. Scale economies restrict the number of firms that can profitably compete in a market, forcing entrants to choose between operation at sub-optimal scale and a cost disadvantage relative to incumbents or operation at optimal scale facing a depressed market price.

By now, we have accumulated a fair bit of evidence on the height of these three entry barriers (for a survey, see Geroski, (1983)). In most cases, scale economies do not seem to pose a substantial entry barrier. Tables 3 and 4 present evidence on scale economies in practice (see also Scherer, (1980)). In most cases, optimal scale involves plants producing less than 5% of EC output, though, where the European market is effectively fragmented into national markets, scale economies may be more important in relation to market size. What does seem to be true is that the capital requirements of building large plants may pose substantial difficulties for entrants, the absolute cost disadvantage arising largely from unequal access to capital markets. Considerable evidence exists in the UK to suggest that the important distinction here may not be entrant versus incumbent so much as unquoted versus quoted firms, (Hay and Morris, 1984). In part, the problem arises from the concentration of financial power, as personal savings are increasingly managed by life assurance firms, pension funds, and building societies. 'The vast funds put at the disposal of . . . institutional intermediaries, by being placed preferentially in large quoted companies, have contributed to financial pressures which have encouraged the formation of large industrial groups' (Prais, 1976). Whereas large quoted companies can raise capital through new issues, unquoted firms generally finance their expansion through retained earnings and short term credit. These financial problems often severely restrict new firm formation. Other absolute cost advantages – control of scarce resources, limited access to new technology, etc. – can be important in particular cases, but it is hard to generalize. Product differentiation advantages are certainly the most controversial to identify in practice, although many industrial economists suspect that they are the most important of all. Although again it is hard to generalize, space packing, product proliferation, the inflation of styling costs, differential access to retailing networks and advertising have all been documented as causes of barriers in particular cases.

While there is a wealth of material documenting the existence of particular types of entry barriers, there are few evaluations of the overall height of barriers in particular sectors, much less for economies as a whole. Nevertheless, our reading of this material suggests that, in general, barriers can be appreciable. This, it must be stressed, is not inconsistent with the observation of large inflows of small entrants, or even the occasional large scale entry attempt in particular industries. Many of the small scale entry attempts that we observe involve firms whose survival probabilities are extremely low, and those that do manage to secure entry often inhabit small market niches and do not pose any kind of substantive threat to their larger competitors. Barriers are not impossibly high in all sectors, but this does not imply that a concerted effort to reduce barriers would not produce much more entry and mobility in Europe.

3.3. Strategic entry deterrence by private agents

Structural barriers may sometimes be sufficient to protect incumbents against entry challenges, as in the extreme example of natural monopoly. Frequently, however, incumbents will seek to reinforce such barriers by strategic behaviour. In our view, such behaviour plays a key role in reducing the flexibility of many markets and in forestalling innovative entry.

Strategic entry deterrence is the adoption by incumbents of strategies which will credibly alter the expectation of entrants about the post-entry profits those entrants will face. To be credible, such threats by incumbents about their own post-entry behaviour must actually be optimal *ex post* to carry out should entry occur. In essence, this requires the incumbent to make irreversible investments prior to entry which effectively commit the threatened course of action should entry occur. (For surveys of this work, see Geroski and Jacquemin, (1984), or Encaoua *et al.* (1985)).

Following Dixit (1982), we can illustrate the argument in a simple way. Suppose in the absence of entry, incumbent earns profits $R0$. Faced with an entry challenge, the incumbent can either fight off the entrant and earn profits $R1$ (which may be low if a price war is expensive), or can accommodate the entrant and earn profits $R2$. If $R2$ exceeds $R1$, any pre-entry threat to fight will not be credible – the entrant can work out that it will, in fact, be in the incumbent's interest to accommodate entry. Suppose, however, that the incumbent first makes an irrevocable commitment with a cost C (perhaps an act of irreversible physical investment) which reduces the post-entry profit from accommodation from $R2$ to $R2-C$. Given entry, the incumbent will now fight if $R1$ exceeds $R2-C$. In this case, the entrant will abandon any thoughts of entry, and, in its absence, the incumbent will earn the pre-entry profits $R0$ minus the commitment cost C. Summing up, we deduce the conditions:

$R1 > R2 - C$:   incumbent would fight, and hence entrant won't bother to enter

$R0 - C > R2$:   payoff to entry deterrence exceeds payoff from admitting entrant without a fight.

Combining these conditions, when $R0$, $R1$ and $R2$ are such that there exists a positive C such that

$$R0 - R2 > C > R2 - R1,$$

then strategic entry deterrence will be successful. By making the irreversible commitment C, the incumbent can credibly deter entry. The essential insight of this analysis is that it may be possible for the incumbent to lock into a post-entry course of action which the entrant must then take as given. In short, such strategic actions during the pre-entry stage seek to alter the conditions of any post-entry game in a way that is favourable to the incumbent.

The most obvious example of this strategy is where the incumbent undertakes prior investment to increase capacity, which enables the incumbent to threaten to expand output and flood the market should entry occur. Without such prior investment, the threat is an empty one. A good illustration of this strategy occurred in the titanium dioxide industry (Ghemawat, 1984). The early 1970s saw a large jump in the price of ore and the introduction of new pollution controls which were widely expected to raise the cost of waste disposal. Of the six major competitors in the industry, one (du Pont) used a ilmenite chloride technology which protected it from the worst of these effects and gave it a cost advantage of at least 20% over its rivals. Our theory predicts that du Pont, acting as the incumbent with the relevant technology, should find it profitable to try to preempt the adoption of this technology by its rivals or by new entrants. And this is exactly what happened. Du

Pont embarked on a massive investment programme of capacity expansion to forestall entry by others. Given a projected total demand increase of 377,000 tons of titanium dioxide, du Pont drew up plans to expand capacity by 505,000 tons, thus establishing the credible threat to flood the market if necessary. In fact, this example illustrates how the commitment strategy can sometimes backfire. Commitment involves the deliberate decision to lock oneself into action for strategic reasons which are privately profitable for the incumbent. But this inflexibility leaves the committed incumbent vulnerable to unexpected shocks. When the demand for titanium dioxide subsequently fell unexpectedly, du Pont were left with more excess capacity than they had bargained for. As Ghemawat wryly observes, 'caveat pre-emptor.'

Other deterrence strategies include investment in reputation. Here the idea is that the incumbent should fight off early entry challenges even if there is a short term loss in so doing. By investing in a reputation for toughness, the incumbent will deter future entry challenges and the discounted value of the additional future profits may more than cover the cost of early fights. A third example is product proliferation by the incumbent, crowding the product market with a variety of brands which leaves little space for entrants. This example combines product differentiation and fixed set up costs, and has been documented for the ready-to-eat breakfast cereal market by Schmalensee (1978).

In these examples, it is the prior appearance and activity in a market that can give the incumbent strategic opportunities for entry deterrence, and these 'first mover' advantages may allow dominant market positions to be maintained for long periods which are relatively free from entry challenges.[4] Natural selection can then be seriously impeded in two distinct ways. First, as we shall see shortly, the prior installation of product-specific, durable, and hence sunk, capital makes the incumbent's own exit less likely, and so increases the entrant's costs of displacing the incumbent completely. A successful supplanting of an incumbent surrounded by high levels of sunk costs requires an even more innovative entry than normal. Second, incumbency may also act to delay innovation and change. To illustrate this argument, we discuss the example of patenting (see, e.g., Gilbert and Newbery, 1982).

Suppose a firm monopolizes a market, earning profits $R1$. Some exogenous change in technology then enables a market expansion in a

---

[4] A firm enjoying a first mover advantage may not always find it optimal to exercise this advantage. An example is the 'fast second' strategy (see Baldwin and Childs (1969), and recall our earlier discussion of IBM) in which the incumbent delays introducing an innovation until the rivals have introduced theirs.

related dimension which complements the incumbent's existing activities. Any firm which patents the technology can monopolize this new segment. If the incumbent patents first, it earns $R2$ on its entire activities. If the entrant patents first, the entrant earns $R3$ and the incumbent $R4$. Since a post-entry duopoly is always less profitable than a monopoly unless the two firms collude perfectly, $R2$ exceeds $(R3 + R4)$. Competition for the patent is a race, and we assume that the firm which spends more in search of the patent will win. The maximum the entrant will spend is $R3$, its expected return to winning the race. For the incumbent, the return to winning is $(R2 - R4)$ and since $(R2 - R4)$ exceeds $R3$, it follows that the incumbent will win, introduce the patent first, and pre-empt the entrant.

What is particularly unsatisfactory about this outcome is that the entrant can appreciate that this result is likely to prevail, and hence either will have no incentive to begin the patent race or will drop out early. This suggests that the mere knowledge that the incumbent is likely to win the race may be enough to prevent the race from being run at all. In any kind of competition in which the incumbent can 'run faster' than entrants because of their first mover advantages, there will be little incentive for entry to occur and so incumbents will not need to search out the new patents; or, if they choose to do so, need not introduce them. It is important to see that this represents a basic bias in how markets work. Markets reward innovative activity on a first come first served basis, and not after a comprehensive review of all possibilities. Hence, being 'quick' is often better than being 'right', and the knowledge that one competitor is quicker than all the rest may be enough to ensure that nothing happens at all.

The empirical evidence that we have on these issues is really rather meagre. The above arguments suggest that positions of dominant market power achieved by early market leaders ought to persist for long periods of time. Direct examination of the decline of positions of dominant market power shows that such positions are often maintained for long periods and that, in general, there can be no strong presumption that market forces operate strongly to erode them (e.g. Geroski, (1985)). The other side of the coin is that one expects first rivals to do particularly well against later entrants. Shaw and Shaw (1982) study late entry into synthetic fibres. Of five late entrants ten or more years after the initial development of the nylon market in the early 1950s, four abandoned production and the last survived with a low market share only by concentrating on a specialist part of the market. Late entrants into the acrylics and polyester sectors showed even less success, and all the late entrants proved to be far more vulnerable to the poor market conditions of the late 1970s than did the early leaders, whose dominant positions were maintained largely intact over the twenty year period covered by the study.

3.4. Strategic behaviour by governments

One cannot analyse the activities of large firms as if they were governed solely by the actions of purely private decision makers. Firms use governments for various types of assistance, and government policies frequently are implemented through large firms. It is therefore of some importance to complement the preceding discussion by looking at the strategic behaviour of governments, and how it affects competition in markets. Most of the interesting actions in this respect are those which governments undertake to improve the international position of their domestic champions.

When trade occurs under imperfectly competitive conditions, trade policy instruments – import tariffs, export promotion, changes in anti-trust policies, research and development subsidies – can be used with effects very different from those expected under competitive conditions. These instruments often constitute an important dimension of industrial policy. The European market has been particularly affected by public actions to replace intra-EEC tariffs by more potent non-tariff barriers designed to maintain market segmentation. The result is that intra-EEC trade is hampered by regulatory and institutional barriers, such as national product standards (officially adopted for technical, safety, or health reasons), which play a major role in reducing the substitutability between products from different countries, increasing unit costs and distorting production patterns. In terms of border controls, the European Commission estimates that companies are wasting 5% of total transport costs getting 7 billion ECU worth of goods across European frontiers. Similarly, although 42% of goods traded in the Community are moved by road, only 10% of hauliers are governed by Community permits allowing hauliers to move goods at will through the Community. Worse still, recent EC statistics show that over 90% of public sector equipment purchases are made from national suppliers, in spite of the obligation to open national procurement to all European corporations. All of these activities suggest that the European market, far from being an integrated domestic market, is still an international market deliberately segmented by national attitudes. There are even indications that the process of market integration has slowed down: for example, since 1974, intra-EEC trade has more or less stabilized. As recognized by the recent White Paper from the Commission to the European Council, there remain many barriers to the free movement of goods, services, capital, and persons, to be dismantled if a truly

Table 7. The post-entry trade policy game

	EC protection	EC free trade
US protection	$(SU1+PU1;$	$(SU1+PU1+PE2;$
	$SE1+PE1-K)$	$SE2+PE2-K)$
US free trade	$(SU2+PU2;$	$(SU2+PU2+PE2;$
	$SE1+PE1+PU2-K)$	$SE2+PE2+PU2-K)$

integrated European market is to be achieved. In its absence, it is essential to recognize that countries are likely to persist with national rather than international policies. Whereas such strategic competition between European governments may be harmful, their collective strategic action may be beneficial.

The following is a simple illustration. Consider a game between the US and EC governments in a world where the incumbent firm is American, and there is a potential EC entrant firm. The US incumbent has sunk costs K which have already been incurred. In the US market, let $PU1 =$ excess of revenue over production cost for a monopolist; $PU2 =$ excess of revenue over production cost for each duopolist; $SU1 =$ consumers' surplus under monopoly; and $SU2 =$ consumers' surplus under duopoly. Define $PE1$, $PE2$, $SE1$ and $SE2$ analogously for the EC market. The problem is the following. The two governments have to choose between free trade and complete protection which bans all imports; the EC government has to decide whether to subsidize the EC entrant's 'sunk costs', the part of its production costs which correspond to the costs already sunk by the US incumbent; and the EC firm has to decide whether or not it wishes to enter.

Given perfect information, we calculate the solution as follows: first, we calculate optimal actions in the second stage game, then we calculate optimal actions in the prior first stage game. A taxonomy of possible outcomes is discussed in Dixit and Kyle (1985). For our illustrative purpose we focus on the post-entry trade policy game. For simplicity, we shall take marginal costs as constant and assume away any international reselling. Table 7 shows the payoffs to different government actions. An outcome labelled $(A; B)$ implies that the payoff to the US is A and to the EC is B. If $SU2+PU2$ exceeds $SU1+PU1$, the US government prefers free trade no matter which policy the EC government selects. Similarly, if $SE2+PE2$ exceeds $SE1+PE1$, the EC government prefers free trade no matter which policy the US government selects. Hence, free trade will be chosen, and the EC entrant knows this in advance in deciding whether or not to enter. Entry is profitable for the EC firm if $PE2 + PU2 - K$ is positive, but, for an industry with large sunk costs K, this expression will be negative and entry will not take place. Dixit and Kyle show that if the EC government is allowed to move first, it could have an interest in making an irreversible precommitment. By paying the EC firm's sunk cost K, the EC government can ensure that the final equilibrium will be free trade with a duopoly, which yields greater benefits to the EC than the alternative policy of complete protection, and also greater benefits to the US than the alternative of protection by the EC. More generally, Dixit and Kyle conclude that the inability of firms to appropriate all consumers' surplus can justify a public policy to alter oligopolistic market outcomes even from the viewpoint of worldwide efficiency.

A good example of industrial policy as strategic behaviour at the international level is the public support offered to the European Airbus consortium in its efforts to challenge the incumbent (Boeing) in the market for intermediate range commercial airliners. The recent deal with PanAm marks a further consolidation of the Airbus foothold in this market, and goes beyond earlier sales in domestic European or third markets. The success of Airbus to date derives not merely from European cooperation in pooling knowledge, thus placing Airbus on a par with the United States where the award of grants and R&D contracts through an open bid system results (particularly in the Aerospace industry) in a common pool of knowledge. The collective governmental precommitment to Airbus has also raised the cost of Boeing of trying to fight off the entry challenge, and thereby increased the chance of successful entry.

3.5. Exit barriers

Thus far, we have focussed largely on entry barriers and on barriers to mobility within industries. However, for change to occur through the introduction of new firms, new ideas, and the expansion of successful firms, there must also be exit. Restrictions on the contraction and exit of unsuccessful firms will only impede the progress of the new.

Three considerations are vital to exit decisions. The first is sunk costs. In their absence, a firm earning less than it could elsewhere would cash in its assets and start up afresh in another industry. But it is in the nature of sunk costs that they cannot be cashed in. Hence, a firm with sunk costs may continue in business even when its operating profit is well below that earned in other industries. Second, as with entry, exit decisions are inherently long run decisions in which expectations about the future play a key role. Thus exit will be more common in a declining industry that in an expanding industry. For an individual firm, the exit decision will be influenced by its beliefs about how many other firms will leave the industry, since the exit of others will increase the profitability of those who remain. This interdependence of firms' decisions means that exit decisions are frequently strategic in nature. Finally, government behaviour also plays a role since government subsidies may enable declining industries to survive with excess capacity and low profitability.[5] Table 8 shows the scale of government subsidies in five European countries in the late 1970s.

Whereas in any entry game the first mover advantage is clearly defined (it lies with the incumbent who is already in the industry), in exit games the question of who goes first lies at the heart of the strategic competition (see, e.g., Nalebuff and Ghemawat, (1984)). As an illustration, consider a classic war of attrition. Suppose there are two firms in a market which has already shrunk to the point where only one firm can operate profitably. Each firm can choose either to exit or to remain. Table 9 illustrates the payoffs to each firm. Thus, for example, the outcome (S, T) denotes a return of S to firm 1 and T to firm 2.

If both remain in the market, each firm gets R. Either firm gets S if it exits. If only one firm remains, that firm gets T. When an exit barrier exists, R exceeds S, and clearly T exceeds R. Consider the decision of firm 1. If it believes firm 2 will exit, firm 1 should remain (since T exceeds S). If it believes firm 2 will remain, firm 1 should remain (since R exceeds S). Hence firm 1 will definitely remain, as will firm 2 by identical reasoning. Neither firm exits even though it may clearly be sociably desirable that one of them should.

A related problem occurs when there are no sunk costs and the returns to both firms are negative when both stay ($S = 0$, $R < 0$). Each firm would like the other to leave and it is not obvious which, if either, will exit. Thus, even when it is clear to all that a market is in decline, each firm may decide to remain and, in such circumstances, there may be persistently low returns and little innovation in the industry over long periods of time. Outside intervention is needed to ensure exit and

---

[5] Shaw and Shaw (1983) present a good example of how government policy can complicate the exit process. The West European Synthetic Fibres industry grew rapidly from the early 1960s to the early 1970s but, by the mid to late 1970s, severe excess capacity began to emerge (average capacity utilization was about 68% over the period 1974–80). The process of rationalization was complicated by extensive Italian intervention which eventually forced the EEC Commission to intervene and coordinate a rationalization agreement. The Shaws suggest that this intervention did not produce anything like a competitive outcome, since small and inefficient plants did not disappear. This seems to be largely irrelevant since it is more than clear that several national governments had no intention whatsoever of allowing the free market to do its work. Under the circumstances the Davignon plan seems to have been far better than any other option that was actually likely to prevail at the time in that industry.

Table 8. Industrial subsidies in five European countries 1978–1980

	Great Britain 1979–80 million £	Italy 1978 billion Lire	Norway 1979 million Nkr	Sweden 1979 million Skr	W. Germany 1980 million Dm
General subsidies					
Export	376	1,688	152	1,507	1,750
R&D	267	75	614	1,643	4,450
Investment	2	240	395	—	650
Employment	209	—	125	396	—
Regional and small firm	388	725	1,205	3,134	12,000
Rescue operations					
Sectoral	77	—	1,109	1,255	2,650
Firm specific	620	2,671	1,192	7,464	400
Total	1,939	5,399	4,792	15,399	21,900
Total					
as % of GDP	1.0	2.6	2.0	3.5	1.6
as % of value added in mining and manufacturing	3.6	7.1	7.6	16.0	4.0

Source: Carlsson (1983).

Table 9. The exit game

Firm 2

Firm 1		Exit	Remain
	Exit	(S, S)	(S, T)
	Remain	(T, S)	(R, R)

raise returns for those who remain. This, in turn, will go some way to encouraging new internal innovations, and will certainly clear the ground for new firms to enter and populate the market. In the absence of such outside intervention, there is no obvious market mechanism to enforce the rationalization of the industry which is required.

3.6. Two examples

In order to illustrate the arguments that we have discussed in the previous sections, we shall now examine in some depth two examples

Table 10. Share of World integrated circuit market by end-use sectors, 1983

	% Share of World end-use	Of which, producer shares (%)		
		US	Japan	W. Europe
Computer/Data Communication	39	86	10	4
Telecommunications	11	71	17	12
Industrial	11	74	21	5
Consumer	30	36	59	5
Government/Military	9	95	—	5

Source: OECD (1985).

which pose crucial questions for the future of the European Community. The first one is in the field of the high technology sectors, while the second corresponds to a mature oligopoly where exit barriers are operating. In both cases, we shall see that the important policy problem is not inadequate corporate size but rather a market structure dominated by a few large firms usually enjoying governmental support.

3.6.1. The semiconductor industry. The semiconductor industry's importance derives not from its share of manufacturing value added (still less than 0.1% for the OECD), but from its role in promoting a wide range of industrial and commercial products, services, and changes in work practices. Semiconductors may either be discrete components (e.g. transistors) or integrated circuits (e.g. microprocessors and memories), the latter being the fastest growing product. Existing data shows clearly that European firms in this industry have lagged behind international rivals (especially in integrated circuits); for example, a recent OECD study (1985) showed that Western European firms accounted for 12.3% of world production in 1978, but only 8.5% in 1982. Table 10 displays the relative shares in the end-use consumption of integrated circuits by companies based in the United States, Japan, and Western Europe, and indicates that Europe is weak in all aspects of the industry. Table 11 suggests that this weakness extends to other high-tech products and Table 12 confirms this impression for trade in integrated circuits, where Europe faces a large and growing trade deficit.

How can we explain the disappointing European performance? As we argued earlier, the size of companies is certainly not a crucial factor, for economies of scale in production appear to be insignificant. (Tilton, 1982, and Coughlan and Flaherty, 1983). Furthermore, even US firms are often reluctant to invest heavily in equipment that may soon be obsolete. In marketing, the opportunities for scale economies are also

Table 11. Shares of firms in sales of high-tech products (%)

Product	US-based	European-based	Japanese
Semiconductors	64	9	27
Computers and data processing	82	9	9
Software packages	89	10	1
Data communications services	62	29	9
Digital public switching products	36	35	29
Satellites and satellite launchers	81	13	4
Satellite earth stations	27	33	35

Source: Ergas (1984).

Table 12. EC (10) trade balance in electronic microcircuits ($000s)

	1978	1979	1980	1981	1982	1983
Exports	209	247	312	730	21	543
Imports	541	659	1,126	909	916	1,172

Source: OECD (1985).
Note: excluding intra-EC trade.

limited; most buyers are final electronic equipment producers who are not susceptible to massive advertising campaigns. Nor does the nature of the product require a large servicing network. Similarly, the vertical integration of semiconductor and final equipment production (another possible source of scale economies) is not very profitable and could even adversely affect the competitive position of both: product decisions are hurt if firms are pressured to use in-house semiconductors when, for their purposes, better or cheaper ones are available from outside firms. In any case, though a size gap exists between EC firms and the largest US firms, they are of comparable size to those of Japan (Locksley 1982). If there is a competitive gap in terms of the innovative abilities of Community firms, it seems likely that it must be explained by other factors.

Such an alternative explanation may be based on the existence of strong first-mover advantages, the presence of sizeable learning economies, the existence of growing investment costs, the strategic creation of barriers to entry by the early entrants, and the existence of a fragmented European market in which existing firms play the role of

national champions. A major factor in the development of this industry
in Europe was the early presence in Europe of subsidiaries of US
corporations whose mother companies have developed through the
help of a large domestic market, with its great demand for new and
sophisticated military devices. This market supported the production
of most new semiconductor devices several years before the European
(and Japanese) markets. By the time sufficient demand arose in Europe
to support local production, new European firms were already at a
competitive disadvantage relative to American subsidiaries that enjoyed
licensing and technical assistance agreements with their mother companies. It is also interesting to note that the foreign subsidiaries which
have diffused new technology in Europe were not old foreign subsidiaries such as ITT, but new ones set up mainly in the 1960s. Thus
Tilton (1982, p. 165) concludes: 'These firms manage to evade the entry
barriers blocking new domestic firms because their parent companies
share with them much of the know-how derived from past production
experience, provide specialists and other professional personnel, and
if necessary supply venture capital.'

Other elements complemented the advantages of first movers in the
semiconductor industry. Although the basic discoveries have diffused
quickly, product development and process engineering of semiconductor technology have diffused much more slowly. Hence, the acquisition
of a patent or licence does not effectively enable the acquirer to capture
the main benefit from disembodied advances in technical knowledge.
Customer–supplier relationships are also very important in semiconductor and electronics subassembly process innovation, as is the necessity
of working extensively with the customer after the product introduction.
Thus, the existing relationships of US subsidiaries with their buyers
may have operated as an important aspect of product differentiation
entry barriers. Moreover, there is a requirement for specialized facilities
and specific production and marketing skills. It takes time for entrants
to acquire these, and this has two implications. First, firms which use
semiconductor process equipment to make semiconductors for end-use
will face significant barriers in trying to move into the production of
semiconductor process equipment itself, barriers which arise from the
high degree of specificity of know-how, organization arrangements,
and production infrastructure. Second, incumbents have important first
mover advantages once they are established with one strong product
in which their costs are largely sunk, on the back of which they can
continue to widen and extend their product range.

A further set of problems has arisen from the characteristics of
European policies towards semiconductors. Within each country, very
few government R&D and production contracts were awarded to new

firms trying to enter the semiconductor industry as this was deemed likely to divert support from the few large firms chosen as national champions to develop viable alternatives to American subsidiaries. This procurement policy raised the barriers to entry in these countries, making it difficult for entrants to pioneer the use of new semiconductor technology. In fact, the number of new European firms entering the industry has been small (particularly relative to the multitude of new American firms). What is worse, in individual European countries, each government has promoted its own national champion in semiconductors, thereby creating barriers which prevent genuine specialization at the European level. US and Japanese companies have been able to make a series of bilateral agreements with firms in each of the European countries, thereby preventing the emergence of serious European competition and reducing much of the European industry to the role of licensing and second-sourcing US and Japanese technology.

These factors lead us to argue for the possible role of a concerted European industrial policy able to help to overcome industry strategies along national lines, to reduce barriers between national champions and to develop a large home *European* market for industrial applications. What is required is not merely an integrated European market at the product level (in which nationally based procurement policies must be abandoned), but also specialization at the European level, in the R&D on, and production of, semiconductors. Indeed, we now see the emergence of such a policy. The ESPRIT programme is intended to provide the European semiconductor industry with an autonomous technology base, and to promote cooperation in R&D not merely in university research laboratories but also within electronics companies.[6] In similar spirit, the project RACE (R&D in Advanced Communications Technology in Europe) is intended to facilitate the transition from a narrow Integrated Services Digital Network to an Integrated Broadband Communications Network by 1995.

3.6.2. The steel industry. The European steel industry is a good illustration of a mature oligopoly characterized by barriers to exit. In the 1960s

---

[6] The ESPRIT programme was set up in February, 1984, following some earlier and limited attempts at intra-Community cooperative research. Conceived as a matching of private and public funds, money is allocated to 'clubs' involving partners from different member states for 'pre-competitive resarch' in five basic areas: microelectronics; software; information processing; office systems; and computer manufacturing technologies. Of 104 projects announced in January, 1985, bringing together about 265 European companies (including the big 12 Electronics giants in Europe), and at least 50% of the projects involve firms of 500 employees or less, and more than three quarters involve universities. A similar if rather narrower programme – the Alvey project – has recently been implemented in the UK.

324   *Paul Geroski and Alexis Jacquemin*

a misplaced faith in continued demand growth led European steel-makers to embark on long-term programmes of plant expansion both to meet demand projections and in the hope of securing scale economies.

Furthermore, firms had only a limited ability to make alterations in production processes once new capacity was in place. Since the 1970s, steel has become a mature industry. With demand stagnating, excess capacity has steadily emerged. The problem has been intensified by the entry of new competitors. These latecomers, mainly from the LDCs and Eastern Europe, and often characterized by lower labour costs and new technologies, have developed export-oriented capacity, able to compete with producers of advanced countries.

Technological changes constitute another important factor. In the 1960s, when demand was on an upward trend, a technology based on scale economies and massive investment programmes appeared to be obvious strategy. However, since then the priority governing technological development and expenditure on R&D has begun to change, moving away from the design of larger-sized plants to focus on increased production flexibility and capacity rationalization. The clearest example of this is the direct reduction of ore into iron, allowing the elimination of the blast furnace; afterwards, the iron is processed into steel by new electric-ore steel furnaces. This process has been adopted mainly for relatively small-scale production, and was called a 'mini-mill' technology to contrast it with the oxygen process. Such mills use scrap as inputs and, with electric furnaces, they can dispense with the upstream process. Since scrap prices are far more flexible than iron ore prices, their cost advantage grows in a recession. The main point is that these and other innovations (such as the continuous-process industry with a direct flow from input to output) offer lower capital and operating costs, smaller optimal sizes, and greater flexibility than the more traditional plants of the 1960s and early 1970s.

Despite the structural changes in the conditions of demand and in the technological conditions, most European firms have not scrapped existing capacity, and have not adopted the new methods of production. Since 1960, there has been a persistent gap between existing capacity and actual production, as shown in Table 13.

With present capacity at around 200 million tons, excess capacity is today enormous, and, as average costs are generally well above marginal costs, we have observed a vicious cycle of falling output and profit. Existing competition is characterized by quality differentials, various degrees of downward integration, distinct external markets, and sufficiently imperfect information to allow extensive price discrimination and rebate schemes. Furthermore, modernization programmes

Table 13. European crude steel production and capacity 1960–82 (million tons)

		Production				Estimated capacity	
	1960	1974	1979	1981	1982	1966	1982
EEC(9):	98.1	155.3	140.1	125.1	110.6	140.6	197.6
of which:							
Germany:	34.1	53.6	46.0	41.6	35.9	48.0	67.7
UK:	24.7	22.3	21.5	15.4	13.8	31.3	25.2
France:	17.3	27.0	23.4	21.2	18.4	23.6	29.6
Italy:	8.5	23.8	24.2	24.7	24.0	17.2	39.8
Belgium:	7.2	16.2	13.4	12.3	9.9	11.1	19.1

Source: Messerlin and Saunders, in Shepherd *et al.* (1983).

have been unduly delayed although the international transfer of technology is relatively easy. As the investment costs of new plants rose, firms found themselves heavily committed to obsolete technological processes that were not suited to the new market conditions. Simultaneously, long-term increases in plant size made it essential that all capacity – new and old – be operated at rates of utilization as high as 90%.

This example illustrates how the search by incumbent firms for large size and scale economies through massive investment in durable, specific capital can initially create high entry barriers, which for some time are successful. But it is a risky strategy, and the steel example shows that it can backfire. On the one hand, technical change has allowed the new, low-cost, mini-mills to overcome these entry barriers and compete effectively. On the other hand, by locking themselves into a particular type of large steel mill, incumbents have left themselves very vulnerable to the unforeseen but dramatic change in both steel demand and energy costs. In such circumstances, the strategy of precommitment has severely reduced the flexibility of the European steel industry, and these sunk costs now form high exit barriers. The first movers have become trapped by their own commitments.

One industrial strategy which may allow a weakening of the barriers to exit is product diversification, for example a shift into the production of high quality and special steel products that compete with substitutes like aluminium and plastics. There is, however, the danger of excess production if too many European, American and Japanese firms move in that direction, as seems probable.

Rather than allowing the twin pressures of shrinking demand and continuing entry to place severe contractionary pressures on large established steel firms, most European countries have tried to protect their own producers and maintain existing capacity, expecting (or at least hoping) that the capacity of other EC countries would be reduced.

For example, in Italy an extensive investment programme was sustained between 1965 and 1978, as the dramatic increase in Italian capacity in Table 13 makes clear. Even where steel industries remain in private rather than public ownership (as in Germany, Luxembourg, and the Netherlands), government subsidies have played an important role in sustaining the existing national capacities. In this regard, the European experience contrasts sharply with the Japanese, where it has proved possible to pursue a consensus strategy for rationalization (see Ballance and Sinclair, 1983).

As we have stressed, the exit game in the European steel industry takes place not merely between individual steel firms but also between their governments whose financial support schemes are vital to the industry as it currently operates. This suggests that it will be important to try to introduce a supra-national element into European decisions so that current 'beggar thy neighbour' policies may be replaced with a cooperative solution. One important initiative in this area is the 'Davignon Plan' which emphasizes the need for greater product specialization, the joint use of plants, coordination of investment plans to eliminate duplication, restriction of national subsidies to inefficient firms, the dismantling of obsolete capacity, and the promotion of joint technical research. In our view, such initiatives should be encouraged. The alternative is to leave everything to the forces of market selection. In this section, we have tried to argue that such selection is likely to be seriously impeded by exit barriers, to be slow and erratic, and to depend as much on private financial reserves and public financial support from national governments as on any innate comparative advantage.

3.7. Internal adaptation and rigidities within European corporations

Thus far we have argued that, because of high mobility barriers, market forces external to incumbent firms may exert only a weak selection process on such large firms. Competitive discipline and the pressure to innovate may be weak. In such circumstances, it is important to consider whether there are powerful forces within the firm which can stimulate efficiency and change. Here, we draw on organizational theories of the firm to examine the internal structure and control of large firms.

The essential feature governing organizational behaviour and the response to change is routine (for an extended discussion, see Nelson and Winter, (1982)). The standard operating procedures which define the activities of firms play at least three important roles. First, they act as a store of memory. Agents, and their specific information and capital, are connected to each other by such routines, and the essential information that they need to coordinate their actions is codified in them.

Second, routines act as a form of truce between competing agents within the firm, setting a compromise between the preferences and desires of each that enables them all to act in concert. Routines thus formalize agreements and the associated set of sidepayments needed to sustain them. Finally, routines act as a norm of behaviour against which performance can be assessed, and towards which behaviour can be galvanized should performance fall short of aspirations. The important point is that conflict colours the dynamic response of organizations and gives all agents an interest in maintaining the *status quo*.

Short term deterioration in performance can generally be financed out of the organizational slack inherent in the truce which determines the firm's activities; if so, standard operating procedures need not be seriously disturbed. However, a more severe and prolonged setback eventually prompts an expensive search for a new compromise. The cost of this search arises from the conflict it can provoke, and tends to bias such organizations against rapid change. Moreover, large firms, protected by positions of market power, may be able to finance performance problems for some time, thereby postponing necessary change still further. There seem two ways in which the dynamic response of large organizations might be improved. First, one can alter the incentives of leading agents within the firms. Secondly, the process of internal bargaining can be affected by the internal structure of the firm. We consider each of these in the European context.

The incentives of leading managers will depend on the behaviour of owners. In most large firms, owners do not participate in the day to day running of affairs, but act only as a check on management's longer term strategic decision making. In one sense, this makes owners ideal arbiters in situations of organizational conflict. However, in practice, the flow of relevant information to owners is severely curtailed, making it almost impossible for them to fulfill this function. In addition, Board members are typically quasi-insiders who generally share an interest in the sidepayment structure embodied in the current operating procedures, and so do not assume the role of independent arbiter. In practice, the share ownership of most large companies is widely dispersed, and most action by owners occurs collectively through the capital market. In principle, this could enable the transfer of control to those with the right ideas and the ability to implement them. In practice, capital market pressures on large firms do not seem a powerful selection process for increased efficiency and improved profitability. Rather, most capital market activity encourages firms to increase their size, usually through merger. The vast majority of empirical studies make clear that the best survival strategy for incumbent managements is to increase the size of their concerns; increasing efficiency and profitability affect survival chances only marginally. In fact, until recently, corporate control in Europe appears to have been largely held in the hands of holding companies, banks, and wealthy families (e.g. Jacquemin and de Ghellinck, (1980)). Indeed, this ownership pattern has often led to the creation of large diversified groupings organized not on an 'industrial' logic but on a 'financial' or 'personal' logic, and has given such firms an unduly high orientation towards defining their goals in terms of short-term financial achievements. (See, de Woot and de Maredsous, (1984)).

Whatever the incentives to change, it is clearly the case that the internal structuring of firms can make the process of change less costly. The best example we have of this is the famous transition in corporate form from U-form to M-form. Most firms at the turn of the century were organized on what has come to be called a unitary-form basis, with the firm internally organized in functional divisions headed by a small overall management team. When deep and severe problems were imposed on these firms by their environment, they proved quite incapable of meeting them. The problems were twofold. On the one hand, the functionally organized divisions were richly interacting units whose lines of communication were routed through the chief executive. When the need for extensive communication between them arose because of environmental adversity, the extra load imposed on that chief executive generally became too much to handle. As a result, internal communications broke down, and the different divisions floundered in an uncoordinated mess. On the other hand, this involvement of the chief executive in day to day administrative affairs generally prevented consideration of the longer term strategic interests of the firm.

The multi-division form innovation was an attempt to solve these particular problems. First, it reorganized the firm into quasi-autonomous divisions centred around particular products and containing all the functional specialists necessary to handle them. The necessity for outside intervention was facilitated by the use of profit centre auditing for each division, enabling outsiders to tell at a glance which divisions were in trouble and which were prospering. Such accounting organization not only facilitates monitoring, but enables chief executives to allocate resources amongst divisions in a fairly rational fashion. Secondly, the M-form structure separated the chief executive more clearly from the day to day running of affairs, and provided the resources both to monitor the individual divisions and to focus on the firm's long run strategy. As an organizational innovation, a fair amount of evidence suggests that this transition has been a success, raising profitability by the more effective control of the overall organization exercised by top management. Its diffusion in Europe, however, has been rather slow. By 1970, M-form structures had been adopted by 54 of the top 100 French firms, 50 of the top 100 in Germany and 57 of the top 100 in the UK; by contrast, 80 of the largest 100 US companies had such a structure.[7]

Of the areas in which the internal organization of firms can be altered to enhance performance, one of the most important is in the organization of the workforce (as we saw earlier, this applies particularly to large establishments). The Japanese experience is rather interesting in this connection. Rather than allocating labour amongst productive activities through the movement of labour among firms which hire and fire in a free labour market, labour allocation in the Japanese economy is largely within the large multi-unit enterprise (e.g. Imai and Itami, 1984). By assuring the employees stability of employment, such firms have acquired, in compensation, the right to flexibly operate their internal labour systems by organizing movement among various jobs within the firm and preventing each worker's skill and know-how from being limited to any single job.

One noticeable consequence of this system is the success of the diversification strategies adopted by Japanese firms. The resources needed for implementing diversification plans are usually not procured from outside, but come from the accumulated technologies, know-how, and knowledge contained in the firm's own human resources. Such a strategy stands in contrast with the usual 'product portfolio management model' much fancied in the West which stresses purely financial (e.g. risk pooling) advantages, and encourages conglomerate diversification too far away from the firms' technological base. More generally, these considerations lead to the notion that the current problem of productivity will be remedied only when firms learn how to manage people in such a way that they can work together more efficiently. In this context, it is interesting to note some preliminary findings on the relationship between worker participation and corporate performance in Britain, France and Italy. This research suggests that profit-sharing and individual capital stakes can have marked effects on productivity even after controlling for all the other possible determinants of productivity. In the specific case of French cooperatives, value added is an increasing function of workers' participation in profits, in collective

---

[7] These notions have been pursued by Aoki (1983), who observed in Japanese firms a 'quasi-tree' structure which is even more flexible and decentralized than the M-form. The principle here is the extensive development of subsidiaries and sub-contracting. Unlike US firms which face a continual drain of key personnel, these Japanese firms have been allowing their own managers to organize new or hitherto internalized functions on a quasi-autonomous basis, tied to the mother organization in a series of overlapping (rather than strictly hierarchical) relationships.

membership and in capital stakes (Estrin *et al.*, 1984, Defournoy *et al.*, 1985).

4. European industrial policy and the current crisis

Our central thesis has been that the root cause of the current industrial crisis in Europe is not the small scale of European firms but rather that they have been too slow in initiating and responding to change. In explaining this, we have focussed on the undue height of mobility barriers which weaken market selection, and on the rigidities within large corporate organizations. Structural and strategic barriers reduce entry, intra-industry mobility, and exit. In so doing, they not merely impede the ability of markets to weed out the inefficient, they also reduce the competitive pressures which promote innovation as the mechanism of, or the response to, entry by new firms. Nor can we rely on the internal dynamics within large organizations to initiate and promote efficiency and change.

From this we deduce that policy must aim to enhance market flexibility, reduce barriers to mobility, and stimulate adaptability within large corporate bureaucracies. This conception of industrial policy can be quite activist but must not be mistaken for planning. Its object is not to pick winners and choose outcomes, but to reinforce the competitive market process in which European firms must operate. It may include the familiar tools of industrial policy – tax credits, accelerated depreciation allowances, R&D incentives, and so on – but it must go beyond these. In our view, a coherent European industrial policy must contain four major features: a vigorous anti-trust and merger policy, an attack on financial barriers to entry, the harmonization of national industrial policies within Europe to reduce government-created barriers between member countries, and policies to promote cooperative ventures in particular areas such as high-tech. Let us briefly consider each in turn.

First, the policy of the 1960s, which gave rise to the super-firms which now populate Europe, was somewhat misconceived. The benefits of large-scale plants and firms have, at best, been limited. Larger size may not be necessary, and is certainly not sufficient, for improved corporate performance. Since the pursuit of larger size was the rationale for a policy stance favourable to mergers, we believe that merger policy should now be reconsidered. In its judgement of February 21, 1973, the Court of Justice established a rule of law to the effect that Article 86 of the Treaty of Rome applies to mergers that constitute an abuse of dominant market positions. However, such an application can be made only after a merger has taken place. We propose that this legislation be strengthened. Specifically, we believe that the Council of

Ministers should adopt the draft regulation on Economic Concentration, and accept the European Commission's proposal for a system of prior notification of mergers above a specified size.

Tougher anti-merger policy may prevent market power being further enhanced, but it is also necessary to deal more effectively with the market power which already exists. Thus, a vigorous anti-trust policy must be an essential component of a successful European industrial policy. As we have seen, dominant positions of protected market power allow large firms to erect mobility barriers which weaken market discipline and the incentives to innovate and respond to change. Anti-trust policy must reduce such barriers by attacking the dominant positions on which they depend.

In comparison with policy in the United States, European anti-trust policy has taken a more benevolent view of inter-firm cooperation. Although Article 85 outlaws such cooperation where it may affect trade between member countries, exemption may be sought if prior notification has been given. Moreover, the European Commission has used its power to exempt whole categories of agreement, for example those relating to standardization, specialization, and R&D. The new EC regulations of December 19, 1984 have further relaxed Article 85 by allowing firms to cooperate in R&D on products and processes, and to extend their cooperation to final products and markets. We do not believe that opportunities for beneficial cooperation have been restricted by existing anti-trust policies and we recommend that continuing pressures for further relaxation of European anti-trust policy should be resisted.

Second, a coherent European industrial policy must tackle financial markets, which presently favour established firms but hamper new enterprises through lack of funding. Private savings are overly concentrated in the hands of a small number of conservative financial institutions. Industrial policy should encourage the development of venture capital[8] markets in Europe since these effectively decentralize financial

---

[8] Of course, investors are as prone to waves of irrational enthusiam as anyone else. The computer industry provides an excellent example of this. In early days, it was generally easy to raise small or moderate amounts of capital because of investor enthusiasm, and this reached its limits of absurdity with a firm named Viatron Computer Systems Ltd. which had a stock market value of 217 million dollars in 1969 before it made any deliveries (it folded in 1971). Brock (1975) argues that up to about 1969 the capital market provided a positive spur to entry for minicomputers and peripherals because of the possibility of making large amounts of money through public stock offerings. By about 1970, this situation had changed, in part due to IBM's aggressive tactics, which led investors to fear that new companies they backed would be driven out by IBM. At this point, Brock reckons that capital costs became a significant barrier to entry in the peripherals market.

decisions to local or regional levels.[9] In addition, and without in any way advocating an attempt to pick winners, we recommend that public support or private incentives be provided to ensure that a larger fraction of total funding is channelled towards new and smaller firms.

Third, it is important to harmonize the industrial policies of different national governments in Europe, thus eliminating many strategic intra-EC barriers to trade and mobility. First, we advocate standardization. We should like to see the abolition of barriers caused by differences in VAT and by differences in health and safety standards. Frequently these act as hidden protection, making it harder for firms in one country to compete effectively in another. We should like to see the adoption of Community-wide standards, and perhaps a Community trade-mark. Second, we should like to see a much stricter adherence to the provisions in the Treaty of Rome against discriminatory practices by national governments, most notably in industrial subsidies and public procurement policies, which tend to favour national champions. Together, these proposals would help reduce the fragmentation of the European market and move us towards a more genuine Common Market. In each country, the large firms or national champions would then be exposed to greater competition and their market power would be correspondingly reduced. To supplement this process, we recommend the harmonization of legal arrangements, especially at the corporate level, to allow the formation of pan-European companies. Such companies would of course be subject to the full force of the anti-trust policy we described above, and we see them as a force for an increase in effective competition rather than for its curtailment.

Finally, European industrial policy must consider carefully the possible benefits of increased cooperation. By this we do not mean a general licence for collusion, of which we have already been critical. However, in previous sections we have argued that interdependence is a key feature of both private corporations and national governments. In such circumstances, cooperative action may well be superior to the outcome of uncoordinated individual decisions.

We have already discussed several examples of this proposition. In spite of our general scepticism about scale economies, there are undoub-

---

[9] The growth of high technology industry around Cambridge, England, is a good example of this. In general, the availability of finance has not been a limiting factor in the setting up and growth of these firms, and much of the cause of this is the active support by a *local regional office* of Barclays Bank. Starting in 1978, this office took a decision to support such firms, and by now has come to dominate lending activity in this area in Cambridge. At a somewhat different level, Carnforth (1984) has noted the spectacular growth of worker cooperatives in Britain (from about 20 in 1970 to about 900 in 1984), stressing that their finance has come almost entirely from public monies through support at local government levels (through the Cooperative Development Agencies): 'It has only been in areas with local CDAs that the number of cooperatives has grown significantly' (p 33).

tedly some activities in which scale economies are important, and aerospace is one instance. Even the world market cannot support six Boeing corporations. Unless there is a concerted European effort on a massive scale, individual national attempts to compete with Boeing are likely to fail. Nor is this simply a question of scale economies. We have also emphasized the strategic value of a credible commitment. In our opinion, one reason for the success of the European Airbus venture is the concerted governmental support which was initially pledged to the project. Had this burden fallen on a single government, Boeing might have taken a more optimistic view of the chances of resisting the entry challenge. Such strategic issues become even more important when we consider competition between European firms and their governments, as in our discussion of the European steel industry. The uncoordinated exit game between national European champions involves strong externalities and an incentive to adopt 'beggar thy neighbour' policies. To this we attributed the problems of rationalizing the European steel industry. Since it is a Europe-wide problem, it needs a Europe-wide solution, and it may require a genuinely supra-European body to impose such a solution on member countries. Even where a collectively beneficial policy can be adopted, not every member may gain in the first instance. Part of the role of a collective European policy would be to devise the side payments which ensure that all participating countries could then share in the gains from the adoption of such a policy. To some extent we already have examples of redistributive mechanisms within the Community. The European Social Fund has provided financial help for vocational training and youth unemployment. The European Regional Fund has helped correct the most serious imbalances within the Community, and since 1984 has participated in the finance of national programmes for aid to industry and for infrastructure investment. In short, the logic which already leads member countries to supplement local and regional policies with industrial policy at the national level should lead us to conclude that there are many larger problems for which the appropriate solution must be a coordinated and cooperative industrial policy at the European level.

The Large Internal Market under the Microscope: Problems and challenges

Michel Catinat

At the same time as it is engaged in intense legislative activity,[1] the Commission has embarked upon a detailed analysis of the economic and social consequences of the large internal market. This is a Herculean and particularly delicate task. A few moments' thought will serve to demonstrate that the completion of the internal market will overturn a good many economic mechanisms, will transform the environment of firms, and will – in some cases profoundly – affect the behaviour of individual actors. The number of parameters to be mastered is huge; any approach meant to be totally deterministic raises insuperable problems. Despite these difficulties, the Commission is settling down to its task and is calling for studies from both inside and outside. To mention only the most recent: the report of a group of independent experts chaired by Mr T. Padoa-Schioppa [20] which describes the economic and institutional conditions required if the large internal market is to succeed; and the report on the 'cost of non-Europe' prepared under the direction of Mr P. Cecchini, which will concentrate[2] on the economic consequences – quantified as far as possible – of the large internal market.

The ideas set out below should be seen in the context of the preparation of this report. Their scope is limited to the problematical aspects. There is no attempt at quantitative evaluation, nor any proposal for priority action as a result of arranging the effects in order of importance.

The article is built around a central argument:

(a) The economic consequences of completing the large internal market will be engendered by *an improvement in supply-side conditions*, and this improvement will occur whatever the four large components[3]

Michel Catinat is Economic Adviser in the Directorate-General for Economic and Financial Affairs of the Commission of the European Communities. The views expressed are those of the author and do not involve the responsibility of the Commission.

[1] Of the 300 Directives listed in the White Paper, the Commission had, by the summer of 1987, presented around 170 and the Council of Ministers had adopted more than 70.

[2] This report is due to be completed right at the beginning of 1988.

[3] This article does not deal with two important aspects of the internal market:

(a) The approximation of indirect taxation as it relates to goods passing through customs (VAT and excise duties). For the Commission this represents a prerequisite for the abolition of frontiers within the Community. In July 1987 the Commission adopted a proposal [24] midway between two incompatible requirements: to provoke the smallest budgetary effect for each of the member states which would lead to a small degree of which we shall analyse in the following order Part I: the opening of public procurement, the abolition of frontiers within the Community, the liberalization of financial services, and what we shall agree to call 'the supply-side effects' (naturally!).

(b) They will bring about *an easing of various constraints:* the constraint of profitable production[4] in the first place but also, in certain conditions, that of the budget deficit and the external deficit. Partly *potential*, they will be realized fully only to the extent that the macroeconomic policies of the member states will be able to provide the political and institutional means of exploiting the room for manoeuvre created (Part II).

1. THE ECONOMIC MECHANISMS OF THE LARGE INTERNAL MARKET

A frontal attack on the problem is doomed to failure, because of its multifaceted nature and its numerous difficulties. First, the statistical difficulties: until very recently the relative importance of public procurement was unknown at Community level.[5] Then the theoretical difficulties: the economist attempting an analysis has to mix a cocktail with ingredients taken from internal trade and customs union theory, company behaviour, inputs from macroeconomics, etc.

The problem has therefore been divided into sections. An economic reading of the White Paper has enabled us to define four areas which are sufficiently independent and typical to permit a partial analysis: the opening-up of public procurement, the abolition of frontiers within the Community, the liberalization of financial services, and the 'supply-side effects'.

A. Opening-up of public procurement

Public procurement relates to all the purchases – intermediate consumption or investment – made by general government, whether central, regional, or local government, and by 'public enterprises' which, because of their status (nationalized enterprises, for example), the nature of their production (public services such as transport, energy) or their strategic position (arms

convergence, and to provoke the smallest distortion of competition of a fiscal nature which, on the contrary, would require full harmonization.

(b) The increase in transnational activities. These are an essential element in company strategies, and concern any contractual or legal link between two firms in different countries which pool one of the four functions (buying, selling, production, and research) while leaving the others entirely autonomous.

[4] At the price level given and imposed by international competition, European firms will be able to achieve sufficient profit to ensure their survival, or even their expansion in the medium term.

[5] A study on the opening up of public procurement contracts commissioned from Atkins-Planning in connection with the Cecchini report on the 'cost of non-Europe' has provided an initial quantitative estimate of the importance of public procurement.

industries), are in a dependent relationship with the public authorities. They represent around 15 per cent of Community GDP (see Table 1). But the opening up of public procurement concerns only part of these purchases, namely those giving rise to invitations to tender or to negotiations; the other purchases made by direct order or payment at a necessarily local level (rents, postal and telecommunications services, etc.) must be excluded. On this definition, public procurement probably represents[6] around 8.5 per cent of Community GDP – some 300,000 million ECU in 1987.[7]

TABLE 1. *Relative importance of public procurement contracts in 1984*

As percentage of GDP[a]	Germany	Belgium	France	Italy	UK	Total (5 countries)
General government expenditure[b]	43.2	48.9	45.1	41.4	39.5	42.8
Public purchases[c] of which:	11.9	17.5	14.1	15.4	22.1	15.5
general government	7.5	6.6	8.6	9.8	12.0	9.1
public enterprises	4.4	10.9	5.5	5.6	10.1	6.4
Public procurement contracts[d]	8.4	9.3	6.0	7.8	11.1	8.3

[a] The different aggregates of expenditure, purchases, and public procurement contracts correspond to a sum of transactions, whereas GDP represents a sum of value-added substantially smaller than all transactions.
[b] All current and capital expenditure.
[c] All intermediate consumption and investment.
[d] Proportion of purchases giving rise to invitations to tender or to negotiation. All purchases by direct order or any service paid for directly (rents, electricity, postal charges, etc.) are excluded.
Source: General Government Accounts and Statistics (1970–84), Eurostat 2–C. Preliminary estimates by Atkins-Planning for the purchases of public enterprises and public procurement contracts (provisional).

(a) Direct effects

For general government and public enterprises, opening-up public procurement means consenting to make full use of the action of intra-Community (or world) competition to make their purchases. They would choose their supplier purely on the basis of economic criteria (the lowest price for the identical quality and service) without interference from other criteria (protectionism, national autonomy, etc.).

This can only mean lower expenditure on an unchanged quantity of purchases. Even if, in the present situation in which public procurement is relatively closed, the unit prices paid by general government and public enterprises may sometimes be lower than the prices under the correspond-

[6] Estimate by Atkins-Planning, outside consultant studying the opening-up of public procurement in connection with the Cecchini report.
[7] Thus distinctly less than the 520,000 million ECU 87 (updating of the 400,000 million ECU 83) mentioned in the Albert-Ball report [1].

ing private market, this is the result either of their power of oligopsony or of differences in the nature of their purchases (e.g. bulk purchasing). The opening-up of public procurement will not change these characteristics;[8] but it would enable every national public department or enterprise to obtain supplies from a foreign contractor offering better terms. Of course in the case of some products which, for example, cost a great deal to transport, national suppliers might still be the most competitive; but taking the average for all products, opportunities for spending less would be created.

So the opening-up of public procurement is synonymous with a fall in prices and at the same time with the intensification of intra-Community trade.

This offers general government an opportunity to improve their budget balance, and public enterprises an opportunity to reduce their production costs, and to strengthen their competitive position, although within the Community everything depends on the relative falls in production costs in one country by comparison with the others.

For the supplier branches (equipment goods intended for telecommunications, transport, and energy in particular), the opening-up of public procurement would make them swing from a relatively sheltered situation to a situation of international competition. Faced with competition on their national territory, these enterprises would in exchange be able to compete with their counterparts on the other Community markets. All the effects of keener competition would therefore appear: first, smaller profit margins as a result of a reduction of monopoly rents, and then changes in respective markets shares in parallel with an intensification of intra-Community trade (and extra-Community trade, in line with the Community's foreign trade policy and the outcome of the Uruguay Round). In the medium term, the industrial production process would be restructured according to the approach of N. Owen's model [14]: the least efficient firms would disappear, since market prices could not cover the cost of their expansion; the most competitive firms would increase their market share, which would strengthen their competitive position even further as a result of them making better use of economies of scale. The maintenance of competition and the freedom of entry to the market would oblige these firms to keep up their research, development, and innovation effort, thus creating a dynamic process of productivity gains. There is every reason to believe that these sectors would undergo substantial restructuring. For these firms there is a considerable amount at stake; and the benefits are considerable for the most efficient.

---

[8] In theory cases could be imagined in which the opening-up of public procurement would reduce general government's power of oligopsony in so far as suppliers of a national department will be able to find other customers with other general government departments in the Community. In this case the prices paid for certain products by general government could go up. But this scenario is entirely hypothetical; in practice it is highly improbable that prices will rise as a result of the opening-up of public procurement.

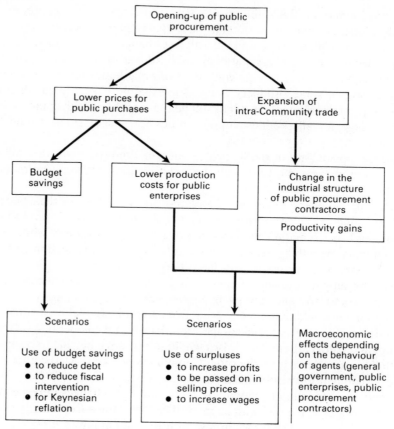

FIGURE 1. *Macroeconomic effects of opening-up public procurement*

(b) Macroeconomic effects

In accordance with international trade theory, the opening-up of public procurement would lead to a reallocation of resources to countries where the public procurement contractors are the most efficient. As a result, at the same time as prices fell the collective welfare would increase with the initial beneficiaries being general government and the public enterprises. The spread of these initial effects to the macro-economic sphere will depend on how general government and the public enterprises behave.

In simple terms, the yet-to-be-determined improvement in the budget balance can give rise to three types of polarized reactions:

1. General government will endeavour to reduce its indebtedness further. There would be no direct effect on the real economy. However, the reduced recourse to the financial markets would limit the crowding-out effects and would put a downward pressure on long-term interest rates,

triggering an increase in demand by productive investment or housing investment.

2. Taxation will be reduced. In this case general government would transfer the benefits of opening-up public procurement directly to firms and to households. This scenario illustrates the State's wish for disengagement, with no adverse Keynesian effect (no initial contraction in the volume of expenditure of general government).

3. The volume of expenditure increases (e.g. through participation in major European projects). This case would then be typical of a Keynesian reflation with no deterioration in the budget balance.

The reduction in the price paid by public enterprises for their intermediate consumption could also produce three types of behaviour:

1. The public enterprises would consolidate their profit, and could then use it either to reduce their debt or to increase their self-financing capacity. The result could be a favourable effect on the investment of public enterprises if they are suffering from solvency problems (see Lévy-Garboua and Maarek [10] or from insufficient self-financing capacity or, more generally, from constraints of profitable production (classical unemployment situation). In these cases the maintenance of surpluses in such enterprises would have the favourable economic effects of increasing production, employment, and in the long run boosting investment.

2. Enterprises would feed the lower prices through to their production prices. This would give rise to a two-fold knock-on effect: the (relative) fall in prices would be spread to all the user agents which, in the case of products such as energy or transport, represents a substantial proportion of the economic agents. The diffusion effect could thus be considerable and could initiate an increase in demand. In this case the surpluses created by the opening-up of public procurement would be shared out between the productive sector and final consumers.

3. Redistribution in the form of wages. Although, in real terms, the transfer of income is identical to the preceding case, the dynamic which it releases is different: there is no disinflationary effect and the initial transfer goes in full to households. Such a redistribution could realize its full effectiveness only in the case of a generalized Keynesian unemployment situation.

The opening-up of public procurement would be one more step towards the economic integration of the member states: the penetration rate of public procurement should gradually converge with the rates observed for private market. If we refer to the assessments presented in the annex, there is room for a broad intensification of intra-Community trade. What should be expect for the trade balance of the Community as a whole? It is too early to reply unambiguously so long as external commerical policy has not been defined, and in particular so long as the problem of how to respect the competence of the Community vis-à-vis each of the member states has not been clarified.[9]

Three hypothetical cases can be envisaged to begin with: (i) the opening up of public procurement would be strictly limited to the Community area; (ii) it would be negotiated on the principle of reciprocity, or (iii) there would be no reciprocity from areas outside the Community. Depending on the case, the economic consequences could differ widely, more for the sectors to be opened up (telecommunications, transport, energy, water services) and their suppliers (equipment goods branches) than for the more open sectors (furniture, building).

The first two cases should lead to an improvement in the Community's trade balance: the restructuring of supplier branches and the productivity gains which can be expected should strengthen European competitiveness – in the first case without increasing non-Community imports, and in the second case with an increase of imports from outside the Community and a parallel increase in Community exports. The opening-up of public procurement would then have three favourable effects: an improvement in budget deficits, an increase in GDP (by a positive contribution from the Community's external balance) and a disinflationary effect.

In the third hypothetical case the consequences would be less certain. Everything would depend on whether the supplier branches were able to withstand external competition on domestic markets. If public procurement was not opened up in the rest of the world, a deterioration in the trade balance could ensue: there would even be a risk of a deterioration in the budget balance of the Community as a whole if the decline in the price of public purchases was smaller than the difference between levels of average taxation and social security contributions on Community production and non-Community imports.[10]

It is difficult at the present time to determine from the outset the right hypothetical case – the one which would actually happen. At the very most it can be argued that the completion of the internal market would reinforce the Community's economic and commercial identity. This would take place in an international setting governed by the rules of the game (GATT), which are applied on the basis of the relative strengths of the different economic entities involved. While respecting these international rules, the Community should therefore improve its negotiating powers.

The least probable and the non-desirable – the opening-up of public procurement with no reciprocity – would therefore coincide. Very fortunately; a great deal is at stake.

[9] According to Article 113 of the Treaty of Rome establishing the European Communities, external commercial policy is within the Community's field of competence. However, for various historical reasons, derogations have been tolerated by the Commission (for example, certain countries have import quotas for Japanese cars) and bilateral agreements have been concluded individually between member states and non-Community countries.

[10] The replacement of Community production by non-Community imports deprives general government of tax revenue, and this loss may more than counterbalance the initial budget savings.

B. Abolition of frontiers within the Community

The existence of customs controls gives rise to extra costs which penalize intra-Community trade: additional transport costs (chiefly customs delays) and administrative costs, whether they are borne by firms[11] (dealing with customs formalities, paying for the services of forwarding agents) or by general government (customs officers).

Customs controls therefore result in the price of goods or services which are traded within the Community being higher than the price of goods and services produced and bought within the same member state.

(a) Direct effects

Reduction of the price of intra-Community trade as a result of the abolition of customs controls would lead to two types of substitution (through price effect):

1. imports of Community origin would be substituted for national production;
2. imports from within the Community would be substituted for imports of non-Community origin.

Not only would intra-Community trade be increased, but also imports of Community origin would gain market shares within the total imports of Community member countries. Beneficial effects . . . but in exchange employment would be lost: a contraction in the number of customs officers (or at the best their redeployment), fewer staff employed in exporting firms to deal with the administrative formalities of passing through customs, reduction in the numbers employed by forwarding agents and by all the suppliers of services associated directly or indirectly with customs activities within the Community.

(b) Macroeconomic effects

The twin substitution effects would mean not only an increase in each member state's imports, but also a reduction in imports of non-Community origin, with both developments being accompanied by a fall in average import prices for each of the Community countries. The result would therefore be a positive effect on Community GDP, because Community production would partly displace imports of external origin[12] and the fall in import prices would increase the purchasing power of the Community's economic agents. The contraction in numbers of employed resulting from the abolition of frontiers should partly reduce the favourable effect on GDP, but this adverse effect should be slight.

An increase in Community GDP, an improvement in the trade balance,

[11] Exporters or importers or both together, depending on how the extra costs are fed through to the prices.

[12] The rise in imports of Community origin are neutral for Community production; they correspond to the exports of other Community countries. The only resultant effect on Community GDP is therefore derived from the fall in imports of non-Community origin.

a fall in prices and a probable increase in employment . . . the squaring of the circle for the macroeconomist!

C. The liberalization of financial services[13]

A variety of barriers at the present time impede the market in financial services: restrictions on the right of establishment, regulatory constraints[14] and controls on movements of capital. The liberalization of capital movements, which is a necessary precondition for any effective liberalization of financial services, is in the process of completion within the Community area, although some countries such as France, Italy, or Spain have as yet been unable to push liberalization to its limit.

These various barriers involve extra costs for the suppliers of financial services. If they were abolished, the prices of these services would

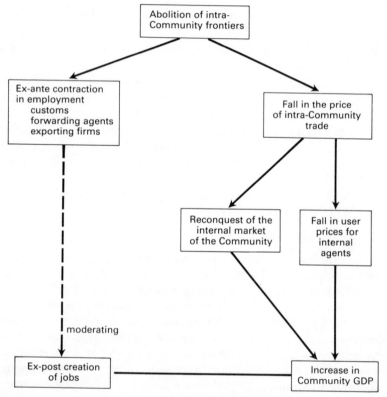

FIGURE 2. *Macroeconomic effects of the abolition of intra-Community frontiers*

[13] Broadly defined: banking, insurance, and stock exchange activities.

[14] A subsidiary or branch of a foreign financial institution must generally respect the national regulations (prudential rules, liquidity ratios, etc.) without being able to consolidate results with the foreign parent company.

therefore come down. But in the case of this sector, prices should be expected to fall more as a result of the removal of monopoly rents which characterize the current European situation, so great is the segmentation of the Community market into as many national markets. Breaking down the barriers between these markets would therefore be decisive in bringing down prices; it would have other advantages as well: a greater number of financial products would be made available in each member state, insurance risks would be better spread over a broader market and, for the same reason, banking services would run a smaller risk of an inadequate supply of credit.

TABLE 2. *Relative importance of financial services[a] in 1985*

As percentage of all branches	B	D	DK	E	F	GR[b]	I	L[c]	NL	UK	Total
Value-added (at 1980 prices)	5.4	4.8	3.3	5.9	3.7	2.6	6.5	11.6	5.0	18.7[d]	7.5[e]
Employment	3.8	3.0	3.7	2.8	2.8	n.a.	1.8	5.7	3.7	3.5	2.9

Source: Eurostat sectoral data bank.
[a] Branch 69A of NACE.
[b] In 1984.
[c] In 1982.
[d] For the United Kingdom, unlike the other countries, the value-added of the financial services branch is much higher (overvalued?) than the value-added of the sector. According to Eurostat sectoral statistics, the value-added of the financial services sector represents only some 6 per cent of GDP.
[e] Estimate (average weighted by the relative size of GDPs at current prices).

In view of the character of financial services which permeate the whole of the production process,[15] their liberalization could have particularly favourable and even decisive macroeconomic consequences for the revival of European growth in the medium term.

In the field of banking services, the pressure of competition and the free movement of capital would stimulate the decline in real interest rates, opening the way to recovery of investment: productive investment which, in the long run, determines the potential for growth, housing investment – an important creator of jobs – etc. The decline in interest rates would also push up share prices and therefore increase the national wealth. All these favourable effects would lastingly stimulate growth and improve the employment situation.[16]

[15] Financial services are situated upstream in the production process. Not only does their price permeate the whole of the productive sphere directly, but also their adaptability in financing projects which vary in complexity, and sometimes carry high risks, is often a condition of the industry's dynamism.
[16] The employment created would stem indirectly from the extra activity generated and permitted by the increase in productive investment. But the decline in interest rates also results in the substitution, all other things being equal, of capital for labour, because the cost

The favourable effects on investment would stem not only from the decline in interest rates which would make a larger number of investment plans profitable while reducing the cost of private indebtedness,[17] but also from the liberalization of capital movements which would lead to a more efficient allocation of financial resources and to them being more closely matched to the most profitable projects.

With regard to the other financial services – insurance in particular – the effects would be felt essentially as a result of the prices for such services coming down in most Community countries. However, given their smaller economic importance in terms of value-added, but also in terms of their effect in permeating the economy, the macroeconomic consequences of liberalizing such services should not be as great as the liberalization of banking services.

D. Supply-side effects

The term 'supply-side effects' covers all the phenomena associated with the completion of the internal market which will improve the efficiency of the Community's production process, i.e. the global productivity of the factors of production.

Essentially, these effects are microeconomic in nature. The transformation of firms 'environment' due to the creation of a large internal market should modify, or even revolutionize, entrepreneurial behaviour. Cumulatively, over several sectors, this is bound to have an effect on the actual macroeconomic situation of the Community.

For the sake of simplicity, but because we wish to concentrate on the phenomena considered to be essential, the supply-side effects will be grouped into three categories:

(a) more efficient allocation of resources and factor mobility;
(b) economies of scale and restructuring the production process;
(c) competition and making firms' behaviour more dynamic.

(a) More efficient allocation of resources and factor mobility

According to the theory of international trade which has been developed on the basis of the law of comparative advantages, the opening-up of frontiers means that each national economy is able to specialize in producing the goods or services for which that economy has either lower unit production costs, or better factor endowment. At the macroeconomic or macrosectoral level this expansion of trade therefore enables a more efficient allocation of resources, and raises global factor productivity on

---

of capital becomes cheaper relative to the cost of labour. This substitution effect would, however, remain relatively weak (see [4] for more details) and could reduce the creation of employment no more than partially.

[17] In proportion to the share of borrowings at variable rates.

average over the various countries: potentially, this reallocation is synonymous with additional wealth, therefore additional GDP.

However, a note of caution must be sounded about the effects of this nature which can be expected from completing the internal market:

1. If we exclude the southern Community countries (Spain, Greece, Portugal), the comparative advantages of the Community's most industrialized countries is fairly small; many studies have moreover shown that the expansion of trade between these countries followed a different logic – that of intra-industry trade.[18] So at the very most we can expect that, on the basis of comparative advantages, intra-Community trade will expand between the countries of the south and the other member states [8].

2. The movement of workers and capital written into the White Paper will partly take the place of the trade in goods and services which results from comparative advantages; the very foundations of inter-industry trade – the existence of comparative advantages and the non-mobility of factors of production – should gradually disappear and the respective advantages of the Community economies should level out.

3. The increase in welfare provided by the expansion of trade assumes an economic situation of competitive equilibrium (in the sense of the classical paradigms). Yet the completion of the internal market would eliminate only part of the non-tariff barriers, and the remaining ones would go on being augmented by other constraints of a macroeconomic nature (budget deficit, imbalance on the labour market, etc.). In other words, each member state's economic situation would shift from one situation of imbalance (or a sub-optimal situation) to another situation of imbalance. In this case, no general theoretical conclusion can be drawn.

On the whole, and leaving aside the southern Community countries, the effects which can be expected from the better exploitation of comparative advantages could be small and, in any event, distinctly smaller than the consequences of factor mobility. If this is the case, the cause of the more efficient allocation of resources would be the mobility of workers and capital towards more productive utilization, rather than the shift of production from one country to another in response to the principle of comparative advantages.

(b) Economies of scale and restructuring the production process

Quite generally, the enlargement of markets from the national level to the Community level would also enable firms to exploit the opportunities for economies of scale more successfully. If we consider the restructuring which followed the creation of the common market we see that company

---

[18] On this point a recent study, taken to extreme sectoral detail [21] has shown that, for France, almost 50 per cent of trade took place within industries (intra-industry trade).

strategies develop in thrse states [14]: investment[19] which permits an increase in size, a price 'war' by reducing production costs, and the elimination of the least productive firms which can no longer cover development costs at market prices.

This strategy may stretch over a relatively long period, in particular where the level of prices imposed by the most competitive firm remains higher than the operating costs, but lower than the replacement cost of the least productive firms.[20] As a result the Community's production process would be restructured and trade inside (and outside) the Community would be intensified. Without being deterministic, the analysis of this phenomenon of the exploitation of scale [14] over the fifteen years which followed the creation of the common market shows, however, that it is generally the firms which are the most productive at the time when barriers to trade are removed which consolidate their initial advantages.

At sectoral level the potential for the exploitation of economies of scale would chiefly concern the industries which at present have their trade impeded the most by non-tariff barriers: the contracting industries for public procurement, and the service branches including financial services.

Aggregating all industries (see Figure 3) the restructuring of the production process resulting from the better exploitation of economies of scale would have three essential consequences:

1. An increase in overall factor productivity. First, the creation of a large internal market would do away with the need to differentiate[21] products by the Community countries of destination.[22] Production runs would lengthen, automatically improving the productivity of existing capital and of the labour associated with it. If production lines are automated, the extra costs involved in product differentiation are, however, low and the anticipated productivity gains could then be tiny. But this case is not typical of the average situation. Second, this time from a dynamic viewpoint, all investments in size and in the greater exploitation of economies of scale would help to increase factor productivity beyond normal technological progress. Lastly, the closing of the least productive firms would reinforce this process further.

---

[19] Either physical if the economies of scale are essentially due to the length of production runs, or physical or financial if the economies of scale are due to the size of firms. In the latter case, economies of scale may be situated upstream of the production process (e.g. research and development) or downstream (marketing network).

[20] The least productive enterprises are then driven out only when their plant and machinery is scrapped.

[21] The fact that each firm will not have to engage in so much product differentiation does not mean that the variety of products available in each national economy will be reduced. On the contrary, an increase in variety should be expected [6].

[22] On the basis of mutual recognition, any product approved in its member state could be freely sold in any other Community country. Mutual recognition is more flexible to introduce than the harmonization of technical standards, but is not a perfect substitute for it. In some cases where problems of product conformity, health and safety rules, prudential rules, or consumer protection are involved, Community standardization remains essential.

2. In parallel with the progressive exploitation of economies of scale, intra- (and extra-)Community trade would expand as the most productive enterprises or those becoming more productive gained market shares. Expansion would be both quantitative and qualitative since, in accordance with the theory of intra-industry trade [6], the variety of goods and services available in each member state would increase, and with it collective welfare.

3. Lastly, the ex-ante contraction of employment. The productivity gains described above would relate to all the factors of production, including labour. In addition, some of the people employed in circumventing the present barriers – whether they be technical, regulatory, or administrative – would have no (or less) 'raison d'être' and would either be made redundant or have to be re-trained for other jobs.

The macroeconomic consequences will be those which can generally be expected from any gain in overall factor productivity: a reduction in unit production costs and an initial loss of jobs. In the short and the medium term the result would be a reduction in inflationary pressures as a result of lower production costs and an increase in GDP as a result of the creation of extra productivity. The consequences on employment would be the result of two opposing forces: an initial contraction in numbers employed but recruitment induced by the extra activity. In the short term the initial loss of employment effect is likely to predominate; in the medium to the long term an increase in employment would be the most likely, although this depends a great deal on the way in which productivity gains are used. For firms or industries which are insufficiently profitable the most favourable effects would come from internal absorption of productivity gains. But firms which are constrained by their outlets would derive most benefit from passing the proceeds of their productivity gains on in their selling prices (and, less effectively, in wages). In either case the right allocation of the extra productivity would increase capacity widening investment, which is essential for any lasting upturn in growth and employment.

(c) Competition and making firms' behaviour more dynamic

There is no doubt that the completion of the internal market would improve supply-side conditions by encouraging productivity gains. But there are two keystones to the edifice! The improvement in supply-side conditions should also be based on an increase in competition.

The many non-tariff barriers which today segment the Community market – technical, regulatory, or tax barriers; closed public procurement procedures; customs controls; etc. – are so many barriers impeding the free play of competition and preventing firms from freely entering each of the national markets. If they were abolished, competition would therefore be bound to increase.

According to the argument recently developed by Geroski and Jacquemin

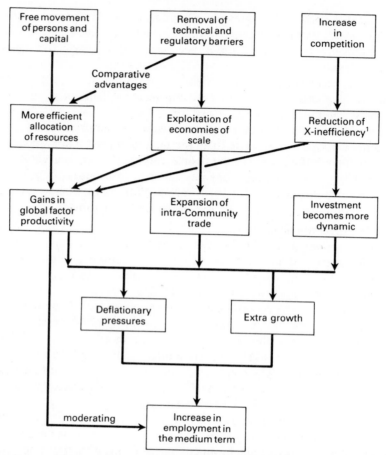

FIGURE 3. *Macroeconomic effects of 'supply-side effects'*

    [a] The term 'X-inefficiency' coined by H. Leibenstein [12] refers the firm's internal inefficiency. A. Jacquemin [7] gives the following brief definition: 'The basic idea is that the existence of monopolistic structures helps to maintain an inefficient staff, obsolete equipment, a top-heavy organization, excessive expenditure, in short the poor exploitation of production opportunities, so that the firm does not fulfil its capacity for production.'

[5], additional competition brings many beneficial effects. First, it obliges firms so eliminate pockets of unproductiveness, to combat what the Anglo-Saxon literature terms 'X-inefficiency', to slim down. A sometimes unsuspected improvement in productive efficiency can be obtained from a simple internal reorganization in order to withstand competition.

    Secondly, the pressure of competition obliges firms to adopt dynamic behaviour in order to survive: the need for product innovation or to reorganize the processes of production, the need to restructure in order to fill supporting and profitable niches and, in return, the obligation to withdraw from declining industries and the need for an aggressive commercial policy.

Lastly, competition prevents or reduces the oligopolistic positions which are liable to be created by the drive for economies of scale, and the concentrations or cartellizations which they imply. From a situation of monopolistic national champions, the large internal market would move towards a situation of perfect or monopolistic competition on a larger market which could be shared by several firms of optimum size.

As in the case of the other supply-side effects, the consequences of additional competition are rooted in the actual behaviour of the individual firms. But unlike the other supply-side effects which have a static aspect (the removal of a barrier reduces production costs once and for all), the pressure of competition continuously maintains the dynamism of enterprises. Macroeconomically, it should therefore, permanently, not only limit the drift of prices but also reinforce the investment effort and increase the potential for growth in the medium term.

II. COMPLETION OF THE INTERNAL MARKET: THE ISSUES AT STAKE

Can it all be that simple? Is the completion of the internal market to be the magic potion which can cure the Community of the Twelve of all its ills?

The examination of the mechanisms and the consequences of the large internal market has shown all its virtues, all the potential which it contains. But if this potential is to be translated into reality a group of conditions, a convergence of behaviour and of economic policies, would have to exist. We shall deal with them, in turn, starting with the most microeconomic and going on to the most macroeconomic.

A. Transformation of the firm's culture

The firm stands at the heart of the process: the large internal market will be created with the firm or it will not be created at all. The elimination of non-tariff barriers, the strengthening of competition, and the free entry to markets will oblige firms to change, to re-think their organization, to re-define their strategy. They will have to keep pace with events or disappear, accept the risk in order to seize new opportunities for expansion or go under.

The collective advantages are great, and so are the individual risks. Yet, firms will accept the new rules of the game and the associated risks if the large internal market is credible and its rules are clear or, at least, felt to be clear. Any excessive delay in the timetable, any obscure compromise or, even more so, any lack of consensus and political will, could block the process. If the internal market is seen as an additional factor of uncertainty on top of all the others (demand prospects, instability of the international monetary system, commodity prices, etc.), there is everything to be feared, in particular the reappearance of other indirect forms of non-tariff barriers.

B. Redistributive aspects and adjustment costs

The regional, sectoral, and social redistribution of the benefits of the internal market is a problem in itself.[23] We shall confine ourselves here to recalling what is at stake.

The completion of the internal market will undermine protected positions in the productive sphere; it therefore contains a risk of social conflicts in the least productive industries and political problems in the least-favoured regions. All these are factors which are liable to frustrate the integration process. As the Padoa–Schioppa report rightly stresses, growth at the time when the large internal market starts to become established is crucial for it to succeed. The higher that growth is to start with, the more cushioned and the more socially and politically acceptable the many adjustment costs will be (restructuring the production process, shifting the centres of employment, the mobility and retraining the labour force).

C. Competition and commercial policy

The strengthening of competition offers a variety of advantages. But if it goes too far it can also become harmful. A price war may create severe downward pressure on firms' profits. The constraint of profitable production, instead of easing as desired, could on the contrary become tighter. A growing proportion of the Community's domestic demand, stimulated by falls in prices, would then be satisfied by imports from outside the Community. Under pressure on their self-financing margin, firms would be liable to underinvest,[24] and the penetration of the internal market by imports of non-Community origin would only be increased in the medium term.

Here we come back to the problem already mentioned of external commercial policy. The unilateral abolition of non-tariff barriers, with no counterpart from non-Community countries, may be dangerous. Although the completion of the large internal market will provide Community firms with the potential to be more efficient and more competitive, they must still be able and willing to translate the opportunities offered into reality. It will take time for them to consolidate their position vis-à-vis other countries, and to turn the benefits which can be expected from the large internal market into a reality. Competition should first be internal before being external, otherwise there is a danger that the disindustrialization of Europe will be irremediably accelerated. This would be the opposite of the objective sought.

D. The transmission of supply-side effects to demand

An examination of economic facts since the first oil shock has convinced many economists that the lasting recovery of growth could not be attained

---

[23] See [20] for the regional redistributive aspects.

[24] In most of the European countries, profit is the prime determinant of investment in the medium term. See [4] for more details.

without a 'supply-side policy'. Observation of the facts also teaches us that this is a necessary but not a sufficient condition. The completion of the internal market, a European-style supply-side policy, will not exert its full effect unless demand prospects for firms improve. Here, the increase in competition could be crucial: it would guarantee that much of the reduction in costs is passed on to prices, thus ensuring that demand is supported at the pace at which supply-side conditions improve.

E. Interdependence and coordination of economic policies

The completion of the internal market would intensify intra-Community trade, whether through the opening-up of public procurement, the liberalization of financial services, the abolition of customs controls, or the elimination of non-tariff barriers.

When examined in the light of the theories of comparative advantages or of intra-industry trade, the economic consequences of this expansion of trade are quite clear: they would turn out to be positive, because the expansion of trade would on average increase the collective welfare of the economies involved in the opening-up process.

However, this conclusion must be qualified in two ways:

1. The expansion of intra-European trade could lead, for the member states, to trade imbalances and consequently to current account imbalances.[25] It is unlikely that the net effects on the trade balance of each of the member states will be nil, and even less likely that these effects will improve the balance between countries (improvement for the countries originally in deficit, deterioration of the countries originally in surplus). With all the necessary caveats on this subject, one might rather be inclined to think that, if trade were liberalized, the surplus Community countries would on average find it easier to strengthen their dominant positions while the opposite would apply to the countries with an external deficit. This statement is admittedly neither general, nor can it be generalized; exceptions could be quoted, be it only the case of the French automobile industry.[26] Nevertheless, a dominant position is easier to defend than to win.

External imbalances could therefore appear, and would be liable to reinforce the imbalances existing between Community countries. In the short or the medium term these imbalances will have to be reduced by appropriate economic policy measures. Yet various studies have shown that, without cooperation, the adjustment towards equilibrium situations tended to occur 'from below', i.e. it is chiefly the deficit countries which

[25] Exchange rate changes could, it is true, reduce these imbalances, but if the large internal market led to an increase in currency adjustments, this would run counter to the objective of parity stability within the Community.

[26] In France in 1960 the unit costs for the automobile industry was around 40 per cent higher than in Germany, and around 5 per cent higher than in the United Kingdom ([14] Table 4.10, p. 63). Despite this the French automobile industry for 15 years enjoyed unprecedented success, so that France ranked as one of the largest producers in the world.

took recessive measures, and not the surplus countries which took expansionary measures. If this deflationary bias were to appear with the completion of the internal market it could appreciably reduce the potentially expansionary initial effects. If the increase in imports from outside the Community were larger, this danger would be all the greater; this brings us back to the Community's commercial policy in relation to external areas.

The expansion of intra-Community trade will increase the interdependence of the Community countries. There are at least two dangers in a high level of interdependence:

1. It encourages the policy-makers to prefer disinflationary policies to expansionary policies [13]. This is a 'beggar-thy-neighbour' policy: all disinflationary policies are partly borne by the trading partners who suffer a loss of competitiveness and a contraction of their export markets, whereas all expansionary policies are partly of benefit to the trading partner countries and also causes a trade imbalance.
2. This means that any incompatibility between partner countries in their choice of economic policy – in particular in their choice between inflation and employment – is resolved by an adjustment which, if there is no cooperation, becomes deflationary for the reasons mentioned above [9].

So, even if the completion of the internal market is potentially a vehicle for an improvement in the Community's economic situation, the improvement would become a reality only if the economic policies of the member states were to magnify the initial effects, and not reduce them, or even neutralize them. Here it seems essential to reinforce and develop the coordination of economic policies; this should form an integral part of the political process of creating the large internal market [20].

The foundations for this coordination already exist at the present time [11]: a consensus on the policy of monetary stability, the European Monetary System, the initial successes of the social dialogue at European level. . . . Is it inevitable that these foundations must be strengthened, as Mr Delors, President of the Commission, has stressed [23]: 'We must now place the European Monetary System at the centre of an economic system which offers higher performance in terms of growth, competitiveness and employment. The spectacular progress in liberalizing capital movements within the Community leaves us with one choice: to widen the area of economic and monetary cooperation'?

CONCLUSION

The completion of the large internal market is a European-style supply-side policy; it has its strength and its weaknesses.

Its various components – the opening-up of public procurement, the abolition of intra-Community frontiers, the liberalization of financial services, the 'supply-side effects' – have one thing in common: they would mean a contraction in unit costs and, at the same time, an expansion of intra-Community trade. These are the two major assets.

The limiting of the administrative formalities at customs posts or the ending of delays at frontiers, the removal of extra costs caused by the many technical or regulatory barriers, the productivity gains generated by the better exploitation of economies of scale – all these elements chiefly affect the non-wage part of production costs: while improving supply-side conditions, they would not ex-ante depress the level of demand. This avoids a first pitfall.

The reduction of unit costs is the vehicle for reducing inflationary pressures. But if it is introduced by a better exploitation of economies of scale it would carry a risk of cartellization, and therefore of exacerbating the monopoly situation. An increase in competition would therefore be essential for the lower costs to be converted into lower prices. The completion of the internal market contains the ingredients for this: the abolition of the many non-tariff barriers would limit the costs of entering the markets of the member states, and would therefore encourage free competition. But the rules of the game will have to be clearly laid down and applied by the member states without ambiguity or exception. Competition would then be synonymous with dynamism for firms, and not with uncertainty. But competition should mean neither lack of control – the risks of cartellization in order to exploit economies of scale should be strictly controlled – nor out-and-out deregulation; the dangers of which are demonstrated by the experience of one of the most advanced liberal countries (the United States in the case of air transport, for example). A second pitfall to be avoided.

The expansion of intra-Community trade has the potential to increase the collective welfare.[27] But its translation into reality depends on two conditions: Community commercial policy and the coordination of economic policies.

The large internal market has to be of benefit first to European firms; this would be permitted by the Community's commercial policy, if it ensured that the abolition of non-tariff barriers remained limited to the Community area or that other areas benefited on the basis of agreements of reciprocity. In either case the internal market would help to remove protectionism while ensuring the consolidation of the European production process. It could be dangerous to abolish barriers between the Community and third countries with no agreement of reciprocity; this could result in excessive import penetration which could destabilize a good many industries, and hold back their restructuring or modernization. In the medium term, a swing of the protectionist pendulum could be the unwelcome consequence.

---

[27] This theoretical result which is valid in the case of a partial equilibrium analysis nevertheless becomes ambiguous in a general equilibrium framework [2].

354   *Michel Catinat*

But the expansion of intra-Community trade would also increase the interdependence of the member states and the dangers of exacerbating their external imbalances. It would become essential to reinforce the coordination of their economic policies. Otherwise there would be an accentuation of the deflationary links which are created between countries which are closely interdependent because of their external trade, but whose economic policies are uncoordinated.

Will the European Economic Community be able to equip itself with the tools for this coordination, as it was able to do in response to the dangers of monetary instability by creating the European Monetary System?

The challenge is great: the potentially favourable effects on Community GDP of the large internal market could be cut down substantially or even totally neutralized.

These are two new pitfalls with a large political content because they imply a transfer of responsibility from the member states to the European Economic Community.

It should be possible to meet all these challenges. And all the more so if we judge the consequences of the large internal market according to the essential criterion of employment: the effects on employment are bound to be weaker than on GDP, since the creation of the internal market would be accompanied by an increase in factor productivity. There could even be fears of job losses in the short term. The starting conditions of growth and employment creation to which the consequences of the large internal market itself would be superimposed, therefore become crucially important from this point of view, as suggested by the Padoa–Schioppa report [20]. On this hinges the social and politicial acceptability of the internal market, even if, in the medium term, it is the vehicle for an improvement in the Community's economic situation on the world stage.

The Commission has considered it its duty to set out the conditions for ensuring that the gamble represented by the large internal market has a successful outcome ('The Single Act: a new frontier' [22]. The Single Act was ratified by the various member states as a political act in the full awareness of the situation. But let there be no mistake, the large European internal market is a medium-term therapy; it will take time for its benefits to become apparent, and patience and political determination will be required if we are not to change course.

REFERENCES

[1] ALBERT, M. and BALL, R. J. (1983) 'Vers le redressement de l'économie européenne dans les années 80', *Rapport présenté au Parlement européen.*
[2] BORGES, A. M. (1986) 'Applied general equilibrium models: an assessment of their usefulness for policy analysis', *OECD Economic Studies*, No. 7, Autumn.

[3] BUIGUES, P. and GOYBET, Ph. (1985) 'La compétitivité de l'industrie européenne: un bilan', *Economie Européenne*, No. 25, September.

[4] CATINAT, M., CAWLEY, R., ILZKOVITZ, F., ITALIANER, A. and MORS, M. (1987) 'The determinants of investment', *European Economy*, No. 31, March: pp. 5–60.

[5] GEROSKI, P. A. and JACQUEMIN, A. (1985) 'Corporate competitiveness in Europe', *Economic Policy*, No. 1, November: pp. 170–217.

[6] KRUGMAN, P. R. (1979) 'Increasing returns, monopolistic competition and international trade', *Journal of International Economics*, Vol. 9, No. 4, November: pp. 469–79.

[7] JACQUEMIN, A. (1979) *Economie industrielle européenne*. Dunod, second edition.

[8] KRUGMAN, P. R. (1987), 'L'intégration économique en Europe – Problèmes conceptuels', *Annexe A du Rapport Padoa-Schioppa*, 'Efficacité, stabilité et équité'.

[9] LASKAR, D. (1985) 'La contrainte extérieure dans un cadre multinational', Note ronéotée CEPREMAP, December.

[10] LÉVY-GARBOUA, V. and MAAREK, G. (1985) *La dette, le boom, la crise*. Paris: Atlas-Economica.

[11] MATTHES, H. (1987), 'La coordination des politiques économiques dans les communautés européennes', *Revue du Marché Commun*, No. 307, May–June.

[12] LEIBENSTEIN, H. (1966) 'Allocative efficiency vs. X-efficiency', *American Economic Review*, 56: pp. 392–415.

[13] OUDIZ, G. (1986) 'Europessimism?', *Bulletin du CEPR*, No. 18, December: pp. 7–9.

[14] OWEN, N. (1983) *Economies of Scale, Competitiveness and Trade Patterns within the European Community*. Oxford: Clarendon Press.

[15] PELKMANS, J. (1984) *Market Integration in the European Community*. Martinus Nijhoff.

[16] SCHERER, F. M. (1980) *Industrial Market Structure and Economic Performance*, second edition. New York: Houghton Mifflin.

[17] VENABLES, A. J. and SMITH, A. (1986) 'Trade and industrial policy under imperfect competition', *Economic Policy*, No. 3, October: pp. 621–72.

[18] VIGNON, J. (1986) 'Sept ans pour construire le vrai marché commun', *Economie Prospective Internationale*, No. 25, 1st quarter.

[19] Livre Blanc de la Commission (1985) *L'achèvement du marché intérieur*. Document CEE, June.

[20] Rapport Padoa-Schioppa (1987) *Efficacité, stabilité et équité*, Rapport à la Commission des Communautés Européennes, April.

[21] 'Commerce intra-branches: Performances des firmes et analyse des échanges commerciaux dans la Communauté européenne', *Rapport d'étape, CEPII*.

[22] 'Réussir l'Acte Unique – Une nouvelle frontière pour l'Europe', *Bulletin des Communautés Européennes*, Supplément 1/87, Commission des Communautés européennes.

[23] Discours du Président Delors au Parlement Européen, compte rendu – séance du 18.02.1987, p. 121; reproduced in Supplement No. 1 (87), of the Commission.

[24] 'Achèvement du marché intérieur – rapprochement des taux et harmonisation des structures des impôts indirects', Communication globale de la Commission COM (87) 320 final du 4/8/87.

ANNEX: *Share (percentages) of intermediate consumption of foreign origin[a] for general government (Gov) and economy as a whole (T)*

	Countries										
	Belgium		Germany		France		Italy		Netherlands		United Kingdom	
Sectors	Gov	T	Gov	T	Gov	T	Gov	T	Gov	T	Gov	T
Agriculture	19.2	36.8	37.1	27.0	4.8	10.6	7.1	23.9	3.5	31.9	4.0	20.3
Energy	24.4	49.5	15.0	36.8	13.6	46.4	8.5	46.9	20.1	63.8	.0	25.8
Intermediate goods	49.1	59.4	14.6	23.6	0.2	33.4	16.0	28.0	13.7	60.0	13.9	29.3
Equipment goods	71.3	69.2	26.6	17.4	11.0	24.1	22.3	20.7	54.9	56.7	12.8	23.1
Consumption goods	25.6	43.7	15.7	19.8	11.5	18.6	9.6	16.9	13.7	38.1	1.7	22.3
Construction	0.3	0.1	14.7	17.0	.0	.0	.4	0.2	.0	.0	.0	4.6
Transport – telecommunications	6.9	11.4	5.0	9.4	7.3	15.4	3.1	6.9	43.4	45.4	0.2	13.7
Market services	8.0	15.4	10.5	5.4	1.9	4.8	2.0	8.7	6.3	3.0	6.3	3.8
Total	23.6	42.7	15.0	18.6	7.2	20.6	7.1	21.5	20.3	39.0	9.1	18.4

Source: Eurostat, National Accounts ESA, Input–Output tables 1980 (or 1975 for Belgium).

[a] Share of intermediate consumption of foreign origin (value including VAT): ratio of imported intermediate consumption to intermediate consumption of all origin (imported and domestic).

A

Economic Integration in Europe: Some Conceptual Issues
by Paul Krugman

This paper presents a brief, non-technical survey of current thinking about the economics of international economic integration, with an emphasis on concepts relevant to European problems. The paper is intended to be useful in thinking both about those moves toward closer integration of the long-standing members of the EC envisaged under the heading of 'completion of the internal market' and to the issues presented by EC enlargement. Thus, the paper reviews not only the implications of international trade but the effect of integration of capital and labour markets as well.

Some of the effects of international economic integration are familiar, part of the common currency of economic discussion. International trade increases world efficiency by allowing countries to specialize in activities in which they are relatively productive, or that use intensively their relatively abundant resources. International factor mobility, whether of capital or labour, similarly raises world efficiency by transferring resources to countries where their marginal product is higher. On the other hand, both trade and factor mobility may have strong effects on income distribution, so that the owners of initially scarce factors—which become less scarce as a result of increased integration—may be left worse off despite gains for the nation as a whole. And the process of adjustment to increased integration may be difficult, involving temporary unemployment of labour or capital.

These effects of integration are well known. The need for a new survey of the economics of integration arises from the growing recognition that there are other effects as well. Much recent work in international economics has been driven by the perception of more complex consequences of economic integration than conventional accounts describe. These additional consequences arise from two sources. First, the *microeconomics* of international markets are now seen as more complex than the conventional view had recognized. Second, international integration has *macroeconomic* consequences that have only recently been fully appreciated.

This paper is in three parts. The first part reviews the microeconomics of international economic integration, with emphasis on the relatively new issues that arise from the interaction between integration and industrial organization. The second part reviews the macroeconomic consequences of integration, with special emphasis on the co-ordination issues that have been the focus of recent work. Finally, the third part of the paper briefly discusses the policy implications: how might the prospects for successful integration be improved using instruments available to the European Community?

1. Microeconomics of integration

There are some common themes in the microeconomics of international integration, whether this integration takes place through trade in goods, capital movement, or labour mobility. First, integration offers countries an opportunity to benefit from their differences, reallocating resources both domestically and internationally to more productive uses. Second, integration offers further opportunities for gains from increased competition and rationalization to realize economies of scale and scope. Third, integration also poses problems of adjustment and income distribution.

Although these themes are common to all forms of integration, however, the institutional and regulatory framework differs considerably among trade in goods, capital, and labour. Thus we consider each form of integration separately.

1.1 Integration of goods markets

1.1.1 Comparative advantage and the conventional analysis

The most basic analysis of the effects of international trade in goods and services has not changed in its essentials since Ricardo expressed the principle of comparative advantage in the early nineteenth century. Countries trade because they are different; each country specializes in activities in which it is relatively efficient, or which use intensively its relatively abundant resources. This specialization raises the efficiency of the world economy as a whole and produces mutual benefits to the trading nations.

Although new developments in the analysis of international trade, described below, have modified this view, the insights from conventional trade theory remain important. In particular, the basic comparative advantage approach to trade is useful to keep in check two fallacies that remain common in popular discussion, and that could easily cloud understanding of the implications of EC enlargement.

The first misconception is that integration is only beneficial to a country if that country is able to achieve productivity comparable to that of its trading partners. That is, the popular concern is that a country will be hurt by enlarged trade if it is too inefficient to be 'competitive'. What the concept of comparative advantage makes clear is that absolute productivity advantage in some areas is not necessary for a country to gain from integration. Even a country that is less productive than its trading partners across the board can gain by specializing in those sectors in which its productivity disadvantage is smallest. 'Competitiveness' is not a long run, microeconomic issue. To the extent that international competitiveness is a legitimate concern, it is a short-run macroeconomic issue of the kind addressed in the second part of this paper.

The second misconception that conventional analysis helps to dispel is the other side of the same coin. This is the fear that international competition will be harmful if it is based on lower wages rather than higher productivity. Again, the concept of comparative advantage makes it clear that gains from integration do not depend on parity in wage rates. A highly productive country may be more efficient than its trading partners in almost everything, yet it can still gain by specializing in its areas of greatest relative productivity while importing goods in which its productivity advantage is smaller from less productive, and hence lower-wage, nations.

The basic comparative advantage analysis, then, remains important and useful. It has become increasingly clear from recent research, however, that comparative advantage by itself is not an adequate explanation of international trade. This is perhaps especially true of trade within Europe. Thus it is necessary to turn to more recent and less familiar concepts.

1.1.2 Increasing returns and imperfect competition[1]

The need to extend the comparative advantage approach to international trade arises from two related observations:

1. *Much trade occurs because of economies of scale rather than comparative advantage.* When there are advantages to large-scale production, costs will be reduced by concentrating production of each good in a single location. Concentration of production would, however, require international specialization and trade even if countries were identical in productivity and resources. In practice, it seems likely that much of the trade in manufactured goods between the advanced nations of Europe (like much of the inter-regional trade within North America) represents specialization to realize economies of scale rather than a response to national differences in technology or resources. This conclusion is based on two observations. First, there is the evident similarity in the countries' economic bases (is Germany or France more capital-abundant?). Second, there is the high incidence of 'intra-industry' trade, i.e. two-way trade in goods produced using similar technologies and similar mixes of factor inputs.

The importance of increasing returns in international markets has an important implication for the structure of these markets, which leads to the second key departure from the conventional comparative advantage approach:

2. *Many international markets are oligopolistic rather than perfectly competitive.* An inevitable consequence of economies of scale is that markets for manufactured goods are rarely composed of a large number of firms. Each of these firms is aware that its actions have an effect on world prices; in many markets, each

---

[1] The theory of international trade in the presence of increasing returns and imperfect competition has experienced explosive growth since the late 1970s. Much of this work is surveyed and synthesized in E. Helpman and P. Krugman, *Market Structure and Foreign Trade: Increasing Returns, Imperfect Competition, and the International Economy*, MIT Press, 1985.

firm produces goods that are sufficiently differentiated from those of its rivals that it is in fact able to set its own prices. The price-setting ability of firms is, however, constrained by competition; the intensity of this competition depends, among other things, on the extent to which national markets are integrated.

The recognition of the related importance of increasing returns and imperfect competition in international markets requires some modification of the analysis of the effects of increased economic integration. Probably the most important consequence for our thinking is that additional gains from integration become apparent. Against these newly appreciated sources of gains, however, must be set the perception of some risks of adverse consequences of trade liberalization.

The direct source of gains from integration that becomes apparent in the light of new models of international trade is that of increased efficiency when trade allows 'rationalization' to realize economies of scale. The point is perhaps best made by example. When the US and Canada liberalized trade in automotive goods in the mid-1960s, the Canadian industry was able to specialize in producing a narrower range of products while maintaining employment through exports. This allowed Canadian auto production to take place for the first time at a scale and efficiency comparable to that of the US. At least at first, the trade in automotive products was roughly balanced; that is, there was little of the inter-industry reallocation of resources associated with conventional gains from trade. Thus the gains from the auto pact represented extra benefits over and above those captured by conventional analyses.

In addition to the direct gains in efficiency associated with rationalization of production, integration can also have a benign effect on oligopolistic markets by increasing competition. Economies of scale that bulk large relative to any national market, and would therefore lead inevitably to highly concentrated industries at the national level, may be much smaller relative to the EC market as a whole. Thus economic integration may in effect serve as an anti-trust policy, curbing what would otherwise be problematic levels of monopoly power.

A recognition of the role of increasing returns and imperfect competition, then, offers extra reasons to expect benefits from moves toward greater integration of goods markets. Indeed, an emphasis on these additional gains is an important feature of current policy discussion in North America. Canadian economists have stressed scale economies and imperfect competition as reasons to move to free trade with the United States. An influential effort to quantify the benefits of North American free trade, by Richard Harris of Queen's University, suggests that the competition/scale gains for Canada would be more than twice as large as the gains from conventional comparative advantage.[2]

---

[2] R. Harris and D. Cox, *Trade, Industrial Policy, and Canadian Manufacturing*, University of Toronto Press, 1984.

Unfortunately, while scale economies and oligopoly increase the *potential* gains from trade, they also open up some possible ways in which trade can have adverse effects. The negative aspects have received considerable attention recently, and thus require discussion.

1.1.3 Potential adverse effects of trade[3]

With growing discussion of the role of imperfect competition in trade, certain possibilities of adverse results have been noted. Most of the concern focuses on the possibility that the benefits of international integration will be divided unevenly, with some countries possibly emerging as net losers. This concern is sharpened by the possibility that nationalistic policies could be used to secure benefits for one country at the expense of others. Finally, there are at least in theory ways in which all parties could end up worse off as a result of trade liberalization.

The possibility of uneven distribution of benefits is associated with the existence of excess returns in imperfectly competitive industries. In industries where economies of scale limit the extent of competition, capital can earn a return higher than it does in alternative uses. (If labour is organized, some of this return may be captured in wages instead). A country that succeeds in getting a disproportionate share of high-return industries as a result of trade can gain at other countries' expense, while a country that ends up with small high-return sectors can conceivably be worse off with trade than without.

While the possibility of actual losses from trade is probably purely academic, there is a real issue of conflict over the division of the gains. Because some industries yield higher returns than others, countries have an incentive to take unilateral measures to secure a larger share of these sectors. Policies aimed at securing national advantage in oligopolistic industries have come to be known as *strategic* trade policies. Recent efforts to quantify the possible scope for such policies suggests that it may be in the national interest to impose tariffs or provide export subsidies at rates as high as 20–30 per cent in selected sectors.[4]

The problem is that while strategic trade policies may be in any one country's interest, if all countries pursue them the result may be to block mutually beneficial integration. Suppose that semiconductors are viewed as a

---

[3] The possibility that countries can use subsidies and other policies to secure a higher share of excess-return industries was pointed out by James Brander and Barbara Spencer in 'International R&D Rivalry and Industrial Strategy', *Review of Economic Studies*, 50 (1983), 707–22, and in their 'Export Subsidies and International Market Share Rivalry', *Journal of International Economics*, 18 (1985), 83–100. The implications of the Brander–Spencer analysis and critiques of its relevance as a guide to policy are covered in many of the papers in P. Krugman, ed., *Strategic Trade Policy and the New International Economics*, MIT Press, 1986.

[4] See in particular A. Dixit, 'Optimal Trade and Industrial Policy for the US Automobile Industry', forthcoming in R. Feenstra, ed., *Empirical Research in International Trade*, MIT Press; R. Baldwin and P. Krugman, 'Market Access and Competition: A Simulation Study of 16K random access memories', forthcoming in the same volume; and A. Venables and M. A. M. Smith, 'Trade and Industrial Policy Under Imperfect Competition', *Economic Policy*, 3, 1986.

strategic sector suitable for special government attention. A single country could then gain by promoting this industry. If every major nation attempts to ensure a strong position in semiconductors through protection and subsidies, however, the outcome will be a fragmented high-cost industry, which benefits no country.

Under the rules of the EC, of course, direct use of protectionist measures with regard to intra-EC trade is ruled out. Indirect measures such as nationalistic procurement and government support of industry, subsidized R&D, and so on can still, however, have similar, although more muted effects. Thus the problem of an industrial policy war that blocks beneficial integration remains a serious concern.

We should also note that since Europe does not trade only with itself, but is also engaged in trade and competition with other regions, European integration itself is a kind of strategic trade policy. Theoretical models of strategic trade policy show that in industries subject to increasing returns, the size of the domestic market can be an important determinant of export performance. Again, recent efforts at quantification provide some support for this view, especially for high technology sectors. Thus, increasing the degree of integration of the European market may produce 'strategic' gains over and above the usual benefits by giving European firms a better base for oligopolistic competition against US and Japanese rivals.

Finally, we should note that in imperfectly competitive markets it is possible in principle that increased integration could leave everyone worse off. The simplest example is the case known as 'reciprocal dumping': oligopolistic firms may restrict sales in their local markets in an effort to keep prices high, while selling at much lower margins in their rivals' markets in pursuit of additional profits. This practice can lead to shipments of the same good in opposite directions, with a consequent waste of resources in transportation costs. If this waste is not outweighed by the gains from increased competition, everyone will be made worse off when markets are integrated.

It remains true, however, that the most likely effect of economies of scale and imperfect competition is to *raise* the gains from integration, and that the major concern is the problem of policy conflict, not direct losses from the integration itself.

1.1.4 Adjustment costs and income distribution

A major obstacle to increased economic integration is the fact that the gains from integration are not shared equally within countries, at least in the short run. The owners of scarce factors of production may command a higher return before trade liberalization than after—one need only mention farmers threatened by low-cost agricultural imports or low-skill workers. Furthermore, it takes time for resources to shift from one sector to another, so that even some of those who stand to gain from integration in the long run may lose at first.

There are three main issues that need to be addressed when we consider the role of adjustment costs and uneven distribution of gains in economic integration. First is the question of whether the costs are purely distributional or represent a net cost to the economy as a whole; if they are purely distributional they do not provide an argument for limiting integration or slowing its pace. Second is the question whether future trade liberalization is likely to present more or less of an adjustment problem than past. Finally, there is the policy question of how to manage adjustment—but this question we reserve for the last part of the paper.

Economic work of the past decade has made it clear that costly adjustment *by itself* does not mean that increased economic integration is of doubtful benefit. It is of course costly for labour and capital to shift from old into new industries. Since these factors have the choice of remaining put, however, their decision to incur the costs of moving can be viewed as a kind of investment project, one in which there need be no divergence between private and and social returns. The costs incurred by factors of production in shifting out of import-competing industries and into new export sectors following a liberalization of trade may therefore be viewed as productive, similar in ultimate effects to the investment needed to take advantage of a new technology. On this view, the costs suffered by workers and firms in industries hurt by trade liberalization are comparable in significance to the losses suffered by buggy manufacturers with the coming of the automobile: distributional effects deserving of compensation, but not a reason to prevent or delay change.

Adjustment costs provide an argument against trade liberalization only if they involve some social cost beyond changes in income distribution. The most important of these would be unemployment. If increased integration leads to a net increase in involuntary unemployment, this may provide a case against moving too fast.

It is not hard to devise stories in which liberalized trade may create unemployment. Suppose, for example, that labour is immobile between sectors and that real wages are rigid downward but not upward. Suppose also that trade liberalization increases the demand for labour in sectors that were already prosperous, while reducing it in sectors that were already suffering high unemployment. (For example, trade liberalization might benefit Southern England while hurting the North.) Then in the prosperous sectors the effect will be mostly a rise in real wages rather than in employment, while in the declining sectors real wages will fail to fall and unemployment will rise. The net effects will therefore be a fall in employment, possibly negating the benefits of integration.

This story need not be right, of course. If even relatively well off sectors have substantial unemployment, they can experience large job gains. For that matter, trade liberalization could benefit high-unemployment sectors at the expense of low-unemployment ones. None the less, the possibility that adjustment costs can turn into real social costs should not be lightly dismissed.

Given that adjustment represents a definite political problem and at least potentially a real cost to the economy, how much adjustment will increased integration require? Here the important point is that the EEC's past experience has been one of increased integration with remarkably easy adjustment. This will unfortunately not necessarily be true in the future.

In its original formation, the Common Market was virtually tailor-made to foster *intra*-industry trade based on economies of scale rather than *inter*-industry specialization that might have posed large adjustment issues. The original Six were all more or less advanced industrial countries (if we exclude the south of Italy), with similar levels of productivity, wages, and capital-labour ratios. Thus the specialization that took place as trade in manufactured goods grew tended to involve concentration on different niches within sectors rather than wholesale concentration of different countries on different industries. Essentially, all of the growth in intra-EC manufactures trade from 1958 to the mid-1960s took the form of intra- rather than inter-industry exchanges.

The one sector where large inter-sectoral specialization might have been expected to occur was agriculture. Here, however, the Common Agricultural Policy, by ensuring prices above world levels, protected the agricultural sectors of countries that in fact were at a comparative disadvantage.

In part due to the relatively benign character of the trade expansion it produced, the EEC in its years of rapid trade growth aroused fewer complaints about problems of adjustment than many had expected. The question now is whether the further extension of trade in progress will be equally easy to cope with.

The unfortunate answer is, probably not. To the extent that unification of standards and a reduction in nationalistic purchasing practices can increase trade among the wealthier nations of the enlarged EEC, this may produce a further round of intra-industry specialization with few adjustment costs. The addition of Southern Europe to the scene, however, means that now trade within the EEC will involve partners with major differences in productivity, wages, and resources. Trade between Portugal and Belgium will surely be more conventional in its character than trade between Belgium and Germany; it will involve specialization in labour-intensive, low-technology products by the one and exports of higher-technology, capital- or skill-intensive products by the other. This will pose adjustment problems for both the heretofore protected Portuguese heavy industries and some traditional industries in Northern Europe.

The point is that the trade expansion produced by EC enlargement is simply not likely to be as painless as the trade expansion produced by the formation of the Community and earlier enlargement. There will certainly be income distribution problems created by the changes, and also quite possibly some real costs in terms of unemployment.

1.2 Integration of capital markets

In a deep, underlying sense, integration of national economies through capital movements is not very different in its causes and effects from trade in goods and services. As in the case of trade, capital movements serve to allow countries to benefit from their differences through long-run transfer of resources to countries where they are more productive. Also like trade, capital mobility can be beneficial through its effects on financial market efficiency even where little net transfer of resources takes place. On the other hand, differences in regulation and the institutional framework make the issue of capital controls quite different in practice from the issue of protectionism.

1.2.1 Long-run resource transfer

The use of capital movement to transfer resources is both the most obvious reason for such movements and the most obvious source of gain. By investing abroad, individuals can shift resources to where they are most productive, in principle benefiting both the recipient of the capital inflow (via increased production that exceeds the repayment) and the donor (via higher foreign investment income).

As Robert Mundell pointed out nearly thirty years ago, long-run resource transfer via capital movement may serve as a substitute for international trade, and vice versa. Capital-abundant countries may either trade capital-intensive for labour-intensive goods, or directly trade the services of their capital for a stream of future goods. Either way, the trade allows countries to gain from their differences.

In the era before World War I, long-run resource transfer was the prime reason for capital movement, and took place on a massive scale. The UK invested 5–10 per cent of GNP abroad for decades, and on the eve of the war its foreign investment income paid for a third of its imports. In the 1980s, however, net resource transfer has been much smaller relative to national incomes. In any case, it is doubtful whether moves currently under consideration will do much to increase long-run resource transfer through capital flows. First, most of the regulations restricting capital mobility that are likely to be liberalized bite most strongly on short-run movements rather than long-term capital. Second, the main likely recipients of net foreign investment within the Community (Greece, Ireland) are already sufficiently heavily indebted that further large inflow seems unlikely.

Thus, the main gains from liberalized capital in the European case seem likely to come not from net resource transfer but from the efficiency advantages of a more integrated European capital market. These benefits are harder to define, but they can be described in rough terms.

1.2.2 Integration and efficiency of financial markets

It is useful, in thinking about integration of capital markets, to draw an analogy with trade in goods and services. Long-run resource transfer corresponds to inter-industry trade: it represents trade of one kind of useful object (purchasing power now) for another (purchasing power in the future), and arises because the relative prices of these two objects (the rate of return) would differ between countries in the absence of trade. Thus it allows countries to benefit from their differences, while at the same time generating income distribution and adjustment problems that may be problematic politically.

On the other side, corresponding to the 'intra-industry' trade that we observe in goods markets, is two-way trade in financial assets and the effect of potential financial flows on competition. Two-way international investment is more subtle in its origins than two-way trade in similar goods, but we can at least enumerate a few main causes.

1. *Diversification*. Since risks are not perfectly correlated across countries, investors in an integrated market will have some incentive to diversify across countries. As each country's investors do this, the result will be financial flows in two directions at once.

2. *Intermediation*. International financial centres provide investors with short-term, safe, liquid assets while acquiring long-term, risky, illiquid claims. As other countries trade assets with financial centres, the result is simultaneous flow of capital in both directions. The role of some cities as centres of international intermediation, in turn, may represent a combination of comparative advantage and economies of scale. Most notably, London acts as a world financial centre partly because of the external economies associated with its already established position (which in turn rests on historical accident).

3. *Information*. When financial resources are traded, since nothing material is being shipped, the cost of information rather than physical costs represents the main natural barrier to trade. Often, however, information will flow more easily between geographically separate but economically linked parties than between physical neighbours. A firm in Italy that seeks additional funds may find that its parent company in the Netherlands or a bank familiar with its industry in London is more able to evaluate its needs than potential sources of capital in Italy itself. Yet at the same time, firms in the Netherlands or England may find that the potential sources of funds that are well-enough informed to provide what is necessary are in Italy. Thus the vagaries of information flow may create a 'geography' of capital markets that differs from actual geography enough to generate capital flows in all directions.

4. *Competition*. Even if there is no reason for net trade in capital, integration of capital markets will create the potential for increased competition. If, say, cartelized banks in one country were to attempt to use their market power to drive a wedge between the rates paid to depositors and the rate charged to lenders, foreign competitors could offer more attractive intermediation and hence induce both export and import of capital. The competition between oligopolistic financial institutions in different countries need not involve much actual capital movement, but it might involve some two-way raiding of each

others' territory, along the lines of the 'reciprocal dumping' mentioned earlier as a possible behaviour in goods markets.

The important point is that these effects on financial market efficiency do not depend on the achievement of large net resource flows. Suppose that Italy and France were to remove all of their restrictions on capital movement. They might not end up exporting or importing large amounts of capital on net (indeed we would hope not). None the less, their integration with the open capital markets of Germany and the United Kingdom could produce significant gains from improved prospects for diversification, economies of scale in intermediation, improved ability of firms to pair up with well-informed investors, and increased financial market competition.

Sceptics would argue, however, that financial markets are so distorted by other government policies that the gains from removal of capital controls are in fact highly uncertain. This is an important caveat, which needs some discussion.

1.2.3 Distortions and questions about the benefits of capital mobility

There is no question that financial markets in all countries suffer from significant distortions. These distortions raise the possibility that increased international trade in financial assets could hurt the economy instead of help it, and correspondingly that restrictions on international capital movements may be desirable as a second-best way of mitigating the effects of distortions.

One main set of distortions comes from the moral hazard problems created by bank regulation. The desire to prevent 1930s-style banking collapses has led nearly all nations to provide a safety net of deposit insurance, together with implicit guarantees that the government will bail out the banking system if necessary. These measures are surely desirable: few would advocate a return to complete *laissez-faire*. None the less, they present moral hazard problems. Banks are offered an incentive to take excessive risks, especially risks that offer a low probability of large losses. If the low-probability disasters do not happen, the bank has earned a high return; if they do happen, depositors are protected, while stockholders can at most lose their equity—and may not even lose that, if the government bails them out. An unconditional provision of deposit insurance is in its effect essentially like a government subsidy to risk-taking, and its effect in that direction is reinforced if bank equity is perceived to be subject to implicit guarantees.

Now in fact the explicit and implicit guarantees of governments to the financial system are not unconditional. They are backed by regulations designed to discourage excessive risk-taking, both prudential regulations on exposure and capitalization requirements that insure that bank equity is large enough to bear much of the responsibility of adverse outcomes. The problem is that internationalization of capital markets can weaken the effectiveness of the regulatory framework. For example, some economists have argued that creation of Eurosubsidiaries by US banks during the 1970s reduced the effectiveness of capital requirements, leading banks into a surge of risky lending that produced, among other things, the explosion in LDC debt during 1978–81. Whether or not this was in fact a major factor, it is clear that integration on financial markets requires revision of the regulatory framework. Without such revision, capital flows will be motivated more by a search for loopholes than a search for real economic opportunities, and reduce welfare instead of increasing it.

A second kind of distortion involves taxation. A recurrent theme in practical discussion of international capital movements is that they may take place as a way to avoid taxation. First, the effectiveness of taxation on foreign capital is uncertain; residents of countries with weak fiscal systems may be able to avoid reporting their income on investments outside the country. If it is easier to avoid payment of taxes on foreign income than domestic, which is likely, capital flight will take place without any gain in economic efficiency. Notably, those European countries with capital controls are also those noted for problems with tax collection.

If fiscal problems make seignorage an important source of revenue, the problem is compounded. A country that relies to a significant extent on inflation for revenue will offer a strongly negative real return on its currency, and a low real return on bank deposits (because banks must in effect pay the inflation tax on their required reserves). Suppose that such a country liberalizes capital mobility. Then there will be some decline in the demand for currency, as new substitutes become available; and also a decline in demand for deposits. This will either reduce inflation revenue or force a higher inflation rate on the government. Since the capital flight would have responded to an inflation tax rather than underlying differences in productivity, it may be regarded as capital movement motivated by tax evasion—and it will lower national income, not raise it.

It is hard to deny that in practice problems of taxation and regulation do bulk large in capital markets, making the gains from liberalization problematic. One counter-argument to this counter-argument would be to argue for a capital market integration accompanied by institutional reform that corrects these problems; some ideas along these lines are discussed below. Another argument would be that capital controls themselves create serious distortions of incentives. Capital controls create incentives to engage in activities that are not socially productive, but that serve as ways to evade the controls. For example, if devaluation is anticipated but capital flight is prohibited, consumers may respond by hoarding consumer durables, a costly activity from the point of view of the nation but one that absence of financial alternatives makes profitable.

Also, like any government regulation, capital controls pose problems of enforcement. On one side, illegal activities such as falsified invoicing are difficult to police. On the other side, the regulations that make controls effective may also throw sand in the wheels of valuable economic activities.

When it is necessary to apply for permission to acquire foreign exchange, the ease that facilitates transactions, especially small ones, will be lost.

1.3 Integration of labour markets

Labour mobility, like capital mobility, is similar in its ultimate causes to trade in goods. On one side we have net migration of labour from one country to another, corresponding to inter-industry trade in goods. On the other we have at least the possibility of exchange of labour in a more balanced way, corresponding to intra-industry trade.

1.3.1 Migration as resource transfer

The role of international migration as a means of transferring resources needs little discussion. When workers move from low-wage nations to higher-wage countries their income rises, and so does the income of the recipient nation. World income is increased because labour is being transferred to places where it has a higher marginal product.

The movement of labour from South to North in Europe during the 1960s and 1970s is, of course, one of the great migrations in history. This migration had social and economic consequences that are beyond the scope of this paper. The important point for the current situation is that the EC enlargement has brought some of the major reservoirs of labour inside the EC, and thus will presumably encourage an increase in the future extent of migration.

1.3.2 'Intra-industry' migration

In the United States, which is comparable in population to and much larger in area than the EC, net inter-regional migration flows are accompanied by large two-way flows of people. It is not uncommon for a house in New York to be vacated by a family moving to California, and for the house to be occupied by a family just moving in from California. This two-way migration is not fully understood, but it may be explained by several causes:

1. *Differentiation in skills.* If one region is abundant in skilled labour, while another is abundant in unskilled, two-way migration is not unreasonable. Something of this kind went on during the 1940s and 1950s, when a large net migration of unskilled labour from the Southern US to the North was countered by a smaller migration of skilled workers in the other direction.

2. *Information networks.* This is an explanation similar to our discussion of information as a cause of capital movement. Suppose that a software firm in California needs more programmers with a specific kind of background. There may be programmers with that background in California, but the firm might well find it easier to hire people it knows through personal ties or past business dealings who happen to live in Texas or Massachusetts. The point is again that the 'geography' of information networks may not bear much resemblance to the geography of a map, so that resources several thousand miles away may in effect be more accessible than those in the same city.

3. *Internal labour markets and the operations of large firms.* Suppose that a firm that operates plants and offices in a number of states decides to relocate some of its operations. Often in such a case the firm will try to provide its employees with job security by offering them the opportunity to take jobs in the new location. Thus the firm creates an internal labour market from which it hires in preference to hiring from geographically localized external markets. The reasons for this preference for internal hiring—like the preference for internal financing—presumably at root come down to issues of information and insurance. The point is, however, that it can lead to substantial movement of people in all directions.

The notable feature of European labour markets as compared with those of the US is that so far this kind of two-way migration flow is relatively absent. Presumably this is mostly because of language and cultural barriers. It might also be to some extent because of social policies, e.g. claims on subsidized housing that migrants cannot take with them. An interesting question is whether over time the EC will be able to create a labour market that is integrated in this way, and reap the benefits of increased efficiency.

1.4 Conclusions

For all three forms of economic integration—goods and services, capital, and labour market—the effects of reduced barriers can be usefully divided into two kinds. On one side is the conventional or comparative advantage motive for trade driven by differences in countries' resources or productivity. Trade resulting from this conventional motive produces mutual gains in efficiency, but also produces problems of income distribution and adjustment. On the other side is trade motivated by unconventional factors: economies of scale, oligopolistic rivalry, informational asymmetries, and so on. The trade that these unconventional motives produce is similarly (usually) beneficial; however, it probably involves less conflict of interest *within* countries and more conflict of interest *between* countries than conventional trade.

The problem facing Europe is twofold. First, the expansion of trade that will be generated by the enlargement of the Community will probably involve an expansion of conventional, comparative-advantage specialization. This represents a break with the past history of the EEC, which was so successful in the 1960s at least partly because of the predominance of 'intra-industry' over 'inter-industry' trade. The new trade expansion will thus present problems of internal adjustment that will be of greater difficulty than before.

Second, and working in the other direction, completion of the internal market will sharpen the potential for national conflict over the distribution of the unconventional gains from trade. There are bound to be sectors that are regarded as strategic by several European countries, but which tend to concentrate in only one or two. The danger is then of an industrial policy war as each country attempts to secure the desired sectors for itself.

2. Macroeconomics of integration[5]

The objective of international economic integration is to reap the microeconomic benefits of specialization, rationalization, and increased competition. Unfortunately, microeconomic objectives can never be fully separated from macroeconomic issues. Recent research has suggested that under certain circumstances increased integration can worsen macroeconomic performance (though under other circumstances it might be an advantage).

The reason why macroeconomic problems from integration are possible is that increased integration means increased macroeconomic interdependence. In and of itself this is not a bad thing; the fact that Ohio's economy depends on the performance of New York's does not pose special problems for US monetary and fiscal policy. The difference is that Europe's nations do not have fully co-ordinated policies. What recent research has shown is that increased interdependence without a corresponding increase in co-ordination can lead to inappropriate policies. At worst, the problems of co-ordination could negate the microeconomic benefits of expanded integration. Even if this is not the case, increased integration makes policy co-ordination more urgent.

2.1 Channels of interdependence

As a first step toward thinking about the macroeconomics of integration, it is helpful to review the main channels of interdependence between nations. These are of course interdependence through goods and service markets; linkage of capital markets, which have a particularly strong role in determining exchange rates; and, in Europe, the direct linkage of employment through policy effects on migration.

2.1.1 Trade and its multiplier effects

The simplest form of macroeconomic linkage between countries is the spillover of demand from one country to another via imports. While much of the attention of economists has focused on the more indirect linkages via financial and exchange markets, this direct and straightforward linkage should not be neglected. In Europe more than anywhere else in the world the spill-over of demand between countries is of vital importance. The average Community nation (which turns out to be France, more or less) imports and exports about a quarter of its GDP and has a marginal propensity to import of more than one-third; but about 60 per cent of these imports come from other European countries, so that Europe as a whole is as closed an economy as the United States.

Until recently most of the analytical attention of economists studying trade linkages was focused on the question of foreign trade multipliers: how much

---

[5] Much of the analysis in this section is simply conventional open-economy macroeconomics, as exposited, for example, in R. Dornbusch, *Open-economy Macroeconomics*, Basic Books, 1980.

does a percentage point of growth in Germany affect GDP in France? These numbers are much larger within Europe than, say, between Europe and the US. None the less, emphasis on trade multipliers is now seen to miss the most important point. What matters is not so much how much a given German policy affects France as the way that interdependence affects the policies pursued by both Germany and France. We shall examine this issue soon, but first we continue by discussing the roles of linkage through capital markets and labour markets.

2.1.2 Capital markets, monetary policy, and exchange rates

Integration of capital markets introduces a more complex and less well understood policy linkage than trade in goods and services. The picture is complicated by the question of exchange rate regime. If exchange rates are flexible, capital market linkages operate in the first instance through exchange rate changes. If on the other hand exchange rates are more or less fixed, the integration of capital markets introduces a direct linkage between monetary policy in one country and the money supplies in others.

In the case of flexible rates, anything that raises the rate of return in one country tends to appreciate its currency against its trading partners, while anything that lowers the rate of return in a country tends to depreciate its currency. The more integrated are capital markets, the more pronounced these effects. It is a familiar proposition from international macroeconomics that in a world of high capital mobility, some effects of fiscal and monetary policy may go in unexpected directions. The two main examples are a reversed effect of fiscal expansion on the exchange rate, and a reversed effect of monetary policy on the current account.

If capital markets are not highly integrated, we should expect a fiscal expansion to raise the demand for imports and thus lead to currency depreciation. When capital markets are closely integrated, however, fiscal expansion that drives up interest rates may induce capital inflow that actually produces a currency appreciation. (This effect of course becomes much more likely when the fiscal expansion is accompanied by tightened monetary policy).

On the other side, we might expect that monetary expansion, which raises demand for imports as well as domestic goods, will lead to a current account deficit. With capital mobility and flexible exchange rates, however, monetary expansion may depress the currency so much that a current account surplus emerges instead. (For what it is worth, most econometric models suggest that things are not quite this perverse. Regressive expectations seem to limit the decline in the currency following monetary expansion enough so that the current account worsens after all).

The combination of flexible rates and high capital mobility creates a direct channel whereby each country's monetary policy has a direct—and perverse—effect on its trading partners' inflation. Tight money in one country appreciates its currency, reducing import prices at home but raising them abroad.

When rates are fixed, the effect of increased capital market integration is to remove the possibility of independent national monetary policies. An attempt to pursue seriously divergent policies will lead to capital flows that cannot for long be offset by sterilized intervention, and eventually one country or the other will have to allow its money supply to be dictated by the other country's.

2.1.3 Labour market linkage

There is not much deep to say about the direct role of labour market integration in creating economic linkages. Clearly, reduced employment in Northern Europe swells unemployment in Southern Europe, as migrants return home and potential migrants choose not to go. In general we might expect migrant employment to be more sensitive to economic fluctuations than overall employment; even with the protection of common EEC labour law, migrants will tend to find themselves in the position of 'last hired, first fired'. The significance of this is that looking at absolute numbers employed may understate the true importance of the linkage. Suppose that one worker in ten in Northern Europe were from Southern Europe, and the one Southerner in ten worked in the North. Then the extent of labour market integration might not seem very large. But if Southerners are in effect the reserve army that fills fluctuations in Northern demand, the marginal propensity to hire Southerners will be much higher than the average. An extra ten Northern jobs might translate into several jobs for Southerners, not just one.

2.2 *Policy problems posed by interdependence*

The essential policy problem posed by interdependence is that policies that affect residents of each nation are made at least in part by governments of other nations. This can lead to two sorts of bad result. First, a failure of governments to predict correctly what others' actions will be can lead to increased uncertainty and volatility in economic policy. Second, there may be a problem of collective action, in which rational policies from the point of view of governments acting on their own sum up to inferior policies at the level of Europe as a whole.

2.2.1 Information and uncertainty

Suppose that France and Germany set their macroeconomic policies independently, and that there is enough of a lag in the policy process that each country must base its policy on a guess about the other's future policy rather than responding to the actual policy adopted. Then uncertainty about the other country's policy can clearly be a problem. If France decides to expand when Germany decides to contract, France may end up with a bigger trade deficit than it bargained on. If France decides to contract, not realizing that Germany has made the same decision, both countries will be surprised at the depth of the recession that results.

This is not just an academic concern. Many observers, including the OECD secretariat, have argued that the severity of the 1982 slump in part reflected just such a failure to forecast other countries' actions. As many countries turned toward restrictive demand policies at the same time, each failed to appreciate how much its export demand would fall as a result of the actions taken abroad. The consequence was a deeper slump than anyone intended. We might also argue that some abrupt U-turns in policy—France being the obvious example—were prompted in part by the initial failure to predict correctly other countries' macroeconomic policies.

If information and uncertainty were the only problem posed by increased interdependence, the solution could lie in a more extensive process of mutual notification. It has become clear in recent years, however, that there are deeper issues of co-ordination that cannot be resolved simply by information exchange.

2.2.2 Co-ordination issues[6]

The essential co-ordination problem is that when interdependence is high, policies that appear advantageous to any one country acting alone may yield poor results when everyone follows them.

The classic example that has attracted a great deal of academic attention is that of how quickly to attempt to disinflate. Suppose that a number of countries have 'inherited' inflation, either as the result of adverse supply shocks or misguided past policies. Suppose also that exchange rates are freely floating. Then to any individual country a policy of rapid disinflation through restrictive monetary policy may appear attractive. Where capital mobility is high, tight money will lead to a large currency appreciation, and this appreciation will at least at first produce a rapid fall in inflation in a highly open economy. Thus the trade-off between reducing inflation and increasing unemployment may appear relatively favourable. (The trade-off will be even more attractive if many of those who lose their jobs are migrant workers rather than national citizens.) So where markets for goods, capital, and labour are well integrated, each country may find that rapid disinflation through tight money is an appealing strategy.

The problem is that if every country pursues this strategy, the results will not be nearly as favourable. All countries cannot simultaneously experience

---

[6] The discussion in this area is summarized in R. Cooper, 'Economic Interdependence and Co-ordination of Economic Policies', in R. Jones and P. Kenen, eds., *Handbook of International Economics*, North-Holland, 1985. An attempt to quantify the gains from co-ordination is G. Oudiz and J. Sachs, *Macroeconomic policy co-ordination among the Industrial Countries*, Brookings Papers on Economic Activity, 1 (1984).

currency appreciation; if they all pursue equally tight monetary policies, none of them will experience much appreciation. Thus, the cheap gains against inflation will be lost.

One might expect that given the failure to experience rapid disinflation, countries would then choose not to use such tight monetary policies. Once the rest of the world has tight money, however, looser money in one country will imply currency *depreciation*, and a risk of accelerating inflation. In other words, the world can get caught in a trap in which all countries are pursuing more restrictive policies than are in their collective interest, yet no one country will gain from being more expansionary.

Once one realizes that co-ordination problems of this kind can arise, it becomes clear that increased economic integration can aggravate them. The more integrated goods markets are, the greater the inflation gains from appreciation and the greater the inflationary impact of depreciation. The more integrated are capital markets, the greater the extent to which monetary policy acts through the exchange rate rather than through interest-sensitive domestic spending. The more integrated are labour markets, the less of a reduction in employment will be borne by permanent domestic residents.

Because increased interdependence can worsen the problems of co-ordination, a move toward increased integration *if not accompanied by an improved framework for co-ordination* could backfire. Worse macro policy could outweigh the microeconomic gains.

The problem of excessive disinflation under flexible rates is, as we mentioned, the most analysed example of co-ordination problems in recent economic work. It is of doubtful direct relevance to Europe at the present time, however. Inflation is less of a concern than it was; furthermore, much of Europe is now either part of the European Monetary System or increasingly adopting exchange rate targets that link it more or less closely to the EMS. Nonetheless, the co-ordination problem can easily reappear in other guises.

Suppose, for example, that we stylize the European situation now as follows: monetary policy is committed to defense of the exchange rate, but fiscal policy remains available as a macroeconomic tool. Fiscal expansion is constrained, however, by a number of factors including concern over its effect on the currency account balance and concern over long-run government solvency. In this situation it is possible that uncoordinated policies could lead to fiscal policies that are more conservative than optimal. For any one country acting alone, fiscal expansion will largely spill over into imports, so that the adverse current account consequences will be large. At the same time the multiplier effects on domestic output will be small, so that little new tax revenue will be generated and the budget consequences will also be unfavourable. If all Europe expanded at once, however, the current account consequences would be less than half as large for the typical country, the multiplier effects will be larger, and hence the budget impact less unfavourable. Thus countries acting in an uncoordinated fashion would be trapped in a fiscal stance that is tighter than their own interests warrant.

In this case, as in the case of excessive disinflation, increased integration and the resulting interdependence can worsen uncoordinated policy. As goods markets become more integrated, the fraction of an increase in demand that spills over to imports rises. Increased integration of capital markets reinforces the reliance on fiscal as opposed to monetary policy. Increased labour mobility makes extra employment seem less valuable to any one country, even though it is as important as ever to Europe as a whole.

2.3 Macroeconomic advantages of integration

The preceding discussion stressed the problems of macroeconomic policy that can arise from increased economic interdependence. These problems have attracted the most attention from economists. Recent work, however, especially in Europe, has stressed some advantages that macro policy can derive from closer integration. These fall under two headings: the use of the rest of the world as a buffer, and the use of external constraints as a way to gain policy credibility.

2.3.1 Interdependence as a buffer

An open economy is exposed to shocks originating in the outside world, but it is to some extent protected from its own shocks. An investment slump will not produce as much a recession if it falls partly on imports. Under fixed exchange rates, shocks originating in shifts in the demand for money or other portfolio shifts may emerge as capital movements with little real effect, whereas in a closed economy they could have generated real output disturbances.

Will the gain from using the rest of the world as a buffer outweigh the cost of exposing oneself to the rest of the world's variability? There is a presumption that the net effect will be to reduce volatility. If we think of Europe as a collection of countries experiencing imperfectly correlated disturbances to private demand, bouts of governmental irresponsibility, and so on, we can expect the *average* of Europe to show less instability than any one country. But each country's rest of Europe is simply an average of the other countries. So there probably is some useful buffering effect of increased integration.

2.3.2 External discipline and credibility

The more important potential source of macroeconomic gains from integration is its hoped-for ability to enhance the credibility of economic policies. For some time, economists have emphasized the importance of public expectations in economic behaviour. Often it is very difficult for a government to carry out a desired change in economic policy if the public does not believe that the change will last. Most notably, stopping inflation is much more difficult both in fiscal terms and in terms of its output cost when the government's determination is questionable.

In situations where credibility is important, it is often useful to restrict one's own freedom of action. Italy, with its history of inflation, would like to convince both the purchasers of government debt and price setters that it will be much less inflationary in the future. Simple declarations that things will be different from now on are not likely to achieve this goal. In order to gain credibility, the Italian government may therefore wish to constrain its own actions. The hope is that by adopting an exchange rate target *vis-à-vis* a country with less inflation propensity, the government of a high-inflation country can make further inflation too costly—and thereby make its announced intention to pursue price stability credible.

Clearly, such a policy works only if it works. That is, making exchange rate adjustment costly is only a good thing if it actually changes both government policy and expectations enough so that the need for exchange rate adjustment is in fact substantially reduced. Otherwise the only effect is to make the inevitable exchange rate changes come too infrequently, and to create targets for speculative attack. The experience of the EMS so far, and the revealed preferences of European governments at the present time, suggest that external discipline can indeed enhance credibility in a significant way.

The impact of increased integration of markets on the credibility problem is double-edged. On one side, increased integration increases the discipline associated with the external constraint. On the other side, if credibility is not established, the costs of that failure are larger with more open markets.

The case is clearest for capital mobility. A country with effective capital controls can for at least a while pursue an inflationary monetary policy without being forced into an immediate devaluation. By contrast, with free movement of capital it could not. It is fairly common now to hear from French sources that 'we now allow our monetary policy to be made by the Bundesbank'. This has however not been quite true as long as French capital markets have been isolated by controls. Once the controls are gone, if France remains in the EMS, it will be fully true. If the commitment to the EMS remains ironclad, there will thus be a gain in credibility.

On the other hand, suppose that the commitment is not seen as ironclad. Then the opening of capital markets presents opportunities for speculative attack. An extreme example may make the point. In 1981–2 both Brazil and Mexico were following unsustainable policies. Brazil had effective capital controls in place, Mexico did not. Mexico experienced capital flight in excess of $20 billion, which was financed by additional debt, while Brazil's capital flight problem was negligible. If credibility is not gained, there is a good deal to be said for *not* having integrated markets.

2.4 Conclusions

Increased integration makes countries more interdependent in their macroeconomic policies. European nations are already strongly linked through trade, but their labour and especially capital market linkages can still be extended.

Increased interdependence creates problems for macroeconomic policy. Failure of countries to communicate effectively about their intentions can lead to increased uncertainty and policy volatility. More important, there is usually a divergence between the policies that are best for each country acting individually and the policies that would be best if countries acted in a co-ordinated way. Increased integration can widen this divergence, possibly leading to macroeconomic problems that outweigh the microeconomic gains.

Against these macroeconomic difficulties we can set two gains. Integration can serve as a buffer against uncertainty; for example, fluctuations in money demand will do less harm if they can be averaged across an integrated European capital market. At a deeper level, integration enhances the ability of countries to appeal to external discipline as a way to enhance the credibility of their policies.

3. Policy implications

It is beyond the scope of this paper (and beyond the author's competence!) to make any kind of detailed recommendations for Europe based upon this very general survey. The most that can be done is to outline a few broad concerns for policy as European integration increases.

3.1 Microeconomic policy

3.1.1 Avoiding conflict over industrial structure

The main danger suggested by the 'new theories' of economic integration discussed in the first part of this paper is that nations will find themselves in an industrial policy war, as each attempts to enlarge its share of high-return sectors. The issue is how to structure rules of the game that prevent procurement, subsidies, and other policies from being turned to this purpose and thus frustrating the goal of increased integration.

Now it is notable that the United States, a highly integrated market with a federal system of government, is relatively free of this kind of conflict. Every state would like to have its own Silicon Valley or Route 128, but the policies they follow towards this end have not noticeably disrupted the free flow of goods and services.

How is conflict avoided? We might note five factors that restrain industrial policy conflict within the US.

1. *Constitutional limitations*. States are forbidden from actions in restraint of inter-state trade, ruling out many barriers that would be legal even in the EEC.

2. *Much procurement is carried out at the federal rather than state level*. While states provide education and other services, a good deal of the procurement in potentially strategic sectors is carried out at a Federal level, most notably defence spending.

3. *Firms have much less of a local identification than in Europe.* Digital Equipment Corporation is a Massachusetts-based company, but the state is aware that the firm is truly inter-state in scope and does not automatically regard it as a state champion that needs to be supported against New York-based IBM.

4. *There is extensive redistribution among states through the federal budget.* States are therefore somewhat cushioned from adverse industrial shifts.

5. *Labour mobility is high.* If a large number of high-wage jobs are created in a state, they are as likely as not to be filled by migrants rather than by local residents.

Europe cannot fully reproduce the US situation. Political union is not on the table; and even if it were, the greater cultural and language diversity would prevent comparable integration. None the less, at least four of these five restraints on industrial policy competition can be institutionalized to some extent. 'Completion of the internal market' is very similar as a slogan to 'no restraints on inter-state commerce', and could be used as a principle to achieve the same end. Rules of the game on procurement, and perhaps some explicit co-operation in the defence area, could reduce the segmenting effect of national bias in this area. Liberalization of capital markets, and in particular of rules regarding direct foreign investment, could help make corporations truly European and thus not the special concern of individual nations. Finally, the EC's own redistributive mechanisms can help reduce concerns about losing out from competition, especially for poorer areas.

3.1.2 Promoting better adjustment

It is obvious but worth saying that all the problems associated with greater economic integration, and all the risks of policy conflict, would be far less if the European unemployment rate were half its current level. There is debate about the relative importance of inadequate demand and structural rigidities in causing the current high rate, a debate that should not be joined here. The point is, however, that integration will be far more successful if other policies are simultaneously doing something about the highly unsatisfactory performance of European labour markets.

3.2 Macroeconomic policies

3.2.1 Monetary policy

As a simple matter of feasibility, Europe cannot have at the same time (*a*) stable exchange rates, (*b*) integrated capital markets, and (*c*) independent monetary policies. The experience of the post-1973 period seems to indicate that (*a*) is not something that can be dispensed with. Given the already close integration of European markets for goods and services, large exchange rate fluctuations associated with divergent monetary policies seem to be unacceptable. Thus creation of a unified capital market will also require adoption of a common monetary policy.

To an outside observer, it appears that this is in fact happening, but not in the most desirable way. It is not too much of a caricature to say that Europe—including the UK!—is starting to look like a Deutschmark area, in which the Bundesbank sets all of Europe's monetary policy. This makes stable exchange rates feasible. The question is whether the arrangement is durable. As long as the need for external discipline to establish credibility is paramount in the minds of the rest of Europe, German centrality works; if and when other considerations become more urgent, the stage may be set for a Bretton Woods-like collapse.

A more desirable arrangement would involve co-operative setting of monetary targets. The difficulties involved in such a project are of course large, but it seems necessary. Though Germany is the largest economy and has a reputation for sound money, it is hard to believe that it is large or sound enough to be ceded control over Europe's money forever.

3.2.2 Fiscal policy

Finally, we turn to fiscal policy. Given mobile capital, it is technically feasible for European nations to maintain fixed exchange rates via co-ordinated monetary policy while pursuing independent fiscal policies. As already noted, however, independent fiscal actions in such a setting may yield suboptimal results—for example, a bias towards excessive restriction because each country ignores the impact of its actions on the others' exports. Given how large European interdependence is already, the further increase in this interdependence makes co-ordination urgent.

Achieving co-ordination of fiscal policies is probably even harder politically than co-ordination of monetary policies. There is not even temporarily a natural central player whose actions can solve the co-ordination problem. None the less, in surveying the problems of European integration, it is hard to avoid the conclusion that this is the systemic change most needed in the near future.

Index